S0-CFK-128

**International Sea Transport:
The Years Ahead**

International Sea Transport: The Years Ahead

S. A. Lawrence
Cornell University

Lexington Books
D.C. Heath and Company
Lexington, Massachusetts
Toronto   London

387.5
L423

134898

Library of Congress Cataloging in Publication Data

Lawrence, Dr. Samuel A.
    Merchant Shipping.
Mass.   Lexington Books

Oct. 1972   5-1-72   72-3544

Copyright © 1972 by D.C. Heath and Company.

All rights reserved. No part of this publication may be reproduced or transmitted in any form or by any means, electronic or mechanical, including photocopy, recording, or any information storage or retrieval system, without permission in writing from the publisher.

Published simultaneously in Canada.

Printed in the United States of America.

International Standard Book Number: 0-669-84319-9

Library of Congress Catalog Card Number: 72-3544

Contents

List of Figures

List of Tables

Foreword

This book began when a bunch of shipping people went fishing not long ago. There being no fish, we fell upon a case of beer and contemplated the mysteries of our trade. "There must be logic somewhere—if only someone could have the time to think it out," we speculated.

These have been rugged days for the world at sea. The past five years have made and broken more than the usual number of fortunes. Shipping executives come and go like migrating birds.

Korea recently suggested that all of her foreign trade should move on ships under the Korean flag. Japan will be content with 70 percent. She contends that this will be won in the open field of free competition. There are doubters.

Tankers are designed big enough to carry the Queen Mary on deck. Engineers are nervous about strength and maneuverability, but still they keep coming in larger sizes.

Malcolm MacLean, a former North Carolina truckman, terrifies the liner package freight world with his Sea-Land containership services. Now there are those who call the container obsolete, fading before other miracles called roll-on/roll-off, LASH, and even the lowly pallet.

Mysterious gentlemen appear in Hong Kong, Singapore, and Grand Cayman with millions of dollars in their pockets for the purchase of tankers, bulk carriers and OBO's. The deals they make look wonderful when the world ship market erupts in a 30 percent rise after New Year's 1970.

After New Year's 1971 the rise evaporates. Shipmen around the world look into their pockets and try to figure out what happened. All of a sudden, there are too many ships and a sick market seems to last forever. Ships are launched and laid up without completion—or even the traditional cocktail party.

Verolome and Mitsui are operating shipyards in Brazil. Days after achieving independence, the new nation of Bangladesh announces formation of its national merchant marine. It joins Nauru, the Maldives, and a half a dozen other small nations on the roll call of national flag merchant fleets. Enterprising gentlemen from Geneva, Rotterdam, New York, and Oslo make a business of organizing new "national flag" fleets in developing nations. In a sick market, these seek profit under the patriotic umbrellas of new nations.

Everywhere there is a jumble of emerging nationalism, rampant automation, old institutions crumbling and new arrangements vaguely described as "consortia" and "NVOCC's."

Is there any pattern? Are there any clues buried in the turmoil? Our spirits rise and fall as we confront this question. Research seems hardly possible in so chaotic a scene. But then, looking behind the froth of today's news and yesterday's headline, it seems that Voltaire could be right: "The more things change, the more they remain the same." How else can one explain that, as this book began, Brazilians were calling urgently for an international conference to write a new set of rules for world shipping. And as it ends, three years later, the news again is that Brazil—now joined by 76 other developing states—is calling upon the United Nations to convene such a Conference of Plenipotentiaries.

The sponsors of this book are an interesting group: The Government of Canada, a Cambridge, Massachusetts research company, two oil companies, several large industrial shippers, and an assortment of Scandinavian, British, and Continental shipowners. We disagree among ourselves on almost any maritime question. We are united only in our perplexity—"What's it leading to? What does it mean?"

Accordingly, we determined to band together in support of this piece of basic research. The person whom we asked to accomplish the impossible, Sam Lawrence, has served both as research director and as author. While he has sought data and advice from us, he has been completely free to conduct the study as he wished and to state whatever conclusions he developed.

Sam is not a green hand at this game; he was author, in 1966, of a Brookings Institution study of United States merchant shipping policies and politics. More recently he served as Executive Director of the Stratton Commission, a special presidentially appointed group to establish United States policies on marine affairs.

We do not pretend that he can produce all the answers. However, we take some pleasure in the fact that this is the first wholly objective, privately sponsored attempt of which we are aware to take a broad look forward at our industry.

Shipping in the "good old days" was a pleasant, gentlemanly proposition. Those days are gone. Hence, both the need for and the excitement of this book.

John L. Eyre
President
Saguenay Shipping Limited
Montreal

August 8, 1972

Preface

This book surveys recent and prospective developments in international sea transport, and considers issues which these developments create for the shipping industry and for public policy. It is addressed both to persons actively engaged in maritime affairs, for whom an overview of the longer term significance of current events may be useful, and to those in governments and universities, whose work and teaching help shape the industry's future.

International shipping has passed and will continue to pass through a period of rapid change fueled by new technologies, shifts in patterns of trade, and enlarging national aspirations. The pace of change has intensified old stresses within the industry and brought new uncertainties regarding its future. Major concerns include persistent tendencies toward overcapacity accompanying introduction of container systems and other technological improvements; competitive relationships between sea, air, and land carriers, and the manner in which ocean shipping may be integrated with other transport modes; the efforts of less developed nations to gain more favorable terms of trade; the use of flag discrimination to advance national flag fleets; unilateral efforts to regulate the terms and conditions of international transport; the need to upgrade port facilities and to establish cargo consolidation and feeder systems; and the increasing dependence of the world economy on the proper functioning of its sea transport component.

The foregoing problems are interrelated. It is the thesis of this study that each can be understood and acted upon only in the broader context of developments concerning the industry as a whole. For example, a proposal has recently been advanced to establish a comprehensive, multi-lateral regulatory system for shipping modeled on the ICAO/IATA system in air transport. Evaluation of such a proposal necessitates a firm grasp of likely technical developments in shipping and of the links between ocean transport and other transport modes. It also requires an appreciation of the strengths and limitations of international organization and of the interests of potential member governments.

At the root of many of the problems confronting the ocean freight industry is the fact that this industry, perhaps more than any other, must provide an international service within a system of nation states. This juxtaposition of national and international business interests is further complicated by the interplay of the public and private sectors.

As with other private activities which impinge on vital national interests, economic efficiency alone does not provide a sufficient criterion for evaluating the industry's operations. But for an international service such as shipping, there are very few models, even of a procedural kind, for identifying the larger public interest.

The matters at issue are numerous and are receiving an increasingly prominent place in international debate. What may be considered the proper rights and responsibilities of national flag fleets in international trade? Can conditions be established which would permit such fleets to compete internationally on a truly equal basis? Lacking fair and equal competition, how can one determine an equitable assignment of trade shares? Could any negotiated system provide sufficient sophistication to cope with the intricacies of this complex industry? What level and type of competition is really desirable in ocean transport anyway? In the absence of governmental intervention, is there reason to expect either excessive competition or that shipping lines will engage in monopolistic action injurious to trade?

This study seeks to examine such questions in the context of the realities of emerging power relationships and business practices. Although incorporating some new data, it draws heavily on technical and trade forecasts, and economic and political analyses performed by others and published in a widely scattered literature.[a] The study is presented in four parts: Part I is an introductory section which describes briefly the structure of the merchant shipping industry and the setting within which it operates; Part II is an analysis of the industry's economic characteristics. This analysis is followed in Part III by a forecast of trade and technological developments during the coming decade likely to affect shipping and a discussion of the manner in which the industry appears to be adapting to these new conditions. The issues which the emerging pattern of shipping operations pose for public policy are treated in Part IV. The book concludes with a brief prospectus for shipping in the 1970s and an analysis of the factors to which future developments appear most sensitive.

A study of this kind inevitably reflects the author's view of the world. One assumption underlying the study is that business operations generally will continue to be increasingly internationalized. Already a full 10 percent of the world's gross production enters international trade, and this percentage is growing at the rate of 0.85 percent per year. Furthermore, trade data only partially reflect the internationality of modern business enterprise. Worldwide investment flows are now on the order of $30 to $40 billion per annum; estimates of the overseas sales of the foreign affiliates of U.S. companies alone run from $125 to $200 billion. International companies think internationally and trade internationally. Their emergence is a factor which must be reckoned with in the future.

---

[a]Other than Carleen O'Loughlin's monograph, *The Economics of Sea Transport* (London: Pergamon Press, 1967), no general handbooks on shipping operations have been published since the 1950s. Several excellent studies have been made of ocean shipping activities within particular countries or regions, and of particular economic and technical problems (such as rate-setting, coordination of container operations, etc.) which affect the industry as a whole. These have been prepared under UN auspices, by special government or industry commissions, and by individual authors. A flow of good short studies of specific problems is provided by the Bergen Institute of Shipping Research, the U.K. National Ports Council, the U.S. National Academy of Sciences Maritime Research Board, the interested departments of several U.S. and British universities, and the Shipping Committee of the UN Conference on Trade and Development. Primary source data are available from hearings before government agencies, ship brokerage and research houses, port authorities, and classification societies. Finally, maritime news is copiously reported in commercial newspapers and business and legal journals.

A second assumption made by the author is that governments will give increasing attention to the impact of international businesses on domestic economics. Unilateral national action will be tried first. As this proves inadequate, nations will seek opportunities through regional and other groupings to develop cooperative programs for advancing common interests.

Third, governments may be expected to respond to international commercial pressures also by collaborating more closely with nationally based firms in order to advance national interests in international trade. The backing given to Fiat by the Italian government in establishing overseas markets provides one example; the Japanese government's cooperative programs with each of its major heavy industries (including shipping and shipbuilding), another.

Fourth, the enlarging scale of industrial organization and of its contributing technologies will require greatly increased coordination between the public and the private sectors, and across national boundaries. We see this in reference to electric grids and communications networks as well as in all phases of long-haul transportation; in resource development and energy policy; and in reference to environmental quality preservation and weather control.

In sum, increasing economic interdependence and the spread of global technologies imply new patterns of cooperation and conflict in years ahead which will significantly influence the political context of decisions regarding shipping problems. Questions involving the terms of access to basic resources, know-how, markets, and transport services appear likely to loom larger in the international dialogue. The major issue—one which lurks behind each of the more specific questions considered in this book—is whether the means will be found to channel this dialogue into constructive action to advance common interests or whether international economic competition will degenerate into a mindless scramble to safeguard narrow national positions.

Certain limitations to the scope of the study should also be noted. It deals solely with the deep sea component of the merchant shipping industry; the important domestic trades, and short sea services, within Europe and the Far East are not considered. Passenger movements similarly are excluded. Emphasis is on ship operations. Matters associated with shipbuilding and other supporting industries are treated only insofar as they bear directly on vessel operations. Detailed critiques of the promotional program of individual nations have been omitted, although such programs constitute a major facet of the overall international problem. Similarly only brief treatment has been possible of the highly specialized activities of the tanker segment of the industry and of the industry's labor organizations.

In preparing this manuscript, the author has purposely strived to view the shipping industry and the public policy issues associated with its operations from an international perspective. The special interests and problems of individual nations, including his own, are treated only insofar as necessary in relation to their impact on the world scene. The inevitable dilemma of every student of international relations and law are faced here—i.e., the frustrating impracticality of reporting on and analyzing the specific terms of each of the national laws and programs which in their totality establish international practice.

This study has been undertaken with the sponsorship of eleven major shipping and industrial organizations, based on both sides of the Atlantic. Their instructions were simply to investigate and report on the industry's present status and outlook with emphasis on the policy issues which developments within the industry may raise, so that these issues may be better understood and more rationally discussed. Within this broad charge, the research was allowed to follow its own directions and lead to its own results.

Preparation of a study of such breadth would, of course, have been impossible without the inputs and helpful comments of a large number of well-informed indiviuals. A generous travel budget for the project permitted interviews to be conducted in Europe, Japan, Southeast Asia, and South America, as well as the United States and Canada. A team of four persons was assigned by the project's principal sponsor, Saguenay Shipping Ltd. of Montreal, Canada, to prepare working papers on selected subjects. Both these papers and successive drafts of the book as a whole were reviewed by representatives of the sponsor organizations and other experts in both the U.S. and abroad. I am indebted to all who participated in this process. In particular, I wish to acknowledge the helpful comments of Gardner Ainsworth, Director of Shipping Policy, U.S. Department of State; Dr. Harry Benford, Chairman of the Department of Naval Architecture and Marine Engineering, of the University of Michigan; Asbjorn Larsen of the Norwegian Shipowners Association; Harvey Paige of the National Academy of Sciences Maritime Transportation Research Board; Paul Fenton of Saguenay Shipping; and John Steele, Shipping Attaché, Embassy of Great Britain, Washington, D.C. Peter Smith and Barbara Johanssen of Saguenay Shipping conducted supporting research in international trade forecasts; James Balfour, now President of Alcan Shipping Services, Ltd., Montreal, prepared the technological outlook. Throughout the project, Jack Eyre, President of Saguenay Shipping and Vice-President of Aluminium of Canada, offered encouragement, counsel, and contacts.

The effort in all of this interchange has been to achieve a breadth, authenticity, and sophistication in dealing with the emerging problems of this complex industry which exceed the capabilities of any person acting alone. I wish to acknowledge my debt to my collaborators and express the hope that the study, strengthened by their contributions, may at least stimulate further interest in this important area of international trade policy and suggest avenues for further research. Needless to say, I take sole responsibility for the contents of this report and the views which I have expressed are not necessarily shared by those with whom I have worked.

S.A. Lawrence
Ithaca, New York
April 1972

Part I:
The Industry and Its Setting

Figure 1-1. Evolution of Merchant Ship Design: Typical Ship Types, 1920-1969.

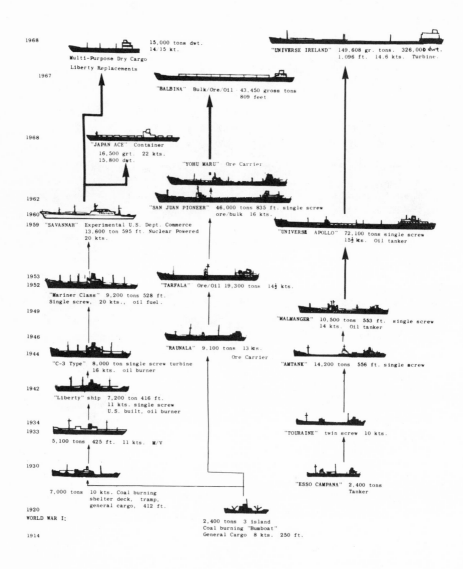

1968   15,000 tons dwt. 14/15 kt.

Multi-Purpose Dry Cargo

Liberty Replacements

1967

"BALBINA" Bulk/Ore/Oil 43,450 gross tons 809 feet

"UNIVERSE IRELAND" 149,608 gr. tons. 326,000 dwt. 1,096 ft. 14.6 kts. Turbine.

1968

"JAPAN ACE" Container 16,500 grt. 22 kts. 15,800 dwt.

"YOHU MARU" Ore Carrier

1962

1960

"SAN JUAN PIONEER" 46,000 tons 835 ft. single screw ore/bulk 16 kts.

1959 "SAVANNAH" Experimental U.S. Dept. Commerce 13,600 ton 595 ft. Nuclear Powered 20 kts.

"UNIVERSE APOLLO" 72,100 tons single screw 15½ kts. Oil tanker

1953

1952

"Mariner Class" 9,200 tons 528 ft. Single screw, 20 kts., oil fuel.

"TARFALA" Ore/Oil 19,300 tons 14½ kts.

1949

"MALMANGER" 10,500 tons 553 ft. single screw 14 kts. Oil tanker

1946

1944

"RAUNALA" 9,100 tons 13 kts. Ore Carrier

"C-3 Type" 8,000 ton single screw turbine 16 kts. oil burner

"AMTANK" 14,200 tons 556 ft. single screw

1942

"Liberty" ship 7,200 ton 416 ft. 11 kts. single screw U.S. built, oil burner

1934

1933

5,100 tons 425 ft. 11 kts. M/V

"TOURAINE" twin screw 10 kts.

1930

7,000 tons 10 kts. Coal burning shelter deck, tramp, general cargo, 412 ft.

"ESSO CAMPANA" 2,400 tons Tanker

1920

WORLD WAR I:

2,400 tons 3 island Coal burning "Bumboat" General Cargo 8 kts. 250 ft.

1914

Introduction to Part I

Merchant shipping is an extraordinarily diverse and buoyant element of the international business scene. The industry includes highly innovative organizations able to gamble tens of millions of dollars on winning a competitive margin by offering the most modern equipment and services. Many of its other members, however, are scantily capitalized companies which depend on low costs, government preferences, or local conditions to secure their trade. Leading figures within the industry include personalities as diverse as Aristotle Onassis, Malcolm MacLean, Lord Geddes, Sigval Bergesen d.y., C.Y. Tung, and Commissar Guzhenko (of the USSR). Established, professionally managed companies based in London, New York, and Hamburg must cope with regulations promulgated in Rangoon, Lima, and Accra, for throughout the world shipping terms are a function of national policies relating to the conduct of international trade.

Historically, merchant shipping operations have been regarded as extensions of national commercial life and of national power and prestige.[1] Even after mercantilism was repudiated, shipping operations in many countries continued to rely upon their governments' patronage and protection; governments in turn have looked to merchant fleets as auxiliaries to their naval services and as instruments for commercial penetration of foreign lands.

The postwar pattern of international business operations has weakened these links. Flags of convenience, which had been used only in exceptional cases prior to the Second World War, now provide registries for 22 percent of the world fleet. An additional 10 to 15 percent of the fleet, although registered under traditional flags, has been placed under such registries by foreign business interests as a matter of commercial policy or to gain some special privilege.[2] Other operators have formed multinational consortia, joined in pools or organized overseas subsidiaries in order to be able to compete internationally in the face of national regulation.

Merchant shipping in reality is not a single industry but a cluster of related industries differentiated both in terms of the ships operated and of the services performed. Significant variations in approach to both operating and policy problems are found in different areas of the world among different owner groups and governments. Counteracting these centrifugal forces, the disciplines of the market, economies of scale, and the necessity for agreement as to some minimum standards of law and practice provide the common elements which give shipping the status of an international industrial enterprise.

The purpose of Part I is to describe this emerging international enterprise and sketch the contours of the economic-political setting within which it operates. The first chapter describes the structure of the ocean freight industry, its conference system, and the patterns of ownership, registry, and manning of ships. This is followed by a brief survey of government interests and roles. In Chapter 3 the focus shifts to intergovernmental arrangements to facilitate international trade and finance, which establish the context for shipping as well. International institutions dealing specifically with merchant shipping problems are surveyed in Chapter 4, while Chapter 5 comments on the unique approaches and problems encountered in different regions of the world. The interplay of nationalism and internationalism in shipping establishes the common thread running throughout the introductory material, and Part I concludes with a comment on these opposing approaches.

1 The International Ocean Freight Industry

The international ocean freight industry may be defined as the composite of the multitude of nationally organized ship operating and supporting services which accomplish the transport of international seaborne trade. The industry has no single, formal, coherent framework of law and public policy to control its operations. The industry's organization and its role in world affairs is, instead, the product of evolutionary development punctuated by wars and periods of unusually rapid technological or political change. The latter portion of the 1960s and the early 1970s have been such periods. The industry today is in flux and is buffeted by intense nationalistic pressures. Its future is uncertain, but the industry is spurred to new high levels of investment by competitive pressures to keep pace with technology, and with a rising volume of seaborne trade.

The accelerated pace of change yields some impressive comparisons. During the last ten years, the average size of new oil tankers placed in service has grown from 28,000 to 130,000 deadweight tons (dwt.); that of dry bulk carriers, from 20,000 to 55,000 dwt. The largest of these ships are three times these sizes. Drydock, ship handling, and cargo loading and discharge facilities have developed apace, while the number of crewmen required for modern, automated bulk cargo carriers has been cut by roughly 40 percent. In the package freight business, container ships have cut port-time by a factor of five and captured over half the prime North Atlantic traffic in less than five years. It sets matters in a useful perspective to recall that the transition from sail to steam occurred over a period of 100 years and that the last sailing vessel was not retired from ocean-going commercial service until 1939.

Merchant shipping is a cyclical industry which over the years has passed through successive periods of feast and famine. In part, the changes now bursting over the industry represent the release of a backlog of improvement opportunities which accumulated during the preceding twenty years when the industry was largely preoccupied with rebuilding wartime losses and adjusting operations to the new requirements of the postwar economy. Services which depended on colonial ties and the prewar dominance of western European capitals in international trade and finance have had to be reshaped to conform to new political and commercial relationships. In addition, during the postwar years, over half of the fifty-plus newly established nations of Asia and Africa have organized new shipping enterprises which have had to be assimilated into the overall system.

Ships themselves constitute only one component of the ocean freight

5

Figure 1-2. Number, Tonnage, and Estimated Revenues of Major Components of the Ocean Freight Industry. Data estimated for ships 5000 gross tons and over in international trade, Dec. 31, 1970.

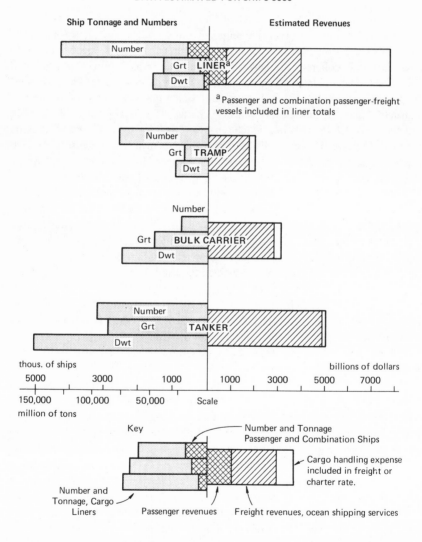

Source: Author's estimates based on foreign trade data, vessel costs, and approximate freight charges. The estimates must be recognized as indicating approximate orders of magnitude only.

industry. Connecting transportation systems and port facilities provide the gateways through which goods move to sea, and a vast complex of agents, freight forwarders, terminal operators, stevedoring companies, customs brokers, ship chandlers, insurance underwriters, financial houses, and admiralty lawyers provides services essential to international shipping operations. In the ports, ship construction, maintenance, and repair are major industries in their own right, which are supported by a network of component suppliers, engineering laboratories, naval architects, classification societies, and educational institutions. Government agencies are concerned with pollution, health and safety problems, maritime labour standards, navigational systems, maintenance of waterways, ship documentation, consular services, tonnage measurement, and nautical schools as well as with security considerations, taxation, and the scope of national flag operations. Any major change in the performance of shipping services requires adjustments in all these related operations. The effect has been to impose a very severe "institutional drag" on the rate at which changes can be accomplished.

An important aspect of the metamorphosis now being experienced in shipping is that this loosely knit complex of activities is being pulled more tightly together into more highly integrated transportation systems. The real "majors" of the industry now command resources sufficient to design and build their own ships; to create ports and pioneer new sea routes; to self-insure against most risks; and to leapfrog the entire network of forwarders, agents, and brokers, if need be, through modern data processing and communications equipment. The pressure from this class of operators is felt throughout the industry, forcing closer attention to coordinated planning, modernization, and the requirements of shipper groups.

Such developments pose a harsh dilemma for the more traditionally minded and poorly capitalized elements of the industry and for the fledgling fleets of the less developed nations. Some have already chosen to phase out of the business. Others have sought to insulate themselves from the pressures of international competition through government action to reserve a portion of the trade to national flag carriers. In other cases, governments themselves are joining the fray, either through heavy direct investments in new equipment or by underwriting such investments by client companies.

Classes of Ships and Services

The term "merchant shipping" recalls the industry's earliest days when merchants built or chartered ships to carry their goods about the world. These early merchants were also armed with letters of patent authorizing them to commandeer the ships and cargoes of foreign powers on behalf of their sponsor government.[1] Independently owned and operated freight lines, offering scheduled services over regular routes, were a development made possible by the

Table 1-1. Composition of the World Merchant Fleet, Dec. 31, 1970. [a]

Portion of the Fleet Typically Employed in:

	World Merchant Fleet (Ships 1000 grt. & over)			Short-Sea Service (less than 5000 dwt)			Transoceanic Service (more than 5000 dwt.)		
	No.	Grt.	Dwt.	No.	Grt.	Dwt.	No.	Grt.	Dwt.
1. Combination, freight and passenger ships	895	7484	4398	331	884	541	564	6600	3857
2. Freighters, all types	11899	67816	92347	5558	15000	21381	6341	52816	70966
3. Dry bulk carriers	2954	47201	77174	571	1568	2251	2383	45633	74923
4. Tankers	4232	88893	153070	955	2127	2977	3277	86766	150093
Total	19980	211397	326988	7416	19626	27152	12564	191771	299836

Freighter Classifications (ships 1000 grt. & over)	No.	Grt.	Dwt.
General purpose liner & tramp	10180	57300	80300
Refrigerated	901	4700	4900
Containerships, full	199	2287	2408
Containerships, partial	123	867	1139
Roll-on, roll-off	38	339	360
Barge carriers	3	100	106
Timber & news-print	377	1740	2420
Other speical types	78	530	620
Total	11899	67816	92347

Bulk Carrier Classifications (ships 1000 grt. & over)	No.	Grt.	Dwt.
General purpose	1894	29820	48500
Ore carriers	395	6300	10400
Ore/oil & OBO	196	7500	12600
Colliers	295	1400	2100
Car carriers	21	320	535
Other specialized types	153	1861	3040
Total	2954	47201	77174

Tanker Classifications (ships 1000 grt. & over)	No.	Grt.	Dwt.
General purpose	3860	86100	149600
LNG/LPG	172	1500	1300
Chemical	113	600	900
Other specialized types	87	693	1270
Total	4232	88893	153070

[a]Includes U.S. Reserve Fleet (786 vessels at 5,750 grt. and 6,970 dwt.)

Source: U.S. Maritime Administration.

introduction of steam in the 1850s and 1860s. During the same period, an auction market for tramp ship charters developed around the Baltic Coffee House in London, which was more formally organized in 1900 as the Baltic Shipping Exchange. Finally, the emergence in the present century of such organizations as Standard Oil of New Jersey, United Fruit Company, Krupp Steel, and other major companies with continuing requirements for specialized transport services has—in a sense—revived the pattern of merchant-owned shipping with which the industry began.[2]

This evolution has yielded three broad categories of shipping service: liner, tramp, and industrial. It must be emphasized, however, that the classifications are not sharply defined, mutually exclusive, or recognized in international law. Liner companies, for example, bear many resemblances to domestic common carriers but are not legally bound to maintain services or accept cargoes unless special provisions are enacted by the individual nations whose trade is served. The feature universally distinguishing liner from tramp companies is that the former advertise a scheduled service between specified ports whereas the latter do not. Generally the liner companies operate faster and more costly vessels, employ a more extensive network of cargo solicitors and agents, and receive for shipment a wider variety of more highly valued cargoes from a larger number of consignees. Liner firms, however, also vary their schedules and bid for bulk cargoes in competition with tramps. Many liner companies have, in fact, evolved from smaller tramping operations and some have continued to operate in both the tramp and liner markets.

Industrial operations are captive services in which both ships and cargoes are controlled by a single entity. But to supplement their own traffic, the industrials may also enter tramp and liner service. Thus, United Fruit for many years offered freight and passenger services to Central America aboard its banana ships, and oil and mineral companies from time to time put surplus vessels on charter. Ordinarily, however, company-owned fleets are sized to (or below) their owners' basic, continuing requirements, and the fluctuations in transport needs are met by time and spot charters from independent owners.

The tanker business strictly speaking represents only a specialized type of industrial and tramping operation, but because of its size is usually considered as a fourth group.[3] In terms of carrying capacity, tankers dominate the ocean freight business. In revenue terms—the more meaningful index—liners remain the largest factor due to the more costly service they provide.[4]

Tankers are only the most prominent of an increasing variety of specialized ships, often coupled with new and specialized service arrangements, which tends to break down the traditional division of the industry into liner, tramp, and industrial carriers. Mechanically refrigerated ships, introduced during the 1920s, constitute another well-established class and tend to be run in a quasi-liner mode to service a limited number of regular customers. More recently, specialized chemical, sulphur, and liquid gas carriers have been developed and placed in a

Figure 1-3. Hull Cross-Sections of Typical Ships.

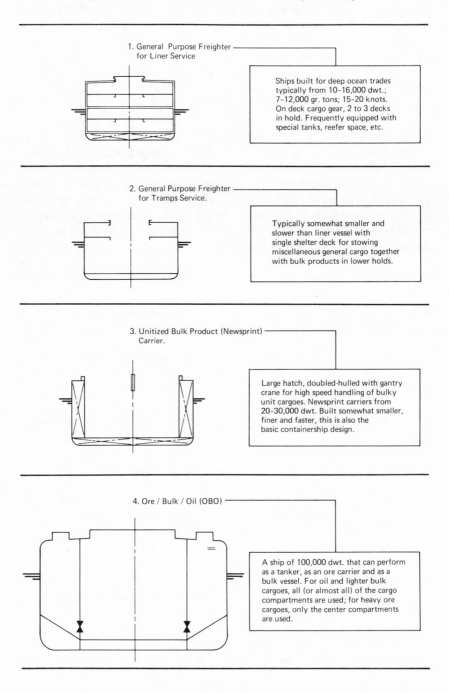

1. General Purpose Freighter
   for Liner Service

Ships built for deep ocean trades
typically from 10-16,000 dwt.;
7-12,000 gr. tons; 15-20 knots.
On deck cargo gear, 2 to 3 decks
in hold. Frequently equipped with
special tanks, reefer space, etc.

2. General Purpose Freighter
   for Tramps Service.

Typically somewhat smaller and
slower than liner vessel with
single shelter deck for stowing
miscellaneous general cargo together
with bulk products in lower holds.

3. Unitized Bulk Product (Newsprint)
   Carrier.

Large hatch, doubled-hulled with gantry
crane for high speed handling of bulky
unit cargoes. Newsprint carriers from
20-30,000 dwt. Built somewhat smaller,
finer and faster, this is also the
basic containership design.

4. Ore / Bulk / Oil (OBO)

A ship of 100,000 dwt. that can perform
as a tanker, as an ore carrier and as a
bulk vessel. For oil and lighter bulk
cargoes, all (or almost all) of the cargo
compartments are used; for heavy ore
cargoes, only the center compartments
are used.

variety of services. Vehicle carriers, usually equipped with roll-on roll-off platforms, operate both as liners and under contract. A new double-hull design, combining large hatches with squared-off holds and high performance cargo handling gear, has found a high degree of acceptance for carrying packaged timber, newsprint rolls, and metal products. Though designed for handling bulky unitized cargoes, these so-called "newsprint carriers" can also rapidly be converted to operate in other trades (for example, by placing rails within the holds to secure automobiles or containers).

Container ships were introduced by liner companies to provide a more economical and efficient method for handling large volumes of small consignments. By placing such cargoes in standard-sized containers, they could be handled with the same ease as a bulk shipment. Although most container services continue to be organized in the liner mode, the economic characteristics of such operations are fundamentally different from their predecessor break bulk services, a fact which is placing severe stress on the liner industry.

In view of the volatile character of shipping, a capability of serving multiple markets has been an objective of many operators, and considerable ingenuity has been displayed in updating outmoded ships and in adapting others to multiple uses. War-built tankers have thus been converted into container ships, tramps into bulk carriers, and multideck, hatch-loaded freighters into roll-on and palletized cargo carriers loaded through doors cut into the side. Ore carriers, which require excess cubic capacity in order to achieve the displacement needed for very dense and heavy cargoes, have been fitted with tanks so that oil may be carried in lieu of ballast on the return leg. Other bulkers have special pumps and cleaning equipment so that they may be shifted from dry to liquid cargo or from molasses to liquid caustic.

One of the most striking developments in merchant shipping has been the escalating size of tankers, the largest of which have grown from less than 50,000 to over 325,000 deadweight tons (dwt.) in the space of only a dozen years. Dry bulk carriers have demonstrated the same pattern, though at somewhat more modest levels, growing from a maximum of 26,000 to 140,000 dwt. during the same period. A 500,000 dwt. tanker and a 270,000 dwt. ore/oil ship are under construction. Container ships similarly are being built substantially larger and faster than the vessels which they replace; with faster turn around in port, these ships are able to do two to three times the work of early post war designs, ton for ton.[5] As a result, while the tonnage of the world fleet has been growing at a rate of 6 percent per year, its carrying capacity has been increasing at an annual rate approaching 9 percent; the number of ship units engaged in deep ocean trades meanwhile has been growing at only 3 percent per year.[6]

New ships are changing the conduct of ocean shipping in a variety of ways. Large investments in specialized cargo handling gear may cause fewer ports of call. Trunk line services may be coupled with local feeder lines. Ore/bulk/oil configurations may lead major industrials to enter trades which previously have

Table 1-2
Selected Freight Conferences—Number and Membership[a]

From \ To		Europe	U.S.A.	Other Developed	Less-Developed	Total
Europe	No. of conferences	25	25	13	69	132
	Total membership	194	186	148	813	1341
	% from established maritime nations	90	92	95	84	87
U.S.A.	No. of conferences	14	2	2	36	54
	Total membership	106	4	20	357	487
	% from established maritime nations	98	100	95	83	87
Japan	No. of conferences	2	1	2	24	29
	Total membership	60	22	23	309	414
	% from established maritime nations	87	86	87	84	86
Other Developed	No. of conferences	6	3	4	16	29
	Total membership	57	22	25	108	212
	% from established maritime nations	90	95	100	81	88
Less-Developed	No. of conferences	41	24	26	43	134
	Total membership	721	206	242	521	1690
	% from established maritime nations	80	78	159	78	78
	Total Number	88	55	47	188	378
	Membership %,	1138	440	458	2108	4144
	as above	85	85	85	83	83

Source: Saguenay Research analysis of conference membership listings published by R.K. Bridges in *Croner's World Directory of Shipping Conferences* (London, 1970).

[a]Includes all major long distance conferences; excludes so-called wayport conferences in which membership is composed chiefly of companies also serving more distant points.

been outside their interests. Further comment on these possibilities follows later in this study. The point here is simply to emphasize that the structure of the international shipping industry is unstable and ill-defined. Concepts which have been adequate in the past to classify types of ships and services will not necessarily be sufficient for the future.

The Conference System

The oldest and most enduring institution of the ocean freight industry is the liner conference system. The conferences are informal associations of liner companies which act collectively to establish a uniform rate structure for tariffed commodities.[7] In addition, many conferences coordinate the sailing schedules of their members, assign ports of call, handle complaints, and monitor business practices in the trade. The conferences may undertake also to fix traffic shares but ordinarily do not attempt to apportion profits, revenues, or specific cargoes and customers among their membership. Although it has some of the characteristics of an international cartel, the conference system is not designed to exercise monopoly powers but rather to stabilize conditions of trade.[8]

In the ninety-five years since formation of the first steamship conference in the U.K.-Calcutta trade, the system has spread to every corner of the world. Approximately 380 conferences are now in operation, of which about 125 regulate conditions on major international trade routes, 150 operate on minor trade routes, and the remainder are concerned with more local or intermediate trades.[9] Conferences control a very high proportion of the total transoceanic liner trade and on many routes face little or no nonconference liner competition.[10] Their membership varies from two to sixty-five firms flying many different flags. Firms operating under the flags of the traditional maritime states (northern Europe, the U.S., and Japan) dominate most conferences but companies based in less developed nations and the communist states also are enrolled (see Table 1-2).

As the conference system has developed, one of the important functions which it has served has been to provide a forum within which competing national interests might be negotiated. The conferences also have served as the vehicles for negotiating terms with major shippers and as a link between the liner industry and other elements of the commercial world.

Traditionally the conferences have sought to emphasize the high quality and reliability of their services. Nevertheless, they have been criticized for maintaining excess capacity, for sheltering inefficient operations, for charging excessive rates geared to the needs of their highest cost members, for being nonresponsive to shipper needs, and for using their considerable economic power to quash competition by nonconference carriers.

For many years, British and northern European companies were able to control the decisions of most conferences, including even those not linked to their national trades. Lines of the traditional maritime nations still exert a powerful influence in many cases, but their control has been diluted by membership in the conferences of a growing number of non-European firms.

The success of the conference systems depends upon the cooperation of its members and a reasonable degree of acceptance within the commercial world. If the conference lacks this support, ways can be found to circumvent conference rules.

The strains and stresses within the system today, due to the proliferation of national flag lines, nationalistic pressures, and the introduction of new container services, have caused many observers to conclude that the system cannot long survive in its present form. Others feel that the fundamental rationale for liner conferences, at least in the major trades, has been washed away by the formation of large, amply capitalized international consortia, which are fully able, individually, to offer services commensurate with those provided by the conferences in the past. Finally, some large shippers in recent years have found it both feasible and advantageous to shift their business from the conferences to their own vessels, or to contract carriers offering specialized services at a lower price.

Government regulations, especially in U.S. trades, have created an additional pressure on conferences. The U.S. program attempts to limit the monopoly powers of conferences by insisting that those serving its ports should be "open" on reasonable terms to any qualified applicant; elsewhere conferences have been free to develop their own rules on such matters and have typically operated as "closed conferences," accepting entrants only at times and upon terms acceptable to the established members. Legislatively-based programs to review conference activities have been established by Australia, New Zealand, South Africa, Brazil, India, and Argentina as well as the United States. Occasional ad hoc reviews of conference practices and informal liaison between conference, government, and shipper organizations have been the rule in other areas.

Yet, despite these many pressures, the conference system has remained as the key means for controlling rates and services in liner shipping. It continues to be the preferred mode of operation for the great majority of the world's general cargo carriers (who apparently prefer the shelter which it provides to the possibility of larger profits through a competitive organization) and of the shippers whom they serve. The need for shipping conferences was formally recognized in 1964 by the United Nations Trade and Development Conference (UNCTAD) despite the disaffection of certain less developed states. More recently, representatives of the major maritime nations have initiated efforts to update and codify conference practices so that the system may more effectively satisfy user needs. Rather than collapsing, the conference system appears more likely to be reformed to adapt it to the new conditions of container trade.

Tramp Ship and Tanker Associations

The evolution of merchant shipping has included several efforts to form conferences of tramp and tanker operators to stabilize rates and practices, but none has been fully successful. One of the earliest of these efforts, designed to support rates in the timber trades out of Russia, Finland, and Sweden, led to the organization of the Baltic and White Sea Conference, which remains the only international conference of tramp ship owners. Since World War II its membership has been enlarged to include almost 2,000 firms operating fifty-nine million tons of shipping, and its program has been reoriented to emphasize such commercial services as the preparation of standard charter parties, arbitration of insurance questions, and notice of objectionable practices.

The International Tanker Owners Association (INTERTANKO), a London based group whose members by the end of 1970 controlled 25 percent of the world's tanker tonnage, also evolved out of a rate stabilization program. Offering a more homogeneous service to a more limited clientele, the tanker operators have been more successful than tramps in coordinating the terms and conditions under which their ships are offered.

During the Depression a large portion of the world tanker tonnage participated in a pooling scheme through which owners whose ships were employed compensated others who undertook to lay up surplus tonnage. The pool was terminated when the tanker industry regained full employment on the eve of World War II but was briefly revived through INTERTANKO in 1963. This time, however, the Association was unable to enroll more than a slight majority of the free tanker tonnage, and the scheme collapsed the following year.[11]

The Baltic Shipping Exchange, which is the most prominent institution associated with the tramp industry, serves a quite different purpose than the conferences in the liner trade. The Exchange is a bourse of owners and shipper's brokers, where information on ships and cargoes is exchanged and charters fixed. It operates under rules similar to those of commodity and stock exchanges and, with a large number of transactions occurring daily, approximates the classic economic model of an auction market.

Ownership, Manning, and Registry Patterns

Despite masses of descriptive data, it is extremely difficult to ascertain with any precision where the real control of ocean shipping lies, the extent to which different nations are represented in the business, or the stake of different owner and user groups. The difficulties relate in part to lack of data, but more fundamentally to the diversity of criteria (e.g., whether we are concerned with operations, management, ownership or control) by which one may measure "participation" in shipping and the great diversity found in national laws regarding registry, citizenship requirements, and overseas investments.[12]

Table 1-3

Ownership and Registry of Merchant Ships: 5,000 Gross Tons and Over as of December 1970

	Ships Registered Under National Flag	Ships Owned by Nationals but Registered Under: Convenience Flags[1]	Other[2]	Registered Ships Controlled By: Nationals of Other Countries[2]	Multi-national Oil and Ore Firms[3]	Net Tonnage Controlled By: Nationals[4]	Nationals and Firms[5]
		(Millions of Gross Tons)					
A. Developed Nations:							
United States	9.8	12.5	3.0	0	2.8	22.5	32.3
Japan	21.7	0	.5	0	.8	21.4	22.2
United Kingdom[6]	23.2	7.6	.7	2.5	6.5	22.5	29.5
Scandinavia	26.7	.5	.8	1.5	1.5	25.0	26.5
W. Europe	38.5	8.4	2.0	2.5	8.5	37.9	46.4
Other	1.2	1.0	1.5	.5	.2	3.0	3.2
Subtotal	121.1	30.0	8.5	7.0	20.3	132.3	160.1
B. Socialist States	12.8	0	0	0	0	12.8	12.8
C. Less Developed States	12.6	2.8	0	1.5	3.2	10.7	13.9
D. Flags of Convenience	40.5	–	0	32.8	7.5	.1	.1
Total	187.0	32.8	8.5	41.3	31.0	156.0	187.0

Source: Author's estimates based on official and company data plus personal knowledge. The estimates should be considered to represent only approximate orders of magnitude.

[1] See Table 1-4 for basis for estimates.

[2] These estimates are particularly tenuous. The data include cross-registrations within the region.

[3] Includes tankers owned by the major international oil companies and detailed in Table 8-1 plus dry bulk carriers owned by such companies as Kaiser, Unilever, and Krupp. Two-thirds of the tonnage controlled by such companies is owned by the eight oil companies listed on Table 8-1.

[4] This column is the arithmetic sum of column one plus columns two and three less columns four and five. It therefore excludes ships owned by multi-national firms.

[5]This column includes ships controlled by multi-national firms but owned by an affiliate domiciled in the area and registered under the applicable national flag. Ships registered under flags of convenience are shown as under the control of the nation in which the multi-national firm is headquartered. Thus, tankers owned by Royal Dutch Shell, the world's largest shipowner, are shown under the country of registry wherever these registries reflect genuine national ties (for example, the German registered ships owned by Deutshe Shell A.G. are shown as German), but are distributed equally to Britain and Holland when the affiliate, such as Shell Bermuda or Hercules Tankers, operates its vessels under flags of convenience. It may be noted that the multi-national companies appear to prefer to register their ships with the nations in which their products are to be sold or processed than under convenience flags.

[6]Includes ships owned by the so-called London Greeks, who have made heavy use of flags of convenience.

Table 1-4

Classification and Ownership of Ships Registered Under Flags of Convenience. Ships 5000 Gross Tons and Over, Dec. 1970

	Liberia	Panama	Bermuda	Bahamas	Somali	Lebanon	Honduras	Total
I. Vessel type:			(thous. of gross tons)					
Passenger combination	278	241	15	0	21	5	0	560
Freighter	2,567	838	220	20	200	79	38	3,962
Dry bulk carrier	10,787	640	254	106	0	0	0	11,787
Tanker	20,203	3,307	531	60	102	0	0	24,203
Total gross tons	33,835	5,026	1,020	186	323	84	38	40,512
Number of ships	1,620	338	95	12	39	15	8	5,988
II. Ownership[1]			(millions of gross tons: estimated)					
U.S.A.	16.4	2.8	.3	*	0	*	*	19.5
Europe:								
London Greeks	6.6	.3	*	0	*	*	0	7.0
Greece	3.0	.3	0	0	*	*	0	3.5
Other	5.2	.8	.4	0	.2	*	0	6.7
Taiwan and Hong Kong	2.2	.6	0	0	0	0	0	2.8
Others	.4	.2	.3	.1	0	0	0	1.0
Total	33.8	5.0	1.0	.2	.3	.1	*	40.5

Source: Author's estimates in collaboration with Saguenay Research. The chart has been compiled from a variety of data and should be considered as representing a best estimate of approximate orders of magnitude.

*Less than 100 thousand tons.

[1]Owner's nationality, if an individual, or business address, if a corporation. Corporations wholly owned or controlled by another entity are shown under the domicile of the parent organization. Ships controlled by multi-national corporations are shown where company has its headquarters.

Table 1-5
Seafaring Manpower[a]

| | Berths on National Flag Oceangoing Ships | | Manned by | | Principal Nationalities Represented |
	Transoceanic[b]	Total[b]	Nationals	Other[c]	
U.S. and Canada	38,000	40,000	40,000	NA	Negligible
UK and colonies	60,000	116,400	95,000	31,400	Indians, Pakistani, & Chinese
Scandinavia	68,000	96,000	79,500	16,500	Other European (40%)
EEC	75,000	133,000	112,000	21,000	Asian (40%)
Greece & Spain	36,000	67,800	67,800	NA	Negligible
Japan	55,000	116,000	116,000	NA	Negligible
Socialist states	55,000	135,000	135,000	NA	Negligible
Convenience registries	95,000	120,000	NA	120,000	Greek, Spanish, Italian, British, Cayman Is., Somali, Indian, & Chinese

Source: OECD, *Maritime Transport*, 1970 and estimates by Saguenay Research.

[a]Data on seafaring manpower are complicated by different assumptions used by reporting countries regarding the ratings and types of vessels included and coverage of seaman who are on leave or unemployed. In constructing this table, the objective has been to report data only for persons actually employed on deep-sea oceangoing merchant ships, 1,000 gross tons and over.

[b]Author's estimates based on an average of 45 berths per ship for all countries except EEC and Scandinavia (40) and Great Britain and other (50 and 52). "Transoceanic" relates only to ships 5,000 gross tons and over; "total" to all ships over 1,000 gross tons.

[c]Data for OECD nations as reported in *Maritime Transport*, 1968, annual report of the Maritime Transport Committee of the OECD.

Registry under flags of convenience is only one of many means used by owners to gain the flexibility needed to remain competitive in an international market. Increasingly shipping companies of all types are reaching beyond national borders for capital, equipment, personnel, and even management. Long term leasing agreements (terms of three to twenty years) are a common feature of the dry bulk and tanker business, and are appearing with increasing frequency in the liner and tramp sectors of the industry—e.g., SeaLand's proposal to take the entire U.S. Lines container ship fleet under charter for a twenty-year term. In other cases, vessels may be assigned to brokers or agents for management purposes or are owned by companies subject to some sort of external affiliation or ownership agreement.

It is virtually impossible to trace all of these interlocking agreements. Indeed, establishing the effective control of a single ship can involve weeks of careful research and raise difficult points of law. Yet by making some broad assumptions, it is possible to develop at least a rough gauge of the extent to which foreign registries are used by ship managers in various parts of the world. Tables 1-3 and 1-4 present the results of such an effort.

Table 1-3 probably substantially understates the tonnage which might validly be considered to be controlled by U.S. and British corporations. For example, according to a list maintained since 1946 by an industry journal, vessels built in foreign yards on behalf of United States companies and their affiliates totaled 48.1 million dwt. by April 1, 1969.[13] Assuming that sales and retirements from this tonnage approximately equal new acquisitions from other owners, the journal's tabulation would suggest that the U.S.-controlled tonnage is well over that shown in the table.[14]

Registry and ownership data, furthermore, do not necessarily reveal how the owning corporation established its nationality, where vessels and financing are obtained, by whom the ships are operated, or the nationality of the officers and crew. International law requires only that there be a "genuine link" between the ship and its flag. The nature of this link is undefined, and in practice considerable latitude in these matters is permitted by most maritime states.[15] Thus, ships are typically built wherever the most favorable arrangements can be made. They may be nominally owned by corporations (often holding a single vessel) formed solely for this purpose and domiciled wherever tax, registry, and national preference considerations may dictate. They may be managed by a professional management organization, by a charterer, or by both with respect to particular functions; and they are operated by the best available crews allowed under the laws of the registering nations (see Table 1-5). At present, about 50 to 60 percent of the world fleet, including most modern tankers and specialized bulk carriers, can in this sense be regarded as essentially supranational in character. And despite nationalistic pressures, this portion is growing.

The many nations and companies involved either directly or indirectly in the Torrey Canyon disaster present an interesting case in point. The tanker was owned by the Barracuda Tanker Corporation of Bermuda and registered in

Liberia under the Liberian flag. At the time of the accident, she was under long term lease to Barracuda's parent company, the Union Oil Company of California but had been subleased for a single voyage by British Petroleum Trading Ltd. (a subsidiary of British Petroleum Company) to carry oil from Kuwait to U.K. The ship had been built in the U.S.A., had undergone extensive structural changes in Japan, was insured in London, and was manned by an Italian captain and crew. After repeated failures to obtain litigation through the courts, the British and French Governments eventually collected $7.5 million when British treasury agents seized the sister ship, the "Lake Palourde," in Singapore and issued an arrest-writ against her, which was paid by her insurers.

In sum, the international maritime economy presents an extremely complex net of international relationships between owners, ship operators, financial institutions, shipyards, and users. Interesting opportunities are available throughout this network to minimize taxes or to gain government financial aid, a preferred position for carrying certain types of cargoes, or more favorable labor rates. In the final analysis, effective control of ships and shipping tends to gravitate to the centers of world trade and industrial organization—i.e., New York, London, Tokyo, Hamburg, and Moscow. The dispersion of ownership for the charter market and of the management of liner shipping, however, has supported the growth of active shipping centers in such secondary cities as Piraeus, Taipei, and Hong Kong. Finally, shipping's outreach through the hiring on of foreign crews has permitted substantial participation in the industry by Burmese, Somalis, and residents of the West Indies and Bahamian Islands.

2 Government Interests and Roles

There is hardly an aspect of merchant shipping in which governments are not in some way involved. Governments finance, own, and operate merchant fleets and participate in mixed-ownership shipping corporations. They directly and indirectly subsidize private shipping, direct its deployment, and set the conditions for its registry. Governments are major users of shipping services and sometimes act also to represent the interests of other users. They may directly allocate cargoes, control inland feeder routes, and influence terms of shipment through state-controlled financial, industrial, and trading institutions. During emergencies most governments reserve the right to requisition ships; in peacetime, merchant ships may be used for training or paramilitary tasks.

Shipowners depend in many ways upon their governments as well—for diplomatic protection and consular services abroad, and for the entire infrastructure of facilities and aids necessary for safe and efficient operations in home ports and along the routes which their vessels serve. Under international law, a vessel operating without the protection of its national flag is subject to seizure on the high seas and may be denied access to ports. In effect, all international trade depends upon the sufferance of governments, and the network of treaties of friendship, commerce, and navigation built up during the past 125 years provides a crucially important, though seldom noted, backdrop to shipping operations.

Promotional Programs

In past years, governmental interest and support has chiefly focused on liner operations, which have frequently been treated as overseas extensions of the internal transportation system. In contrast, the tramp and industrial sectors of the world fleet have been relatively free of governmental intervention. There are signs that this situation is changing. Several countries are already subsidizing construction of bulk carriers; others are applying pressure in various ways to bring such vessels under national control.

Government support to shipping operations is infectious; advantages granted by one party tend to cause compensatory actions or retaliation by others. Unfortunately the basic cause of the infection lies beyond the control of shipping authorities—in fact beyond the control of anyone, given the present state of international economic affairs. Costs of operating under different

21

registries vary widely, depending on registry requirements and on the underlying economic strength of the host country. Local currencies, in which wages usually must be paid, may be severely inflated or available for only limited use. Tax policy is a variable which always complicates international comparison. When governments themselves operate shipping fleets, it is usually impossible to calculate true costs.

Inasmuch as there is no agreement as to what constitutes a "normal and appropriate" relationship between national flag shipping operations and their host governments, there is no commonly accepted reference against which one can assess the impact of alternative public policies. The flags of convenience offer the most neutral benchmark, since countries having them do least either to assist, tax, or regulate the ships flying their flags. In addition to such longstanding convenience registries as Liberia, Panama, and Honduras, Lebanon and Somali registries are popular with certain southern European shipowners, while Bermuda, Hong Kong, Cyprus and the Bahamas offer havens from pyramiding of British and commonwealth taxes. Other nations have from time to time adjusted their registry laws in hopes of attracting foreign tonnage (e.g., Costa Rica, Tunisia, and Morocco). For the Greek government, the problem was to devise a tax program which would cause Greek citizens to repatriate their ships without at the same time wholly renouncing the possibility of imposing future taxes on the ships which were enrolled. In Japan and India, economic conditions are in any event relatively favorable to shipowners, but the governments of these nations have adopted more far-reaching promotional programs to stimulate the expansion of national flag services.[1] In Scandinavia, West Germany, and the Low Countries, operating costs are higher, but a strong commercial position coupled with long experience in ship operations (and, in certain of these countries, with selective tax and credit advantages) has permitted owners to compete successfully with little or no positive public intervention.[2] In Great Britain, favorable provisions for tax write-offs were for a time translated into a direct subsidy to underwrite 20 percent of the purchase price of new vessels but, with British shipping now enjoying relatively favorable results, this aid has been repealed.[3] Modest construction and operating subsidies are granted by Spain; more substantial amounts by Italy and France.[4] In less developed nations, primary reliance tends to be placed on state operation or government assignment of cargoes to national flag carriers at preferential rates rather than on direct subsidy aid.[5] The United States, of course, maintains the most comprehensive program with direct and indirect operating subsidies now running in the range of $400 million per year—roughly 40 percent of the total cost of fleet operations excluding cargo handling expense.[6]

Deep sea merchant shipping is conducted wholly through public corporations only in the socialist countries of Eastern Europe, Asia, and the Caribbean (Cuba); in Burma, Ghana, Nigeria, Ethiopia, Kuwait, Venezuela, Peru; and in certain of the smaller African states. Governments, however, hold a controlling interest in major portions of the fleets of Brazil, Ecuador, France, Iceland, Indonesia, Ireland, India, Israel, Italy, Mexico, Turkey, the United Arab Republic, Venezuela, and the United States. In more than a dozen other countries, they are minority participants in mixed ownership corporations or bear responsibility only for a small portion of the national flag fleet.

There is no apparent correlation between the intensity of government support for shipping and the competitive strength of national flag fleets. Backed by their governments, the Japanese and Russian fleets have achieved impressive results. The Scandinavians have achieved comparable growth without such backing. For the United States, massive subsidization has sustained only a static level of operations.

Regulatory Programs

Governments also may intervene in shipping matters to assure that services are available on a fair and reasonable basis to carry import-export trade. Usually such programs are carried out in collaboration with the national flag carriers. However, a few nations (the U.S., India, Japan, Brazil, and Argentina) have established formal procedures for reviewing rates and practices of all carriers serving their foreign trade while the governments of others (Australia, New Zealand, and South Africa) work with quasi-public shipper groups to negotiate terms of shipment with conferences dominated by foreign flag carriers.[7]

The unilateral efforts of the first group of nations cited above (and particularly of the United States) to impose their judgments regarding the conduct of international shipping on carriers domiciled elsewhere and protected by treaties of commerce and navigation have caused untold turmoil in the shipping industry during the 1960s. The most notorious controversies have revolved around the U.S. Federal Maritime Commission and its largely unsuccessful efforts to obtain information upon which to base rate judgments from foreign flag lines.[8] However, an objectively more serious interference with extraterritorial shipping activity was successfully consummated by Brazil, which in 1968 unilaterally dissolved the major conferences serving its trades and replaced them with new bodies organized more to its liking.[9] India's more cautious approach has attracted little notice but has had some success in limiting rate increases, which would have had a major impact on its foreign trade.[10] All of these actions—successful or not—created direct confrontations of national interests which still are not wholly resolved.

Other Intervention

The conduct of the ocean freight business is conditioned by government policies in other ways as well. Port operations in most nations are controlled by public bodies. Visiting vessels must contend with port fees, pilotage requirements, berthing preferences, consular fees, and clearance procedures and taxes. In the less-developed world, such regulations are often administered in a discriminatory fashion to favor national flag ships. Exchange controls often present additional complications.

Health and safety considerations (including pollution control) have also led to extensive governmental regulation. In these fields there has been considerable international coordination. The size and qualifications of ships' crews, however, continue to be a matter for national determination, and important variances are found in national approaches to this and other matters.

National governments from time to time intervene in shipping in more dramatic ways. Consider the impact on the shipping world of the closing of the Suez Canal, the UN-endorsed embargo on trade with Rhodesia, or the U.S. unilateral blacklist on shipping to Cuba, China, and North Vietnam. So long as wars and tensions are a condition of mankind, shipping's international operations will be vulnerable to disruption from overriding political considerations and to redeployment in the interests of national defense.

Interests at Stake

Clearly there is a very great range of concerns which may arouse governments to become involved in shipping affairs and which may vary from time to time and place to place. For some nations, shipping is an important source of foreign exchange; for others, a major source of employment. Norwegian shipping generates 10 percent of that nation's GNP and over one-third of its export earnings. The British industry still provides seafaring employment for 85,200 persons although the number has recently been falling at a rate of 5 percent per year. Revenues from tonnage taxes and fees meet 10 percent of Liberia's annual central government budget.

Compared to other industries, however, shipping for most nations is a relatively minor factor in the domestic economy. Worldwide deep-sea employment, at approximately one million jobs, is dwarfed by employment in other facets of the maritime industry (i.e., ports and shipyards) and wholly insignificant as compared to employment in such basic industries as fishing or farming. There is a wise saying, "Where there are rich farms, there are no seamen." For those nations where poverty of domestic resources has turned attention to the seas, however, there may be few options to absorb the impact of a downturn in shipping activity.

Also shipping everywhere is an important factor in foreign trade calculations, both to assure access to foreign markets on fair and reasonable terms and as a source itself of foreign exchange. Ocean freight payments, at some $15-18 billion worldwide, are in the range of 8-10 percent of the f.o.b. value of merchandise entering international seaborne trade and the freight entry looms large in almost all nations' external payments accounts. Closer examination, as we shall see in Part II, usually reveals that shifting cargoes from foreign to domestic flag carriers will not affect the greater portion of payments receipts and costs, but such examination is not always performed.

Finally the relatively intangible considerations related to national prestige, power, and commercial penetration have an important influence upon national shipping policies. The precedents of history include too many instances in which control over shipping has determined the wealth or safety of nations to be wholly ignored. It is difficult to relate these precedents to the foreseeable realities of the modern world. However, it is also difficult to dismiss entirely the possibility that nations could face prolonged periods of international tension in which national shipping would be essential to the continuation of overseas trade or the possibility that they might have to contend with unfriendly shipping monopolies as the sole vehicle for commercial contact with the outside world.

Trends in Exercise of Government Powers

Governmental interests are and always have been one of the basic facts of life in the international shipping business. The manner and vigor with which these interests are expressed ebb and flow to a rhythm set by changing international trade conditions and the ravages of war.

World War II substantially eradicated the tangle of preferential and anticompetitive practices which had beset international shipping throughout the 1920s and 1930s. Furthermore, at the war's end, there was a strong sentiment among the leaders of the allied powers that the conditions which had typified prewar trade should not be allowed to recur. As negotiators began to come to grips with the hard realities of competing interest, however, many of the lofty objectives toward which their conferences had been convened gave way to compromises which have proved to afford inadequate protection against the revival of nationalistic and discriminatory practices.[11]

Reconstruction of war-ravaged economies and merchant fleets required many special measures which, for the most part, were administered with sensitivity and restraint by the United States in cooperation with other affected, friendly powers. By the mid-fifties, this reconstruction was substantially complete and the merchant fleets of all major shipping countries other than Germany and Japan had regained or exceeded their prewar level. Restrictions within the Atlantic Community were relaxed and both trade and shipping doubled in less than ten years.

Differential rates of growth during this period are now revealing maladjustments which threaten a recrudescence of restrictive practice. In particular, the nonindustrial countries of Asia, Africa, and South America have failed to keep pace or in many cases to achieve the targets which they themselves had set for their development. In an effort to regain lost ground, many of these countries have abandoned liberal trade policies in favor of experiments in more aggressive exercise of government power. A common result in the shipping field has been the extension of discriminatory regulations designed to channel cargoes to national flag ships and to build up this facet of their domestic industry. In a recent survey, Phillip Franklin shows how flag discrimination slowly spread between 1946 and 1965 to become a significant aspect of the official maritime policies of forty-two shipowning countries.[12] In the years since 1965 the practice has continued to grow with a vigor which is causing informed industry sources to be fearful that the entire system of free access to commercial cargoes may become unplugged.

3 International Trade and Financial Policies

Governmental attitudes toward shipping are but one element of more far-reaching international trade and financial policies, and shipping policy inevitably is influenced by developments in related fields. Thus the broader framework of international trade policy sets the tone for economic concourse among nations and the standards of trade practice generally are likely to be reflected in the shipping field.

Shipping of course depends totally on a growing trade for its own growth and prosperity. It also requires efficient international financing mechanisms for the conduct of its own business and a reasonable degree of clarity and common understanding in such matters as taxation, commercial law, and liability.

Though shipping and trade policy are related, it should not be assumed that they are necessarily consistent with one another or even in themselves. Several western European exponents of liberal shipping policies are also leading protectors of domestic agriculture. Israel, with a rapidly developing and entrepreneurial domestic economy, conducts its shipping activities largely through state institutions. The Soviets frequently concur with the United States in shipping matters, and so it goes.

Such contradictions should surprise no one. The pervasive characteristic of international trade and financial affairs is their extraordinary ambiguity and complexity. As one seasoned expert, Jan Tinbergen, describes it, "Viewed in toto, trade policy is a monster with a multitude of dimensions and degrees of freedom. An exact description of its state would require thousands of figures at the least."[1] Tinbergen argues that "this situation is undesirable if for no other reason than it enables pressure groups to operate in the dark: almost nobody else knows his way around the subject. If in the past, trade policy had been less opportunistic and more systematic, a greater degree of public control would have been possible. . . . [But] trade policy is in chaos."[2]

Trade Agreements

Some minimum agreement among governments regarding the terms and conditions of international trade is a necessity for the planning and conduct of business operations. Postwar planners had anticipated forming an International Trade Organization to meet this need. The failure of the ITO to secure adoption created a gap in international economic machinery which has only partially been filled by the General Agreement on Tariffs and Trade (GATT).[3]

The General Agreement was drafted as an interim measure intended only to set out basic principles regarding the conduct of trade (including trade in "invisibles" such as shipping). It has evolved into an institution, loosely affiliated with the UN, which sponsors a variety of activities to facilitate trade and encourages the formation of new trade agreements among its members. Although its membership does not include any of the Communist states, the sixty-seven contracting parties to GATT account for over 80 percent of world trade.

The Agreement embodies four principles: (1) nondiscrimination in setting terms of trade, subject to the right in certain circumstances to form free trade associations and customs unions; (2) progressive reduction in the tariff barriers to trade and prohibition of quantitative restrictions, discriminatory licensing arrangements and so forth, except those agreed upon by contracting partners as temporary expedients to overcome a balance of payments deficit; (3) compulsory consultation as a means for arbitrating trade disputes; and (4) continued collaboration in advancing the objectives of the Agreement. GATT has served effectively as a forum within which successive tariff reductions have been negotiated and it has sponsored a number of successful arbitration proceedings. But it has failed to stem the tide of import quotas and restrictive trade practices or to reconcile the divergent doctrines of "most-favored-nation" versus preferential regional trading.

During the past half dozen years the focus of trade policy has increasingly shifted away from tariff equalization and reduction towards formulation of special arrangements to regulate the terms of trade in specific commodities, within regions, or between specific nations.[4] Furthermore, the diffusion of economic activity has increased the role in international trade of such nations as Japan, which subscribe to GATT rules but approach trade from a perspective quite alien to that of the Western powers. Also, an increasing volume of trade, particularly with socialist and less developed nations is based upon special arrangements worked out through intergovernmental agreements rather than private market channels.

The building pressures within GATT and the UN Conference on Trade and Development for preferential arrangements to improve the access of the less-developed states to industrial markets may be regarded as a logical outgrowth of the changing attitudes toward the conduct and purpose of trade. If nondiscrimination principles may be set aside in order to hasten the economic and political development of a European Common Market, why can they not be set aside for African and Latin countries? If the affairs of the world truly have become so intertwined that the closing of the gap between the rich and poor nations is among the most urgent of the world's priorities, as the Pearson Commission suggests, does it not also stand to reason that trade should be used as a positive instrument for getting on with the task? And if trade, why not shipping services? Such developments in trade policy are therefore of keen interest to the shipping world.

Commercial and Tax Law

A second requirement for the successful conduct of international trade and business activities is a framework of reasonably clear, consistent, and enforceable commercial and tax law. Enactment and enforcement of such law is a responsibility of national governments. Private groups, however, have also long been active in a continuing effort to codify and publicize decisions, harmonize legal principles, minimize conflicts amongst national approaches, clarify jurisdiction, facilitate enforcement, and provide for arbitration of international disputes. Proposals developed through consultation within such groups as the International Law Association and the International Institute for the Unification of Trade Law (UNIDROIT) frequently have been given effect through national legislation and through bilateral and multilateral agreements amongst nations. In 1966, additional impetus to such activity was provided by the formation of a continuing Commission on International Trade Law (UNCITRAL) by the United Nations.[5] The United Nations, through its International Law Commission, also has developed and secured adoption of a Convention on the Recognition and Enforcement of Foreign Arbitral Awards. Through its regional commissions, it has worked effectively to promote commercial arbitration in Europe and the Far East.

That almost $300 billion of business (merchandise and services) is now successfully transacted across national boundaries each year demonstrates the existence of an internationally workable system of commercial law. It is a system, however, which depends heavily on good faith and cooperation and which can hardly be considered adequate as a framework for our exploding global enterprise. The dramatic difficulties (e.g., expropriations) reveal only the top of the iceberg. More typical problems—and it will be noted that each has implications also for shipping—arise in connection with such matters as: interpretation and enforcement of contracts; limits of liability and provision of insurance; protection against pollution; access to the resources of and under the high seas; identification of jurisdiction and citizenship; and validation and simplification of documents used in international trade.

The tax field presents special problems, which are gaining increasing prominence and attention. For businesses, tax inconsistencies may lead to double taxation or to financial burdens which diminish their competitiveness in foreign markets; for governments, the international character of modern business enterprise creates problems in identifying activities subject to taxation and in making levies effective. Efforts to harmonize tax policy are making some progress in Western Europe, and recent years have brought a surge in bilateral tax treaties among industrialized countries. However, numerous difficulties are still encountered in tax matters in the less developed world and there is little prospect that any tax conventions, either formal or informal, could be developed which would gain anything approaching universal acceptance within the next decade.[6]

Efforts to come to grips with the gaps and inconsistencies of international commercial and tax law, in shipping and in other fields, are severely hampered by the inherent complexity of the subject matter, the economic significance of the points at issue, the sluggish responses of national legislatures and judiciaries to recommend practices, the refusal of certain leading commercial nations to commit themselves in advance to abide by arbitral procedures, and the general undertone of mistrust between governments and between the private and public groups collectively engaged in the coordination effort. It is clear that these constraints will not be surmounted easily. Similarly, it is unrealistic to expect any comprehensive rationalization of the legal environment for the conduct of the shipping business within a period as brief as the ten years here under review. Those engaged in the effort instead seek progress by chipping slowly away at specific problems in the uncertain hope that these practices can be updated more rapidly than others are made obsolete by change.

International Monetary Arrangements

A third necessary element to the conduct of international commerce is a system for currency stabilization and exchange which reflects the changing economic position of nations but which also provides a cushion to temporary fluctuations. Prior to World War II, there was no governmentally-backed system for international settlements and most currency exchanges took place within bilateral agreements on essentially a barter basis. The Bretton Woods Agreements of 1944, coupled with the formation of the International Monetary Fund the following year, constituted an enormous forward step and for the first time institutionalized the commitments of the contracting parties to assist one another in stabilizing the international valuation of their currencies. To this end, the Agreements set forth certain rules regarding the manner in which exchange rates should be set and adjusted to keep pace with changing conditions, set up criteria for evaluating the permissibility of temporary restrictions on trade and currency convertibility, and provided mechanisms both to maintain an international pool of currency reserves and to monitor the domestic monetary policies of debtor states.[7] However the Agreements did not establish a self-executing system which could operate successfully without the active participation and cooperation of its members.[8]

Like other elements of the international trade apparatus, the monetary system has worked, but it has many imperfections and limitations. The chief difficulties have related to its sluggishness in achieving currency revaluations. Since it is politically easier to use stopgap measures to prop up currencies at artificial values than to revalue or achieve domestic economic reforms, deviations from the Fund's objective of a nondiscriminatory, freely functioning, multilateral system for currency valuation and exchange have in some areas of the world been less the exception than the rule.

Nations having recourse to such devices can argue that they are a necessary response to certain underlying conditions: inadequate amounts of liquid reserves; maladjustments in the value of other currencies; and discrimination in the conduct of trade. The use of exchange restrictions, of course, exacerbates one of the problems (discrimination) which it seeks to solve and, over the medium to long term, may undermine the ability of the nation electing this course to earn the foreign exchange it needs to finance essential imports.

There is no question that fundamental disequilibria have developed within the international monetary system within the past decade. The vast expansion of international business and capital flows has put stresses on the adjustment process which have significantly altered the conditions within which the Fund must work.[9] Fortunately, international money managers are coming to recognize that excessive emphasis on currency stability creates conditions which negate the very purpose of the system—i.e., the conduct of trade.[10] Authorization of Special Drawing Rights was visualized as one way of reducing pressure on the system by allowing more time for nations to accomplish adjustment without resorting to artificial props. More aggressively negotiated revaluations provide a second means for bringing currencies more in line with their real worth. In the aftermath of the August 1971, revaluation of the dollar, intensive attention is being given to still other methods, such as the "crawling peg," to facilitate exchange rate adjustments.

The manner in which the international monetary system is reshaped in the years ahead will have important implications, both direct and indirect, for shipping. The use and exchange of many currencies is an inescapable feature of international shipping operations. When currencies are blocked or pegged at unrealistic values, shipping companies are forced to hedge their financing or adjust their pattern of operations.[11] But more important, it has been the extreme pressure on payments balances and the consequent premium that states have placed on foreign exchange earnings which have provided the principal economic motivation to governments to use subsidies and cargo preferences to promote national flag merchant marines.

Relaxation of payments pressures through monetary system reform is probably a prerequisite to any real progress in controlling the aids which governments extend to shipping. Fortunately the outlook for reform is reasonably good. Those in charge clearly are not ready to consider anything approaching a free market in currency exchange.[12] Nor are national governments likely to surrender any powers relating to internal economic management of their territories.[13] But all concerned do appear to be edging towards a more self-executing system which will make it easier for national governments to fulfill the commitments regarding currency adjustments to which they are pledged under the 1944 Agreements.

Links Between Trade and Shipping Policy

Shipping has a compelling interest in international trade policy, and in several nations the industry has assumed an active role in policy formulation. Yet when international questions are considered, the shipping interest typically is taken up last, as a sort of afterthought to the larger enterprise. Neither national governments nor international organizations are therefore likely to give shipping questions the sustained and forceful attention which their resolution requires. The industry in turn has traditionally preferred to be left to work through its own channels in shaping its private destinies.[14]

The difficulty, of course, is that shipping affects too many interests to be left alone, and some of these interests look to governments to support their cause. Recognizing that nationalistic tendencies are being expressed with alarming vigor, industry leaders during the past decade have swung around to the view that they must seek an active role in strengthening international cooperation as the only alternative to balkanization of shipping into a medley of inefficient national endeavors. European shipowner associations are working hard to articulate a doctrine of "workable competition" in shipping which will preserve the essential flexibility and international character of shipping within a framework of self-regulation designed to achieve a more equitable environment for the conduct of international trade. In this effort, shipowner groups are emphasizing close cooperation with shipper interests in the belief that the competitive need to have free access to the cheapest and most efficient shipping services will "cut across all irrational tendencies, thus making governments reaffirm that a major objective in the future, as in the past, will be to preserve the freedom of choice of shippers."[15]

This widening horizon is leading the industry to assume a more active role in reference to a broader range of commercial and political concerns. The 1969 Annual Report of the Norwegian Shipowners' Association, for example, examines such matters as European unification and international currency stabilization, arguing that "for a globally oriented industry such as shipping, it is of central importance that the broadest possible market solutions are established . . . and that sensible stabilization of international currency markets . . . should be given high priority."[16] The need to assist in the growth of less developed countries is recognized and the contribution which more technologically advanced nations, such as Norway, can make to this objective, noted.[17] The tone of such statements is sharply different from that of only a few years ago. The metamorphosis reflects the recognition that overall arrangements for international commerce will significantly affect the conduct of shipping, even as the manner in which shipping approaches its obligations will affect the conduct of trade.

4 International Shipping Institutions

Although shipping officials have for many years consulted informally on matters of common interest, the level and number of multilateral maritime organizations and activities have sharply escalated during the past dozen years. This apparatus shows every sign of playing a growing role in years ahead, as more problems outstrip the capacities of individual companies, conferences, and national bodies. It includes both public and private bodies organized on both a global and a regional basis. A comprehensive description would require some hundred pages, for nearly that number of groups are in some way involved.[1] What follows therefore can only identify and briefly describe the most prominent.

United Nations Agencies

The United Nations is sponsor to a great variety of programs and instrumentalities, at least a dozen of which have important implications for shipping. In recent years UN economic programs have been heavily slanted towards meeting the needs of less developed nations. In addition, the UN Secretariat, through its Department of Economic and Social Affairs (Resources and Transport Division) and its Center for Planning and Projections, has assumed an active role in providing basic planning data, in trade facilitation, and in standardization of transport systems. The Secretariat arranges technical assistance, sponsors conferences and publication programs, attempts to coordinate related work throughout the UN family, and provides direct support to those elements, such as the UN Development Programme, which do not maintain a separate transport staff.

Regional economic commissions have been formed under the aegis of UN Economic and Social Council in Europe (ECE), Africa (ECA), Latin America (ECLA), and Asia and the Far East (ECAFE). The latter two have been particularly active in shipping affairs. The Economic Commission for Europe in cooperation with the Council of European Ministers of Transport also has been substantially involved but with emphasis on the facilitation of intermodal transportation and container systems.

Amongst the various UN special programs and related bodies, the work of the International Law Commission, the UN Commission on International Trade Law, and the GATT merits note. The Law Commission, for example, developed the 1958 Conventions on the Law of the Sea, which codified the rights and responsibilities of shipping in the various zones of marine jurisdiction. Special-

33

ized agencies of the UN having programs related to transport include the World Bank and its affiliated agencies, the International Civil Aviation Agency (ICAO), the World Meteorological Agency (WMO), the Food and Agricultural Organization (FAO), the International Telecommunications Union (ITU), Intergovernmental Maritime Consultative Organization (IMCO), the Shipping Committee of the UN Conference on Trade and Development (UNCTAD), and the International Labor Organization (ILO). The last three bodies are discussed in more detail below.

Figure 4-1. United Nations Agencies Dealing with Transport Matters.

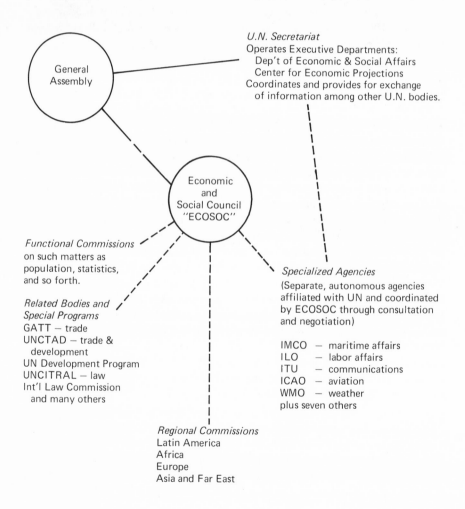

U.N. Secretariat
Operates Executive Departments:
  Dep't of Economic & Social Affairs
  Center for Economic Projections
Coordinates and provides for exchange
  of information among other U.N. bodies.

General Assembly

Economic and Social Council "ECOSOC"

Functional Commissions
on such matters as population, statistics, and so forth.

Related Bodies and Special Programs
GATT – trade
UNCTAD – trade & development
UN Development Program
UNCITRAL – law
Int'l Law Commission and many others

Specialized Agencies
(Separate, autonomous agencies affiliated with UN and coordinated by ECOSOC through consultation and negotiation)

IMCO – maritime affairs
ILO   – labor affairs
ITU   – communications
ICAO – aviation
WMO – weather
plus seven others

Regional Commissions
Latin America
Africa
Europe
Asia and Far East

Intergovernmental Maritime Consultative
Organization

IMCO is the smallest of the UN specialized agencies (with a budget of one million dollars per annum and a staff of roughly twenty professionals), but it is the agency with the widest role in maritime affairs. Its membership of sixty-nine nations includes all major countries, other than Communist China, which register ships under their flag. Since its formation in March 1958, it has concentrated on technical, legal, and facilitation problems and has established an impressive record of achievement in these fields. IMCO has sponsored conferences leading to the adoption or amendment of four major international conventions.[2] The agency also has issued a number of recommended practices to advance the safety and efficiency of sea transport and has conducted technical studies on a variety of practical ship construction and operating problems.

The charter for IMCO was written during the immediate post-war years during a period of high hopes for achieving permanent improvement in international relations through strengthened international organizations. Initially it was anticipated that the functions of a UN shipping organization should be twofold: first, to promote adherence to standards of fair competition set up along the lines specified in the Havana Charter for an International Trade Organization, and second, to act as a successor to the wartime United Maritime Authority by providing for cooperation in technical and operational matters. The final drafting of the IMCO convention, however, revealed such differences in approach amongst the participating governments that the commercial and economic policy objectives of the organization were substantially diluted, both through revisions in the language of the charter and, subsequently, through declarations filed by several governments conditioning their adherence to the Convention.[3] Thus, although the IMCO Charter includes in its aims the "removal of discriminatory action and unnecessary restrictions by governments," the organization has in fact attempted very little in this field.

Within the last several years mounting commercial problems have begun to cause some reconsideration of IMCO's role. For example, a Legal Committee, formed in 1967 following the Torry Canyon disaster and charged initially only with studying liability questions, has since been empowered to consider any "legal problems" arising within the scope of the IMCO Charter.[4] IMCO also has assumed an active role in control of marine pollution and is the chief focus of international efforts toward this objective.

Shipping Committee, UN Conference for
Trade and Development

UNCTAD was established as a continuing organization of the United Nations General Assembly in December 1964 upon recommendation of an ad hoc UN

Conference on Trade and Development held earlier that year. Its role is to consider means for accelerating the economic development of less developed states through revised international trade policies. The Committee on Shipping is one of five standing committees of the Conference and is open to all states participating in the parent body. At present forty-five nations are enrolled, including all major shipping nations other than Mainland China. A staff of approximately twenty professionals has been assembled to conduct the work program, which is heavily oriented toward economic studies and questions of trade policy. Attention is also given to port facilities, container systems, and future developments in shipping technology.[5]

Questions relating to terms of trade and economic development have a high political content, which inevitably affects all the organization's work. Lacking formal authority, UNCTAD must rely on persuasion to give effect to its positions and, on most issues, has attempted to find formulas which could gain the support of each of its three major blocs (developed nations, less-developed economies, and socialist states). This means that progress has been slow and marked by increasing frustration. UNCTAD's role is further weakened by the fact that its mission is entirely supplementary to that of UN bodies, including particularly the UN Social and Economic Council, through which UNCTAD makes its reports to the General Assembly.[6]

UNCTAD's work in the field of shipping is based on a Common Measure of Understanding, adopted by the 1964 Conference,[7] which:

1. acknowledged the necessity of the liner-conference system in order to secure stable rates and regular services;
2. called for closer cooperation between conferences and shipper groups;
3. assigned priority to improving port facilities; and
4. stated that the decisions of developing nations regarding promotion of national flag merchant fleets should be based on sound economic criteria.

The Shipping Committee has been relatively successful in stimulating more meaningful consultation between conferences and shipper councils, and in stimulating economic analysis and discussion of the unique sea transport problems of less developed states.[8] It has been less successful in its effort to use economic analysis as a means for identifying factors which enter into the determination of shipping routes and freight rates. This latter work has been impeded both by the inherent difficulty of the subject and by concern within the shipping industry that such analyses might create a leading wedge for unwanted government intervention in conference rate-making.[9]

Unlike IMCO, the Shipping Committee's work cannot directly result in the adoption of any formal international agreements or action. At its 1969 meeting, however, the Committee acted to establish a Working Group on Shipping Legislation with a mandate to "review economic and commercial aspects of international legislation and practices in the field of shipping from the standpoint of their conformity with the needs of economic development . . . in order to identify areas where modifications are needed."[10] Charter parties, marine insurance, and bills of lading and related matters are identified as matters for priority attention.

As this volume goes to press, the UNCTAD Shipping Committee is engaged in a debate concerning basic features of conference operations. Because vital interests are involved, it seems unlikely that UNCTAD will be able to translate this debate into any effective action.

International Labor Office

The ILO is one of the oldest intergovernmental agencies now operating under the UN. From its beginnings in 1919 it has taken an active interest in maritime labor problems and, through its Joint Maritime Commission, it has developed some twenty-seven conventions and fifty recommendations, which together constitute a comprehensive Maritime Labor Code. These instruments have achieved a high measure of ratification and brought about progressive improvement and international standardization of working conditions aboard ocean-going ships. The conventions include provisions on manning, hours of work, pensions, vacation and sick pay, and even minimum wages. However, the latter are geared to the social and economic development of the seaman's country and in themselves, therefore, have done little to close the gap in costs of operating ships.[11]

ILO's success rests upon the unique tripartite procedures through which it conducts its work. The Joint Maritime Commission includes both shipowner and labor representation together with public members appointed by the ILO. Both the International Shipping Federation (owners) and the International Federation of Transport Workers (labor) have supported and participated in the work, although owners stress the need for flexibility in the formulation of labor standards, while labor seeks specific commitments. Labor shortages in many European countries, which are increasingly causing the employment of mixed crews, add to the pressures for internationally similar treatment of seafaring personnel.

Other International Governmental Organizations

Several international, intergovernmental agencies which contribute significantly to the legal-political framework for merchant shipping operate independently of the United Nations. These include the Brussels Diplomatic Conference for Private International Law, the Permanent Court of Arbitration at the Hague, and the International Hydrographic Bureau. The first of these bodies was the vehicle for extensive work during the first half of the century in standardization of national commercial law. It was, for example, the group which promulgated the Hague Rules.[12] The second, despite its resounding name, simply provides a mechanism through which a distinguished and nonpartisan panel of technically qualified arbiters can be empaneled at the request of the parties to a dispute. Like the UN-affiliated International Court of Justice (World Court), it limits its activities to disputes between states requiring interpretation of treaty law; although both bodies have taken cases bearing on merchant shipping, their ponderous procedures have limited their use.

Other important intergovernmental organizations are the OECD Maritime Committee and the thirteen-nation Consultative Shipping Group. Strictly speaking both are regional groups representing a particular point of view, but they have gained a standing in shipping affairs which transcends their regional status. An interesting aspect of the OECD Maritime Committee and the Consultative Shipping group is that both, while oriented toward European interests, also include Japan.

The OECD Committee sponsors research in shipping problems, provides a forum for exchange of views among the maritime officials of its member governments, and attempts to identify and discourage discriminatory practices within the industry.

Although lacking any staff or permanent organization, the smaller, thirteen-nation CSG is now emerging as an effective policy group. It had its origins in discussions in the early 1960s among European governments as to how they might counter actions of the U.S. Federal Maritime Commission which Europeans regarded as an improper assertion of foreign authority over their national trade. Members are the senior shipping officials of twelve West European nations plus Japan. The group has been meeting once or twice per year. At its Tokyo meeting in May 1971, it developed suggestions for formulation of a Code of Shipping Conference Practice which are now being carefully studied by public and private groups throughout the world.

Nongovernmental International Associations

There is a plethora of private international associations concerned with specialized aspects of shipping or organized to represent the interests of certain groups or owners but there are only a dozen or so which attempt to respond to worldwide interests and to enroll a global membership. Three of these, the Baltic and International Maritime Conference, the International Tankers Association, and the International Shipping Federation have been briefly noted above.[13] Others are:

Comité Maritime International

The CMI was established in 1896 under the sponsorship of the International Law Association and has been very active over the years in drawing up draft instruments for consideration as international conventions by the Brussels Diplomatic Conference and by IMCO. Its membership includes a substantial representation from insurance and financial houses as well as shipping companies and is principally, though not exclusively, drawn from the established maritime countries. A belief among officials of less developed states that the CMI had failed adequately to recognize their needs was a principal motivation for the organization of the UNCTAD Shipping Committee Working Group on Shipping Legislation.

International Chamber of Shipping

Founded in 1921, the ICS is a London-based organization representing ship-owners from Great Britain, Scandinavia, the EEC countries, the U.S., Japan, Greece, Spain, and a half dozen other states. It has full-time observers sitting in as advisers on the ad hoc committees of UNCTAD, IMCO, and similar organizations and is directly concerned with national shipping policies, shipping regulation, and technical and legal matters affecting shipping. The ICS is the most broadly based of the several shipowner groups and espouses the traditional liberal viewpoint of the established maritime nations. The Chamber is colocated with the younger and more compact Committee of European National Steamship Owners Associations (CENSA formed in 1963) and has a partially shared staff.[14]

International Chamber of Commerce

The ICC has a broad membership based in eighty countries and supports a wide range of activities in support of expansion in international trade. Shipping has long constituted a major interest of the Chamber and it maintains both a Commission on Sea Transport and a Commission of Transport Users among its twenty-five boards and committees. The special contribution of the ICC is that it bridges shipowner and user interests. The organization has worked actively to provide joint consultation and improved machinery for self-regulation in industry. The ICC has also taken strong positions opposing flag discrimination as inimical to trade and has worked actively with the CMI and other bodies in the field of shipping legislation.

International Cargo Handling Coordination Association

ICHCA is a relatively new (1952) and active group with 1700 members in seventy-four countries. Its major function is to stimulate communication on handling methods within the transportation community—a function which it discharges through local, regional, and international symposia and the publication of a monthly journal.

International Standards Organization

The ISO is an association of the national standards bodies of fifty-three countries. Growing use of containers in shipping has caused the problem of container standardization to become one of the key issues before the ISO. Recommended ISO standards are not binding on either the national standards organizations or upon the governments of the nations which they represent unless specific action is taken by government to give such standards legal effect.

International Association of Ports and Harbors

First organized in 1955, the IAPH membership now includes 206 public and corporate members from fifty countries. The organization's aim is to increase the efficiency of ports and harbors through information exchange and technical assistance. It conducts (biannual) international conferences and publishes a quarterly journal.

International Federation of Forwarding Agents Associations

FIATA is another international body dedicated to maintaining communication amongst its members and to representing their point of view before other international bodies.

Council of European Shippers' Councils

The CESC represents European national shipper councils in negotiations with CENSA and has been assuming a growing role in shipping affairs. During the past year CESC has observer status at meetings of the CSG and UNCTAD Shipping Committee.

In sum, the shipping industry does not lack for consultative mechanisms on an international scale. Like most international bodies, shipping organizations lack effective decision-making power in reference particularly to economic and commercial issues. Because the collaborative machinery has evolved out of voluntary associations, the membership of most groups tends to emphasize the more established sectors of the industry. However, shipping's international machinery is maturing with action within the past decade to focus the interests both of less developed states and of shipper groups.

5 A Regional Review

As a worldwide undertaking, merchant shipping must be attuned to a variety of disparate traditions and local economic conditions. The industry has been approached quite differently in different lands. Also, in shipping as in other branches of industry and trade, regional organizations are assuming a growing role.

Arrangements for regional economic cooperation, led by the formation of the European Common Market in 1958, have proliferated during the last dozen years. (See Table 5-1.) Some, such as the Central American Common Market and East African Community, already brought substantial economic integration. Others have moved more slowly. In general, the experience of successful groupings has been that a quickening of intraregional exchange supports a growing external trade as well.

Europe

The major issue for European trade policy is, of course, whether arrangements can be successfully concluded to bring Britain and its EFTA associates into the EEC. Shipping interests in the EFTA countries strongly favor this move. They believe that membership in the market is crucial to assure continued access to continental cargoes and will buttress Europe's commitment to liberal shipping policies in its dealings with other nations.

Ocean shipping occupies an ambiguous position vis-à-vis the Treaty of Rome. The industry is clearly excluded from the application of the EEC countries' common transport policies until affirmative action may be taken by the Council of Ministers to extend their effect.[1] However, there is no specific exclusion of ocean shipping from policies and programs which may be adopted to implement such other objectives of the Rome Treaty as harmonizing national legislation and developing a common policy for foreign trade and regulating competition.[2] Some observers conclude that integration of other aspects of the national economies of Common Market states inevitably will build pressures for implementation of common policies in merchant shipping.

Lacking British and Scandinavian participation, the EEC nations have been net importers of shipping services. With the participation of EFTA nations, the Market will be an exporter of shipping and, through the coordinated action of its expanded membership, will both have a strong incentive and be in a powerful

41

Table 5-1
Regional Trade Agreements

I.	Customs Unions—aiming toward free trade within the area and a common tariff externally
	European Economic Community (EEC)
	East African Common Market
	Central American Common Market
	Central African Customs and Economic Union
	West African Customs Union
	Arab Common Market
II.	Free Trade Areas—aiming at internal free trade only
	European Free Trade Area (EFTA)
	Caribbean Free Trade Area (CARIFTA)
	Latin American Free Trade Area (LAFTA)
III.	Other Regional Economic Groupings
	Council for Mutual Economic Assistance (CMEA · COMECON)

Source: Saguenay Research.

position to promote the maintenance of liberal shipping policies by its trading partners.[3]

All of the European states, of course, have proud maritime traditions. Great Britain, the Scandinavian countries, Holland, and Greece have built the largest fleets in comparison to their trade and have over the years maintained the highest levels of operating efficiency. Germany has made successive efforts to extend its shipping beyond the requirements of its national trade in order to assume a global role and, during the past fifteen years, has made considerable progress toward that objective. France, Italy, Portugal, and Spain have emphasized liner services linking the metropolitan state with colonies and dependencies and with other trading partners. In these latter countries, the government has assumed a prominent role both through direct participation in the business and subsidies to national flag lines.

Prior to World War I, European shipping (in particular, British vessels) accounted for almost 80 percent of the world fleet. Today its portion is a bit less than half. For most European states, national flag shipping has nonetheless kept pace with a growing national trade.

Great Britain presents a special case. Her extraordinarily dominant role in shipping during the early years of the century reflected unique circumstances which could not possibly have been sustained.[4] By the mid-sixties, British and Commonwealth shipping (at 17 percent of the world total) had stabilized at a level equivalent to their trade. Since then, there has been growing optimism that British shipping, spurred by more aggressive management and modest government aids, may regain its former profitability and growth. Long concentrated in conventional liner and tramp service, firms now are shifting to container ships, dry bulk carriers, and tankers.

All European nations—particularly the Scandinavian countries and Britain—impose heavy taxes on personal and corporate income. Because ships may be acquired with modest cash outlays and depreciated on a flexible (Britain and Sweden), or accelerated (Norway and Germany), basis, they are an attractive vehicle for investment of surplus funds. Greece has in effect suspended taxation altogether on new construction and on ships repatriated from convenience flags. In Norway, Sweden, and Finland capital gains from ship sales may be placed in special funds for reinvestment in the industry which may both reduce and defer taxation.

These programs are not considered as "subsidies" because in most cases they are consistent with tax principles applied to other industries by these countries. Their particular utility in reference to shipping has, however, been a powerful stimulus to investment.[5]

Because the European nations have a large stake in the shipping business, they have been particularly concerned about the effect which changes now convulsing the industry may have upon their fleets. In Britain, a royal commission under Lord Rochdale was appointed to study the organization and structure of British shipping; the Commission's 500-page report offers almost 100 recommendations for strengthening company finance, increasing productivity of seamen, and improving cooperation between shipowners and shippers.[6] A similar study was prepared in 1968 for the Dutch Shipowners' Association.[7] In Scandinavia, research on the industry's economic position and outlook is being privately supported.

Commonwealth Nations and Crown Colonies

The fortunes of shipping throughout the British Commonwealth are closely tied to those of Europe. Some of the Commonwealth nations (notably Canada) have extensively used the British flag as the vehicle for their own shipping operations; in other cases a colonial flag (notably Bermuda) may offer tax advantages for services that are chiefly managed from London.[8]

British maritime traditions have taken root in most of the Commonwealth nations. Substantial fleets (including tankers and bulk carriers) are based in India (2.3 million gr. tons), Pakistan (0.6 million gr. tons), and Cyprus (0.9 million gr. tons); smaller but respectable national flag liner operations are maintained by Singapore, Ghana, Malaysia, Nigeria, and Malta.

Although heavily involved in seaborne trades, Australia and Canada have encountered adverse labor conditions which have inhibited use of national flag ships. Australia, however, is now making a modest entry into container shipping through participation in container consortia serving her trades. Canada appears, as a matter of deliberate policy, to have decided to avoid development of a deep sea shipping industry under Canadian flag.

In India and Pakistan strong interests in national development, coupled with long-standing maritime traditions, have combined to give merchant shipping high priority in national investment plans. Although confronted by desperate domestic problems and chronic shortages of development capital, these two nations' merchant fleets have been expanded during the past decade at rates of roughly 12 percent per year, which are among the most rapid growth rates of any national flag. India now ranks sixteenth among the world's shipowning nations and is developing the nucleus for a supporting shipbuilding and ship repair industry. Pakistan's progress has been more erratic, but her shipping is now moving aggressively into the conferences serving her national trade.

United States

The United States is probably the single most important factor in the world shipping scene and one of the most unpredictable. The U.S. participates as either the shipper or receiver of almost one third of the world general cargo trade; its Federal Maritime Commission conducts the most far-reaching program of unilateral shipping regulation found in any country; U.S. representatives play a leading role in most intergovernmental trade and shipping organizations; the national flag merchant fleet, although relatively small, includes a high proportion of the world's most advanced liner-type vessels; American firms have spearheaded the introduction of container shipping; and American owners are the largest users of convenience registries.

A profound uncertainty surrounds most aspects of the U.S. shipping scene. After years of debate, extensive revisions of the U.S. subsidy laws were enacted in October 1970, but the real impact of the amendments—intended to de-emphasize dependence on operating subsidies and government cargoes by stimulating investment in new container and bulk cargo vessels—will depend upon the readiness of American firms to build ships for operation under U.S. flag.[9] To date (May 1971) only a half dozen vessels have been placed under contract and most of these are of conventional design.

American liner companies were the leaders in introducing container systems. The extraordinary success of the SeaLand Company set a standard which the U.S. subsidized lines have found difficult to follow. The challenge of container shipping has convulsed the managements of the subsidized lines. Every one of the twelve companies remaining in the program at this date is led by a president appointed within the past five years; three companies have had two or more new presidents during this period. Four of the companies have been absorbed into larger conglomerates and three have undertaken substantial nonshipping investments.

Except for the SeaLand and Seatrain companies, the nonsubsidized portion of the U.S. flag fleet is composed almost entirely of overage vessels. Their obsolescence will, within a very few years, force their owners to decide whether to invest in new U.S. flag tonnage or shift to other registries.

U.S. regulatory programs also are in transition. Following a burst of zeal for protecting competition in the middle sixties, the Commission appears now to be accepting cargo sharing and pooling arrangements, at least in the South American trades. It also has seriously considered asking for authority to establish rate minimums in U.S. foreign trade. Though the Commission's focus remains on the at-sea portion of maritime transport, attention now is being given to means for bringing the entire point to point process, including the role of terminals, brokers, and forwarders, under some sort of regulatory control.

In past years, the requirement that 50 percent of all government and government-financed shipments be via U.S. flag ships has been a particularly contentious element of American shipping policy. European governments have argued, probably with justification, that this requirement has provided a model for similar discriminatory practices abroad.[10] Sole access to these cargoes (at inflated freight rates reflecting the higher cost of U.S. flag operations) has, however, become critical to the survival of America's aging tramp fleet. As the old ships are replaced by modern bulk carriers, it is expected that U.S. companies will become less financially dependent on the "cargo preference" system. The requirement that at least half of the Government's shipments be via U.S. flag vessels, however, will in all likelihood be maintained.

Over the past two decades, the tonnage of U.S.-controlled shipping registered abroad has grown so that it now exceeds the tonnage of the active privately owned fleet under U.S. flag by a factor of three to one. Including this tonnage, U.S. shipping is in approximate balance with U.S. foreign trade. The national flag portion of the fleet concentrates on liner cargoes and (including all government shipments) in this sector achieves a 25 to 30 percent share.[11] U.S.-controlled ships registered abroad are utilized almost entirely for offshore bulk movements (coastwise and intercoastal shipping being reserved for U.S. flag), and probably handle about a third of this trade.[12]

Japan

The growth of Japan's export-import trade and shipping during the past decade has outpaced even the astounding growth of the Japanese economy at large. Japanese shipping, which was totally decimated during World War II, began its slow recovery under the Occupation and, upon conclusion of the peace treaty in 1952, had grown to 2.6 million gross tons. Rapid expansion, spurred by shipping shortages during the Korean War and later by the Suez crisis, brought Japan's fleet to 5.3 million gross tons by 1958—capacity sufficient to carry roughly 50 percent of her fast-growing foreign trade. During the succeeding ten years, while gross national product was increasing between 8 and 9 percent per year, the tonnage of Japanese foreign trade expanded at a compound rate of 20 percent annually, and its shipping at 12.5 percent per year. To fill the gap, Japanese companies have chartered 3 million gross tons foreign flag shipping (six month

Figure 5-1. Ship Tonnage and Cargoes by Geographic Region.

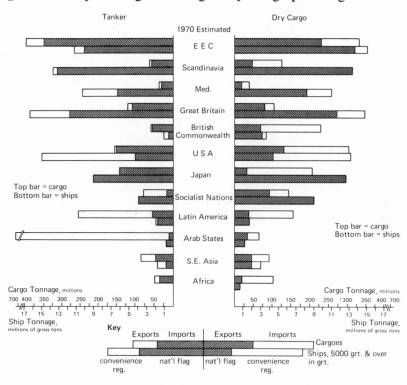

Source: Ship tonnage by U.S. Maritime Administration; for estimates of ownership of convenience registries see Table 1-3, this study. Cargo estimates from UN data.

term and longer) and, with this supplement, now carry an estimated 59 percent of their trade.

Japanese industrial and trade expansion has been achieved through a close partnership between industry and government and between the major industrial combines. The achievements of the past ten years have substantially exceeded the nation's economic plan adopted in 1960.[13] Japanese trade and shipping experts appear to feel that trade expansion during the coming decade may also exceed the 8.5 percent annual growth rate anticipated in the government plan, perhaps coming closer to 10.5 percent. This plan, incorporated in a 1969 White Paper, proposed construction for Japanese owners of 20.5 million gross tons of shipping during the six-year period through 1974, permitting an approximate doubling of the tonnage held in 1968. The plan is geared to balancing the Japanese freight payments account and to bringing 70 percent of the nation's foreign trade onto national flag ships. In actuality, a more realistic estimate is that Japanese flag vessels will continue to handle only their present 50 percent because trade will expand more rapidly than anticipated in the plan, and because Japan's growing participation in cross trades will divert a portion of the tonnage.[14]

However the numbers may be construed, they point towards Japan's emerging during the very near future as the world's leading shipping and trading nation. With this in mind, it is well to note several unique characteristics of the Japanese situation:

1. Japan's trades are heavily imbalanced (inbound tonnages exceed outbound by a factor of ten to one) but diversified both as to commodity and trading area. Although there is a heavy concentration of activity in the regions of Southeast Asia and Oceania and with the United States, Japan's trade reaches every corner of the Communist and non-Communist world.
2. Control of Japanese shipping is concentrated in only six nucleus companies, which in turn are closely associated with other elements of the nation's heavy industry and finance.
3. Japanese management demonstrates strong interest in economic research, new technology, and advanced production planning methods. Furthermore, it employs the large numbers of researchers and engineers needed for these activities.
4. The operating philosophy of the Japanese industry reflects a unique blend of strong national loyalty and cooperation in reaching common goals. The Japanese have been strong supporters of the conference system and are full-fledged participants in the major European shipowners' associations. Although not pioneers in either field the Japanese have been quick to capitalize on the economies available in supertankers and containers.

Japanese shipping enjoys an efficient and low wage maritime labor force, but has nonetheless been subsidized throughout the postwar period. This subsidy has been directed chiefly at buttressing the financial structure of companies which had been encouraged to expand very rapidly on narrow equity margins and has been provided chiefly through low interest rates and deferred repayments of government loans. The 1969 plan, however, will require the Japanese shipping industry to meet a larger share of its financing through its own resources, although liberal credit terms are still offered by Japanese yards.

Communist Nations[15]

Maritime transport does not play a major role in the trade among socialist countries; however, it is very important to their overseas and Western European trades. The latter have been growing rapidly since Nikita Krushchev liberalized

Soviet trade policy in 1956, and socialist shipping has grown apace. Between 1958 and 1968 the average annual compound growth rate in shipping tonnage under registries of Council for Mutual Economic Assistance (Warsaw Pact) countries was 13 percent per year, a rate which approximates the group's expansion of seaborne trade. The rate of fleet expansion has eased during the latter portion of the period and, as of December 1968, the tonnage of ships on order for socialist registries indicated a slower rate of expansion during the next several years than for the world fleet as a whole.

The socialist states of Eastern Europe conduct their foreign trade through bilateral trade agreements which commonly contain a shipping clause. To the extent that national flag ships are insufficient to meet shipping needs under these agreements, supplemental tonnage is chartered on the international shipping exchange. Because national flag tonnage still falls short of shipping needs, such chartering is very common, involving several million tons each year.

Shipping policies within the CMEA bloc are coordinated through a Permanent Commission of Transport of the Council, located in Moscow. An operational unit of the Commission (Shipchartering Coordinating Bureau) coordinates the actual use and acquisition of ships. Although operated within a single system, there is some diversity of operations amongst the socialist fleets and within the Soviet merchant marine. This latter sizeable fleet is actually managed through fifteen "companies," each under the general jurisdiction of the Soviet Ministry for Merchant Marine.

The growth in socialist shipping has generated considerable apprehension in Western shipping circles, in part due to uncertainty about Soviet plans and intentions. To date, however, these vessels have limited their activities principally to their own foreign trade. Where participating on a regular basis in cross trades, the socialist liner operators have generally been willing to observe conference practices and even to join these organizations. Within IMCO the socialist representatives have cooperated in technical matters; in UNCTAD they have generally remained aloof from the developed-less-developed nation contest.

Soviet shipping has gained a reputation for efficient, unspectacular operation (ice-strengthened vessels and ice-breakers are an exception). Vessels are mostly conventional types and concentrated in the small to medium-sized dry cargo categories. Although the Soviets have not yet acquired any container capacity, they have recently announced a plan gradually to introduce such services. The public statements of Soviet maritime officials express a pragmatic outlook and an inclination to seek an accommodation of competing interests through negotiation with other governments.[16] Within the past year the Soviet Union has signed treaties of navigation with several Western European countries. In the treaty with Great Britain, a reference is made to the necessity of maintaining freedom of competition in international shipping.

Less is known of the shipping activities of mainland China. Ships registered under her flag are reported at 888 thousand gross tons (chiefly small coasting vessels). Her seaborne foreign trade (exports) is estimated by Saguenay Research at seven to eight million tons, about 30 percent with Japan, and most of the remainder with other nations within her immediate environs.

Latin America

Although officially classed among the world's less developed areas, large sectors of Latin America are moving rapidly towards an industrialized economy and participate in a substantial foreign trade. A strong desire to expand national flag merchant shipping, particularly in Brazil, is a natural concomitant of the drive towards industrialization. The impact of Latin maritime expansion programs so far has been felt chiefly in the form of political action to establish a firmer position for national flag lines. The extent to which the Latin nations will be able to follow through with actual ship operations of a scale commensurate with their aspirations depends, as do other aspects of their development plans, on the availability of capital (and particularly foreign exchange), on attitudes toward foreign investment, and on internal political stability and leadership.

The larger and more advanced South American nations have operated deep ocean fleets since World War I. Their fleets however have been small, relatively old and inefficient, and stagnant in size except when pressed into wider service by the exigencies of war. Latin states have never commanded more than 4 percent of the world shipping tonnage—an amount sufficient to carry roughly half the area's intraregional commerce (and roughly half of the fleet is so employed) but only 10 percent (in terms of freights paid) of the area's external trade.[17]

A mixture of government and private ownership characterizes almost all of the South American fleets. Government controlled operations dominate the overseas liner services; privately owned fleets, local cargo services and petroleum trade.

Lacking resources to provide direct subsidies, Latin states interested in maritime development have resorted to a variety of preferential and discriminatory devices to advance national flag shipping. Although all the seaboard South American countries have legislation reserving a portion of their foreign cargoes to national ships, waivers of the requirement are commonly granted by the West Coast states. A more aggressive discriminatory posture was adopted in 1967 by Brazil, and its model has since been followed by Uruguay and Argentina.

The South American nations (particularly Brazil) are active and articulate proponents of trade and shipping policies geared to the needs of developing economies. Their dependence on overseas trade and their vulnerability to shortages in world shipping, painfully demonstrated in two World Wars, has caused them to place high priority on maritime development. In this cause, they can be sure of the attention, if not the concurrence of the United States, which is caught between its desires to assist in Latin development and to promote international competition in shipping.

By exercising raw commercial pressure, Brazil has been able to introduce bilateral cargo sharing agreements in most of its overseas trades. Bilateral arrangements also exist between Brazil, Uruguay, and Argentina for carving up the coastal trade. But, interestingly, the South American states have been unable to develop a comprehensive agreement for sharing cargoes moving in intra-regional trade despite intense negotiation on the problem.

Arab States and Middle East

Deep sea shipping appears not to fire the imaginations of the residents of the desert lands stretching along the south and east coasts of the Mediterranean, the Red Sea, and the Persian Gulf. Of the nineteen recognized states in the region, only three—none typical of the Arab League—operate more than fifty ships of over 1,000 gross tons. These are Israel, with a diversified foreign trade fleet of 750 thousand tons, Turkey, with a fleet of 566 thousand tons concentrated in short sea services, and Lebanon at 441 thousand tons, mostly under Greek ownership. Moves toward providing convenience registries have also been initiated in past years by Tunisia and Morocco but without success. In the late 1950s a complicated negotiation between Aristotle Onassis and the Saudis for placing a tanker fleet under Arabian flag was also aborted. The United Arab Republic maintains a small fleet for local service purposes but has so far demonstrated no disposition to expand it as a vehicle for an intensified intraregional trade.

Southeast Asia

Southeast Asia is a major trading area which generates a great variety of cargoes, about two-thirds of which are absorbed in Japanese markets. The nations of the area are themselves diverse, and, despite the leadership of such groups as the regional UN commission and the Asian Development Bank, there is little evidence of intraregional cooperation.

This situation, coupled with the region's geography and the continuing commercial ties of prewar colonial relationships, has produced a very mixed pattern of maritime development. Burma has essentially attempted to achieve maritime self-sufficiency to the great disadvantage of her trade. Indonesia also has followed a separatist policy, but its requirements for marine transport are so large and urgent that it has had to invite the services of foreign flag carriers until it can build its own fleet to a sufficient size. Hong Kong vessels, reportedly largely financed abroad, engage in international trading operations, whereas the substantial fleets of the Phillippines and Taiwan are employed chiefly in servicing national needs. Singapore's fleet provides distribution and feeder services. Other nations in the area rely almost entirely on foreign flags.

As an area which is crisscrossed by major international trade routes, Southeast Asia is uniquely exposed to overseas maritime influences and expectantly awaits being caught up in the container tide. Under the pressure of new operating methods and more strident nationalism, the old European-dominated conference system in the area is breaking down. The pattern toward which the industry is moving in this area is particularly unclear.

Africa

Of the thirty independent states of Black Africa, none has a national product as large as a typical medium-sized American city.[18] A dozen of these new countries, however, have responded to the lure of owning a deep-sea merchant marine. In total, fifty-seven ships (1,000 gross tons and over) totaling 400 thousand gross tons operate under these African flags. The Black Star Line of Ghana maintains the largest of these operations and, with 14 ships (plus chartered tonnage), has carried up to 20 percent of the Ghanese trade.[19] The Nigerian Line, which has close ties to that nation's Marketing Board, also has achieved a substantial trade share. The remaining operations are of subcritical size and appear not to have received much emphasis in national development plans.

The foregoing data exclude Liberia, which serves as the country of registry for the world's largest merchant marine. The Liberian government holds a 50 percent interest in three of the 1,547 vessels which fly its flag.

Concluding Remarks: Nationalism versus Internationalism in Shipping

Any effort to portray in an overall way the character of the international ocean freight industry founders on the extraordinary diversity of this global industry, the strong crosscurrents of interests within which it operates, and the instability of the international trading system it serves. The present turmoil clearly marks a period of transition in shipping, whose outcome is still obscure. The stresses within the industry are of the same kind as those acting upon the international community at large: national versus international approaches, developed versus emerging nations, competition versus accommodation, and governmental versus private action. The increasing interdependence of the world economy lends urgency to the resolution of these stresses.

Pressures for change in the conduct of ocean shipping are being advanced from both ends of the development spectrum. On the one hand, the most advanced container ship and bulk carrier operators have in effect outgrown the established conventions of such institutions as the liner conference and the Baltic Exchange. On the other, many less developed nations have concluded that existing conference and chartering practices are prejudicial to their trade and to their efforts to establish national merchant fleets. Not surprisingly, the leading ship operators prefer to work through commercial channels to update shipping practices; the governments of the less developed states, seek action in the political arena, where they enjoy more leverage.

Neither public nor private authorities enjoy a well-defined status in international trade and shipping affairs. In legal theory, the nation state is sovereign; in fact, its practical authority in shipping matters is severely limited by the alternative available to shipowners to shift their operations to another flag. But, whereas economic interests may in the normal case be controlling, shipowners face the risk that their business could at any time be wiped out through a governmental action which bars them from a nation's ports or requires a certain proration of its cargoes. With no functional avenue for appeal in such cases to international authority, owners must rely for help and protection upon their national governments, just as governments must rely upon shipowners for fair and efficient transport of their trade.

The phrase "shipping nationalism" is often used to refer to governments and ship lines which adopt a policy of close mutual support and protection to the exclusion of other interests. An international or "liberal" shipping policy favors a system in which governments accord equal privileges to shipping companies of any flag and intervene minimally in the affairs of those companies which happen to be domiciled within their jurisdiction.

There is a considerable body of opinion which holds that it is both futile and counterproductive for governments to attempt unilaterally to control international trade and shipping affairs. Those holding this viewpoint cite the rise of international business, the economic advantages to be gained through free international trade, and the self-interest which businesses have in the responsible conduct of their affairs. Others argue that any business activity requires groundrules, that governmental authority is needed to make such groundrules effective, and in any event governments are so enmeshed in shipping affairs that it would be unrealistic to project any system which did not recognize their role.

The economics of international shipping, as will be demonstrated in the next section of this study, place a high premium on flexibility and rapid market response. Were there only one world government, it would be difficult enough to devise a regulatory system to provide an appropriate framework for the industry's operations. In a system which depends on the separate actions of the world's 145 sovereign states, over half of which support an active foreign trade and shipping industry, to establish such a framework through deliberate action may prove impossible. Yet, international shipping is very much a going concern and an industry which has prospered and expanded rapidly over the past twenty-five years—despite its difficulties.

**Part II:
The Economics of Sea
Transport**

Introduction to Part II

Within the more general context of strategic and political interests, the most important factors shaping the development of international shipping have historically been economic. It is economics that determines which trades will prosper and which sets the threshold of technological change. Even when other considerations (e.g., security or prestige) take priority, economics establishes the "price" which must be paid to achieve their realization. In fact, since this price often is regarded as an investment needed to secure future prosperity, economic, political, and strategic considerations are blurred over the longer term. In an internationally competitive industry such as shipping, economic power and economic efficiency are the dual bases for industrial leadership and control.

Recent years have brought a quickening of interest in shipping economics in efforts to understand better the consequences of alternative policies, to improve the efficiency of maritime investments, and to anticipate future developments. A substantial literature has been amassed on conference operations and rate-making, on the impact of shipping investments on national balances of payments, on appraisal of port investments, on criteria for making the most efficient use of ship design, and on relationships between shipping supply and demand.[1] However, as in most areas of industrial economics, the data for such studies are frequently inadequate. While general principles can be identified, their application is often made difficult by the realities of specific situations.

The chapters which follow deal with the demand for and the supply of shipping services; the organization of freight markets; competitive relationships; and the economics of ship subsidization. They draw both upon the published literature and on certain unpublished materials prepared by Saguenay Research.[2] The treatment is analytic and is presented in order to provide a basis for our later estimates of trade and technological developments in shipping, their likely impact on the industry, and their implications for public policy.

6 The Cargo Base: Demand for Shipping Services

Despite the growth of overland and air transport, the great weight of international trade—85 to 90 percent of total dry cargo transport performance—moves by sea.[1] Similarly, about 85 percent of the world's deep-sea shipments move in international commerce.[2] Except for cargoes which can be taken by air, long distance interregional trades are, of course, virtually entirely seaborne and almost always involve international commodity exchange.[3]

The postwar growth in deep sea shipping has been paced by a truly remarkable expansion in world trade. In other periods the relationship has been reversed—improvements in shipping services provided the basis for the growth of trade. The trade-generating effect of new bulk cargo and container services is at the moment a question of great importance for certain, potentially over-tonnaged segments of the maritime industry. Unfortunately it is a subject on which very little is known.

In shipping terminology, international trade is differentiated in terms of the physical and economic characteristics of the cargo and the size of shipments, as well as in terms of the routes on which transport services are required. Expansion of trade has been selective, affecting different segments of the industry in different ways. Furthermore, the balance and stability of trade flows have important implications for the organization of shipping services, as will be noted below.

Growth Rates: Production, Trade and Shipping
1948-1967

	Growth	
	Total percent	Compound percent
World Population	45.5	2.0
World Domestic Product	140.4	4.7
Int'l Trade (Value)	264.8	7.1
Int'l Seaborne Trade (Tonnage)	284.8	7.3
Merchant Shipping (G.R.T.)	297.5	7.4

Pattern of International Seaborne Trade

World seaborne trade is an extraordinarily far-flung enterprise involving an enormous variety of cargoes and all parts of the world. Shipping companies will undertake to handle almost every conceivable cargo from elephants to asphalt and from locomotives to lace. A typical liner tariff in fact announces rates for one to three thousand commodities. Transport performance, however, is concentrated in a very few commodities—principally petroleum, iron ore, grain, and coal—which move in very large volume over a limited number of well-defined routes. Of these commodities, petroleum dominates the scene, occupying a position in international shipping somewhat analogous to coal 40 to 50 years ago. The tonnage of the three major dry bulks enumerated above is only slightly more than one third that of crude oil and petroleum products shipped in interregional trade, yet these three dry bulk products represent over 40 percent of world interregional dry cargo movements (see Figure 6-1).

The remainder of the dry cargo movements is more difficult to categorize. Wood products, fertilizers, natural phosphates, bauxite and alumina, sugar, salt, and manganese ore move in substantial quantities but over more widely dispersed routes and in a greater variety of forms than the primary bulk products. Iron and steel products and scrap represent another major class of cargoes which is shipped throughout the world. Coffee, tropical fruits, and rubber fall into more easily defined geographic patterns and often require special handling, establishing the basis for separately identifiable trades. Manufactured goods, transportation equipment, processed foods, and such other high valued goods, provide only a tiny 6 percent of the tonnage of interregional dry cargo shipments handled by ocean carriers.[4]

The diversity of cargoes is accompanied by a diversity in shipment and packaging techniques and by considerable variance in the compilation of statistics and definition of terms. For purposes of this study, "petroleum" or "oil" shipments include both products and crude. The "major dry bulks" include iron ores, slurries, and pellets; grain (wheat, rye, and barley); coal; phosphate rock; bauxite and alumina; manganese ores; and sugar. All other cargoes are described as "general cargoes." This includes many cargoes which are conventionally shipped "in bulk"—defined as cargoes loaded "without mark, line, or count"—as well as those classed as "break-bulk." Even this final category includes many cargoes of relatively low value which may be simply offered in a unitized form (e.g., aluminum ingots or steel bars) as well as "packaged cargoes" in boxes, casks, bags, and crates. It is probably only this last category which persons ordinarily think of as "ocean freight." Although of relatively high value and carrying a high rate, "package cargoes" are confined almost entirely to liners and represent only a small portion of "general cargo" tonnage.

In order to analyze trading patterns for this study, Saguenay Research arbitrarily divided the world into fifteen regions (see Table 6-1 for their identification). For general cargoes, trade conducted wholly within a region (intraregional) accounted for 21 percent of the total international traffic, reflecting the propensity of nations to select neighbors for their trading partners if possible. An additional 10 percent of the general cargo tonnage was carried for a relatively short haul interregionally to an adjacent region. These intraregional

Figure 6-1. Estimated Commodity Composition of Inter-Regional Seaborne Trade, 1960 and 1969.

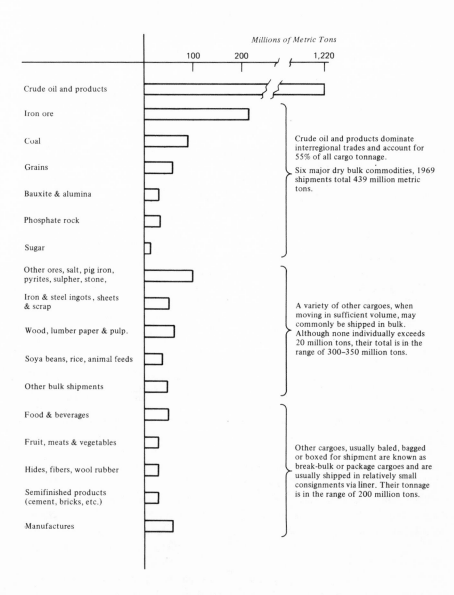

Millions of Metric Tons

| | 100 | 200 | 1,220 |

Crude oil and products

Iron ore

Coal

Grains

Bauxite & alumina

Phosphate rock

Sugar

Other ores, salt, pig iron, pyrites, sulpher, stone,

Iron & steel ingots, sheets & scrap

Wood, lumber paper & pulp.

Soya beans, rice, animal feeds

Other bulk shipments

Food & beverages

Fruit, meats & vegetables

Hides, fibers, wool rubber

Semifinished products (cement, bricks, etc.)

Manufactures

Crude oil and products dominate interregional trades and account for 55% of all cargo tonnage.

Six major dry bulk commodities, 1969 shipments total 439 million metric tons.

A variety of other cargoes, when moving in sufficient volume, may commonly be shipped in bulk. Although none individually exceeds 20 million tons, their total is in the range of 300–350 million tons.

Other cargoes, usually baled, bagged or boxed for shipment are known as break-bulk or package cargoes and are usually shipped in relatively small consignments via liner. Their tonnage is in the range of 200 million tons.

Source: 1960 and 1969 data for major commodities from Fearnley and Egers Chartering Company. Data on other commodities from Saguenay Research study of 1966 national trade statistics.

Table 6-1

Regions Defined for Cargo Analysis with 1966 Cargo Tonnages (mil. of metric tons)

	Exports				Imports			
	Gen.	Dry Bulk	Oil	Total	Gen.	Dry Bulk	Oil	Total
1. USA, including Alaska, Hawaii and Puerto Rico	59	82	10	150	54	62	126	242
2. Canada	26	43	–	69	7	9	19	35
3. Caribbean, including north coast So. America, Central America & Mexico	21	43	220	285	14	2	71	87
4. South America, west coast	7	19	–	26	4	1	4	9
5. South America, east coast	10	24	2	36	7	6	18	31
6. United Kingdom & Eire	22	4	12	38	39	29	94	162
7. Western Europe, incl. Turkey	120	33	47	200	142	131	358	630
8. Eastern Europe, incl. Yugoslavia	33	22	48	103	13	22	4	39
9. Africa, West Coast including UAR, Libya, Algeria	17	47	123	188	13	5	18	36
10. Africa, south & east coasts	10	7	–	17	5	1	14	20
11. Near East, Persian Gulf & India-Pakistan	9	14	411	435	18	13	19	50
12. Southeast Asia	10	8	36	54	3	1	25	29
13. Far East, south	14	6	–	21	8	1	16	25
14. Far East, north, including Japan, China, & Korea	28	3	–	32	63	89	105	257
15. Australia & Oceania	11	24	2	37	7	5	24	37
	398	378	914	1690	398	378	914	1690

Source: Saguenay Research, special study of *Cargo Statistics in International Seaborne Trade*, 1966. Data from national trade statistics, compared with cargo tonnages reported by UN (total dry cargoes loaded and unloaded, Fearnley & Egers (origins and destinations of dry bulks) and British Petroleum (oil) in order to determine "best fit" estimates.

and short sea trades are concentrated in Europe, the Far East, and along the east coast of North America (see Table 6-2).

Petroleum and dry bulk cargoes tend to move between regions and over longer routes than the "generals." Thus, the average shipment distance of petroleum moving in interregional trade has been calculated to be 4,200 miles and the average for the major dry bulks, 4,000 miles. For general cargoes, an average of 3,500 miles has been estimated for interregional movements.

More than half of the world's long distance petroleum shipments originate in the Middle East with destinations concentrated in the U.K. and Western Europe (51 percent) and Japan (26 percent) see Table 6-3). Caribbean oil is shipped largely to the U.S. and Canada; African production, almost entirely to Western Europe. Although the Communist states are increasing their oil exports to other

Table 6-2
General Cargo Short Sea Trades, 1966 (Millions of Metric Tons)

	Tonnage of goods loaded
1. Within:[a]	
Western Europe	64.2
Far East, north	13.4
Caribbean	4.2
Other regions	3.3
2. Between:[b]	
UK-Eire and W. Europe	9.8
Eastern and Western Europe	17.0
Canada-US (excluding Great Lakes)	12.1

Source: Saguenay Research.

[a]Saguenay found a total of 85.1 million tons of general cargo to be reported as moving within the fifteen regions used to organize data for its cargo study (see Table 6-1). An additional 10-15 million tons, which is not recorded in national trade statistics, may also move intraregionally.

[b]These short-haul shipments, which involve movements between regions, are included by Saguenay Research in its data for interregional trade.

Table 6-3
Interregional Shipments of Petroleum, 1969 (Millions of Metric Tons)

From To	W. Europe and Britain	U.S.A. and Canada	Japan	All Other	Total
Caribbean	33.7	114.0	2.5	19.8	170.0
North and West Africa	209.2	19.5	-0-	8.5	237.2
Middle East	287.2	17.2	150.0	112.8	567.2
Southeast Asia	.7	3.5	15.8	6.8	26.8
USSR	45.0	-0-	-0-	7.2	52.2
All Other	4.0	42.8	1.7	21.3	69.8
Total	579.8	197.0	170.0	176.4	1123.2

Source: *BP Statistical Review of the World Oil Industry*, 1969. Data exclude local transshipments and overland movements, especially between the U.S. and Canada.

nations, it appears that such shipments represent only 5 or 6 percent of the world seaborne total.

Almost one quarter of the world's six major dry bulk cargoes was shipped in 1968 out of the U.S. and Canada (see Table 6-4). Australia's rapidly expanding bulk exports accounted for 10 percent of the dry bulk traffic and shipments

Table 6-4
Interregional Shipments of Major Dry Bulk Cargoes[a] 1968 Data (Millions of Metric Tons)

From: To:	U.S. and Canada	U.K. and W. Europe	Japan	All Others	Total
U.S. and Canada	7.9	40.0	18.9	29.2	96.0
South America and Caribbean	34.0	20.2	19.0	5.5	78.7
Africa and Asia	5.6	45.1	34.0	7.5	92.2
U.K. and Western Europe	0.6	38.6	0.8	1.9	41.9
Eastern Europe	–	15.1	3.8	.3	19.2
Australia	1.2	4.0	27.6	5.3	38.1
All others	1.0	15.5	6.5	13.3	36.3
Total	50.3	178.5	110.6	63.0	402.4

Source: Fearnley & Egers Chartering Company.

[a]Includes iron ore, coal, bauxite and alumina, grains, phosphate rock, manganese ores, and sugar.

from other developed nations for about 15 percent. The remainder of these cargoes—half the total—were shipped from the less-developed nations. Destinations were heavily concentrated in the U.S., Europe, and Japan.

The main interregional general cargo movements fall within two broad categories:

1. Industrial and agricultural commodity exchanges between Western Europe, North America, Australia, South Africa, and Japan which form a belt of high-value trade encircling the world and account for about 30 percent of the interregional general cargo trade volume.
2. Trades between developed and less-developed nations, which tend to run north-south and to emphasize such commodities northbound as timber, organic material, tropical fruits, and high cost ores. This category accounts for about 40 percent of the interregional general cargo tonnage and requires a widely dispersed network of service.

Relatively short hauls between the British Isles and the Continent, and the U.S., Canada, and the Caribbean (essentially short-sea trades but classified here as interregional) move 10 to 15 percent of the tonnage, and the overseas trades of the Communist states (also concentrated in short sea services) another 10 to 15 percent. Only very minor amounts of general cargo tonnage are reported to move between less developed regions (see Table 6-5).

All things considered, the United States in 1966 was the world's leading trading nation in terms of her impact on the ocean freight industry. Japan ranked second and was closing the gap rapidly. The U.K. was a poor third with

Table 6-5
World Seaborne Trade 1966—General Cargo (In Thousands of Metric Tons)

Area	From/To	1	2	3	4	5	6	7	8	9	10	11	12	13	14	15	Total
1.	United States		2,061	3,489	1,521	1,525	2,498	17,315	1,291	1,929	724	6,570	223	2,277	15,771	1,400	58,594
2.	Canada	12,121	13	970	73	230	4,431	4,362		318	267	535	31	172	1,973	824	26,320
3.	Caribbean	9,258	1,434	4,163	395	644	1,002	2,069	222	157	19	36	–	47	1,557	241	21,244
4.	West Coast S. America	2,354	90	197	195	441	301	2,222	194	–	3	18	–	2	1,169	17	7,203
5.	East Coast S. America	901	235	180	418	1,113	889	4,369	734	71	46	144	1	8	668	7	9,784
6.	United Kingdom and Ireland	2,097	664	571	135	250	1,412	9,803	1,066	451	1,216	1,281	263	284	1,129	915	21,537
7.	Europe	10,708	1,354	3,093	815	1,906	15,858	61,185	4,594	7,672	2,055	5,601	778	897	2,800	894	120,210
8.	Europe – Eastern Bloc	1,082	161	295	125	640	3,204	16,669	3,579	1,616	–	1,519	17	92	4,457	10	33,466
9.	West Coast S. Africa	973	156	80	–	13	2,223	11,570	625	419	372	181	10	162	542	38	17,364
10.	South and East Coast S. Africa	1,855	196	16	4	12	2,020	2,319	10	318	174	10	1	–	2,784	106	9,825
11.	India, Persian Gulf, Red Sea	1,087	146	7	25	107	1,593	3,477	–	40	9	107	16	28	1,904	116	8,662
12.	Malaysia, Singapore, Indonesia	1,275	–	28	4	32	400	1,295	49	6	–	290	–	474	5,774	226	9,853
13.	Far East South	1,885	57	41	2	5	238	2,225	30	87	58	–	8	501	8,979	37	14,153
14.	Japan, Korea, China	7,431	539	549	215	264	390	1,792	671	257	211	1,104	939	2,656	10,400	1,054	28,472
15.	Australia and Oceania	1,148	154	73	11	44	2,705	1,258	91	27	111	511	250	314	3,113	1,465	11,275
	Total	54,175	7,260	13,752	3,938	7,226	39,164	141,930	13,156	13,368	5,265	17,907	2,537	7,914	63,020	7,350	397,962

Sub-total, Intraregional trade 84,726

Sub-total, Interregional trade 313,236

Source: Saguenay Research. Amounts reported in the table are only shipments positively identified in national trade statistics and may understate the volume of movements between less-developed states and between Communist nations. Overall, the volume of such unidentified cargoes is estimated to lie in the range of 30-35 millions tons, of which about 20 million tons are estimated to move intraregionally and the remainder to move between regions as defined for this study (see Table 6-1).

only about half the impact of Japan. These rankings are based on estimated freight payments for all categories of import-export trade, less the portion of freight attributable to longshore costs.

Intensity and Balance of Cargo Flows

The character of seaborne trade flows has important implications for the organization of international shipping services. The handling of many cargoes, for example, can be expedited through investment in specialized facilities in the ports and onboard the ships serving the trade. When these cargoes move in sufficient volume to be handled by shipload lots, they can provide the basis of a specialized service. Such specialized services have been established to move automobiles, timber, cement, sulphur, wine, and military equipment as well as the conventional bulk cargoes, petroleum, iron ore, coal, and grains. The economies gained through moving shipload lots in special-purpose ships may justify a shuttle service with the return leg in ballast, or the shipowner may adapt his vessel so as to be able to bid for a variety of different cargoes which might be taken on a more roundabout route and, by arranging successive charters, reduce his amount of ballast steaming. General-purpose liner operations, in contrast, are almost always more economic if they can be based on a balanced trade.

Any single specialized movement is, of course, imbalanced by definition; ships still do not carry coal to Newcastle, and the Middle Eastern countries do not import oil. Furthermore, the tendency of major bulk movements to originate either in extreme north latitudes, in the tropics, or from the southern hemisphere nations, makes it difficult to devise voyage itineraries which provide cargoes on the return leg from Europe, Japan, and the U.S. Some ballasting is therefore unavoidable in virtually all of the bulk cargo trades.

Examination of cargo flow data indicates that severe imbalances are a chronic condition of seaborne general cargo trades as well (see Table 6-6). Thus of the fifteen largest trades (accounting for almost two-thirds of the total general cargo traffic) ten were imbalanced by a ratio of more than 2:1. The average ratio of inbound to outbound cargoes in these ten trades in fact exceeded 3:1; in none of the fifteen leading trades was the ratio less than 1.5:1. These data identify a major need for shipping capable of moving among a variety of areas to handle cargoes which cannot be economically handled by regular liner services geared to reasonably balanced trades.[5]

Table 6-6 highlights also the extent to which general cargo shipping is concentrated on a limited number of major trade routes. The fifteen routings for which data are presented in the table generate 60 percent of the general cargo tonnage estimated to move in interregional trade. Of the 105 regional pairs which are yielded by classifying the world into 15 major trading areas, over

Table 6-6
Major General Cargo Trades, 1966 Data (Millions of Metric Tons)

	Heavy Leg	Light Leg	Tonnage Difference	Index of Imbalance[a]
10 Large Imbalanced Trades				
East to West Europe	16.7	4.6	12.1	3.6
Canada to U.S.A.	12.1	2.1	10.0	5.8
U.S.A. to Far East North	15.8	7.4	8.4	2.1
Far East South to Far East North	9.0	2.6	6.4	3.5
Caribbean to U.S.A.	9.3	3.5	5.8	2.7
U.S.A. to India, Persian Gulf, Red Sea	6.6	1.1	5.5	6.0
Malaysia, Indonesia to Far East North	5.8	.9	4.9	6.4
East Europe to Far East North	4.5	.7	3.8	6.4
Canada to U.K. and Eire	4.4	.7	3.7	6.3
Canada to Europe	4.4	1.4	3.0	3.1
Total Tonnage	88.6	25.0	63.6	
5 Large Relatively Balanced Trades				
U.S.A. to Europe	17.3	10.7	6.6	1.6
Europe to U.K. and Eire	15.8	9.8	6.0	1.6
West Coast Africa to Europe	11.6	7.7	3.9	1.5
Europe to India, Persian Gulf, Red Sea	5.6	3.5	2.1	1.6
Europe to Caribbean	3.1	2.1	1.0	1.5
Total Tonnage	53.4	33.8	19.6	

Source: Saguenay Research.

[a]Equals the ratio of heavy leg to light leg tonnage.

one-third generate less than 300 thousand tons of cargo per year; the 15 routes shown in the table each generated over 3 million tons. If the data were organized on a country-to-country basis, an even more striking asymmetry would be revealed. Thus, amongst the world's 145 recognized nations, there are in excess of 13,000 potential trade pairs, roughly 8,000 of which are principally linked by sea. At most only 3 to 4 percent of this latter number generate sufficient general cargoes to support a weekly sailing by a conventional general cargo vessel.[6] For all but a few nations, service must be organized on a regional basis to permit any reasonable frequency of sailings. The introduction of container ships, capable of carrying twice the cargo each sailing and of making two to three times as many sailings each year, will exacerbate the problem and emphasize the need in a very high proportion of the world's trades to approach scheduling regionally rather than on a bilateral basis.[7]

Trade Growth and Stability

Due to the absence of any consistent historical data for many trades, it is difficult to establish long term trends in aggregate worldwide cargo movements. The substitution of oil for coal has been the most dramatic shift with the most pervasive effects. Iron ore, bauxite, and manganese also have demonstrated strong growth during the post-World War II years, fed by the rapidly growing capacity of the world's industrial plant, the depletion of nearby resources, and the relatively cheaper cost of sea transport in relation to other factors of production. Grain shipments, heavily dependent on the two factors of climate and the ability of consumer nations to grow their own crop requirements, have followed an irregular pattern (see Figure 6-2).[8]

Although international trade in finished products, measured in value terms (reduced to constant dollars) has been growing at some 11 percent compounded annually over the past 20 years, the impact of this trade expansion on sea transport has been diluted by the tendency of trade in manufactures to be concentrated in areas served by overland carriers and by the introduction of air freight. Also, the value of manufactured products even after correction for inflation, has probably increased faster than either their weight or volume. The result of these factors has been to hold the growth rate in package cargoes, measured by weight, to a relatively unspectacular 2 to 3 percent.

Figure 6-2. Growth in World Seaborne Trade of Selected Bulk Commodities, 1960-1968.

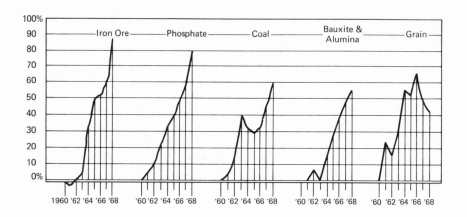

Source: Fearnley and Egers Chartering Company, data adapted by Saguenay Research.

Furthermore, the growth of these "liner-type" cargoes has been concentrated in a relatively few trades. Thus between 1951 and 1968, liner shipments from the U.S. to the Far East (principally Japan) approximately doubled and imports increased from 650 thousand to 2.0 million tons. Most other Japanese trades showed comparable increases. But liner exports from the U.S. to northern Europe and the U.K. dropped from 4.4 to 2.0 million tons between 1951 and 1968, while the imports to the U.S. on this route fluctuated in the range of 1.5 to 2.2 million tons. Exchanges between the United Kingdom and Australia moved in a virtually steady flow during these years (roughly 2.5 million tons westbound and 500 thousand tons easterly). In the trade between U.S. Gulf and Atlantic ports and the East Coast of South America, nonliner carriers have not only captured all the increase in cargo flow but have contributed to an absolute reduction of liner loadings by one-third.

The instability of trade flows is a major problem throughout the industry. Certain of these instabilities are seasonal and are repeated year after year, providing the basis for a recurring pattern of tramp operations. Thus, grain shipments out of the St. Lawrence and Hudson Bay are heaviest during the summer and fall; December marks the beginning of compensating grain movements from Australia and the River Plate. Requirements for oil movements to Europe and North America peak during the winter heating load. Ore shipments are stronger during the summer when materials can be handled more easily, and ports in northern latitudes are free from ice.

In other cases, changing trade patterns are the product of more or less predictable economic developments. Thus, necessary adjustments in shipping operations can be planned well in advance of the commissioning of a new pipeline, the enlargement of a major steel works, or the opening of new mines. Major commercial developments, such as the growth of the Japanese trades or of automobile exports from Europe to America, often also can be anticipated in their broad dimensions, although forecasting specific year to year and month to month changes presents difficulties.

For many bulk materials, a prediction of overall demand provides little guidance regarding the likely specific sources of supply for specific markets, and considerable variation is experienced from year to year in trade patterns. Grain provides the most obvious example, but sales competition and political considerations can also cause violent changes in the seaborne movements of fertilizers, coal, scrap metal, cement, and sugar. Accommodating these shifts in trade obviously requires a highly flexible system of international shipping services.

The most elusive instabilities are those which result from political factors. Aside from the Suez Canal closures and the Korean War, such factors appear to have had relatively minor effects on world freight markets.[9]

The Suez closures have caused dramatic shifts both in the sources of European crude oil and in the routing of that still shipped from the Middle East. In 1966, Europe received 53 percent of its annual petroleum requirement from the Persian Gulf; almost 75 percent of these shipments were through Suez. Closure of the canal caused Europe to increase its imports from North and West African sources by 50 million tons. About 200 million tons of Middle East oil was rerouted around the Cape of Good Hope requiring seventeen additional days steaming time on the round voyage. Accommodating these shifts increased requirements for tanker tonnage by roughly 15 percent between 1966 and 1968.

Variations in transport requirements are amplified as one looks more closely at the finer-grain structure of trade. The factors creating instabilities in specific trades—variances in production requirements, transport tie-ups, work stoppages, climate, competitive factors, and so forth—are themselves too numerous and too varied to permit any easy generalizations. Together they create a major challenge for the supply of shipping services and a requirement for the greatest possible flexibility.

7 Ships and Services: Supply

Considering the tasks which it is called upon to perform, the ocean freight industry has achieved a quite striking record of efficiency and technological progress. The industry has made these gains despite the instability in its operations, intermittent (tanker) or generally low (tramp and liner) levels of profitability, frequent labor difficulties, and pricing policies (in liner shipping) generally considered to be unscientific. The record of the different sectors of the industry, of course, varies considerably, and the progress of bulk transport has been markedly greater than that of the liner industry, in which economic pressures have been buffered by the conference system and by governmental protection.

Vessel Capacity and Utilization

In twenty years since 1948 the carrying capacity of the world merchant fleet has quadrupled. Tanker capacity has grown most rapidly, from 24 million dwt. with an average speed of 14 knots in 1949 to 125 million dwt. and an average speed of 16 knots as of December 31, 1969. Expansion of dry cargo capability has been led by a burst in the construction of dry bulk and ore carriers, beginning in about 1958 and continuing through the present. Tonnage of conventional freighters, reefers, container, and pallet vessels has expanded at a rate of only 2 percent per annum (from 52 to 85 million dwt.) over the past 20 years, but the carrying capacity of this sector of the fleet has more than doubled, due to better design, higher speeds, and faster turnaround of ships in ports.

In both the tanker and dry cargo sectors of the industry, shipping capacity would appear to have outpaced demand for shipping services. Yet except for brief periods in 1949-50 and between 1958 and 1961, tonnage in lay-up has been held at very modest levels (see Figure 7-1). The apparent inconsistency is explained in part by the increase in ballast voyaging in order to move vast quantities of bulk materials from less developed countries to the industrialized nations of the north temperate zone. In part it reflects a lengthening of average voyage distance and changes in the composition of trade. However, there also now is less intensive utilization of general cargo ships than in the years immediately following World War II when space was at a premium. Because it may be preferable to keep a ship in service, even if not fully employed, so long as there is a reasonable expectation of more profitable future employment, data

Figure 7-1. Comparative Growth in Ship Tonnage and Cargoes; with Ships in Lay-up, 1954-1969.

1954—1969

Tanker (Wet Cargo)

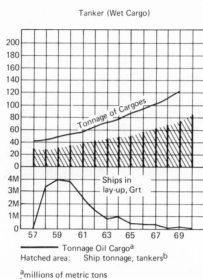

——— Tonnage Oil Cargo[a]

Hatched area: Ship tonnage, tankers[b]

[a]millions of metric tons
[b]millions of gross tons, ships 100 gross tons and over.

Bulker and General
(Dry Cargo)

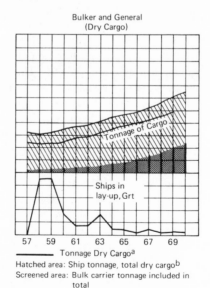

——— Tonnage Dry Cargo[a]

Hatched area: Ship tonnage, total dry cargo[b]
Screened area: Bulk carrier tonnage included in total

Source: Organization for Economic Cooperation and Development, Maritime Transport Committee.

on ships in lay-up do not really provide a reliable measure of the utilization of the world fleet.[1]

Comparison of shipping capacity and demand is complicated by the opportunities for ships to cross over into different service modes and into different cargo markets. Thus tankers have from time to time entered the dry cargo market to carry grains; combination oil/ore carriers may be used to move petroleum. Conventional freighters and tramps share many of the bulk commodity markets, with routing determined by the availability of ships and cargoes and the size and stability of cargo flow. Modest amounts of package cargoes normally considered the province of liners, move via tramp; liners in turn take on bulk commodities when more lucrative cargo is lacking.

Figure 7-2 depicts an estimate of the manner in which cargoes moving in interregional seaborne trade were handled in 1966.[2] This model of world shipping activity necessarily rests on a variety of assumptions, but by relating fragmentary information compiled from several sources in a reasonable way, it can help to validate the data and to test the assumptions from which it is compiled.[3]

Among other matters, the model assumes the following pattern of vessel utilization.[4]

	Days in Port	Days at sea, total	Days at sea with cargo	Percent cargo capacity utilized while at sea
Liner	175	175	175	70%−cubic
Tramp	140	210	160	80%−weight
Bulk and Ore Carriers	85	265	160	98%−weight
Tankers	60	290	150	98%−weight

Data are for 1966 and do not reflect the later impact of container operations. For that year, a 70 percent utilization of the cubic capacity of liner vessels was consistent with the actual experience of U.S. flag ships in U.S. foreign trade, the only trade for which such data have been compiled.[5] It probably substantially overstates the utilization liners now enjoy. Foreign flag vessels participating in U.S. foreign trade, however, have had less utilization than their American competitors. The apparently low utilization of liner vessels of course reflects the severe imbalance of cargo offerings on many trade routes and the greater difficulty of finding sufficient cargoes to permit liners to sail "full and down" on each departure required by their relatively fixed schedule.

Disregarding periods in lay-up and ballast voyages, the utilization of tankers and bulk carriers may be assumed to be very high, since the cargoes which they carry are available in quantity and sailings ordinarily can be scheduled in a manner which allows the vessel to be loaded full and down. For tramp operations, there is little or no data to describe actual use. The figures shown simply fit the model and relate to reasonable expectations.

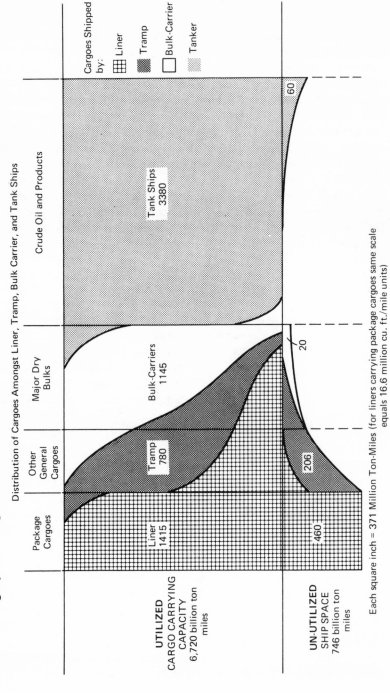

Figure 7-2. Ton Miles of Transport Performance in Inter-Regional Trade, 1966, by Ship Category and Cargo Classification.

Distribution of Cargoes Amongst Liner, Tramp, Bulk Carrier, and Tank Ships

Cargoes Shipped by:
▦ Liner
▨ Tramp
☐ Bulk-Carrier
░ Tanker

Crude Oil and Products

Tank Ships 3380

Major Dry Bulks

Bulk-Carriers 1145

Other General Cargoes

Tramp 780

Package Cargoes

Liner 1415

UTILIZED CARGO CARRYING CAPACITY 6,720 billion ton miles

UN-UTILIZED SHIP SPACE 746 billion ton miles

460

206

20

60

Each square inch = 371 Million Ton-Miles (for liners carrying package cargoes same scale equals 16.6 million cu. ft./mile units)

The model brings out clearly the impact which cargo loadings and discharge have upon the efficiency of shipping operations. Port time may consume up to 60 to 65 percent of potential carrying capacity of liner vessels. In poorly developed and congested ports it is still not unusual for vessels (usually operating as tramps) to wait two to three weeks simply to get on berth.[6]

The amount of ballast voyaging which is required in order to obtain cargo is a major variable in both the tramp and bulk carrier portions of the industry. In all cases, industry averages mask an enormous range of variation in circumstances encountered by operators and in their ability to copy with the peculiarities of particular trades.

The model also highlights the extent to which liner operators have found it necessary to reach out into relatively low-value and bulk cargo categories in order to obtain sufficient custom to support their service. It is generally acknowledged that one of the principal results of the conference system is to create a tendency towards over capacity.[7] However, a conclusion which one might draw from the model is that liner overcapacity is more a matter of misuse of liner capabilities (through routing via liner of cargoes which might, were there not surplus space, be routed more economically via tramp) than of nonuse of liner space.

The deep sea tramps, potentially the most flexible instrument of the ocean freight industry, must compete with both liners and bulk carriers for their cargoes. During the 1960s the latter have rapidly expanded their share of dry bulk movements and enjoy a solid economic advantage in those trades in which cargoes may be handled in very large large lots.[8] The division of the remainder of the market between tramp and liner services, however, is less clearcut and depends in part on how hungry the liners are to take on low rated, semi-bulk goods. Reinhard Schultz has estimated that 60 percent of the cargoes classified as "sometimes bulk" in Figure 6-1 move in sufficient volume to justify handling in shipload lots.[9] This is substantially more than are now actually so handled. It remains to be seen whether the development of container shipping will release more of these cargoes to tramps or whether containerization will become a major means for moving such commodities as hides, copra, fertilizers and wool.

Investment in Shipping

A tendency towards overcapacity in shipping reflects conditions which create a systematic tendency toward overinvestment in new tonnage. Since 1965 the scale of such investment has more than doubled and is now some 5½ billion dollars per year (see Table 7-1). The type of ship acquired for this investment is shown in Table 7-2.

Like other branches of industry, the capital equipment used in shipping is rapidly becoming more sophisticated and expensive while the direct labor input

Table 7-1
New Vessels Delivered, 1965–1970

I. Ship Completions (thous. of grt. of ships 100 grt. and over)

	1965	1966	1967	1968	1969	1970
Dry Cargo	6,518	7,989	10,518	10,598	9,874	10,576
Tankers	5,245	5,862	4,367	6,247	8,864	9,976
Total	11,763	13,851	14,885	16,845	18,738	20,552

Source: OECD, *Maritime Transport*, 1970.

Table 7-2
II. Ships on Order (thous. of dwt. of ships 1,000 grt. and over), Dec. 31, 1969

	No. of Units	Dwt.
Dry Cargo, freighter and reefer	1,241	9,220
Container ships	162	3,463
Tankers over 150,000	219	51,358
Tankers less than 150,000	428	11,542
Dry bulk carriers	399	15,038
Ore/oil and ore/bulk/oil	107	13,876
Total Cargo Vessels	2,556	104,497

Source: *Fairplay*, annual supplement, "World Ships on Order," 26 February 1970.

is being reduced. On an overall basis, the investment in shipping per shipboard worker approximates $14,000, ranging from a high of $500,000 for seamen employed on new 20,000 dwt. containerships or on 200,000 dwt. supertankers to a low of $3-5,000 for those operating fully depreciated "handy vessels" and tramps. Considering the additional shoreside labor required to support at-sea operations, these per capita investment rates are reasonably in line with other heavy industries in the developed nations (see Table 7-3).

Investment in shipping is stimulated by direct subsidies to nationals in some nations and, for buyers throughout the world, by the direct and indirect credit aids which have been extended by the major shipbuilding countries to promote the export business of their yards. During most of the 1960s credits were provided for ship sales on terms covering 80 percent of purchase price at 6 to 7 percent interest with repayment over eight to fifteen years. During the last several years, financing arrangements for ships have tightened roughly in proportion to the improvement which has been achieved in builders' order books.[10]

Additional financing assistance has often been available to nationals or persons planning operation under national flag. For example, Japan has provided mortgage money at 4 percent interest on 80 percent of construction cost and has

Table 7-3
Investment Per Industrial Worker, Selected Nations and Industries, 1965

	Manufacturing	Mining	Gas and Elec. Power	Construction
1. Developed Countries				
U.S.A.				
W. Germany	$15,179	$18,614	$12,107	$5,373
U.K.	9,686	4,450	6,871	3,083
Japan	8,622	4,268	9,864	N/A
2. Less-Developed Countries				
Malaysia	5,432	4,094	N/A	1,434
Ghana	3,753	2,015	1,864	N/A
India	3,462	N/A	1,041	N/A

Source: United Nations.

subsidized commercial bank loans on the remaining 20 percent to hold their interest cost to approximately 6 percent.[11] In 1963 the government also granted a five year grace period on all loans then outstanding to it from companies which agreed to participate in a plan to consolidate management within the industry.[12]

In Britain, a 20 percent investment grant, originally conceived as a means for supplementing depreciation reserves to meet equipment replacement needs in an inflating economy, was sufficient while applicable (1966-1970) to meet the cash requirement in new building projects. A government-owned Israeli Shipping Bank covers the entire construction loan and guarantees the ship mortgage for 80 percent of the purchase price when sale is to an Israeli national. The Brazilian Merchant Marine Commission covers construction financing and a subsidy to equalize the construction cost when a ship is built in a domestic instead of a European yard. It is also reportedly planning to provide mortgage financing in selected cases for up to 95 percent of the ship purchase costs, repayable over 15 years.[13]

Favorable tax treatment also has stimulated investment in shipping. Like real estate, ships are both a depreciable and a readily transferable asset. New vessels enjoy a competitive margin which usually is sufficient to generate a cash flow adequate to meet an accelerated depreciation schedule. In an inflating economy, the sale of a ship after 5 to 7 years may yield a return adequate to cover the initial cost; an owner can then raise his equity in the next generation fleet of vessels, assisted by generous credit aids, and by reinvestment can avoid most capital gains tax. This pattern of operation has been an important stimulus to shipping investment in the high-tax countries of Northern Europe.[14]

A third stimulus to investment in shipping arises from need of certain companies to find outlets for investment abroad either to utilize blocked currencies or to avoid repatriation of funds earned abroad. These factors are particularly important to American corporations with multinational interests, which under legislation enacted in 1962 are allowed to convert certain overseas earnings into equity in foreign built and registered ships without payment of tax.[15] Many of the agreements through which multinational companies conduct their overseas operations (particularly in less-developed countries) provide also that some portion of earnings must be locally reinvested. Shipping offers an attractively flexible method for meeting such requirements.[16]

Fourth, shipping possesses certain characteristics—the relatively modest investment required for entry, the absence of any extensive infrastructure requirements, favorable credit terms, and the ability to balance cash flows of various currencies—which make the industry an attractive vehicle for investment by less developed countries. The ability to capitalize effectively on these characteristics underlies the success in shipping of such poorly endowed nations as Greece and Norway. The relevance of these characteristics in relation to the shipping interests of today's less developed world today will be examined further in Chapters 10 and 15.

Finally, the participation of many independent shipowners in the industry is undoubtedly a factor in the continued flow of investment funds, even in situations of high risk and inadequate economic return. Many such owners, including some commanding substantial fleets, are essentially still small businessmen in that they feel a need to stay in the industry in order to support their own interests and their business organizations. These motivations may outweigh strictly economic considerations. They are reinforced in lands in which alternatives are limited.

Costs, Pricing, and Profits

Substantial variances are found in the costs of operating ships of various types depending on the character of the ship itself, the trade in which it is employed, the flag of registry, and the operating policies of the owner. These variances affect both the competitive position of the vessel and the trades in which it can be profitably employed. As recently as ten years ago, ships commonly were written off over a period of twenty (tankers) or twenty-five (tramps) years. Amortization now is generally geared to a ten to fifteen year economic life, and some operators are turning over their equipment in an even briefer cycle. The fact that new equipment can be paid off so quickly is powerful evidence of the great improvements which have been achieved in maritime technology.

The prices which may be obtained for both new and used ships are notoriously unstable, depending more on market demand than upon any intrinsic value of the equipment. Thus, despite pronounced inflation, the price of new buildings actually declined by about 10 percent between 1958 and 1961

Figure 7-3. Comparative Costs of Ships, 1969 data.

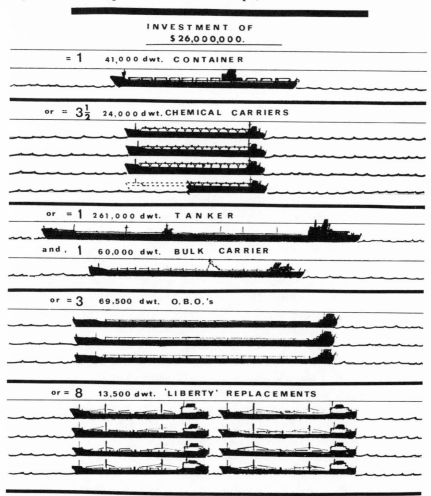

INVESTMENT OF
$26,000,000.

= 1   41,000 dwt. CONTAINER

or = $3\frac{1}{2}$ 24,000 dwt. CHEMICAL CARRIERS

or = 1 261,000 dwt. TANKER

and, 1 60,000 dwt. BULK CARRIER

or = 3 69,500 dwt. O.B.O.'s

or = 8 13,500 dwt. 'LIBERTY' REPLACEMENTS

Source: Saguenay Research.

and did not reach their post-Suez level again until 1966. The demand for new ships induced by the 1967 Suez crisis again pushed prices sharply higher, and prices now may be as much as twice the price applying three years ago. Costs of used vessels fluctuate even more sharply, approximately in phase with rates for long-term charters. Proper timing of ship purchases and sales is accordingly a major factor in the success of a shipping business, and many companies appear to have established their profitability almost entirely on this basis.

A decade ago vessel operating expenses (exclusive of depreciation, cargo expenses, and overhead) were chiefly determined by crew's wages. The number of crew, furthermore, was reasonably consistent from ship to ship, falling somewhere in the range from thirty-eight to forty for a Liberty ship to as many as sixty or even sixty-five for vessels with extensive gear and/or access to cheap labor. Introduction of improved machinery and automatic control devices now permits ships to be operated with as few as twenty-one men on board; the typical crew of the new vessels of North European operators is in the range of twenty-five to thirty. Most of the saving has been achieved in semi- and unskilled ratings and is partially offset by higher wages for those remaining onboard. Nonetheless, on new, semi-automated ships crew costs are some 30 percent below those of older, fully-manned vessels operated under the same flag. Concurrently, investment-related costs (particularly the cost of money and insurance) have increased. These fixed costs are now likely to outweigh the direct operating expenses of almost all new ships; for very large or expensive new vessels, they substantially outweigh operating expenses. (See Table 7-4.)

The cost characteristics of shipping have commanded much attention from economists, who consider these characteristics to be fundamental to the pricing policies and competitive relationships of shipping firms. In liner shipping, direct out-of-pocket costs of taking on additional ton of cargo are a tiny fraction of the average costs which must somehow be covered in order to make the transport service viable over the long run. Hence the general desire of liner companies to cooperate in administering a price system which will check the competitive impulse to secure any revenue which yields a margin over the out of pocket cost.

Tramp companies operate with smaller overheads than liners and, having no commitment to maintaining a regular service, enjoy greater flexibility in the use of their ships. In past periods, when fixed costs constituted only a small portion of tramp vessel operating expense, owners might lay up tonnage which could not be profitably employed without incurring excessive costs. With capital costs now looming as a relatively larger factor in tramping as well as liner shipping, owners must be more concerned about means for stabilizing income. Hence the tendency toward time in lieu of voyage charters and toward advance contracts for freighting services in the bulk carrier component of the industry.

Liner firms have used the economic power which the conference system affords to establish demand-based price systems through which rates are set largely in terms of what the traffic will bear. Although many factors may be considered in setting individual freight rates—R.T. Brown has cited a list of twenty-eight—a thorough study for the U.N. Economic Commission for Latin America has concluded that there are only three—the value of the shipment, competitive conditions on the route, and the costs of service—which exercise a determining influence.[17]

A substantial range is found within most liner tariff schedules. The highest rates typically are assessed on mail, high value cargoes for which shipping costs are essentially irrelevant to the final selling price, and general cargo moved in small quantities for individual customers who lack the bargaining power to win a

Table 7-4
Economic Characteristics of Ship Operating Costs, 1970

	20,000 dwt. Containership	14,000 dwt. Conventional Liner	150,000 dwt. OBO Carrier	14,000 dwt. Tramp (new)	14,000 dwt. Tramp (fully written off)
Voyage Characteristics:					
Speed	20 K.	17 K.	15 K.	16 K.	12 K.
Ports of call	2	4	2	4	4
Distance	3,500 nm	3,500 nm	3,500 nm	3,500 nm	3,500 nm
Sea time	7.3 days	8.6 days	20 days	13 days	18 days
Port time	3.0 days	10.0 days	5 days	4 days	8 days
Voyage Time	10.3 days	18.6 days	25 days	17 days	26 days
	Typical Voyage Costs Per Cargo Ton[a]				
I. Variable Costs Load and discharge cargoes and other costs in port	$10.55	$18.85	$1.14	$2.14	$2.15
II. Voyage Costs Crew costs, stores, insurance, fuel at sea	1.81	2.76	.47	2.08	3.40
III. Carrying Costs insurance, admin.	.48	.44	.09	.31	.53
IV. Debt. Service	4.31	2.89	.98	2.03	0
Total Cost per 1000 tons of cargo....	17.15	24.94	2.68	6.56	6.08

Source: Saguenay Research. All cost data above must be regarded as only gross estimates of costs likely actually to be incured since actual cost will be seriously affected by the longshore wage scales and work practices in the ports of call, the type of cargo worked, the manning on board ship, and so forth.

[a]Liner data for measurement tons, tramp and bulk carrier data for metric tons.

separate tariff classification. More moderate rates apply to commodities which move in volume, especially in those situations in which the shipper has substantial bargaining power and where a reasonable tariff is necessary to assure a market for his goods. The lowest rates apply to semi-bulk and bulk commodities for which liners compete with tramps. Such commodities usually are omitted from the conference tariffs in order to allow liner operators to negotiate the rate on an individual basis.

Numerous studies have been made of trends in liner and tramp rates.[18] The former have been demonstrated to be far more stable, reflecting the conferences' long-term commitments to servicing their trades. Even the most celebrated rate wars appear not to have significantly jarred the overall rate structure of the competing lines.[19] However, a general scarcity of cargoes does appear to depress liner rates although far less drastically than such scarcity affects tramps.

Like other industries with administered price systems, liner shipping operates with substantial unused capacity. There has been virtually no analysis to establish the extent to which this surplus capacity may be economically justified in order to cover occasional surges in cargo offerings, to provide services to out of the way ports, or to provide a frequent schedule.[20] Economists instead have usually assumed that the surplus represents an economic waste created by artificially inflated rates which attract excess investment to the trade. Extra quality features, such as high speeds, also are generally held to be the product of an institutional structure which minimizes direct price competition.[21]

Cross-subsidization of cargoes in liner shipping also has been held to be an economic waste by some authors.[22] The more prominent view, however, is that demand-based pricing policies are justified if their result is to facilitate the flow of trade, since the comparative advantage to be gained through trade outweighs any loss in the efficiency with which shipping space is employed.[23] Thus, if the profits gained in handling a high-rated cargo like watches permit a tariff to be set for aluminum castings at a level which induces new trade to move, there is assumed to be a benefit to the world economy which outweighs any possible loss of sales to the watchmaker due to his slightly higher transport costs.

The theory is sound, although it seldom can be tested by analysis of specific cases. Furthermore, liner operators may feel compelled to subsidize high volume "open-rate" cargoes in order to meet competition for these cargoes from tramps. This competitive situation has forced liner companies to look almost entirely to tariffed commodities for revenue gains sufficient to meet their increased costs, since rates for tramp charters have been essentially flat throughout the period from 1958 to 1968. The rates on these tariffed commodities have consequently increased at a pace which many shippers find to be unacceptable.[24]

The conference system has not yielded monopoly profits to liner firms. Indeed their managers claim that over prolonged periods they have barely been able to cover expenses, considering the likely increases in equipment replacement costs due to inflation.[25] During the past five years, some European firms have actually withdrawn from liner services. Profits in the tramp industry also are believed to be extremely low, but owners who have shifted their investments to modern tankers and bulk carriers have fared well. The great fortunes in shipping, however, have not been made on the margins of day-to-day operations but through the occasional coup, the good luck of having ships available at a moment when demand has exploded, or through pioneering new technologies, business methods, and services.

Elasticity of Supply and Demand

In the short term, both the demand for and supply of shipping services are considered to be relatively insensitive to shifts in price—i.e., they are inelastic.

For most processed or manufactured goods (and some raw materials) the cost of transportation accounts for only a small proportion of the ultimate sales price (Table 7-5), and rate increases appear to have little impact on demand.[26]

Transport costs loom much larger in relation to the delivered price of bulk commodities. Yet the demand for these goods is also a derived demand likely to be relatively unaffected by changes in transport prices. The people of India must be fed; the steel mills of Europe, coked; and America's eighty million automobiles, supplied with fuel regardless. In fact, the transoceanic movement of the raw material is often only a first stage in the production of finished products for ultimate sale, and shifts in transport price are absorbed in other stages of the production process or in a relatively small adjustment of price to the ultimate consumer.

The supply of shipping also has proved relatively insensitive to shifts in price. At no time during the postwar period has more than 8 percent of the privately-owned sea transport capacity been in lay-up. Although an upturn in charter rates will immediately bring this laid-up tonnage back in service, it takes from one to three years for additional new vessels to be ordered and deployed.

The inelasticities of supply of and demand for shipping space cause relatively small variations in the one to be sharply amplified in the price required for the other—at least when these fluctuations are not muted by an administered price system. "In no other industry," states one authority, "can a small shift in utilization cause so disastrous impact on profits." Here lies the root of the feast-or-famine character of the industry noted earlier.

Yet a superficial view of the industry's operation can overstate these inelasticities, particularly for the long run. Ship operators can and do use a host of fine-tuning devices to adjust their services to requirements. When business is slow, more port calls may be added, routes adjusted to avoid canal dues, cargoes placed aboard with less attention to maximum efficiency of stowage, and deferred maintenance accomplished. Oil companies employ all of these devices and more to take up the slack in the summer months when demand is low. Shippers can take similar steps, stockpiling goods when ships are scarce, routing their cargoes through alternative ports, shifting to other, nearer sources of supply providing slightly more costly or lower grade ores, or—over a longer period—reorganizing their production to minimize transportation requirements. As world trade becomes increasingly diversified, it becomes increasingly sensitive to economic factors.[27] Both producers and consumers of goods in trade may accordingly be expected in coming years to pay closer attention to transport costs and to adjust their activities more promptly in response to changing rates and services.

Phase-out of the large U.S. Reserve Fleet should also encourage private owners to hold more of their tonnage in reserve during depressed freight markets in expectation of profits when conditions improve. Having a reasonable pool of reserve capacity in private hands should help to stabilize trading operations and would remove the uncertainties associated with trying to predict when the U.S.

Government may activate its fleet. Only large owners or consortia of owners, however, can afford the drain on operating income which maintaining ships in lay-up entails. The phase-out of the U.S. Reserve Fleet therefore may operate also to stimulate consolidation within the shipping industry.

Table 7-5
Rates on Commodities from Kingston to Montreal (In $ U.S. per ton)

	Naptha	Canvas Shoes	Gloves
F.O.B. Value, Kingston	$ 78.00	$2,111.00	$11,414.00
Kingston-Miami (Ro-Ro)	25.00	53.19	28.08
Miami-Montreal (Truck)	20.00	42.56	22.47
Insurance	.27	12.14	52.79
Total, transport costs	45.27	107.89	103.34
Transport cost as percent of F.O.B. value	58.0	5.1	.9
Final retail price (tax excluded)	131.50	4,411.00	22,960.00

Source: Saguenay Research.

8

Organization of Sea Transport Markets

Aggregate economic data and use of such shorthand terminology as "liner," "tanker," and "tramp" tend to obscure the complex realities of ocean shipping markets and services. Although convention and convenience still lend some validity to the traditional categories, it is more accurate to think of the ocean freight industry today as a congeries of specialized facilities and services responding to the requirements of a similarly diversified range of shipper requirements. Such specialization yields significant economies; it also requires great flexibility in the use of facilities in order to adjust services to changing demand conditions. The incentives to both shippers and carriers to build such flexibility into their operations create numerous opportunities for interpenetration of related markets. These crossover points establish the links which shape the behavior pattern of the system as a whole.

The organization of shipping markets and services is in constant flux. The changes now being experienced are fundamental in the sense that they are affecting not only the pattern of services but also the long-established institutions through which markets have been organized and business conducted. The old institutions, i.e., the liner conferences and ship charter brokerage exchanges—are still vigorous but are losing ground to such new arrangements as intermodal through-transport systems, long-term affreightment contracts, and captive industrial services. Full discussion of the manner in which the industry is adapting to these new conditions is deferred until Part III; here we will deal only with the economic forces at work.

Economics of Specialization

Establishing the design for a ship is very much like designing a building. A ship's basic function dictates its overall configuration, size, speed, and hold arrangements. Additional utilities and equipment may be added to increase the efficiency with which the vessel may be used, and amenities introduced in order to make it a more attractive place to live and work and/or to satisfy its customers. Like shoreside structures, ships may later be modified should the original design become obsolete. Being mobile, they are readily transferred to other owners or shifted to new services.

Design features which are particularly important to the suitability of ships for particular trades include:

83

Size	Cargo capacity and draft.
Configuration	Weight/measurement relationships.
Speed and range	Block coefficient, propulsion, machinery, bunkers.
Cargo hold design	Size, number, internal decking, clearances, bulkheads, securing devices, and so forth.
Cargo keeping equipment	Refrigeration, tanks, etc.
Cargo handling equipment	Boom type, location, and capacity.
Access to cargoes	Hatch size and location, internal stowage procedure.
Convertibility for use in multiple trades	Hold cleaning equipment, layout.

Certain of these features are interrelated. Thus, the propeller sizes and shaft torque loads necessary to drive very large ships in excess of sixteen knots are so great as to render higher speeds for ships over 200,000 tons impractical in the context of existing technology.[1] Investments to increase the ships' efficiency at sea and in port also are linked, since the one affects the time during which the other can be effective. High speeds are appropriate for vessels able to achieve fast turnaround; lower speeds to those which in any event would be required to spend much of their time in port.

The economic advantage to be gained by achieving an optimum match of a ship and cargo is substantial. This advantage is most dramatically evident in the savings to be achieved in the bulk trades through capitalizing on economies of scale. (See Figure 8-1.) But the same principle works in other ways as well. Each extra knot of speed adds from $200 to $300 to the daily operating expense of a 20,000 dwt. vessel; this expense must be balanced against the savings in both ship operating and cargo costs which may be realized by reducing days in transit. Similarly, investments in specialized cargo handling gear may be balanced by handsome savings in operating cost. The expenses of loading packaged timber, for example, are about 30 percent less on ships designed for this business than on a multipurpose tramp. Systems to ship iron ore in slurry form are estimated by their sponsors to reduce investment requirements by one-third and cargo handling expense by a factor of ten.

Many cargoes can be transported only in specialized ships, or in ships incorporating special facilities. Cargoes requiring refrigeration are the most common example. Others must be protected from excess moisture, from shifting and settling, or from spontaneous combustion due to inadequate ventilation. Phosphorous, ammonia, sulphur, and other chemicals require specially fitted vessels used only in these trades. Although automobiles may be crated or carried on deck by any ship, export of cars in volume requires either specialized hold fittings or a roll-on, roll-off ship.

Gaining maximum efficiency through specialization usually requires optimization of the total transport system, from the shipper's plant to the ultimate distribution points. Size and timing of production runs, type of packaging, inland transport and terminal arrangements, cargo handling functions, warehousing, insurance and finance must all be harmonized with the mode of sea transport, if maximum efficiency is to be obtained in the overseas shipment of processed goods. In handling raw materials, the volume of production, stockpiling and storage facilities and costs, channel depths, and load and discharge capabilities are critical factors in setting the parameters for ship design.

Figure 8-1. Shipment Cost Related to Ship Size and Distance of Ore Source.

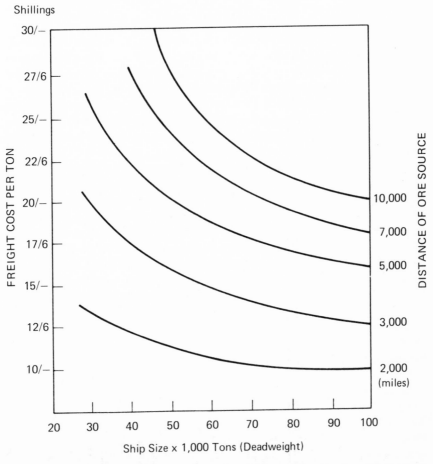

Source: W.G. Meredith and C. Wordsworth, "Size of Ore Carriers for the new Port Talbot Harbour," *Journal of the Iron and Steel Institute*, 204 (November 1966), p. 1077.

Table 8-1
Owned and Chartered Ships of Major Oil Companies, Ships of 6,000 Dwts. and Over, Dec. 1969

Company	Owned & Captive Dwt. (thous.)	No.	Time Charter Dwt. (thous.)	No.	Consecutive Voy. Charters Dwt. (thous.)	No.	Single Voy. Charters Dwt. (thous.)	No.
Shell	10,359	210	9,412	141	722	17	1,494	35
Standard Oil of New Jersey	7,241	138	6,171	135	1,827	41	1,852	61
British Petroleum	5,333	138	6,465	126	3,345	54	2,132	38
Texaco	3,214	84	3,111	42	426	6	2,108	55
Socony Mobil	1,984	35	2,542	38	–	–	147	6
Standard Oil of California	2,037	52	430	9	542	12	447	16
Gulf	1,693	51	2,560	16	255	6	1,053	26
Getty	1,033	19	70	1	–	–	–	–

Source: Compiled by Saguenay Research from data supplied by Standard Oil of N.J., Logistics Coordination Department

aIncludes bareboat charters.

The advantages to be gained through optimizing the design of a total transport system operate as a powerful force towards the use of "closed systems" by such industrial firms as have the transport volume to justify it. Thus, Texaco has established the 255,000 dwt. class to be the most economic for its service and has geared its shore facilities to this capacity. Gulf has entered long-term charters for D.K. Ludwig's 326,000 dwt. ships and will forward its refined products on smaller vessels out of Bantry Bay. The Marcona Company is designing its facilities in Peru for export of iron ores in slurry form aboard tankships which can bring a return cargo of oil.

The growth of specialization in ship type has encouraged the major firms to meet a larger proportion of their tonnage requirements through company-owned ships and long-term charters. Among the "majors" of the oil industry, this proportion now stands at roughly 40 percent (see Table 8-1). Time and voyage charters of suitable ships are used to supplement these nucleus fleets as needed to meet variable requirements occurring in the company's operations about the world.

For industrial firms which do not have the predictable volume of shipments to justify company investment in a closed system, economic advantage may lie in making a long-term arrangement with a ship operator who specializes in meeting the transport requirements for a particular class of product. Thus, while United Fruit still maintains a company-owned fleet of thirty vessels, its smaller rival, Standard Fruit, has shifted almost entirely to charters. U.S. Steel, Bethlehem, and Krupp each maintain shipping subsidiaries, but the British and Italian steelmakers contract for shipping services on the private market through industry-wide procurement organizations. The independently-owned Klaveness fleet provides a specialized service to the aluminum industry, which supplements the capacity directly controlled by Kaiser, Alcoa, and Alcan. The Oedfjell and Lorentzen interests serve a similar role for the petrochemical industry; the Kosangas and Transkosen shipping companies, for the liquified petroleum gas (LPG) industry; and so forth.

The economics of specialization operate to divide the ship charter market into numerous sub-markets each with its own characteristic mode of operation and price behavior.[2] This is not a wholly new development, since both geographic and technical factors always have created variations in the market. Nor are the many submarkets wholly independent of one another. For example, because supertankers were being used in the U.S. to India grain trades prior to the 1967 Suez crisis, charter rates in this trade immediately rose by 30 percent when the canal was closed; on the other hand, draft limitations at the entrance to the River Plate prevent use of supertankers in moving grain out of Argentina and rates in this trade did not react to the canal closing for several months. (See Figure 8-2.)

A vessel of some sort can usually be found to carry any cargo. The availability of such alternatives helps to check runaway rates in narrow markets. Yet the fact

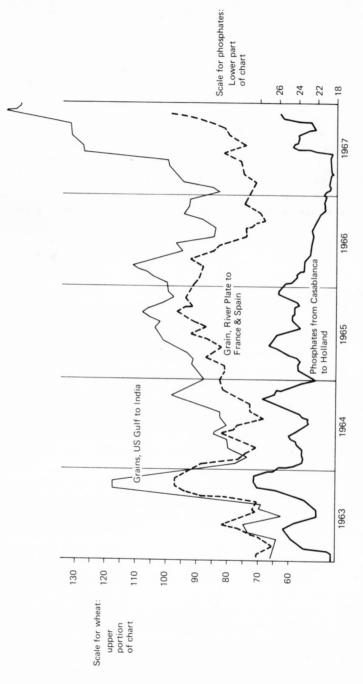

Figure 8-2. Tramp Charter Rate Performance in Related Trades, 1963-1967.

Source: C.F.H. Cuffley, "Monthly Freight Review," as cited in *Freight Markets and the Level and Structure of Freight Rates,* UNCTAD Shipping Committee, p. 85, 95.

that rates do react so sharply to changes in local supply and demand provides a vivid demonstration of the advantage which is gained through the use of the ships best suited to the particular trade. In sum, shipping's technical characteristics segment the market for many types of ships to the point that rates show considerable natural instability. Any further restrictions on market size, as for example through flag discrimination, are therefore likely to exact an unacceptably high price by forcing shippers to employ vessels unsuited to the trade whenever its composition or volume may change.[3]

Dry Bulk Carriers and Their Use

One of the most striking developments in shipping during the 1960s has been the construction, virtually from scratch, of a fleet of some 2,100 ships and sixty-five million dwt for transport of commodities in bulk. This new fleet of bulk carriers accounts for 80 to 85 percent of the total growth in dry cargo tonnage during the period. It was a development stimulated by a widening realization of the economies to be gained through size and specialization and accompanied by a rapid growth in the flow of suitable cargoes and improvement of cargo handling facilities.

The dry bulk fleet, defined as all single-deck ships of over 10,000 dwt., embraces a variety of ship types and sizes. Ore carriers, which are the oldest type, now represent only 12 percent of the total; combination oil/ore and oil/bulk/ore vessels are increasingly popular designs which constitute 10 percent of the present fleet but 45 percent of the bulk ships on order; other general purpose bulk carriers make up the remainder. This last group includes 1,078 "handy-sized" ships (less than 25,000 dwt.; twenty-one million dwt. in total) which have been designed as replacements for the shelterdeck tramps built prior to 1960 and which are engaged in trades similar to those serviced by their predecessors.[4]

The ownership of this new fleet, and particularly of the larger ships, is heavily concentrated in the U.S. (operated under Liberian registry), Norway, Japan, and Great Britain. Although only a small number of dry bulk carriers are owned by industrial companies, long-term charters are common, and on the order of 25 to 30 percent of the tonnage operates under industrial control. These industrial carriers appear to enjoy more intensive utilization than bulkers operated on the charter market.[5] Although they show a higher tendency to be used in a shuttle service than the independents, their use is not usually confined to a single trade or even to a single cargo. In fact, there appears to be a rather similar use pattern for the industrially-controlled ships, taken as a group, and for the larger vessels which are operated under affreightment contracts and short-term charters by the independents (see Table 8-2).

Were Table 8-2 to be extended to include the 547 additional vessels in the

Table 8-2
Patterns of Use of Large Bulk Carriers, 1968

	Industrially Controlled Vessels	Independents	
		18,000 to 35,000 dwt.	35,000 dwt. and over
Shuttle service (1 leg usually in ballast)	115	87	55
One cargo but various trades	75	33	80
Two cargoes but various trades	33	55	160
Three or more cargoes	37	305	135
Total	260	480	430

Source: Special tabulation provided to the author by Mr. Birger Nossum, Fearnley & Egers Chartering Co. Ltd. Estimates were developed from a 20 percent sample of the 170 ore carriers and 1,000 general bulkers, 18,000 dwt. and over, trading during 1968 (combination carriers were excluded from the sample). About three-quarters of the industrially controlled tonnage covered by the survey was in ships of 35,000 dwt. and over; for the independents, the percentage was in the range of two-thirds.

10,000 to 18,000 dwt. range also classified by Fearnley and Egers as bulk carriers, we might expect to see an even larger proportion of these vessels taking multiple cargoes under short-term charters. The carrying capacity of the bulk fleet, however, is heavily weighted to the larger ships which have a more limited trading interest. Owners participating in only one or two cargoes may be presumed to be providing a specialized service to a single industry, with occasional entry into other markets in order to reduce the ballast voyages of their ships.

Short-term and voyage charters of the smaller bulk carriers are typically fixed in the traditional manner on one of the shipping exchanges. The business of the larger ships and those providing a pledged freight service to industrial firms, however, is now more commonly negotiated directly between the shipper and shipowner. The size of the transaction and the many special problems which must be considered in tailoring large scale shipping services to the customer's facilities and cargoes make direct negotiations preferable to working entirely through an auction market.

During the 1960s bulk carriers largely displaced tramps and liners in movements of major, high volume products (see Figure 8-3). With the introduction of larger ships, bulk cargo handling techniques have been greatly improved; for example, internal belt conveyor systems and shoreside cranes are now capable of handling up to 15,000 tons per hour. At the same time, bulk carriers have been entering an increasing number of cargo trades. By 1967, they had captured 85 percent of the iron ore shipments, 54 percent of the grains,

Figure 8-3. Penetration of Bulk Carriers into Major Dry Commodity Traders.[a]

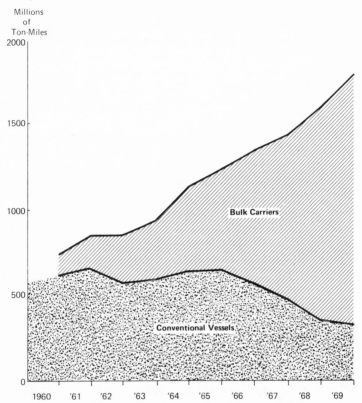

Source: Fearnley and Egers Charting Co. Ltd.

[a]Tonnage of five principal dry bulk commodities (iron ore, coal, grains, bauxite and aluminia, and phosphate rock) shipped in bulk carriers of 18,000 dwt. and over.

one-third of the phosphate rock cargoes, 68 percent of bauxite and alumina, and significant proportions of other ores, sugar, softwoods, pulp, and even steel products, pipe, and automobiles. The economies gained through shipment in large lots via these modern vessels are such as to impose an important penalty on those trades, such as grain exports from Argentina and those into India/Pakistan, in which terminal facilities and harbor depths prevent their being employed.[6]

An increasing saturation of the potential market for shipments in large bulk carriers has led many owners during the past several years to hedge their investments in this class ship by building into it capabilities to handle a variety of cargoes. The spiritual parent to the modern combination bulk carrier may be considered to be the all-purpose tramp, which was the previous generation's answer to the need to participate in many markets in order to assure employment. Modern use of a large bulk vessel in combined trades began with the fitting out of tankers to carry grains in the late 1950s, when reopening of Suez burst the bubble of their natural market.[7] The successor to the dual-use tanker was the oil/ore ship, designed with separate holds to handle these two cargoes without the need for cleaning. The most recent development is an oil/bulk/ore (OBO), designed for grains and other bulk cargoes as well. The additional structure adds about $1 million to the vessel's cost and slightly diminishes its efficiency, but also adds significantly to the flexibility with which the vessel can be traded.

Although much attention has been given to developing itineraries which capitalize upon the OBO's special features by loading several cargoes in the course of a single voyage, this has actually been accomplished by very few owners.[8] On the other hand, the OBO's have shifted frequently from wet to dry cargoes and back again as freight rates have favored the one use over the others. Over the three year period from 1966 to 1968, some 85 to 90 percent of this class of ship was used in both markets; in any one year, the proportion still was in the range of 50 to 60 percent.[9] The emphasis on flexibility causes most of these vessels to be chartered for relatively short terms. However, it is of interest to note that several OBO's have been acquired by oil companies.

Tramp Markets and Trades

The division between the tramp and handy-sized bulk carrier categories, as indicated above, is somewhat uncertain, and statistics do not reliably differentiate between their activities. Although the doughty old 12 knot, shelter-deck tramp no longer holds its former sway in the world's trades, it appears that the tramp sector of the industry (broadly defined to include some portion of the smaller bulk carriers) has been able to about hold its own despite the massive increase in cargoes shipped in very large lots. The cargo mix, however, has clearly changed from the days in the early sixties when the tramps found the majority of their business in grain, coal, and ores.[10] These cargoes are still important, but it is probably sugar, fertilizer, scrap metal, pellets and ingots, copra, and timber that now form the backbone of tramp activity. Unfortunately, authoritative data are not available.

The tramp business still is done chiefly on a trip charter basis through the Baltic Shipping Exchange. However, even in this category there is a noticeable trend towards longer term arrangements; by 1967, probably half the tramp tonnage was being fixed for multiple voyages. A number of tramp vessels under these longer term charters have been taken up by liner firms to supplement their own fleets. Others are chartered to industrial firms for periods of three months to one or two years. Yet, despite the erosion of the classic tramp trades, some 70 to 80 million tons of cargo still are estimated to be lifted by tramps each year on single trip fixtures, often at prices well above those applying in more stable services, to satisfy the erratic and unpredictable margin of the world's cargo flows.

Contract Terms

The increasing diversity of ship types and services during recent years has been accompanied by an increasing diversity of contract terms. The shipowner is concerned not only with the period of the charter, but also with the terms regarding loading and delivery of the cargo, lay-over time, insurance, safety measures, and clean-up costs. In longer term arrangements, the construction of escalation clauses, allowance for time off-charter, and requirements regarding the condition of the ship and her crew become critically important.

Aristotle Onassis is credited with having pioneered the now common practice of arranging a long term charter so that it can be accepted as security for the mortgage financing of the ship.[11] Such charter agreements are used by major industrial firms which do not wish to commit their own capital to ships or to become involved in the operating side of the business. They create a vehicle through which shipowners can acquire tonnage on minimum equity. To the financing institutions, they offer a high-quality investment secured by a pledge, underwritten by the charterer, of charter payments sufficient to meet the amortization of the loan.

Some such contracts are written for bareboat charters in which the nominal shipowner serves essentially as a broker to the deal. The more usual arrangement is for the shipowner to operate the vessel at a stipulated charter rate, with the charterer sharing in some measure in the risks associated with the enterprise. On occasion, the shipowner operating under such a time charter assigns the actual operation of the vessel to yet another party, who fulfills his obligations for him.

The price levels at which charters are fixed reflect both the particular terms of the charter and the expectations of the market. Time charters tend to be placed at higher rates than voyage charters in a rising market, since shipowners will demand more money if required to commit their ships for an extended term. In falling markets, the charterer will seek a discount on the going rate for voyage charters if he offers a multiple voyage or term contract.

Considerable negotiation enters into any charter arrangement. The negotiation of short and intermediate-term charters, however, is far more affected by the immediate tone of the market than is the negotiation of a long-term charter-and-build contract, which is geared more to costs, risks, and rate of return.

"Freight service" or "affreightment" contracts are a recent innovation in ship contracting which are designed to permit the more flexible use of specialized ships in a changing trade situation. Under a freighting contract, the shipowner contracts to supply a stipulated volume of transport service for a period into the future without specifying the particular vessels through which his obligation will be met. Ships employed under such contracts can be loaded with the cargoes of several shippers within a region and their dispatch can be controlled by the shipowner in a manner which minimizes ballast steaming. It also becomes possible for several shipowners to pool their resources in order to establish a fleet of sufficient size to undertake a number of affreightment agreements, which together permit a more economic mode of operation than would be possible to any one of them acting individually. Ship brokers may act as middlemen to such arrangements by taking ships on charter to fulfill service agreements which they negotiate.

The shipping community lacks information on the use of various charter arrangements, and the mix is in any event constantly changing. As a generalization, it may be said that the affreightment contract is enjoying a growing popularity, while single voyage terms are declining in importance.

The Geography of Liner Services

The organization of liner services and markets is a function of historical factors, cargo flows, and geography. The liner world is only indirectly linked to the volatile markets for tramp and bulk carrier shipping. On the other hand, there appears to be quite close linkage in the price and service patterns of liner companies throughout the world.

The high correlation between liner rate movements in diverse trades may be ascribed, in part, to the fact that large liner firms frequently offer services in many trades; in part, to the similar pressures on operating costs throughout the industry; and, in part, to coordination among conferences of rate actions.[12] The rapid pace at which such new service arrangements as containerization have spread through the liner industry is at least partly a result of the close ties among the liner services.[13] Thus, while each route has a separate identity, it is sensitive to changes occurring elsewhere in the system.

The world deep sea liner industry embraces approximately 300 firms domiciled in fifty countries and operating 2,400 to 2,500 ships in excess of 5000 gross tons. All told there are probably on the order of 600 to 800 separate liner services being offered to carry interregional general cargo trade. Although each service may provide different itineraries, ocean liners tend to cluster on about fifteen principal trading routes. The hubs from which these services radiate are, of course, Europe, the United States, and Japan, and approximately 90 percent of the vessels in liner trade operate under the flags of the developed nations. The service areas of these vessels are defined partly by geography, partly by trade flows, and partly by political factors. Thus trade with such geographically isolated countries as New Zealand and Australia and such politically self-conscious states as Indonesia, Communist China, and Burma is conducted chiefly by ships serving only these nations, while the remainder of the Southeast Asian region is considered to be a single trading area.[14]

Some twenty-five less developed states now operate national flag lines in transoceanic trade. Of this number, half are Latin American; about one-quarter, Southeast Asian states; and the remainder, located in South Asia, Africa and the Middle East.[15] About half of the liner tonnage maintained by less developed nations is employed in intraregional trade. The remainder tends to operate in parallel with the ships of the developed nations with whom the great proportion of their external trade is conducted. Only very limited liner service is offered between the world's less developed regions, and this, chiefly as "way cargo" by vessels in other services.

Most liner service is offered over routes which have sufficient trade to support the participation of five or more firms and to provide at least weekly sailings (see Table 8-3). In the main trading areas (e.g., over the North Atlantic and the North Pacific and from Europe to the coasts of Africa, South Asia, and the Far East) there are opportunities for great diversity in patterns of port calls and routings. This diversity broadens potential market areas and encourages the participation of a much larger number of operators. However, although they are insignificant as a proportion of world liner traffic volume, there are also numerous trades in which market size limits the number of firms able to share in the business to two or three and the number of sailings to less than one per week. In these trades, a specific ship coming on berth enjoys an effective temporal monopoly.[16]

Table 8-3
Market Size for Liner Service

Interregional Pairs[a]	No. of Pairs	No. of Vessels	Annual Cargo Tonnage (mil. tons)	Percent
Supporting 5 or more sailings per week	15	1500	105	62
Supporting 2-5 sailings per week	25	640	43	25
Supporting 2-8 sailings per month	28	325	20	12
Supporting less than 2 sailings monthly	37	35	2	1
Total	105	2500	170	100

Source: Author's estimates based on Saguenay Research study of 1966 shipments of general cargoes in interregional trade. The cargo data shown are for general cargoes only and assume that about forty-five percent of these cargoes are handled by bulk carriers, industrials, and/or tramps. The estimate of number of liner sailings is geared to the assumption that on the average each liner will be able to make about six to seven outbound voyages per year. It should be emphasized that arraying the data in terms of regional pairs substantially overstates the service which can be expected over any particular port-to-port route within the region and that introduction of container services with ships capable of carrying substantially greater cargo volumes per voyage similarly will reduce the number of sailings which a particular route can support, as well as very sharply reducing the number of ships required to provide the service.

aPairs of regions as defined in the Saguenay Research study of 1966 cargo flows and reported in Table 6-1.

In contrast to tramps, most liner services have some link to their home country. Many lines, however, depend heavily on cargoes traded between the way ports in their systems. Also, there are several round-the-world liner services which depend almost entirely on "cross-traded" cargoes.

The economic geography of the liner system embraces a substantial volume of strictly nation to nation service, since—where cargo volume is sufficient—it is advantageous to limit the number of port calls to be made at both termini of the voyage. From the fragmentary data on the portion of national trade carried in national flag ships, it would appear that on the order of 30 to 40 percent of the liner business is currently conducted in this mode. However, there also are strong pressures toward multilateralism in liner operations where:

A. Several small nations are located within a single trading area.
B. Cargo volumes are small, volatile, or of a character that requires particularly frequent service.
C. The trade is most efficiently handled as "way cargoes" to another service.
D. National flag fleets are seeking to gain a foothold in the trade and must, at least initially, look to several trading partners to generate sufficient cargoes to fill their ships.

In view of the fact that these factors apply more frequently in the trades of the less developed world, it is ironic that it has been these states which have pressed most vigorously for recognition of the legitimacy of bilateral systems based on flag discrimination. Applied world-wide, bilateralism would prove far more costly to small nations than to large nations and would probably cause the termination of a large proportion of their trade connections, which, on a bilateral basis, could no longer be profitably served by liner firms.

The economies of scale realized through container shipping and the desire of many less-developed nations to assume a larger role in liner shipping lend added weight to the economic advantage of a system which allows ships of any flag equal access to the cargoes of all ports. With the very large investments required for container shipping, service areas will need to be enlarged both to generate sufficient cargoes and to assure a more stable cargo flow. Supplemental services with conventional liners similarly will be forced to search out cargoes over wider areas, while other companies will conclude that their best hope is to be represented in a consortium or joint service. Efforts to organize integrated global systems already are much in evidence.

The geography of liner shipping, therefore, is experiencing a fundamental transition about which more will follow later in this book. The liner system's historical development has yielded a large number of firms, representing many flags and dispersed over many routes, whose coexistence has been facilitated by the protective umbrella of the conferences. Within the conferences, national flag lines have tended to focus attention chiefly on their national trades. But powerful economies of scale inherent in container shipping are forcing these lines to redefine their markets in regional terms and to consolidate their operations with other companies which can assure their access to the region as a whole.

9

Competition in Shipping

Competitive relations amongst firms are a key element of an industry's anatomy, which influence its adaptability and the pattern of its growth. Ocean shipping is clearly a competitive industry in the sense that a great number of firms, driven by profit motivations, share in servicing a diversity of markets within which there is substantial opportunity for product substitution and for reward of economic efficiency. But the industry also has oligarchical features. In liner trades, the conference system has been the vehicle through which leading firms have broadened their influence; in the bulk business, the control of shipping services tends to reflect the structure of the industries it serves.

Shipownership and Economic Control

Except in a few protected enclaves, shipowning is a game of high risks and high rewards. It has long attracted a highly diverse breed of individualists and entrepreneurs. Despite the increasing level of sophistication and of capital required for participation in the industry, truly independent operators may still be found in every branch. They largely populate the tramp and brokerage ends of the business and play a major role in financing and management of bulk carriers. Often, they are the organizers of national flag fleets in remote, less developed countries, even in the liner trades. The competitive impulses of these entrepreneurs, although not always appreciated by their more conservative colleagues, play an important part in checking monopolistic tendencies in shipping.

A second factor which enlivens decentralization of the industry's economic control is the geographic dispersion of its management. There is almost no trade or market within the industry which is not shared by nationals of several countries and usually by nationals of regions widely divergent, not only in geography but also in business traditions and aspirations. Thus, the Japanese join with the Americans and Europeans in liner conferences, but nevertheless maintain a stiff competitive stance beneath their cooperative facade. Greeks are to be found throughout the world operating low cost services in competition with the established lines. Russian, Polish, and East German companies join the conferences in some trades but do not hesitate to compete in others. The shipping lines based in less developed countries are now almost all conference members but within the conference may adopt a highly independent point of view.

97

A third circumstance working against monopoly in shipping is the large number of separate units remaining in the industry despite the management consolidations of the past decade. Many, of course, are phantom corporations formed for tax reasons or to limit liability by treating each ship as a separate unit. Others are linked through intricate networks of joint stock companies, purchase options, financing agreements, long-term charters, and other arrangements, which permeate large sectors of the industry and confound efforts to pinpoint the locus of economic control. A Saguenay Research project, directed to identifying the number, domicile, and type of firms capable of exercising independent action in each sector of the industry, has been only partially successful in charting this intricate scene. Tables 9-1 and 9-2, which present the results of the Saguenay Project, do however consolidate tonnage listed under coporations known to be components of larger units and represent the best available estimates of the size and number of independent shipping firms. By any measure, this number is sufficiently large to bar any likelihood of worldwide monopolization of any major sector of the sea transport industry.

Fourth, there is still a place in the shipping industry for the innovative small firm. Several of today's giants (e.g., SeaLand, Marcona, Maritime Fruit, Star Bulk, and Orient Overseas Lines) were hardly known when the 1960s began. Within the industry, small firms and large operate and compete on apparently equal terms. The giant may enjoy distinct advantages in diversifying and rationalizing his operations; in obtaining insurance, stores, and financing on favorable terms; and in advertising his services. These advantages are offset, however, by higher overhead costs and more ponderous decision-making procedures, and therefore appear not to establish insuperable obstacles to the small competitor.[1]

Finally, the enthusiastic and often belligerent nationalism of the less-developed nations seeking to enter or expand their maritime shipping creates a destabilizing factor and a goad to the established elements of the world fleet. To date, the pressures of the less-developed world have been directly felt in only a few trades and chiefly in liner services. There are indications that these pressures will expand and force a more conscious catering to the national needs of the "under-half" in other sectors of the industry as well.[2]

Yet many shipping people will argue that these decentralizing tendencies are essentially peripheral to the stronger centripetal forces in the industry. These persons point to the small group of firms which have both the economic power and political influence to affect the future development of the industry and emphasize the close relationship which these firms appear to enjoy with one another and with the cargo interests, financial institutions, and government bodies which collectively determine the industry's fate. The proposition that it is a few "Mr. Bigs" which shape the industry's destinies is one which merits examination.

In liner shipping, there is a fairly sharp discontinuity in the spectrum of firm

Table 9-1
Number and Size of Shipping Firms

Activity in Which Firm is Chiefly Engaged	Number of Firms Controlling:					
	Less than 100 Thous. Grt.	100-400 Thous. Grt.	400-1,000 Thous. Grt.	1-2,000 Thous. Grt.	Over 2,000 Thous. Grt.	Total
Liner service	260	32	8	0	0	300
Tramp	310	20	0	0	0	330
Dry bulk	115	15	0	0	0	130
Tanker	256	18	6	5	5	290
Two or more of the above:						
Government-owned	6	8	10	2	1	27
Privately-owned	104	45	18	10	3	180
Total	1051	138	42	17	9	1257

Source: Saguenay Research. To the extent possible in determining both firm size and the number of independent firms, subsidiary companies have been consolidated with their parent organizations. Companies linked through overlapping boards, joint ventures, management agreements, and the like have, however, been counted as separate entities unless there is a parent company holding majority control. Data are for 1970 and relate only to firms operating ocean-going vessels of 5,000 grt. or over engaged in deep sea freight service.

Table 9-2
Number and Tonnage of Vessels (5000 grt. and over) Operated by Firms of Various Sizes

Activity in Which Ship is Chiefly Engaged	Number of Ships Operated by:					
	Small Firms <1000 grt.	Firms of 100-400 grt.	Firms of 400-1000 grt.	Firms of 1-2000 grt.	Firms of >2000 grt.	Total
Liner service	1550	575	500	0	0	2625
Tramp	1200	350	0	0	0	1550
Dry bulk	460	225	0	0	0	685
Tanker	800	220	160	380	620	2180
Two or more of the above:						
Government-owned	30	180	600	300	600	1710
Privately-owned	750	920	720	725	700	3815
Total	4790	2470	1980	1405	1920	12565

Source: See notes on Table 9-1.

size between the very numerous small and medium-sized firms (from two to twenty-five ships) and the few giants of the industry. These latter, with from forty to eighty ships in liner service each, include only a half dozen or so firms, based in Europe, the U.S., and Japan.[3] Unquestionably each of these companies wields a large influence in the industry. Several of them also have joined in consortia with other smaller lines to establish a broader base on which to pioneer such new systems as containerization. In fact, the rapid, worldwide spread of this system simply could not have been accomplished without the active participation of the industry's largest firms.

Oligopolistic tendencies in liner shipping are strengthened also by the existence within many conferences of pooling arrangements designed to reduce or eliminate even service competition among the participating lines. There is no information on a worldwide basis to indicate the extent of such practices. The pool may include all members of the conference or only the lines of trading partners or affiliated national flag lines. The entire trade may be involved or only certain ports or cargoes. The pool may run to the total revenue earned through carrying the categories of cargo covered or include only a portion of this revenue. On the other hand, it may not be concerned with revenues at all, but rather only with the volume of cargo carried. Whatever the form, however, the intent is to reduce competition by stabilizing the participation of the member firms and, in this way, to advance the fuller and more profitable utilization of equipment in servicing the trade.

Although most conferences and pools operate on a one-firm, one-vote basis, power within them tends to gravitate to the large firms, which have the most at stake and the greatest flexibility for initiatives in rate and service matters. The six giants of the liner industry collectively participate in virtually all of the major transoceanic conferences and many conferences include three or four of these firms among their membership.[4] However, except to the extent that the large liner companies may share common economic interests and a common cultural heritage, there is no evidence to suggest that they tend to act collectively in opposition to the interests of the smaller firms. Indeed, such evidence as does exist tends to support the proposition that conference politics are centered on regional groups, embracing both small and large firms.[5]

None of the major liner companies at present directly controls or is controlled by other modes of transportation. Working arrangements have of course been developed between the major ocean freight carriers and domestic truck and rail lines for receiving and forwarding containers and other cargoes from inland destinations. However, U.S. anti-trust policy requires that these be "arm's length" arrangements and equally available to all carriers; a similar doctrine is beginning to evolve within the Common Market. Although intermodal ties seem certain to gain increasing importance in years ahead, preferences in inland transport appear for the present not to be a major factor in the competitive structure of the ocean freight industry.[6]

In the bulk shipping world, ties to cargo interests and the scale of movements count for most in establishing the competitive structure. The "Class A Bigs" are the industrial giants—such as Kaiser, Krupp, Jersey Standard, and Shell,—which each move more than 10 million cargo tons. Being big, these organizations can think in very different terms than companies concentrated in the movement of nickel, chrome, copper ores or other relatively low volume commodities. The supercarriers and local distribution ships employed in the transportation systems of the Class A industrials compose more than half of the world tanker tonnage and perhaps 10 percent of the dry bulk carrier fleet. Although much of this tonnage is owned by independents (on the order of 60 percent), it is often leased on long-term time charters on terms which give the lessee virtually complete control during the life of the lease.

The increasingly capital-intensive nature of bulk shipping coupled with inherent economies of scale tend to strengthen the position of the Class A industrials and it is significant that certain of these firms are moving out from their own base of cargo movements to employ their considerable capacity also in other trades. But while the balance may be shifting, there remains considerable scope for the smaller operator who may be able to tailor his service more sensitively to the natural instabilities of the market and the specialized needs of cargoes moving on a less dramatic scale. Even in oil, the seven majors control only on the order of 60 to 70 percent of the international movements. The smaller oil companies and most bauxite, iron ore, and grain shippers are dealing in the range of only one to ten million tons of cargo annually. Many of these latter companies are locked into systems involving service to upstream ports and relatively unstable cargo flows. They may dream of integrated systems and owning ships in the 200,000 ton class, but in fact depend heavily on the charter market to meet their transportation requirements.

In several countries—most notably Japan and Germany—control of ocean shipping rests in financial houses whose interests extend through wide swaths of heavy industry. In the U.S. also, shipping is increasingly being absorbed into industrial conglomerates whose investment in marine transportation reflects at least a vague perception that control of shipping can facilitate distribution and provide a market for other products of the enterprise as well as generate profit itself. In a groping and complex way, these moves may be leading toward a better correlation of production and transport activities. Such correlation, of course, has long been the objective of the socialist countries whose ships now constitute almost 10 percent of the world fleet.

Where vertical integration is successful, pressures for greater efficiency in sea transport may actually increase due to the competitive pressures on the parent companies. Even nationally owned shipping enterprises are likely to feel the wrath of other trading interests if their services are inferior to those of their competitor lines. Thus, economic pressures may be buffered by holding companies and sponsoring governments but are inescapable in the end. The interplay of these forces is such as to defeat monopolization of economic power on an industry-wide scale and greatly to complicate efforts to monopolize even local sub-markets.

Workable Competition and the Conference System

It has for some years been recognized that economic definitions of pure competition provide a poor model for describing the competitive realities of transportation (and many other) industries. Instead, the concept of "workable competition" has been formulated to establish a standard for analysis. The criteria for workable competition are elastic but assume: prices which respond quickly to changes in conditions of supply and demand; sufficient heterogeneity in the market to create uncertainty regarding competitive reactions; the possibility of substitutes; prompt application of new technology to improve efficiency; and a price structure adequate to cover long-run marginal costs without permitting monopoly profit.[7] Perhaps most important, workable competition should not sustain excess capacity or shield permanently the relatively inefficient producer. The conference system in liner shipping is often criticized for doing exactly that.[8]

The shipping conferences did for many years substantially monopolize the break-bulk traffic on most transoceanic trade routes and continue to hold a strong, though weakening position. Their purpose was essentially anti-competitive: to support a stable price system regardless of supply-demand fluctuations, to reduce uncertainty, and to limit the opportunities of their customers to employ substitute services. The device frequently used to achieve this last objective was a system of loyalty contracts, which allowed a 10 to 20 percent discount on tariffed rates to customers pledging their total traffic over a period of time.

The conferences also have consciously maintained some measure of excess capacity on the grounds that this cushion is needed in order to maintain frequent scheduled sailings during good years and bad. Coupled with relatively high fixed costs, this excess capacity creates a condition in which affirmative protective action is required to maintain tariffs at compensatory levels. Rate agreements are developed which, over time, may tend to be geared to the costs of the most inefficient member. Discrimination in rates between shippers and ports also becomes possible, and in some cases necessary, in order to avoid a drain of traffic in those sectors of the trade more sensitive to competition. In effect, the desire to protect some surplus capacity in the trade almost inevitably requires the conference lines to weave a net of noneconomic practices around their operations.

Within the conference the member lines, barred from direct price competition, emphasize extra speed and services in order to increase their share of the market, placing further pressures on costs and rates. As compared to a perfectly competitive model, the system clearly imposes significant economic costs.[9]

The relevant standard, however, is unlikely to be perfect (or "pure") competition. Ocean transport services bear too intimately on national interests and the reliability and stability of services are too important to the orderly flow of foreign trade to risk the vicissitudes of an auction price system. At a minimum, in order to have a workable situation, the lines providing service must have a sufficient stake in the trade to take a long view of their position and independently structure their prices to recover long-run marginal costs. In a growing trade this would imply rates sufficient to build reserves for ship replacement and to provide capacity sufficient to meet normal fluctuations in demand.

Economists argue that greater opportunity for rate competition would wring out sufficient excess capacity in liner shipping to permit the remaining, more efficient elements to lower rates to a level that would be deterrent to any casual operators and still meet long-run marginal costs. The conferences have countered that deterrent pricing would be unstable, and therefore unsatisfactory, and that the gap between short-run opportunity and long-run service is in any event too large. Government groups investigating the conference system have generally supported the latter point of view.[10]

The more persuasive consideration, often obscured in the economic dialogue, is the important political role played by the conferences. Competition in liner shipping is not simply between firms but between national flags supported by governments and national commercial interests. Quite apart from their economic role, the conferences provide a vehicle through which these interests may be arbitrated in a quasi-private setting and trade practices held to a reasonably healthy standard of commercial practice. Recognizing this role, many conferences have now adopted formal machinery for arbitration of rate and service questions; under 1961 legislation, such machinery is mandatory in conferences serving U.S. trades.[11]

For so long as liner shipping has been characterized by large numbers of relatively small firms, which are divided by sharp national interests and which sometimes take a rather short-run, opportunistic view of the business, the conferences have found support as the most workable means for curbing excessive competition. With conditions in the industry changing, the conferences themselves are finding their role increasingly difficult, and the possibilities of other, more workable arrangements for assuring a long-run, commercial perspective among firms competing in the industry will need to be examined. This is a matter to which we will be returning later in this book.

10 The Economics of Government Aid

Government outlays to support commercial enterprise may be designed to shield favored firms from external competition, to assist the formation of infant industries, or to respond to such specific national interests as defense, economic development, and balance of payments. In shipping all these elements are present, although the defense argument has been pressed openly only by the U.S.A. and certain of the South American nations. In this volume we will not attempt to examine the complex and often emotional issue of the strategic importance of national flag shipping; suffice it to say that no major maritime power is likely to be willing to permit the disintegration of its national flag merchant fleet. The economic bases for maritime subsidies, however, often are not well understood and require at least brief discussion.

Economic Bases of Shipping Subsidization

Until recently, economic doctrine has held that no valid *economic* basis can be established for governmental action to divert resources from one sector of the economy to another—i.e., to provide subsidies.[1] Justification had to be found on other grounds. Within the past decade or two, however, economists have come to acknowledge that in particular situations subsidies can be used to advance economic welfare.[2] This is so especially if subsidies are viewed from a solely national perspective, but an economic basis even for shipping subsidization can also be advanced from the viewpoint of international comparative advantage in selected situations. Those cited are as follows:

To Correct for Inequalities in Market Values

"With the world-wide proliferation of distortions of money cost levels due to tariffs, trade restrictions and to monopolies owned or blessed by governments," writes Professor Sturmey, "comparisons of money costs of similar undertakings in different countries tell us very little about the comparative real resource input."[3] In a homogeneous market economy, any policy which displaces low cost suppliers by higher cost suppliers will cause economic loss, but there can be no presumption in the real world that this will be the case. Indeed studies which have attempted to probe this difficult area have found very large differences—

ranging up to 100 percent—in the resource value of money in different economies.[4] A subsidy designed to offset such anomalies may be economically justified if used in support of enterprises in which the sponsoring nation enjoys a comparative advantage vis-a-vis other industries in which it might invest. High tax and tariff countries may also need to assist export industries whose products must compete with those produced in countries where there is little or no governmental overburden on the factors of production.[5] In other cases, temporary maladjustments in currency valuations may require that assistance be given industries capable of generating foreign exchange.

In recognition of such situations, economists now counsel the use of "shadow prices" in calculations of investment value.[6] In effect, since real world markets are not free, it becomes necessary to create an artificial model of real resource values in order to test the economic validity of particular enterprises; government assistance may well be justified to fill a gap between the real and monetary return of the undertaking.

A crucial difficulty in this approach, of course, is the difficulty of making valid calculations. If large sectors of the economy are governed through this approach, as the socialist states have discovered, the entire system loses its underpinnings. There are risks of this situation developing in foreign trade and shipping. As efforts to correct distortions in one area are matched by counter-action to meet the distortions of another, a subsidy race may develop which profits no one and simply creates an overabundance of shipping service.[7] On the other hand, from the viewpoint of a particular country whose economy has become dependent upon freight revenues, there may be no alternative but to provide the subsidies necessary to stay in the race.

To Correct Imperfections in
Pricing of Transportation Services

Distortions in the pricing of ocean freight services create yet another potential basis for subsidization. Certain nations have believed, for example, that conference rate structures were so arranged as to discriminate against their foreign trade. Even though the effort were costly, it might pay in such situations for the aggrieved nation to organize its own shipping service—especially if this action were taken in a manner which placed leverage on the conference to adjust its rate policy. Ports also frequently claim that liner freights fail to recognize their natural advantages and place pressures on their national governments to allocate funds to bring service to their doors.

To Stimulate Economic Development

Theoreticians once took a static view of the world economy; they do so no longer. Man's experience has been one of a changing and increasingly effective utilization of resources. Investment which can bring idle resources into the economic stream may be justified, even if initial costs are high, in reference to the future development of the world economy.[8] This is the basis of the well-established infant industry doctrine and also of the pressures by the less-developed nations to enter industries for which they may know they are not presently competitively equipped.

An important role of government in less-developed nations is to mobilize savings and attract foreign aid to productive domestic investment. The government may take this investment on its own behalf or extend incentives to private firms to engage in the business and initiate a self-sustaining stream of income, savings, and tax payments from which to generate further investment. What counts in this situation is not the efficiency of the industry in reference to its external competitors, but its productivity in income, employment, and taxes as compared to the alternative opportunities available to the less-developed state. In this respect, shipping has certain advantages but also many disadvantages, regarding which we will have more to say later.

To Stimulate Trade

A key aspect of development is provision of sufficient infrastructure, in pace with productive facilities, to gain the comparative advantage available through economies of scale and the exchange of goods both within the national economy and in intraregional and international trade. As noted above, there are many routes between less developed states on which there is insufficient trade to attract a regular shipping service. Public investment to initiate such services may well be a valid component of an overall development program of a less-developed economy. Such investment frequently also has political overtones owing to the multiple interests which typically are involved in drawing outlying portions of a large country such as Chile, Indonesia, or Brazil into the national economy or in advancing the cause of regional integration.

The trade development argument for shipping subsidization in this context is quite different from that often advanced by a nation such as the United States, Great Britain, or Japan. In these cases export markets already are large enough to command the full services of the world merchant fleet.

To Assure Continuous Service and Enhance
Domestic Economic Stability

A certain amount of instability is a necessary and desirable aspect of any market economy and not in itself a valid basis for government intervention. In a few situations, however, where national economies are heavily dependent on export trade, government action may be justified to protect export and import interests from undue oscillations in the costs of shipping services. A national flag fleet may offer a partial answer to this problem, particularly if the subsidy is so administered as to encourage owners to maintain reserve capacity to be available in times of high demand.

To Diversify Sources of Foreign Exchange Earnings

For some countries with limited export potential, investment in shipping offers desirable diversification of foreign exchange earning sources. Such shipping should not however be designed to service the countries' own foreign trade, since a depression in commodity exports will then be accompanied by depression in shipping revenues as well.[9]

In sum, numerous features are built into our economic system which create real and valid motivations for government support of merchant shipping; additional motivations are found in political and strategic interests. Government patronage appears to have been extended to maritime ventures for as long as ships have gone to sea; it will undoubtedly be continued in the future.

Shipping subsidies which have a valid economic basis and are provided in a manner which does not restrict the freedom of all flags to compete for cargoes in international trade are generally not opposed within the industry. Nor are they considered improper under the fragmentary international law existing on. this subject.[10] Even the U.S. operating differential subsidy has been accepted by most maritime states as a proper and necessary means for assisting U.S. flag ships to compete in international commerce and for meeting its defense responsibilities. The ultimate check on such subsidization is simply the evaluation of individual governments of the priority of this use of their limited funds.

Subsidy Methods and Effects

A ship subsidy may be extended to establish service where none exists. More commonly, however, the subsidy is aimed at enhancing the position of national vis-à-vis foreign flag lines. Furthermore, no system has yet been devised which does not also generate side effects ancillary to its avowed intent. Subsidies may create repercussions by tempting other nations to take counter actions. Subsidies may also lead to increased costs, excess capacity, or inflexible service patterns, which frustrate the very object of the grant.

Over the years, there has been much experimentation with alternative subsidy techniques, and a great variety of measures—none entirely satisfactory—are in current use.[11] In terms of their economic effect, they may be categorized as follows:

Investment Aids

Investment aids include favorable credit terms, depreciation allowances, tax deferrals and exemptions on reinvested gains, and outright capital grants. These measures tend to increase the total shipping tonnage in world trade as well as to increase the share owned by citizens of the sponsor nation. Were such grants to be provided with no strings attached, they would have little other economic effect. Typically, however, the subsidizing nation requires owners benefitting from the grant to employ national crews, use the vessel in national trades, or in some other manner operate so as to create flows of income back to the sponsoring state. Constraints may be imposed regarding the type of ships to be acquired and the timing of purchases. Nonetheless, assuming that owners are permitted to obtain their tonnage at commercial terms on the world market, the economic distortions associated with investment grants are relatively minor and hence unobjectionable to the shipping community.[12]

Concessions in Taxation of Current Income

Tax incentives are another means of inducing shipping investment which are very commonly employed. As with investment aids, to which they are closely related, the effects are to increase somewhat worldwide investment in shipping and to tilt flag shares in favor of the subsidizing state. From another viewpoint, such concessions may be regarded as simply exempting shipping from the distorting effects which the need to levy taxes ordinarily imposes. From this perspective, the very liberal terms offered by the convenience flags may be regarded as setting a standard for the industry which other nations may feel forced to follow in order to keep shipping operations under the national flag.[13]

Other Concessions to Reduce Ship Operating
Expenses and Payments to Increase Income

This category includes a host of measures—exemptions from consular and pilotage fees, preferred exchange rates in purchase of stores, training and social welfare aids to seamen, promotional contracts for carriage of mail and other goods, and of course direct subventions to reduce cost or increase income. In free markets, such aids would permit the benefiting ships to reduce rates and capture a larger share of the market. Within the conference system, where rate competition is barred, subsidies may operate chiefly to inflate costs by inducing demands by the benefitting firms, workers and suppliers for a larger slice of the pie. Where the government aid is provided on a cost-plus basis, as has been the pattern in the United States, these pressures are particularly severe.[14]

It might be supposed that the stronger financial position which a subsidized firm enjoys might encourage it to leave the conference and seek to maximize profit through lower rates. This has not been the actual pattern of experience, however, in part because sponsor governments have encouraged conference participation and, undoubtedly in part, because the companies themselves have preferred the relative security of operating as a conference line.

Guarantees of a Minimum Rate of Return

Government-owned shipping companies and those in which there is substantial government interest are in effect guaranteed an income sufficient to sustain their operations so long as they enjoy their sponsor's support. Ordinarily, of course, such support will tend to reflect the companies' economic performance, yet the political factor does make these companies a relatively unpredictable element of the international shipping scene. In these companies also costs have proved difficult to control and service may be geared more to political interests rather than commercial realities.

Flag Preferences[15]

Measures affecting the routing of cargoes are usually sharply distinguished from subsidies as a technique for providing government aid. Indirectly, however, such measures also create costs to the sponsoring nation and enhance the profitability of the benefiting firms. The chief difference lies in the fact that flag preferences directly limit competition for certain categories of cargo and only indirectly provide monetary aid, whereas subsidies involve direct aid and only indirect effects on shipping markets.

There is a host of techniques through which flag preference (or flag discrimination—the two terms are used interchangeably in practice) may be effected. Some extend an absolute monopoly to national flag ships, some reserve only a certain portion of the trade, and others simply offer inducements to shippers to patronize the national flag. Some form of preference to encourage use of national flag ships is reported by Franklin to be used by over half the world's maritime nations.[16]

Flag discrimination is difficult to control, in part because it is difficult to define. Opportunities to exercise a preference for national shipping are present whenever shipments are arranged. Government officials may be expected to

Cargo Allocation Techniques

	Mandatory	Preferential
Direct	• Laws instructing shippers to employ national flag lines • Conditional grants of export	• Measures to lower cost to shipper using national flag ship – differential import duties

licenses, foreign exchange,
or commercial credit
- • Transport clauses in int'l
trade agreements
- • Limitations on or total exclusion
of foreign shipping from the trade

- differential exchange rates
- improved export credits
- insurance concessions
- differential rates for inland transport
- waiving of various sorts of fees
- tax remissions

Indirect
- • Conference agreements and pools
establishing cargo shares
- • Procedures permitting government
and quasi-government agencies to
control cargo routing

- • Other measures favoring national flag
service
- berthing privileges
- expedited customs clearance
- national promotional campaigns

favor national ships, particularly if the merchant fleet receives other forms of government aid. Quasi-governmental agencies—national trading corporations, export banks, and forwarders—may also favor the national flag, and a natural bias to home-based shipping is likely to be found throughout the foreign trade communities of such nations as Britain and Japan, where shipping is an important export industry. In liner shipments, routing via national flag can usually be accomplished at no added cost to the shipper, and it is in this sector that preferences are accordingly most frequently encountered.

Flag preferences appear to impose little *direct* cost; hence they are a popular device, particularly to nations with limited tax resources, for promoting national flag shipping. However, they create large *indirect* costs which may be felt very widely through the maritime industry and the foreign trade community. These are most severe when the requirement is mandatory. As a result, laws imposing a national flag requirement generally allow for waivers in the event that shipment cannot be arranged within a reasonable period of time or at reasonable rates. On the other hand, economic preferences extended shippers employing national flag vessels may be so great as to allow very little actual choice.[17]

The most obvious economic cost created by flag discrimination results from channeling business to a carrier which may be presumed, in view of its dependence on this aid, to offer a less adequate or more costly service than its competitors. Where delays or poor handling are involved, these also produce additional costs. Furthermore, on many routes there will be only one or two national flag firms offering service. The shipper required to ship via natural flag is then confronted with a virtual monopoly. Cases have been alleged in which carriers enjoying this position have influenced conference rate structures to extract higher rates on this portion of their business.[18]

The administrative overhead of policing cargo allocation systems creates additional costs. Every shipment involves both a buyer and a seller, and sometimes additional parties as well. Establishing the terms of shipment is only one, usually minor, element in establishing the terms of trade and one which is difficult to bring under control.[19] Where large costs are associated with complying with flag preference decrees, both the opportunities and temptation to circumvent the law are large as well.

The most important economic effect of flag discrimination, however, is that it segments markets and undermines the international shipping industry's flexibility. As we have stressed throughout this section, such flexibility is essential in order to achieve balance between inbound and outbound shipments, adjust to changing trade patterns and seasonal fluctuations, capture economies of scale, bring the efficiency of specialized ship types to bear in handling many cargoes, and optimize the routing and scheduling of vessels within broad trading areas. Furthermore, the diseconomies inherent in artificially restricted and segmented markets are not confined to single trades but have ramifications throughout the industry. Thus, Brazil's insistence on bilaterilizing her ocean transport services will not only create costs for Brazil (which appears to feel that these costs are outweighed by benefits to her economy), but also for Uruguay and Argentina, who gain no benefits but will be isolated from the main stream of world shipping service. This increases the pressure on these latter nations to increase their own national flag fleets and hence to resort to discriminatory practices, launching a spiralling cycle of protectionism which could have disastrous effects on the organization of the entire ocean freight industry.

The present and potential impact of flag discrimination of the costs of ocean shipping has so far eluded exact calculation. Phillip Franklin has estimated that about 20 to 25 percent of general cargo tonnage, 10 to 12 percent of dry bulks, and 2 to 3 percent of the world's petroleum shipments were routed through cargo allocation procedures favoring national flag ships.[20] His estimate of the economic cost associated with these procedures is in the range of $500 million to $1 billion per year.[21] However, the extent of such practices, particularly in the liner trades, is sufficient to affect the entire character of the industry. Such situations defeat quantification.

In sum, the manner in which government assistance is extended makes a crucial difference. A direct tax or investment subsidy, properly administered, may operate only as a mild corrective whose effect is to draw vessels likely to be operated, anyway, home to the national flag.[22] But, as we have seen, assistance programs which cause governments to intervene actively in the functioning of shipping markets, particularly through measures to control cargo routing, have serious effects which increase costs and in the long run tend to frustrate the very objectives they are designed to serve. Furthermore, these effects appear likely to be most severe in small, developing trades, where they now are both most prevalent and least able to be supported.[23]

Shipping in Relation to Balance of Payments

The factor which appears to be most influential in causing the less-developed states to risk extreme measures in order to expand their national flag fleets is the expectation that such action will relieve some of the strain on their balance of payments. Due to a quirk in international payments accounting, the total outlay for export shipments carried on foreign flag ships appears as a debit item; the payments to national flag carriers for freight on imports appears as a credit.[24] The realities of the flow of funds, however, are quite different and may yield very little net foreign exchange gain—indeed even a loss—to a nation which attempts to launch a shipping fleet from an inadequate industrial and commercial base.

Shipping may be developed either as an export industry to pioneer new services or as a substitute for foreign flag vessels currently serving national trades. In the former case, vessels are placed in trades in which they appear most likely to achieve commercial success and to maximize their earnings of foreign exchange. The total earnings of foreign currency in such cases, net of the foreign exchange outlays necessary to provide the service, is returned to the home economy. If, on the other hand, national flag shipping is developed to replace foreign vessels, the calculation is more complicated, since the foreign vessels have probably been inserting a substantial portion of their freight earnings into the local economy through purchases of goods and services which now are simply shifted to the domestic line. (See Table 10-1.)

From data developed for the UNCTAD Shipping Committee, it appears that at most only about half of gross freight earnings can be considered to accrue as a gain to the balance of payments.[25] And even this percentage assumes that the sponsoring nation is well-endowed with shipping facilities which would not be employed in the absence of a national flag fleet—a most unlikely assumption. Elements of a national maritime capability do tend to grow together, but at differential rates. A newly developing country cannot expect initially to build and repair ships in its own yards, cover its own insurance needs, or raise its own capital. Even the seamen employed in a new or expanded national flag service may be recruited initially from other ships. And as national seafaring skills and facilities are developed, they are used by other nations as well; then expansion of the national line is likely simply to cause a shift in the sale of services from one client to another.

For a nation with well-developed maritime facilities, shipping can be a substantial source of employment and earner of foreign exchange. It will be able to maintain this position, at least for a time, even though its own sea-going fleet is losing ground by making its yards, finance, and technical skills available on the world market. For a nation not itself equipped with manpower, ships, and facilities necessary to support a fleet, investment in shipping initially represents a high-risk venture geared to capturing whatever profit the enterprise may provide and to providing a foothold necessary to begin a more far-reaching maritime development. It may be argued, however, that this development might be more modestly initiated by training personnel aboard foreign flag ships and providing an increasing range of shore-based services than by taking an equity position in the industry itself, a matter discussed further in Part IV.

An attraction of shipping investment to the poorly endowed state is that it

Table 10-1
Balance of Payments Effects of International Shipping Operations

	Total Cost	Portion Paid in Foreign Currency If:		Currency Outlay Shifted	Notes
		National Flag	Foreign Flag		
Cargo handling, agencies and port charges	52	25	25	0	Payments effect a function of the volume of cargoes rather than flag of ship
Fuel	6	6	6	0	Payments effect a function of where specific purchases made and of the portion of seamen's pay which is spent abroad.
Crew wages	7	2	6	4	
Subsistence and supplies	2	1	2	1	
Maintenance and repair	6	2	5	3	
Insurance	7	4	7	3	Depends entirely on arrangements for financing and build.
Interest and amortization	15	?	?	?	
Administration and other	5	0	5	5	
Total cost	100	?	?	15→30	
Profit and taxes	?	?	?	?	Depends entirely on the success of the venture.

Source: Author's estimates. Cost incidence assumes a liner operation serviced by a fairly new ship serving regions with moderately high port costs and operated by a nation with scantily developed maritime industries. See also Table 7-4.

may be organized with minimum capital and minimum physical infrastructure, particularly if the investment is directed towards participating in cross trades or contract bulk carriage. Ship mortgage money is widely available on liberal terms; alternatively, vessels can be leased, agents hired, and technical assistance obtained from abroad. A highly-leveraged situation is therefore available, but the prospect of profit diminishes in proportion to the additional expenses incurred in order to hire in necessary facilities and services.

Finally, nations considering investment in shipping must consider the opportunity costs of this application of their resources and the effect which it may have on other portions of their foreign trade. If the investment is built on a base so weak that the new enterprise must be nurtured through subsidies and flag discrimination, it almost surely will create difficulties which outweigh its contribution as an earner of foreign exchange.

It may be that certain less-developed nations have no better avenues than investment in shipping supported by a requirement that foreign trade cargoes be carried on national flag ships to improve their earnings of foreign exchange. But if true, this is a sorry state of affairs.

In sum, assessing the economics of government aid can be a slippery business. In an international industry like shipping, there are circumstances in which government assistance, judiciously applied, can have a positive economic effect. There are many others in which such intervention operates chiefly to upset or limit markets and to inject an additional, unnecessary uncertainty into business calculations.

Dealing with the balance of payments effects of aid to promote national flag shipping is especially tricky. In general, anticipated benefits of artificially stimulated fleet expansion are muted in unanticipated reactive and secondary effects. Clearly, there is no immediate, certain corrective in fleet expansion for a broader economic malaise. Strong national flag shipping instead tends to be linked with a rigorous domestic economy and ineffective fleet operations with a weak one.

Concluding Remarks: Policies to Advance Economic Efficiency

Part II has been concerned with the economics of sea transport. Its findings have been presented in terms of economic standards, which are not necessarily the standards by which judgments are reached in the real world. Still, it is useful, as a point of departure for the remainder of this analysis, to sum up the manner in which the ocean freight industry must operate in order to achieve maximum economic efficiency in providing its vital transport service to the world's commerce.

In general, this discussion has supported a liberal policy towards ocean shipping, in which shipowners have equal access to the world's cargoes and are free to compete however they see fit on equal terms and without either government aid or intervention. The need for the flexibility to adapt services to dynamic markets, to capture economies of scale, and to experiment with new types of ships and services has been repeatedly stressed. Both the supply of and demand for shipping services were found to be exercised through highly differentiated but interrelated markets, sensitive to price factors, which provide sufficient opportunity for alternative routings (absent flag discrimination) to establish a check on exercise of monopoly powers. Free and unregulated competition has been advanced as the best means to achieve the delicate adjustments which freight markets require and as an approach which is viable wherever the market is large enough to support multiple firms—the situation pertaining to the overwhelming preponderance of world cargo movements but not always achieved in liner trades.

The preceding chapters, however, have not supported a wholly laissez faire approach to shipping regulation. In liner shipping, particularly, the number of parties in interest—shipping lines, conferences, ports, and export houses—and the crucial role to many nations of their foreign trade make government intervention inevitable.

The governmental role in shipping regulation is varied and ambiguous. No single government has a sufficient scope of authority to oversee in a comprehensive way the pattern of shipping rates and services in its national foreign trade nor, except in a few specialized situations, have governments felt impelled to assume this role. Their interest instead has been directed to promoting conditions favorable to the national flag fleet, to arbitrating intraindustry and shipper conflicts, and to preserving at least some minimal opportunity for independent action among shipping lines interested in pioneering new ways to serve the trade.

Divergent national interests, in fact, are proving to be the strongest check on the tendency toward cartellization of liner trades. Their presence aids in maintaining a healthy diversity of approach within the shipping industry but carries also a heavy risk that economic standards of performance will be displaced by a competition between governments in the support extended to national flag lines.

From a solely economic perspective, a system which provides a realistic opportunity for liner operation outside the conference system and for service competition within it is clearly preferable to the alternative tendencies: on the one hand of permitting cartellization to occur through private accommodations or, on the other, of allowing chaos to develop as a product of unchecked national rivalries. Politically, it is unclear how this is to be accomplished. Bilateral agreements in most cases provide too narrow a base upon which to organize an economic system of liner services. Multilateral arrangements may be ponderous and too difficult to establish.

A basic difficulty is that the international economy does not offer an adequate setting for equal competition on exclusively private terms. Distortions in factor price levels and trading arrangements will impel government support to national shipping firms, unless shipping is to be disassociated entirely from national ties. To achieve economic optimization this support should be provided exclusively through "reverse tariffs" or investment grants which are non-discriminatory in their effect on foreign flag operations and free of strings on the recipient firm. But the amounts which would be required to accomplish this limited purpose tend to elude quantification, and such solely cost-equalizing subsidization in any event would probably be insufficient to overcome the barriers which developing nations encounter in seeking to achieve equal standing as competitors in the international shipping world.

Economists some years ago adjusted their vision to abandon the theoretical niceties of pure competition in favor of achieving workable systems; more recently, they have acknowledged the need to adjust even workable systems to stimulate the growth of less-developed economies and to promote their expanded participation in world trade. The shipping industry has run up hard against both rocks: what framework of public and private institutions will sustain a healthy, workable level of competitive enterprise? and how can the requirements for a private, competitive international shipping industry be reconciled with the accompanying need to stimulate the economic development of the disadvantaged nations of the world? These are questions which must be answered in a manner which is compatible with changes, spurred by developments in trade and technology, affecting the fundamental structure of the industry. The next several chapters assess these changes and their implications for the future development of the industry as a prelude to our return in Part IV to the public policy issues created by the admixture of economics and politics to be found in international transport.

Part III:
Developments in Trade and Technology

Introduction to Part III

Preoccupation with the affairs of today coupled with uncertainty as to what lies ahead draws most policy debate into a retrospective frame of reference. This is unfortunate, since institutional change should be oriented more to future needs than to past experience.

Shipping in the seventies may need very different institutional arrangements than have sufficed to date. Assessment of these needs requires an estimate of the situation to be faced by the industry—in patterns of world trade, in the cargoes likely to be available to shipping, and in transport technology—and an estimate of the manner in which the industry is adapting to these new conditions. To offer such an assessment is the purpose of this part. The material is based on extensive consultation and review of available literature. No new forecasts have been prepared specifically for this study and no special claims are advanced with respect to the foresight—or lack of it—which may be represented here.

It is instructive before attempting our view into the seventies to consider how sharply the world has changed over the past fifteen years. World affairs in the mid-fifties were dominated by the post-World War II readjustment. The U.S. was still embarassed by excessive credits in its balance of payments; Marshall Plan aid was being extended to the reconstruction of European economies. An authoritative trade forecast published at the time anticipated a 2.8 percent annual growth in U.S. imports and asserted that over a twenty-five year period these rising purchases abroad should permit a gradual solution of the so-called "dollar gap" then believed to be inhibiting European development.[1]

The actual growth of trade during the past fifteen years and the extent to which international trade and investment have reshaped the entire international economy have, of course, exceeded all predictions. The Affluent Society, celebrated by Dr. Galbraith in the U.S. in 1958, had by 1970 spread to embrace much of Europe and was on the threshold of becoming a reality for Japan.

Commentators today suggest that in the '70s the impulses of the world's industrialized nations may shift from achieving economic growth to enhancing the quality of life. The old dichotomy of East and West may be displaced by a new polarity between the "have" nations of the North Temperate Zone and the "have-not" nations to the south. Resource scarcity is expected to be a growing problem, and in selected areas food supplies may be outpaced by population growth.

These factors are sufficient to assure continued international tension. Economic issues appear likely to loom larger in international affairs during the coming decade than in that just past. Political considerations likewise will assume a larger role in international business decisions.

It is against this background that the estimates of the next several chapters have been developed. They deal successively with trade policies, cargo flows,

121

shipping technology, and adjustments within the industry to changing methods and needs. The part concludes with a brief comment on the challenge which the more rapid pace of change poses for shipping management and the implications which the dynamism of the seventies may have for different sections of the industry.

11 Outlooks in International Relations and Trade

The over capacity of the international shipping industry of today makes it essential that seaborne trade maintain its recent 9 percent per year annual growth rate into the mid-1970s and beyond. Should this growth rate be undermined, the repercussions would shake the industry from stem to stern, creating a painful shakeout of the weaker elements, and reviving within the industry the cycles of boom and stagnation which have marked its past.

Trade growth is critical to shipping in other ways as well. Over the past two decades the substantial rate of trade growth has provided the elbow room which has permitted the former Axis powers to rejoin the family of maritime nations and the new nations of Asia and Africa to gain at least a toe-hold in the industry. If the less developed states are to build up their shipping in the years ahead, it is critical that such elbow room remain available.

Not only trade growth but also the quality of international trade relations is important to the future of the shipping industry. The quality of trade relations sets the tone for the conduct of international shipping. Where there is a productive exchange of goods and services, shipping companies find ways to compromise on their differences in order to share in the bounty; where there is not, shipping follows suit.

Although the odds appear favorable, trade growth at past rates is by no means assured. In the first place, the basic economic determinants of international trade simply are not sufficiently well understood to permit confident projections of future trade flows. In the second, trade amongst sovereigns is inevitably sensitive to unpredictable political factors. Within the commercial community one now finds real apprehensions that current stresses could presage a retreat away from the gradual liberalization of trade conditions accomplished since World War II. Underlying this concern is the fear that the increasing parallelism in the economies of the industrialized nations (which are involved in over 70 percent of the world's commerce by value), may have weakened their dependence on exchange and opened the way for more autarkical policies.[1] As one writer puts it: "A narrowing of the gap of comparative advantage . . . tends to produce a state of affairs in which there is a relatively large volume of foreign trade trembling, as it were, on the margin of advantageousness, and liable to be blown to one side or the other of the margin by small changes in the wind of circumstance."[2]

This chapter therefore begins with a brief report as to the economic factors to which trade appears most sensitive. It then reviews the political (or trade policy) questions which appear likely to be addressed during the coming decade. The chapter concludes with a report of the forecasts of trade growth which have been prepared for the OECD nations and with some comments regarding the interactions between international trade and politics.

Economic Determinants of Trade Flows

Since the time of Adam Smith, economists have been grappling with the question, "what factors determine the volume and composition of international trade flows?"[3] The answers which they have advanced have varied in terms of the cultural context within which they were writing and the industrial practices which provided data for their observations. During the past twenty years, the classic theories based on comparative advantage have been largely displaced by analyses geared to demand potential, market size, technological advantage, consumer preference, and the organization of production for economies of scale.[4]

As a matter of analytic convenience, students of international trade distinguish between studies of the system in a condition of equilibrium (statics) and studies of its responses to disequilibria (dynamics). Statics is concerned with the effects on the level, composition, and geography of trade imparted by natural endowments; comparative factor costs; economies of scale; industry structure, location, and distribution policies; tariff and nontariff barriers; cultural factors; and transport costs. Dynamics deals with the interactions between trade flows and domestic economic conditions, transmission phenomena within the business cycle, and mechanisms for national and international adjustments. Quantitative studies have been attempted in both areas. By identifying factors to which trade volumes are most sensitive, such econometric studies are both of considerable intrinsic interest and may potentially be used in trade predictions.

"Static" Determinants

Perhaps the most ambitious econometric analysis of the statics of world trade flows available in the published literature is the work of the Dutch economist, Hans Linneman.[5]

Linneman concludes that at any point in time the allocation of trade among nations is primarily a function of market size and accessibility. Growth in GNP enlarges the scale on which a nation can both import and export, but diminishes the proportion of domestic product likely to enter foreign trade. Thus, as population increases, an increasing proportion of a nation's needs met through domestic production.[6] Enlarging the size of economic units through political or economic integration has the same effect. By Linneman's calculation, complete economic integration of the EEC would cause a reduction in the external trade which would otherwise be conducted by EEC countries by roughly 20 percent.[7]

Linneman finds the distance factor to be especially powerful. Amongst nations situated close to one another the level of trade in 1958-60 was about six times greater (compared to that which might have been expected on the basis of the remaining predictors) than the trade of nations located on the periphery. The gap is not entirely a matter of transport costs, which Linneman recognizes to be in any event only loosely related to distance, but of transport time and of limitations in businessmen's "economic horizon"—the barriers of language, culture, and difficulties of establishing physical contact with trading partners.[8]

The role of cultural ties is reinforced in many trades by preferential trade relations. The combined effect is dramatic, creating trade flows eight times greater than otherwise predicted within the British Commonwealth, twenty-five times greater within the French Community, and one thousand times greater between Portugal and her dependencies. Linneman acknowledges that the intensity of these trades may in part reflect diversion of a potential for trade with other partners but argues that the security which political association provides for investment also operates to create trade.[9]

The Linneman study did not attempt to analyze the trade-reducing effects of tariff and nontariff barriers to trade. Such analyses have, however, been attempted by others. Perhaps the most ambitious studies are those of Johns Hopkins economist, Bela Belassa. Using 1960 data, Belassa estimated the increased trade in manufactured products which might follow elimination of tariffs among industrial countries. His rather startling results, which conservatively are calculated on the basis of nominal tariff levels and ignore the secondary stimulus which increased trade would provide, are shown in Table 11-1.[10] These and similar estimates have provided the basis for the prediction that trade in affected products may increase roughly 10 percent as a result of tariff reductions achieved in the Kennedy Round.[11]

Dynamic Determinants

The international trade network is a highly complex, interactive system. Changes within any part of the system can have wide reverberation and multiplier effects. The most obvious connection exists between export income and capacity to import. Among less developed nations, 95 percent of export earnings are estimated to be translated into import demand. In the industrialized countries, the proportion is lower but never less than 50 percent. Thus, any shift in the level or composition of trade is likely to be amplified several times over through multiple "spillover effects" on other potential suppliers and consumers within the trade network.[12]

International trade also is closely coupled to domestic economic activity. In

Table 11-1

Estimated Trade-Generating Effect of Eliminating Tariffs on Industrial Materials and Manufactured Goods

	Industrial Materials			Manufactured Goods		
	1960 Tariff Level	Impact of Tariff Elimination on		1960 Tariff Level	Impact of Tariff Elimination on	
		Exports	Imports		Exports	Imports
		(percent)			(percent)	
U.S.	2.6	1.7	3.0	13.2	26.0	35.9
EEC	1.3	3.2	2.2	12.2	26.9	28.3
U.K.	3.3	2.0	2.3	16.5	24.0	30.8
Japan	4.2	3.7	1.9	17.1	48.5	37.0

Source: B. Belassa, *Trade Liberalization among Developing Countries*, (New York: McGraw Hill), Table 4.1. Belassa prepared estimates based on two assumptions: first, that export prices rise to partially offset elimination of tariffs and, second, that such prices remain constant. The estimates cited in the above table are derived from the latter calculation.

the short term, inflationary upturns in domestic economic activity tend to be amplified in foreign trade. F.G. Adams, who has modeled the interactions of the foreign trade sector with domestic business cycles, reports that one percentage point increase in domestic production will be accompanied by about 1.7 percent increase in imports (to support the additional production and satisfy the additional demand).[13] Concurrently, the price inflation likely to accompany the expansionary phase will bring a temporary decline in exports, further enlarging the nation's trade gap. This creates secondary effects on trading partners, whose own expansion in response to the new opportunities for the trade tend to dampen the cycle and return the system to a new equlibrium.[14]

Unlike most national systems, the international sector has—at least until the institution of the new system of Special Drawing Rights on the International Monetary Fund—lacked institutional mechanisms for moderating cycles in trade.

The sluggishness of the international economy in adjusting to changing economic conditions has yielded "artificial" differentials in prices of goods in different parts of the world which have contributed significantly to the postwar growth of foreign trade. But concurrently such differentials create pressures for protective measures to insulate domestic production from the rigors of international competition, which are distinctly restraining in their trade effect.

Overseas Production and its Effect on Trade

The surge of acquisitions of overseas production facilities to serve overseas markets may be regarded as another response to the artificial price differentials which have grown up during the postwar years. Judd Polk has estimated the overseas production of U.S., European, and Japanese companies at some $400 billion, about 20 percent of the aggregate production of the world's non-Communist countries and some 60 percent greater than the worldwide flow of export trade.[15] Furthermore, this production is growing rapidly—about 10 percent per year from 1950-1967 and 15 percent per year in Europe—and at a rate which substantially outstrips the 7 percent annual growth in trade.

This vast surge of overseas investments by multinational corporations creates a new and uncertain character to international trade relations. The scale of the phenomenon is only now beginning to be recognized, and its implications have not yet been absorbed. Most less developed nations desire the stimulus to their local economies which American, European, and Japanese capital and technology afford; both the Americans and Europeans have preferred to host foreign production on their own soil than to face the possibility that the same market might be captured by a product fabricated abroad. However, all countries—industrialized countries as well as their poorer relations—are wary of the possibility of excessive foreign participation in their domestic affairs.

Very little hard data exist upon which to judge the impact of the multinational corporation on trade. The occurrence of sharp growths in trade volumes concurrently with even sharper growth in the flow of investments overseas creates a powerful presumption that the one has reinforced the other, a viewpoint which also enjoys the considerable weight of history. As in the days of the great trading companies, much of the accumulated present day foreign investment (at least 33 percent and perhaps as much as 50 percent) is in facilities designed to feed the industrial activities of the investing nation. This type of overseas investment clearly adds to the volume of trade. But during the past decade, investment funds have been shifted away from raw materials processing facilities, frequently located in developing nations, to manufacturing facilities constructed to tap rapidly growing markets in already industrialized states.[16] Here the trade effect is not so clear.

From such data as are available, it appears that even these overseas manufacturing affiliates, rather than dampening trade, have actually been more active in trade than in the typical American company and perhaps also than the average European firm.[17] The trade arises in three ways: when the overseas affiliate operates as a conduit for other finished goods of its parent company, when it imports components from the parent company for use in its manufacturing process, and when it is used by the parent as an instrument to manufacture for the home market. A consulting organization, Business International, reports that these patterns are becoming so common that the overseas affiliates of U.S. companies now account for some 25 percent of the total U.S. export trade in the commodity classes in which they are represented.[18] On net, the trend toward multinational businesses appears to have strengthened trade flows as well as bringing a substantially more international cast to the management of the world's economy.

Trade and Economic Development

From reviewing long-term trends in foreign investment and trade, analysts have been convinced that economically rational exchange stimulates the development of the trading partners and is an important stimulant to world economic growth.[19] The Pearson Commission has noted that statistically "the growth rates of developing countries since 1950 correlate better with their export performance than with any other single economic indicator."[20]

The synergistic effect of trade and development has been particularly strong during the early stages of growth and when markets also were expanding in the industrialized nations. An expanding world economy yields surplus funds for investment in less developed areas; the equipment for new facilities moves southward from the industrialized nations; and a portion of the expanded output moves north until an adequate domestic market for the new production can be established.

During the past decade, lowering of trade barriers, together with significant reductions in the cost of transport relative to other factors of production, has strongly favored nations such as Israel, Korea, and Japan which have staked their development on an export-oriented strategy. The contributions of these nations to world cargo flows emphasize the importance which economic growth within the less developed world can have for international shipping.

The Trade Policy Outlook: Expansion or Retreat

To realize the potential for expanded trade during the 1970s will require that the stresses now threatening the system of international trade and finance be resolved in a manner which continues to permit a rational exchange of goods. Although the economic forces underlying a growing international trade are strong, they are not impervious to the impact of political measures which, either directly or indirectly, complicate the business of trade.

In general the postwar era has been one of considerable improvement in the international trade climate.[21] Progress, however, has been intermittent as the attention of world leaders and their foreign offices has shifted focus in response to changing needs. Thus the immediate postwar years were chiefly devoted to creating the necessary institutional structure; the late forties and early fifties, to overcoming exchange restrictions and to building the necessary industrial base and financial reserves; and the late fifties and early sixties, to overcoming narrowly nationalistic economic orientations through regional associations. In more recent years, efforts have been made to lower tariff and nontariff barriers through the Kennedy Round of trade negotiations and to establish more favorable terms of trade for the less developed countries (LDC's) through commodity stabilization schemes and multilateral technical and financial aid.

The rather sporadic nature of world attention to these several matters has created frustrations which tend to obscure the real achievements of the past twenty years. For example, the LDC's have been frustrated by the failure of the developed states to remove restrictions on exports of particular interest or to extend expanded unrestricted aid. This frustration deflects attention from the quite extraordinary increase (12.7 percent per year over the past six years) in exports of manufacturers from the LDC's to the industrialized world made possible by selective improvement in trade terms. Likewise, difficulties within the EEC in reaching accords on agriculture have tended to push into the background the really remarkable steps made towards integration of the Community's economic policy. Agriculture and nontariff trade barriers proved a stumbling bloc to the GATT negotiators of the Kennedy Round, but nevertheless overall tariffs among the GATT partners were reduced by almost 40 percent. Similarly, it is the occasional, spectacular expropriation which captures the headlines, rather than the agreement of some thirty-three LDC's to abide by an OECD–framed Convention for the Protection of Foreign Property.

The headlines as this book goes to press concern the Nixon Administration's actions to force a turnabout in the deteriorating balance of payments of the United States. A stiff increase in duties has been imposed both to restrain imports and to force attention to basic issues relating to currency valuations and the distribution of the security burden among the NATO allies. Meanwhile, in Europe negotiations are continuing toward the admission of Great Britain into the EEC and toward further relaxation of the barriers to East-West trade. A proposal to extend nonreciprocal tariff preferences to certain broad categories of exports of special interest to the less developed nations is under discussion in UNCTAD and the OECD.

The outcome of these specific negotiations cannot be forecast. Yet there are a number of reasons for confidence that today's problems, like the problems of the past decade, will be resolved in a manner which permits continued internationalization of the world economy, accompanied by a rising foreign trade: (1) foreign trade and international business enterprise fill real and needed economic roles; most public leaders are sufficiently sophisticated to appreciate their benefits and to resist popular nationalistic pressures; (2) foreign trade and business interests are also increasingly sophisticated and are gaining an important voice in host-country politics; (3) the enlarging network of international financial agencies may be expected to lend its weight to adoption of liberal trade policies and toward creating conditions which make such policies feasible; (4) liberal trade arrangements tend to apply to the most rapidly growing sectors of the world economy and will therefore increasingly dominate trade with the passage of time; (5) certain tariff and trade restrictions are scheduled for progressive reductions or are bound at specific amounts which gradually will be swamped by price inflation; (6) in any event, business interests have demonstrated considerable ingenuity in circumventing restrictive measures when these are applied; and (7) in an economic system as complex and interconnected as that which applies in international investment and trade, there are considerable inertial forces which should be sufficient to overcome local, intermittent attacks on the system. In effect, today's economy is such as to give an ever-increasing number of persons a stake in gaining freer access to foreign markets in order to extend their operations on a multinational scale.

Negotiation of international trade questions is a slow, time-consuming process even when all parties are working towards a common end. Although new issues undoubtedly will emerge during the years ahead, the areas in which new agreements are likely to be reached during the 1970s are probably already the objects of international discussion. Thus it is reasonable to anticipate that the next several years will yield more flexible arrangements for adjusting currency reserves and valuations, and some strengthening of the role of international agencies in stabilizing prices of major commodities entering international trade. The slow work of harmonizing national laws relating to commercial practice, taxation, and protection of intellectual and other property should gain momentum with visible results by the end of the decade. Collaborative efforts to simplify documentation and reduce customs formalities promise to yield practical payoffs which could very significantly stimulate the flow of trade. Special regional arrangements will undoubtedly continue to receive favorable attention, as will the trade links between groupings of industrial nations and elements of the less-developed world.

In sum, the outlook for trade policy over the next decade appears to this observer to be one of slow and faltering progress toward a more international economy. The policy structure undergirding this economy, however, may be quite different from that anticipated in the GATT agreements of 1947. Differential tariffs will be more prevalent. There will be more emphasis on special regional and commodity arrangements. More attention will be given to the terms applying to foreign investments and to the conduct of multinational business activities. Distinctions between governmental and commercial operations will be further blurred by state trading, export subsidies, and government controlled production and pricing. Some of the characteristics of domestic economic management, in short, may be reflected in the international sphere. Such developments may reshape trade patterns in various unpredictable ways; they will not, however, fundamentally affect the supply and demand forces pushing forward the progressive enlargement of international exchange.

The Outlook for World Trade

The range of uncertainties facing international trade is such that responsible research groups refrain from publishing global forecasts. Trade forecasts have, however, been announced for individual nations and groups of nations.[22] Those examined in connection with this study all show the foreign trade sector expanding more rapidly than wholly domestic transactions.

Throughout the postwar period the rate of growth in trade has been set chiefly by the economic growth and trade policies of the OECD nations. The increasingly outward orientation of these nations is indicated by a consistent expansion of exports at roughly 1.4 times the growth rate of their GDP. For the most competitive of these countries (Italy, Japan, Germany, and France), trade in manufactures has grown even more rapidly in this sector whereas Britain and the U.S. have fallen somewhat behind.

The OECD nations are anticipating a continuation, and in some instances acceleration, during the 1970s of the growth rates achieved from 1955-1968.[23] At least during the early portion of the decade ahead, trade should continue to expand more rapidly than domestic product as the new trade opportunities created by the phased tariff reductions agreed to in the Kennedy Round are realized.[24]

The Kennedy Round tariff cuts were designed, inter alia, to maintain the basis for *worldwide* trade by narrowing the advantage which EEC and EFTA nations have enjoyed in their *intraregional* exchange. Small adjustments in tariffs, however, appear unlikely to offset the advantages of dealing with relatively nearby markets and suppliers if local sources can satisfy demand. Thus as the new centers of mass production in Europe and Japan (and eventually South America and South Asia) approach the scale and diversity of the U.S. industrial base, distribution systems can be expected increasingly to be focused within the surrounding region.

Also, in view of the strong demand within all advanced nations for increased emphasis on public service and local infrastructure investment vis-à-vis consumer goods, foreign trade cannot forever be expected to grow more rapidly than domestic product. The saturation level for the type of goods handled in trade may indeed be quite near. Although it is true that some nations (e.g., Luxembourg or Kuwait) rely on trade to support virtually their entire domestic consumption, the proportion of imported goods to local manufacturers has for the world's larger nations seldom exceeded 30 percent. Several large trading nations have already passed this mark and, as indicated in Table 11-2, others are rapidly approaching it. For this reason, a levelling off of trade expansion to a rate approximating GDP growth appears likely in the 1975-80 period.

There is, however, one major uncertainty in relation to this projection, which concerns the movement of intermediate factors of production. Some of the world's most active traders—Japan, the Netherlands, and Israel are examples—are not themselves the final consumers of the goods they import but instead reprocess a major portion of their imports for subsequent sale abroad at a higher stage of fabrication. Most finished products involve four or five production stages. If the new multinational firms should find it economic in a world of freer trade to handle each stage in a different country—and there is evidence that

Table 11-2
Foreign Trade in Relation to Value Added in Production of Traded Goods

	Traded Goods as a Percentage of Domestic Production, Similar Goods:			Correction for Re-Export	Multiplier to 1980	Estimated 1980 Foreign Trade in Relation to Domestic Production of Traded Goods; (Average of Imports and Exports Corrected for Re-Exports)
	Exports	Imports	Average			
United States	12.6	9.7	11.1	.05	1.05	11.3
Canada	54.6	53.4	54.0	N.A.	1.20	about 50.0
EEC External Trade	20.0	22.3	21.1	N.A.	1.10	about 22.0
EFTA External Trade	33.2	43.4	38.3	.17	1.00	34.0
Japan	27.1	32.2	29.6	.21	1.30	39.4

Source: 1964 data from B. Belassa, *Trade Liberalization among Industrialized Countries* (New York: McGraw Hill, 1967), p. 17. Belassa has compared the value of trade (exports at f.o.b. prices, imports, c.i.f.) to the value added (at market prices for the U.S., France, and Germany; factor prices for others) in mining, manufacturing, and agricultural production. He notes that the ratios are deficient insofar as they fail to include services and imported inputs as factors in the total value of production. Column 4 attempts to correct for the latter by diminishing the foreign trade figure by the estimated import content of each country's exports (Linneman, *An Economic Study*, p. 204; numbers shown in the table represent the percentage by which the trade factor is reduced.) Multiplier to 1980 is an estimate of the relative annual increase in foreign trade vis-a-vis total GDP increase less services. The net impact represents estimated net 1980 imports, reduced by re-export as a proportion of total imported and retained domestic production.

many already do—then the potential for trade is substantially greater than that suggested by the table's calculations.[25]

Political factors as well as trade terms, scale economies, and transport costs now shape the staging of such production. Adjustments to such political realities are necessarily approached with caution, so it would be unrealistic to expect any sudden release of new sources of trade through the operations of large, vertically-integrated, multinational firms. Furthermore, these companies may also be removing some consumer products from the trade stream by arranging their fabrication in the country (or region) of their final sale. The combination of these two trends—decentralization of the stages of production and final fabrication near the point of sale—does however suggest a reshaping of world trade to emphasize shipments of semifinished goods for further industrial processing in lieu of consumer goods.

Development along these lines will tend to strengthen the trading role of nations located in the path of raw material movements and to de-emphasize trades depending on the surplus manufactured product of the major industrial centers. Thus for the 1965-68 period, strong growth was being experienced in the export activity of Canada (15 percent), Taiwan (21 percent), Hong Kong (16 percent), South Korea (39 percent), and Israel (14 percent), as well as Japan (15 percent) while exports of manufacturers from the United States to Europe increased only 5 percent.

During the late 1950s and 1960s Japan's extraordinary 14 percent annual foreign trade growth provided a stimulus to international trade throughout the world and contributed significantly to the expansion of international shipping operations. Although there has been considerable skepticism whether such a rapid expansion can be sustained, the OECD has projected a 10 percent annual growth of Japanese GNP, the same rate of increase which was the basis for Japan's surge of overseas activities over the past fifteen years.

Extremely rapid trade growth has also been achieved by about one quarter of the world's less developed countries, including a half dozen whose foreign trade is at a scale to cause these increases to make a significant mark on world trade. As more nations shift from import substitution to more outward looking policies, the positive contribution of the less-developed world to trade may be expected to increase. Since these nations, like Japan, depend almost entirely on sea transport for their trade links, this development can be important to world shipping.

A potential sleeper in the international trade picture looking toward 1980 is Mainland China. An active trader prior to World War II, China under the Mao regime has directed its overseas transactions toward financing capital goods necessary to its internal development. During the latter portion of the 1950s such trade grew rapidly, to a level exceeding $4 billion per annum. This growth was interrupted by the disastrous economic policies of the early 1960s but has been resumed in the later portion of the decade, so that China's trade now exceeds that of India and Pakistan combined.[26]

Finally, analysts anticipate that the USSR and Eastern European nations will be more active participants in international commerce in the years ahead. Because much of this trade will move overland to Europe, the effect may be to diminish slightly Western Europe's dependence on overseas sources.

International Trade and Politics

Conduct of trade across national borders depends, in the final analysis, on the sufferance of sovereign governments. Governments have full power to regulate the flow of export and import commerce; agreements between them are necessary to establish the rules of the game; and it is by and large independent national governments which are called upon to enforce the rules.

The increasing proportion of the world's total production entering into international trade and the increasing competitiveness of world markets appear certain to plunge governments more prominently into commercial issues during the decade ahead. This will force a closer collaboration between national governments and commercial interests. Because the dominant industries increasingly require access to global markets for both materials and sales, there will be strong pressures on governments to adopt liberal trade policies and to collaborate in developing a more effective framework of international law and institutions to facilitate the growth of trade.

The essentially political basis of economic affairs is reflected in the growing role of regional organization. Even where there is little natural economic complementarity, friendly nations have found that they can collaborate with one another on matters that they have been unable to negotiate with trading partners who do not share their cultural values.

The creation of regional groupings has a complex effect, both positive and negative, on patterns of trade. The hope and expectation is that economic regionalism, by strengthening the economic strength of the participating nations, may gradually evolve into an expanded trade between regions and a liberalization of trading terms throughout the world. But extension of preferential trading arrangements within groups of cooperating nations also holds the potential for discrimination against outsiders and autarky on a regional scale.

What happens in trade policy will be reflected in shipping. This industry, like the commercial scene in general, is constantly threatened by the prospect of economic warfare and touched by its practice as well. But fast and convenient cargo transportation, with the jet plane and overseas phone and telex services, are rapidly forging a global economy. The businesses operating in this economy will create powerful pressures to be supported by the most efficient services which can be provided.

12 Cargo Trends and Implications

Although trade sustains shipping, trade forecasts are seldom directly convertible into estimates of cargoes likely to be available to maintain transport. Shipping companies need to know what kinds of cargoes will move under what conditions and over what routes. Their concern is with tonnage and cubic measurement as well as the value of trade. The manner in which cargo is presented, the size and schedule of individual parcels, and the regularity of the cargo flow determine the type of service which will be desired.

In sum, cargo forecasting requires extensive specialized analysis of trade and industry data. In this chapter we shall review the present state of the art, set forth estimates of developments which may be anticipated in the general cargo and major bulk cargo categories, and explore the implications which these developments may have for the provision of shipping services in the decade ahead.

Cargo Forecasting: The State of the Art

Over the past several years the shipping world has sharply increased its efforts to forecast cargo flows. The level of effort remains modest, however, in even the most forward-looking companies, and many operators continue to believe that shipping markets are simply too volatile and elusive to yield to scientific analysis. So far, actual experience seems to support this point of view. None of the published studies—and to our knowledge, no unpublished analyses either— anticipated the strong surge in demand which sent charter rates skyrocketing during the spring of 1970.

The difficulties of cargo forecasting are many. As noted in Part II, we are dealing not with a single homogeneous market but with large numbers of loosely linked submarkets. In this respect, forecasting shipping demand is like forecasting securities' prices; though the market may create its own momentum, the totality represents only a composite of individual companies operating in industries with widely varying outlooks.

Second, the cargo forecaster faces severe data problems. Despite the best efforts of the international statistical agencies, reporting of import-export trade remains spotty.[1] Those data which are reported are often not available for more than a year after the fact. Commodity classifications still are not fully standardized and reporting errors remain a fairly common occurrence.

Third, there is no single unit which adequately measures the revenue potential to shipping companies of cargoes moving in trade. In some cases, the value of the cargo is most important in determining rates, in others the cubic measurement, and in others the weight. Data reported in one mode unfortunately are not easily converted to another. Unfortunately also, most economic studies of international trade outlooks, on which cargo forecasting ultimately depends, are stated in value terms—the measure least pertinent to the shipping man. For this reason the forecasts actually used by the shipping industry are seldom linked to any systematic analysis of the dynamics of the broader international economy, but are based instead on industry studies and commercial intelligence regarding their clients' plans. These "seat of the pants" methods are probably the most reliable available for the short-term but offer little insight with respect to the time period (in excess of five years) lying beyond their customers' own commitments.

Use of quantitative methods for forecasting a phenomenon as complex and volatile as the international demand for shipping space is an expensive and time-consuming operation. The sheer scale of the problem requires a level of aggregation which severely limits the usefulness of results and may pass over aspects of the problem which are critical to the forecast. As a practical matter, the constant changes in trade patterns are likely to outpace the preparation of the forecast, undermining its credibility when finally published.

Liner operators face a particularly difficult situation. Their business in most cases is highly diversified and may involve a number of countries as well as a large number of clients. The diversity is such that the interested government agencies and shipowner associations have been unable to extend much useful research assistance. A handful of firms in the U.S. and abroad have invested in economic studies, usually directed to specific commodities of particular interest, and others have established research staffs to stay in touch with trade trends and forecasts developed outside the firm. To a large extent, however, the liner companies have relied upon their ability to make reasonably rapid adjustments in capacity (through ship charters or shifting vessels among routes) to compensate for an inability to project long-term demand.[2]

Bulk operators are more favorably positioned to draw upon government and industry analyses of trade potentials in the commodities in which they are interested, and a large proportion of the bulk fleet, of course, is directly linked through ownership or long-term charter to its markets. Independents offering vessels for short term and voyage charters must deal with the marginal shifts in residual demand and have in the past demonstrated an inclination to be heavily influenced by transient conditions. This class of owners, who now are faced with a need to make larger investments in more specialized ships, have in recent years moved away from entirely speculative building in favor of construction for specific users or to meet market potentials fairly clearly defined through economic research.

The problem which is faced by all elements of the international trade community is underscored by the generally poor verification of past forecasts and the widely disparate conclusions advanced in forecasts being made today. The difficulty of the problem has created considerably wariness about publishing those estimates which are developed, and this further compounds the problem. In sum, although more advanced work is going forward, there exist no satisfactory intermediate or long-term forecasts of the cargoes likely to be available to international shipping, and no agency capable of producing one.[3] The shipping operator is forced to rely chiefly on secondary sources, industry studies, and his own intuition in considering the future of his enterprise.

Outlook for General Cargo Seaborne Trade

The general cargo category, as we use the term here, includes all movements other than those of the seven major bulk commodities—oil, iron and manganese ores, coal, grains, bauxite, and phosphates—for which separate data are provided later in this chapter. Such general cargoes on a tonnage basis constitute about 45 percent of the total interregional dry cargo trades. About 30 percent of this business moves laterally linking the U.S., Europe, South Africa, Australia and Japan; about 40 percent is associated with shipments between these nations and the less developed states; 10-15 percent involves the Communist nations; and an additional 15 percent the short sea trades around Europe and the Far East, which are not further considered here. Shipments between the less developed nations currently comprise less than 5 percent of world general cargo trade flows.

Cargo Categories

The general cargo trades are functionally as well as geographically diverse and are shared by proportions (by weight) of about 60:40 by liners and tramps. In assessing the outlook for their growth, it is useful to distinguish between three broad categories of business.

The first and most important to the liner segment of the industry covers products for direct consumption or use, including most manufactures, food products, textiles, and household and military goods. These shipments account for more than half of all seaborne general cargo trade by value although for only 10-15 percent of its tonnage. Trade in consumer goods is sensitive to income levels, consumer preferences, the capacity of domestic industry to meet consumer demand, relative factor costs, and national trade policy. Although highly diversified, the level of such trade is unstable and quite sensitive to prices of imported goods versus domestic production. Ocean freight however is a negligible factor in this equation, usually amounting to less than 5 percent of the final selling price of consumer articles.

The increase in population (estimated during the 1970s by the U.N. at 1.2 percent annually in the U.S. and Canada; 0.5 percent in Western Europe; and 0.7 percent in Japan) sets a floor under the increase in consumption which may be anticipated in the developed market economies. Imports of food staples such as vegetable oils, coffee, and rice cannot be expected to rise much faster than population, although luxury foods do show some sensitivity to increased disposable income.[4] Rising incomes, however, can give strong support to an accelerating trade in manufactures, providing that nations do not react to the "competitive" nature of these trades by imposing import quotas. Transportation of military equipment, now chiefly important to U.S. shipping, may be expected to decline barring outbreak of new hostilities.

The second category of general cargoes, also important to liners, may be defined as embracing semifinished articles, such as chemicals, steel bars, machinery, electronic components, and subassemblies. This is the most footloose category of goods moving in trade, since their production is not directly tied to resource endowments nor their use directly to consumption. It appears also in recent years to have been the most rapidly growing. Its growth has been spurred in part by lower transportation costs and tariff barriers and in part by the geographic spread of industrialization, the growth of multinational firms, the diversity of product lines in manufacture, and economies of specialization and scale. Price may assume a crucial role in these movements, although availability to meet production schedules also is important.

The factors which have spurred the growing trade of semi-finished or "intermediate" products appear likely to persist through the coming decade. Furthermore, as the developing nations are drawn increasingly into the main-stream of the world economy, these shipments may be geographically diffused, with semiprocessed goods in part substituting for the raw materials now exported by the less developed country to developed markets.

Finally, the general cargo category includes a large traffic (approximately half of all such shipments by weight) in such products as zinc, copper, and aluminum ingots, scrap iron, metal concentrates, wool, timber, pulp, paper, copra, and cotton. These cargoes are sensitive to overall levels of industrial activity and to trends in the organization of production. Their transport is shared by liners, tramps, and specialized carriers. Freights comprise a fairly high percentage of the landed value of these commodities (on the order of 10 to 20 percent) and demand should respond to a longer term trend toward lower freight charges. Reliable data and forecasts for this category of cargoes are hard to come by, since in value terms the trades are relatively small and require analysis on a commodity by commodity basis. Such analysis is also beyond the scope of this book.

Service Trends

Aggregate trends indicating a 6 to 7 percent annual growth factor in general cargo shipments since 1960 mask very large shifts in cargo mix and routings. Within the latter portion of the decade, increasing use of bulk carriers and the introduction of container ships have caused further dislocations in general cargo trade. Use of such specialized carriers appears certain to continue to develop strongly for at least another five years. By the latter portion of the 1970s, serious competition to ocean carriers of general cargo may also be anticipated from aircraft and "land bridge" services. A useful forecast of cargo potentials for liner and tramp shipping must take all of these variables into account.

The number of uncertainties in the situation is such as to defy any fully scientific methodology to balance out all the interacting factors which need to be considered. However, it is possible to project certain general trends with reasonable confidence.

Geographic Shifts

General cargo trades are likely to develop most rapidly around the eastern and southern rim of the Asian continent, spurred by Japan's extraordinary growth. Short sea trades should enjoy a strong boost from accelerating development in the Far East and other less developed areas poorly served by other transport modes. Factors which will particularly affect the routes which now carry the largest general cargo tonnage are noted on Table 12-1.

Concentration of Cargoes

Expanding trade and new techniques for preparation, storage, and handling of cargoes will permit more cargoes to be concentrated into larger lots. The most powerful factor likely to force concentration of cargoes, however, is the relative disadvantage to which small shippers will be placed by the economies of scale enjoyed by competitors able to ship in bulk or via container ship. These disadvantages will be reinforced by a feedback effect as conventional liner services, losing patronage to small bulk carriers and container operators, stretch out routes and schedules (and hence incur higher costs) to service the remaining trade.

Increasing Pressure on Costs

The increasing number of suppliers for almost all goods falling in the general cargo category will make both importers and exporters more sensitive to

Table 12-1
Outlooks for General Cargo Trades to 1980, Selected Major Trade Routes

Route	Export-Import Tonnage (Mil. of Metric Tons)		Assumed Rate of Growth	Comment
	1966	1980 Est.		
U.S.-Canada-Europe	46.0	60-80	2-4%	Moderate growth; slackening of military cargoes. Agricultural shipments from No. America important and uncertain
U.S.-Canada-Japan	28.0	60-80	6-8%	Strong growth assuming continued satisfactory trade relations
North-South America	20.5	30-45	3-6%	Growth likely, despite sluggish commodity trades and political differences
Europe-South America	19.5	25-30	2-3%	Weakness due to increasing orientation toward African and Asian sources
Europe-Africa	31.6	60-80	5-7%	Satisfactory growth as major raw materials source
Europe-India, Persian Gulf	13.4	20-30	3-6%	Moderate growth paced by Indian export potential
Europe-Far East, including S.E. Asia & Australia	23.2	60-85	7-10%	Strong growth with manufactures and semimanufactures taking increasing share
Japan-Southeast Asia and Australia	22.5	85-100	10-12%	Very strong growth reflecting step up of economic activity throughout the area
Subtotal	204.7			
All other interregional trade	52.3	100-120	4-6%	Strong growth, reflecting EEC-EFTA activity and stepped up East-West European trade
Intraregional and short sea trades[a]	185.0	420-550	6-8%	
Total	442.0	920-1200	5-7%	

Source: Author's estimates of likely orders of magnitude.

[a]In this analysis, trade between the U.S. and Canada and among the nations of Europe, Africa and Latin America is classified as short sea.

transport costs in order to maintain and build markets. Additionally, the availability of alternative transport modes and routings will force ship operators to keep on their competitive toes.

Continued Rapid Expansion of Container and Roll-on, Roll-off Services

In 1970, approximately 12 percent of all liner cargo was forwarded via container ship, by 1975 this seems likely to grow to 35 to 40 percent and by 1980 to 50 to 60 percent. These estimates are supported by the published plans of major operators and analytic studies of container cargo potentials on selected routes; they assume virtual saturation by 1975 of the container potential on the major routes on which containers have already been introduced and, by 1980, the spread of container services to all trade routes generating more than 2 million tons of export-import cargo per year.[5]

Diversion of Cargoes from Sea to Air Carriers

Air cargo already is a major factor in international transportation. Revenues of ICAO carriers for international transoceanic cargo services approximate 12 percent of the estimated $8 billion freight revenue of liner operators. Because air cargoes are almost entirely small, high value items, they continue to represent only a negligible portion—about 2 percent—of seaborne general cargo tonnage. Furthermore, a significant proportion of the shipments now made by air might not have moved at all in the absence of this quick, convenient form of transportation. Future expansion of international air freight shipments is likely to be largely at the expense of surface carriers.

The surplus cargo capacity of the Boeing 747 passenger aircraft expected to be placed in service over the next several years will roughly double the present international air cargo carrying capacity. Really significant expansion of air operations, however, depends upon introduction of the L-500 and B-747 all-cargo aircraft. To date, despite their manufacturers' glowing expectations, operators have been extremely reluctant to undertake firm commitments for these planes. Even optimistic estimates place per ton-mile costs of operation for the jumbo jets at eight times that of a container ship.[6]

There are numerous operating problems—terminal facilities, landing rights, pricing agreements, and noise and air pollution control, to cite a few—which must be overcome before the jumbo freighters can be successfully operated in large numbers. Nonetheless, the advantages of point to point air service are such that serious consideration already is being given to shipment by air of such products as automobiles, farm equipment, bananas, and processed meat prod-

Table 12-2
Comparative Costs of Alternative Transport Modes

Approximate Costs per Ton Mile[a]	
Air (DC-7 or equivalent)	.2000
Air (L-500 Est.)	.1000
Truck	.0600
Rail	.0130
Containership	.0080
Bulk carrier	.0010
Pipeline (40" diameter)	.0005
Supertanker	.0002

Source: Author's estimates drawing on various sources.

[a]Estimates for U.S. carriers in long haul (3,500 mile) nonstop service, including costs of loading and discharge. Assumes return cargo in all cases but the bulk carrier, and includes allowances for profit and equipment amortization. Foreign carriers have sharply higher costs for air; somewhat lower costs for sea movements.

ucts, heretofore shipped almost entirely by surface transportation. When all-cargo jumbo jets are placed in service (probably in the range of 1973 to 1975) they will be serious competitors for such shipments wherever conventional surface transportation has become mired in high handling costs, pilferage and damage problems, or en route delays. If ocean carriers allow these conditions to develop, air carriers might claim up to 6 to 7 percent of liner cargoes by 1975 and up to 15 percent by 1980.[7] Conversely, if container ship operators are able to hold the line on costs and achieve their promised improvements on service, the present accelerating trend toward air may be deflected, and orders for the new jumbo jets further, and perhaps indefinitely, deferred.

Role for Conventional Liner Services

In terms of freight revenues earned, conventional liner services as of 1970 still dominate the international shipping scene. Despite the rapid growth during the past decade of bulk cargo and container services, cargo liners have been able to maintain and even expand their patronage in most trades. But during the 1970s an absolute decline in services by conventional liner seems inevitable, despite continued growth in general cargo offerings. On the main container routes, conventional vessels may be squeezed out almost completely. In less developed regions, liners will continue to perform an important role but cannot expect to maintain unchallenged control of cargo movements.

Table 12-3 presents an estimate of general cargo shares likely to be handled by different classes of shipping service in the mid-decade. It is based on an overall 6 percent annual growth factor and assumes that commodities moving in

Table 12-3

Cargo Share Estimates, 1966-1975, by Transport Mode, General Cargoes in Interregional Trade

	Trunk Routes Linking Developed Nations		Other Interregional Trade		Total	
	1966	1975	1966	1975	1966	1975
	(Millions of Metric Tons)					
Bulk carrier	10	40	20	70	30	110
Tramp	45	73	60	74	105	147
Conventional liner and palletship	55	35	60	55	115	90
Container ship, Lash and ro-ro	–	50	–	15	–	65
Air Freight	–	2	–	1	–	3
	110	200	140	215	250	415
Assumed Growth Rate	7%		5%		6%	

Source: Author's estimates based on studies by Saguenay Research, "Cargo Statistics in International Trade," for overall cargo volumes (adjusted to exclude intraregional and short-sea services); by Reinhold Schultz for the estimated distribution of cargoes between parcel and vessel lots; and by Lambert Brothers, "Displacement of Conventional Liner Tonnage," for the diversion of cargoes from conventional liners to containerships.

volumes of over 300 thousand tons per year over a particular route will be handled in vessel lots either by tramps or bulk carriers.[8] In fact, specialized shipping services are likely to be economic for substantially smaller cargo flows. UNCTAD economists in particular have stressed the very significant savings in transportation costs which can be realized by small shippers in less developed countries if new institutional arrangements are developed to facilitate consolidation of cargoes for shipment in vessel lots.[9]

Should general cargoes fail to maintain their past rate of growth, the liner operators will be even more badly hurt since economics will tend to favor alternative modes to the extent that they are prepared to offer service. Container and roll-on ships already in service or on order for delivery by 1973 have sufficient capacity to handle some fifty-five to sixty million tons of general cargo or roughly 40 percent of the high value package cargoes now shipped via liner.[10] The investment in the new vessels is such that these owners will be forced to keep them fully employed. If severe rate competition is to be avoided, substantial amounts of liner tonnage will have to be diverted into contract services, laid up or scrapped.

Among the many imponderables in this equation is whether the introduction of container ships will itself be a stimulus to trade. Optimists cite the sharp increase in cargo tonnage which accompanied SeaLand's introduction of container services to Puerto Rico in 1957-58. This, however, was also a period of rapid growth in the Puerto Rican economy, the new SeaLand service was accompanied by a reduction in rates, and there were no tariff or other barriers to trade expansion. Although new cargoes have been generated by international container services, there is as yet no evidence to suggest that this more convenient and rapid service will do more than sustain the 6 percent growth rate already built into our projection.

In sum, the outlook for general cargo trades is one of highly selective growth with important shifts, in part impelled by the character of the trades themselves, in the manner in which cargoes are transported. For individual operators, local conditions will overwhelm global trends. Worldwide trade conditions, on the other hand, will determine the overall demand for different types of tonnage, influence the rate at which container services will spread to secondary trade routes, and establish the general tone for shipping competition. As always, rapidly changing conditions will create unique opportunities for the most technically advanced, well-financed and flexible operators and penalize those not able to adapt to change.

Outlook for Bulk Commodity Trades

Historically security considerations and questions of political strategy have heavily influenced trading patterns of bulk commodities. There have been indications of some relaxation of these restraints within recent years. However, importing countries continue to look to multiple sources in order to avoid excessive dependence on a single supplier and raw materials exporters seek to diversify their markets. These considerations contribute to the extraordinarily far-flung network of bulk commodity shipments which has developed over the postwar years.

Diminishing shipping costs also have stimulated the search for more distant markets and suppliers, reflected in a steady increase in the average distance for shipments of each of the six major bulks over the past ten years. With the exception of oil, ton miles are expected to continue to grow faster than cargo tonnage. In oil, scale economies of shipping have already been stretched close to their maximum so that transport savings must be found in other ways.

The data which follow draw heavily on studies performed by various consulting groups.[11] The estimates developed by different groups may differ by as much as 100 percent. In these cases, the author has used the projection based on assumptions which appeared most consistent with his own estimate of overall economic developments as reported in Chapter 11.

Petroleum

Oil is the most politically sensitive of all commodities. The natural stresses and strains within the industry seem doomed indefinitely to be exacerbated by

Figure 12-1. Petroleum Movements in Inter-Regional Trade.

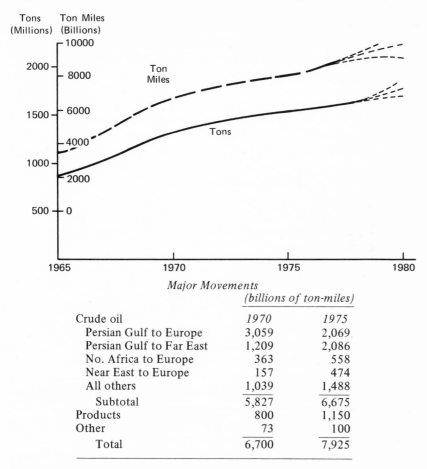

Major Movements		
	(billions of ton-miles)	
Crude oil	*1970*	*1975*
Persian Gulf to Europe	3,059	2,069
Persian Gulf to Far East	1,209	2,086
No. Africa to Europe	363	558
Near East to Europe	157	474
All others	1,039	1,488
Subtotal	5,827	6,675
Products	800	1,150
Other	73	100
Total	6,700	7,925

Source: Saguenay Research.

turmoil in the Middle East. Closure of the Suez Canal disrupted the flow of some 170 million tons of oil moving from the Persian Gulf to Europe. Now during the past year, the closure of the Trans-Arabian Pipeline and curtailment of Libyan production closing of the Suez Canal have added some 185 billion ton miles to annual tanker requirements.[12] It is impossible to say when these artificial stimuli to the tanker industry may be removed.

Demand for petroleum is expected to continue to increase for the next decade and beyond but at rates of increase below that of the past twenty years.[13] The slowdown in rate of growth reflects tapering off of oil's penetration into traditional coal markets, anticipated substitution of other fuels for oil (especially nuclear power and North Sea gas), the maturation of the large

Figure 12-2. Iron Ore Movements in Inter-Regional Trade.

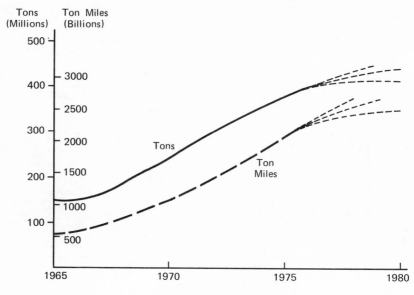

Major Movements		
	(billions of ton-miles)	
	1970	*1975*
So America to Japan	231	491
Australia, Malaysia & India to Japan	218	417
Brazil to Europe	106	175
W. Africa to Europe	102	113
All other	443	922
	1,100	2,118

Source: Saguenay Research.

industrial economies, and, in selected cases, development of more close-at-hand petroleum sources.

The largest oil movements by far are now out of the Persian Gulf to Europe and the Far East. Over the next decade, both North African and Eastern Mediterranean sources are expected to overtake the Persian Gulf as suppliers to the European market while Iranian and Arabian oil will be directed increasingly to Japan. North Sea and Arctic wells should be sufficiently developed by mid-decade to meet up to 5 percent or 10 percent of European and U.S. requirements; by 1980 production from these fields should reach levels which will significantly affect world-wide distribution patterns.

The need to be protected in the event of disruption of supply lines, coupled with memories of the extraordinary surge in charter rates during the spring of 1970, is likely to keep demand for new tanker tonnage at high levels. Barring unforeseen developments, a surplus of tanker capacity may therefore be

Figure 12-3. Coal Movements in Inter-Regional Trade.

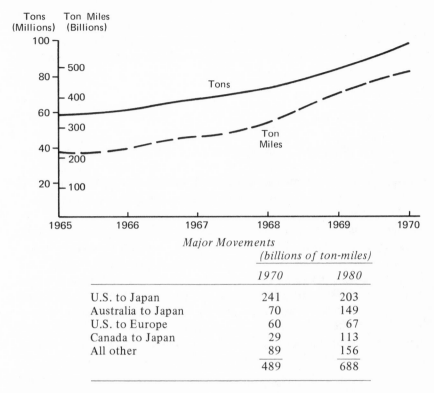

Major Movements		
	(billions of ton-miles)	
	1970	*1980*
U.S. to Japan	241	203
Australia to Japan	70	149
U.S. to Europe	60	67
Canada to Japan	29	113
All other	89	156
	489	688

Source: Saguenay Research.

expected by mid-decade. OBO's and other tankers equipped to handle dry bulks may then be expected to enter the grain and ore markets.

Iron Ore

World production of steel has surged forward since 1963, growing at a rate of 7 percent per year. Almost all of this increased production has been based on imported ores. Concurrently, the great ore discoveries in Australia and reductions in transportation costs have permitted imports to be drawn from greater distances. These factors have stirred a once stable cargo to a growth rate (in ton-miles) of 15 percent per year.

Experts differ in their assessment of whether this rate of growth can be maintained. An UNCTAD study notes that improvement in steel technology is progressively reducing the amount of ore required per finished ton of steel, which may lead to a decline in iron ore demand by 1975. The study notes also that iron ore is increasingly being beneficiated at or near the mine site so that the portion of waste shipped is much reduced.[14] Based on a survey of production and shipment plans, however, Saguenay Research projects that the past rate of growth will actually accelerate as producers all over the world try to keep pace with demand.

Iron ores, like all other raw materials, have sharply different qualities from one another. Low shipping costs permit users to shop around for the particular qualities necessary to their production. Low shipping costs therefore may operate to support the high estimate provided by Saguenay Research.

Coal

Coal shipments slacked off in the middle sixties, but during the latter part of the decade have demonstrated strong growth. Forecasts of international trade in coal for the decade to come anticipate that growth will continue, spurred chiefly by the extraordinary pace in Japan's development, but estimates differ widely both as to rate of growth and as to sources of supply.

During the past year worldwide shortage of energy fuels has once again focused attention on coal. The traditional sources have been unable to satisfy demand, and European buyers as well as the Japanese have turned to new mines being opened as far away as Australia to fill a portion of their requirements. Coal therefore appears likely to be imported in greater quantities and carried longer distances to support steel-making and energy uses in a growing world economy. Substitution of alternative fuels may now have leveled off so that the only deterrents to continued rapid growth in international trade of coal will be improvements in combustion and metallurgical technologies.

Grains

Climate and politics combine to confound reliable forecasts of grain movements. Shipping patterns in the past years have been erratic and will probably continue so for the indefinite future. The apparent breakdown of the International Wheat Agreement complicates the forecast problem. Because the outlook is so uncertain, grains are the only major bulk cargo category which is moved almost entirely by chartered ships.

Bauxite and Alumina

The burgeoning aluminum industry is expected to maintain its leadership in world industrial growth, and consumption of bauxite is likely to double during the decade of the seventies. Concurrently, the major consumers of this ore are faced with diminishing reserves and will need to look to more distant mines to meet supply requirements.

Offsetting these growth factors, aluminum companies are locating more of their ore processing facilities near the minehead. The refined ore, alumina, weighs about half that of the bauxite from which it is drawn. This conversion will tend to slow down an otherwise high growth rate in total bauxite/alumina shipments.

Bauxite trades originate largely in less-developed nations and constitute a highly reliable cargo flow. Due to mine locations, bauxite now is mostly carried in 20,000 to 25,000 dwt. vessels which typically operate in a shuttle mode, returning to the mine area in ballast. In some cases, a general cargo business has been developed on the return leg. However, the opening of new mine fields is now being accompanied by a shift in bauxite/alumina trades to larger bulk carriers, and efforts are being made to tie these shipments in with contracts to carry other products in order to reduce ballast distance.

Phosphate Rock

Demand for fertilizer has stimulated a large and vigorously growing world trade in phosphate rock during the past two decades, with growth averaging approximately 12 percent per year. The material, however, is temporarily in oversupply, and some slowdown of production is indicated over the next several years.

At present, movements of raw phosphate rock dominate the trade. It is possible, however, that in the years ahead there may be a shift to shipping this material in more concentrated form which would result in a commensurate reduction of bulk shipping requirements.

Phosphate deposits are quite widely dispersed throughout the world, but only the U.S., Morocco, Nauru, and Ocean Island now are major producers. As additional mines are opened up for quantity production, shipping distances may be reduced.

Implications for the Shipping Industry

Factors determining cargo potentials have been examined here at some length because they create the very basis for the international shipping industry. The picture which emerges is one of a widely diversified and growing international seaborne trade subject to innumerable economic and political constraints, local variations, and possibilities for error. If there is one characteristic of international shipping which stands out in any effort to forecast cargo potentials, it is the inherent uncertainty of the business. Shipping always has been an unusually risky enterprise. Today the risks of the business are taking on new dimensions. The very factors which promise a growing trade—i.e., world-wide industrialization, increasing disposable income, instantaneous communication, and relatively diminishing transport costs—are creating a chronic instability in trade patterns, an increased sensitivity to domestic economic conditions and trade policies, and a greater vulnerability to disruption from political causes. Concurrently, in order to stay in the race, shipowners are required to risk vastly greater sums in order to drive their costs to the lowest possible competitive level and to offer shippers a flexibility and convenience in their export-import business commensurate to that provided in domestic commerce.

One of the key unknowns in the future of shipping is the extent to which introduction of more rapid, convenient, and economical sea transport services may themselves induce additional goods to flow in international trade. On a cost basis, container ship cargoes already can be moved more cheaply from Great Britain to New York than from New York to Chicago. If the paperwork for international shipments can also be made as easy as for domestic freights and tariff barriers held down, routes linking the industrialized nations could see a burst of traffic reflecting major shifts in patterns of trade. Releasing this traffic potential, however, requires that container ship tariffs as well as costs be competitive with overland movements. With large new capital investments to write off, container ship operators in most trades have resisted rate reductions which would pass on to shippers the economies in operating costs made possible by their new equipment.

In the bulk cargo trades the disparity between overseas and overland shipments has become even more startling. Coal, for example, can be moved from Australia to the U.S. West Coast for substantially less than the cost of rail shipments to California from Rocky Mountain mines. In this sector of the industry, the savings achieved through introduction of very large ships and improved handling methods are fully reflected in the transport price. The declining costs of bulk cargo transport (both overland and at sea) clearly have been a major factor in the rapid growth in these categories of cargoes, since they have made it economically realistic for raw materials suppliers to open up new mining operations at greater distances from their markets.

The relative decline in marine transport costs is beginning to change the world's economic geography.[15] For shipping an increase in coastal industry means both additional cargoes and a more competitive environment. The pricing decisions of liner conferences may henceforward have an important influence on whether machinery can be imported by Brazil more economically than from the U.S., Europe, or Japan. The size of vessels which can be loaded with ore may determine whether Jamaican or Guyanan bauxite is fed to Norwegian smelters.

The exploding internationality and mobility of the world economy are of course heightening pressures on all elements of the international trade system. A satisfactory export position is crucial to every nation. Since adequate and inexpensive sea transport service is an important factor in the competitiveness of exported products, governments may be expected increasingly to interest themselves in shipping rates and services, port facilities, and connecting transport links. The margin of industrial efficiency gained by Japan through her enormous investment in deep water harbours and port facilities serviced by a modern and efficient fleet may well set a model which other nations will seek to emulate. A growing recognition of the importance of shipping to trade should serve to improve the environment for shipping investment; it may also add to pressures for discriminatory policies geared to a narrow concept of national interest in maritime affairs.

The pace of the industry's development also is such as to make it unlikely that shipping rates and services could ever be brought under government regulation without substantially impairing the industry's performance. Shipping men, sensitive to the crucial role played by sea transport in trade, readily acknowledge that important public interests may be affected by the manner in which they conduct their business. But they argue persuasively that a regulatory system along the lines used in U.S. domestic transport or in international air operations would destroy the very flexibility which is most needed to assure that services meet commercial needs.

Looking into the seventies, it is apparent that a wider range of transport options will be available to most export shippers than has heretofore been the case. Also, in an increasingly competitive world economy, price pressures felt by importers and exporters may be expected to be translated into increased pressure on shipping companies to enhance the competitiveness of their services. The know-how to do so is now available. If free to respond to commercial needs, shipowners should be able to introduce new techniques and services that will enhance the natural competitiveness of the industry. The range of options being made available through technology is the subject of the next chapter.

13 Developments in Marine Technology

For many years merchant shipping was regarded as one of the world's most technologically conservative industries. The natural reluctance of many shipowners to experiment with new techniques was reinforced by archaic trade practices, labor agreements, conference regulations, and lack of attention by cargo interests to transport costs. During the immediate postwar years, emphasis necessarily was placed first on rebuilding ships and services. With little time or incentive for experimentation, fleets were rebuilt in the 1940s and 1950s along largely traditional lines.

The contrast to the shipping world of today is startling, so much so that the industry is said to be in the grips of a technological revolution. The pace of change already has fundamentally altered the nature of the industry and the requirements for successful operation within it. Time-tested methods and precedent once offered security and the prospect of reasonable earnings. They do so no longer.

Before attempting an estimate of what further changes may occur during the next decade, it is useful to note the factors which have joined during the past ten years to impel this remarkable transformation of the shipping industry. Probably the most important has been the changing character of the international trade serviced by shipping. The increasing competitiveness of trade has created a variety of pressures on shipping to follow suit. Some of these pressures have been transmitted through governments, which have sponsored research and development programs and in other ways encouraged transport innovation as one means for increasing export trade. Others have come from shippers, particularly the large industrial firms concerned with the costs of their delivery systems.

Changing patterns of trade and the growing volumes of cargo also have facilitated the introduction of new technology.[1] In bulk commodity trades, new transport systems are now routinely designed as new productive facilities are commissioned in order to create total "mine to market" capabilities. Rapid growth in seaborne trade not only has created opportunities for new investment, but it has attracted into the industry new personalities, who have brought new perspectives and ideas to shipping operations.

Change, once initiated, tends to gain a momentum of its own as ship operators, shippers, port authorities, shipyards, and research and development interests contest with one another to offer the most modern service and efficient techniques. This synergistic process will continue so long as an economic basis can be established for innovation, and perhaps a bit longer. Technological development within large systems therefore typically follows an S curve, a principle which is much used in technology forecasting.[2]

Thus the present status for marine transportation technologies can be represented as in Figure 13-1. This chapter offers a brief statement regarding likely developments in each field of interest. Its purpose, like the preceding chapters dealing with developments in trade policies and practices, is to establish a basis for the judgments offered later in this volume regarding the probable future organization of shipping activities and requirements for new institutional arrangements.

Technological Potentials: an Overview

The directions in which new technology is likely to be developed and the rate at which it will be applied are a function of needs, opportunities, and know-how. Thus, the cargo expectations just reviewed establish one of the basic elements for a technological forecast. Need exists or will develop for: (1) still larger and safer ships to handle high volume flows of both bulk and general cargoes; (2) a greater variety of ship types suitable for serving an increased diversity of trade in semimanufactures and for carrying some of the higher volume general cargoes in bulk; (3) increasingly speedy, efficient, and low cost package cargo services to prevent diversion of high value cargoes to air carriers and to assist nations to maintain their position in an increasingly competitive trade in consumer goods; (4) means for extending the advantages of containerization to less-developed areas lacking expensive port facilities; and (5) improved methods of cargo routing and control and for transferring cargoes between transport modes.

Research and development organizations can offer an abundance of ideas for meeting these and other needs. But before new technology can be applied, there must be a considerable period of development, testing, and systems adaptation. Barring some sudden and dramatic breakthrough, it is therefore likely that technological applications in the next decade will revolve around processes that are already widely known and being actively pursued in some part of the world.

The time required to introduce a new marine transportation system is now on the order of three to six years. Most significant innovations, however, must be expected to take considerably longer both to complete development and to deal with the numerous institutional barriers likely to be encountered. Nonetheless, the pace of change is accelerating: container systems have required more than a decade to gain general acceptance; the newer lighter-on-ship concept has been developed and widely adopted in half this time.

During the past decade, ship design has been freed by computer techniques from its historic dependence on incremental adjustments, tested by experience. Radically new designs are now being conceptualized and structures, which a

Figure 13-1. Status of Marine Technology.

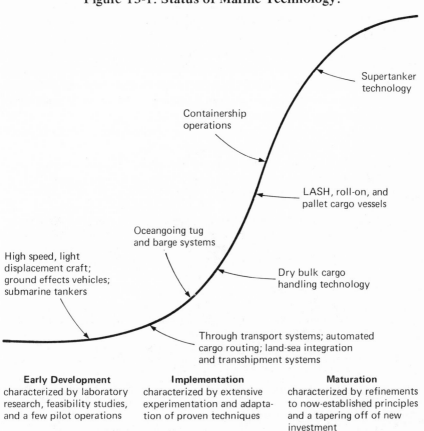

Supertanker technology

Containership operations

LASH, roll-on, and pallet cargo vessels

Oceangoing tug and barge systems

High speed, light displacement craft; ground effects vehicles; submarine tankers

Dry bulk cargo handling technology

Through transport systems; automated cargo routing; land-sea integration and transshipment systems

Early Development	**Implementation**	**Maturation**
characterized by laboratory research, feasibility studies, and a few pilot operations	characterized by extensive experimentation and adaptation of proven techniques	characterized by refinements to now-established principles and a tapering off of new investment

decade ago might have required years of study by classification societies, are certified for construction in a matter of months. It is therefore entirely within the realm of possibility that some of the advanced ship types, such as the straddle carrier or the submarine tanker, could be placed in limited operation by 1980.

Computer studies can provide a basis for other more modest design improvements as well. Using simulation techniques, naval architects can now tailor ship characteristics much more tightly to service requirements. Operations research programs and systems analysis techniques can be used to define these requirements to assure that the right ship and supporting facilities are designed for the trade. The efficiency gains which can be achieved through such analyses will in many cases surpass the savings possible by building standardized ships. To gain the benefits of both construction economy and maximum operation efficiency, naval architects are now emphasizing use of standardized components within ships which are tailored to the particular requirements of the trade.

Although technology has its most dramatic effects when a whole new system is introduced, its most pervasive continuing influence may be through the stream of small improvements being achieved in materials, propulsion systems, navigation and shipboard control equipment, and hull design. Although extremely difficult to measure with any precision, it appears that the productivity gains made in shipping over the past ten to twenty years through such improvements exceed the estimated 3 percent per year improvement in productivity in industry at large.[3]

The pace of these improvements, particularly in shipboard automation, may be confidently anticipated to increase during the 1970s.

It is impossible in this volume to assess the entire range of technological advance being pursued in conventional ship design and construction. A few examples will have to illustrate the point:

1. Hull design. As the wavemaking properties of the bulbous bow have become better understood, the use of the bow has broadened permitting power savings of up to 10 percent. Similar improvements in stern transoms, including the use of bulbs, are yielding additional savings. Use of flat plating for ships' midbodies has significantly reduced costs and simplified cargo stowage.

2. Hull materials. Great improvements have been achieved in the strength and workability of steel plate and members, permitting lighter, tougher ships. Improved welding properties have permitted construction of large, single plated, all-welded ships. Aluminum and fiberglass have been introduced into superstructures for lower weight and improved durability. Significant improvements in antifouling paints have minimized frictional resistance.

3. Fabrication techniques. Introduction of numerically controlled plate burning equipment has greatly reduced construction cost by eliminating need for wooden templates. Very large cranes permit assembling 500 ton modules. Sophisticated computer systems for production control cut inventory requirements and improve labor productivity.

4. Propulsive machinery. Improvements are continuing both in slow speed diesel and turbine systems based on improved engineering and materials. Propellers have grown larger and contrarotating and controllable pitch equipment has been introduced. Efficiency improvements in the range of 3 to 5 percent have been gained from improved siting of propellers and enclosure within a molded hull.

5. Cargo Handling Equipment. Large automatic hatch covers have both reduced time required to prepare for cargo operations and speeded actual loading and discharge by reducing the amount of handling required in the holds. Large hatch covers have been accompanied by introduction of shipboard gantry cranes with precise cargo spotting capabilities and short cycle times. Sixty to 80 tons of breakbulk cargo can be loaded per hour by such equipment or about twice the capacity of conventional port cranes or boom/mast rigs. Comparable improvements have been achieved in dry bulk cargo handling devices and in centrifugal pumps for discharging oil.

6. Service Speed. As port time is reduced, greater investment to shorten time at sea is justified. The average service speed for new bulk carriers and tankers has risen from 14 to 16 knots; for new breakbulk liners from 16 to 19 knots and for container ships to over 22 knots.

7. Automatic Control Devices. The technology for shipboard automation has been available for many years but is only now becoming sufficiently compact, economical, and reliable to make widespread use likely. Concurrently, labor shortages in many of the major maritime nations (e.g., Norway, Germany, Japan) are providing both impetus for and acceptance of the use of automatic controls. In the 1970s ships manned by twenty-five or less men will become commonplace. By 1980, manning tables of ten to twelve personnel are likely to be typical for newly constructed ships, and full automation may be introduced in a few, small test vessels.

8. Navigational Equipment. Increased use of LORAN and DECCA and the outlook for cheap, accurate satellite navigation will both enhance safety and reduce operating cost. Improved weather forecasts and computer-calculated ship routings to avoid storms and seas are claimed to yield approximately 5 percent savings. Positive traffic control in congested areas is gradually being introduced and should significantly diminish accidents.

Because conventional monohull displacement vessels are the principal focus for continuing refinement and technological improvement, they are likely to be the principal vehicles for sea transportation for many years to come. The margin of advantage gained through use of the most up to date technology will increasingly stimulate new capital investment in shipping and favor those fleets which are able to utilize the most modern technique. Norwegian owners already typically sell their ships after only eight to ten years use. By 1980 ships may be rendered economically obsolete by third and fourth generation designs as rapidly as jet aircraft or computers.

Rationalization of Cargo Services

The criteria for technological advance are rationality and efficiency. An important byproduct of increased attention to technology has been a shift in attitude within the industry from one which regarded shipping as an end in itself to one which views sea transport in wholly functional terms. The emphasis now is on systems engineering. Romance has been displaced by the slide rule, and economic calculations increasingly are being directed to the overall costs of cargo—or, in some cases, to the total production function—rather than simply to shipboard costs.

Rationalization tends to proceed incrementally along reasonably well-defined lines as total systems take shape. However, within such clear trends as the search for scale economies and cargo unitization, there are numerous variations which respond to particular conditions. This situation makes any forecast of the likely composition of the 1980 merchant fleet highly tenuous. It will be useful, however, to review some of the principal trends.

Bulk Transport Services

Scale economies have been the dominating feature of bulk transport technology over the past decade. Marine architects have concluded that bulk carriers three times the size of the present 326,000 dwt vessels are technically feasible.[4] Japanese builders have geared their facilities to handle ships in the 500,000 dwt range and beyond. One such ship is now under construction and more are planned. However, scale economies follow a flattening curve which provides only modest advantages beyond 300,000 dwt. (See Figure 13-2.) Additionally, ships with drafts in excess of the present seventy foot maximum would be greatly restricted in their operations. Entry to Europort through the English Channel would be hazardous to vessels of any larger draft, as would transit of the Strait of Malacca.

For most services, ships in the 225,000 dwt. region appear for the next several years to offer the most practical arrangements, and new orders are heavily concentrated in this range. As dry docking, offshore mooring facilities, and longside docks are improved and as numerous projects for deepening harbours to the 65 to 70 foot drafts necessary to accommodate ships in the 250,000 to 300,000 dwt range are completed, the median size of new tankers can be expected to move progressively upward. Continued improvement in hull forms, propeller arrangements, machinery design, and so forth, coupled with further improvements in offshore mooring, are likely meanwhile to create a few situations in which still larger ships will be economic, just as the Gulf Oil's development of its Bantry Bay and Point Tupper facilities provided a unique opportunity to exploit the potential economies of a 326,000 dwt. ship.

Figure 13-2. Tanker Size and Shipping Costs; Operational Considerations.

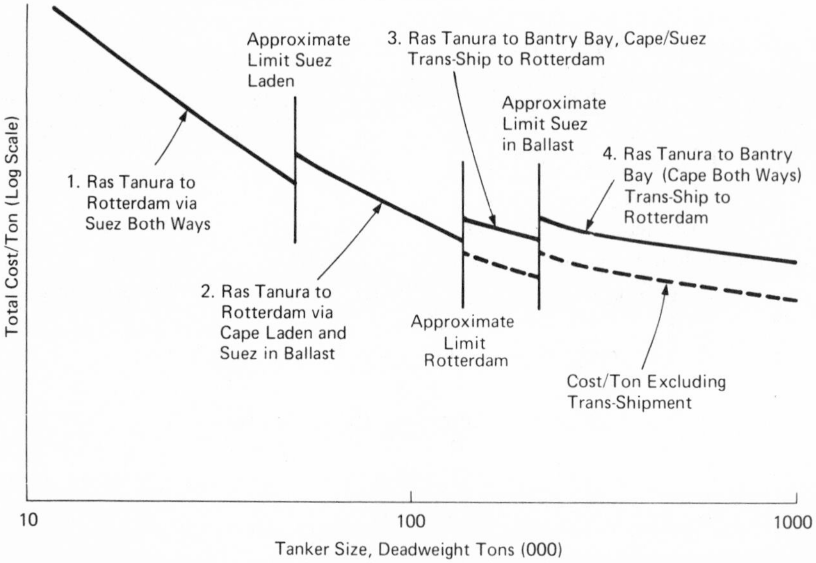

Source: Litton Systems, Inc., *Oceanborne Shipping: Demand and Technology*, pp. 4-11.

Storage problems and inventory costs are a factor in gauging the optimum size of any bulk shipment, but they loom less large in reference to petroleum than to dry bulk commodities. In addition, the loading of dry bulk is geographically more dispersed than oil and seldom favored with the natural deep water found in Persian Gulf ports. Consequently, both the maximum and medium sizes of dry bulk carriers have substantially lagged the tanker classes. The largest dry bulk carrier now in operation is a 250,000 dwt. OBO; the largest ship designed for dry bulks only is 160,000 dwt.; OBO tonnage under construction is concentrated in the 75 to 175,000 dwt. range; ore/oil ships, in the 150 to 250,000 dwt. bracket; the few plain ore carriers still being built in the 60 to 80,000 dwt. range; and other bulk carriers in the 18 to 25,000 dwt. bracket.[5]

The use of large bulk carriers appears now to be concentrated in iron ore, coal, and grain movements, but is spreading rapidly to bauxite and even timber. The potential for further scale economies seems certain to cause the average size of bulkers to continue their increase, though not to the spectacular levels found in tankers.

New construction of small (less than 25,000 dwt.) dry bulk cargo ships tends to fall into two groups: one composed of relatively fast, automated carriers, designed for use in particular trades where cargo can be handled through sophisticated coupling of shipboard and on-shore discharge and loading facilities; and the second of smaller, less costly and conventionally geared ships designed to service the varied requirements of tramp trades. In both groups, numerous design improvements are giving modern bulk carriers a substantial competitive edge over the ships which they replace.

As cargo flows assume larger proportions, increased opportunities may be found for using bulk carriers. Medium-sized bulkers already are finding employment in transporting pipe, steel shapes, and timber. Several 35,000 tonners fitted with appropriate gear and decks, have long-term charters as carriers of automobiles. Such applications appear sure to expand in the near future.

The economy of bulk movements should also be improved through improved cargo handling technology. Handling of ores in slurry form is currently being perfected. On-board belt conveyor systems have been developed with capacities of up to 20,000 tons per hour. Pneumatic systems, now used extensively for cargoes such as grain and cement, may in the future find wider applications.

Ship and Barge Systems

A desire to realize economies of scale while still preserving the flexibility of smaller consignments has generated great interest during the past five years in systems for consolidating barge-sized cargoes for their transoceanic movement. Such systems may also be used to advantage in serving lighterage ports and ports located at river mouths. Docking and terminal expenses are lower. In some trades, tug-barge operations also offer substantially lower crew costs, because such vessels operate under different manning scales than merchant ships. Such systems also permit fuller use of their expensive power plant, since minimum time need be spent awaiting cargoes in port.

The popular lighter-on-board system, called LASH, represents one type of ship and barge configuration. The LASH's seventy-three barges, each weighing 450 tons with cargo, are lifted on board with cranes, which may also be rigged for handling containers in a portion of the ship's holds. Several of these vessels are already in service and orders have been placed by European and American owners for additional LASH ships for use in trades to the Mediterranean, the Rhine and Mississippi deltas, South America, and the Far East.

Another system is the SEABEE, developed by Lykes Brothers, which uses an elevator to lift its thirty-eight carrying units, each with an 850 ton cargo capacity, into the ship. Other designs anticipate floating barges into floodable compartments within the hold of the ship or lowering the entire body of the vessel below water level to allow barges to be floated on.[6] The Stevens Institute is also seriously working on the development of a massive 128,000 dwt straddle carrier which would enclose ten 200 by 90 foot barges within a catamaran hull.

With less fanfare, U.S. inland waterways operators have extended substantial numbers of more conventional push and/or tow-train tug and barge operations out into the waters surrounding the U.S. coasts and beyond. Several regular pull tow services operate from the U.S. West Coast to Hawaii, and Teasdale reports over 20 tows of 10,000 to 15,000 dwt. barges from the U.S. East Coast to Vietnam.[7] A 26,000 dwt. barge is being used to haul phosphate from the West Coast of Florida across the Gulf of Mexico to Louisiana. Such open water tows are accomplished with tugs of up to 5,800 HP and at speeds in the range of 10 to 12 knots. The economies of their operation rest on low crew costs, the low capital costs of both the power unit and the barges, and the flexibility which operators enjoy in the use of their equipment.

In January 1970, the first order was placed for a large, deep sea pusher tug and barge system—a configuration which provides greater propulsive efficiency and directional control than the cable tow but which also necessitates a relatively sophisticated nesting and coupling system between the tug and barge. The 11,000 HP pusher tug is 140 feet in length with a forty-six foot beam; the barge is 532 by 87 feet and is designed to carry 280,000 barrels of petroleum products in the U.S. coastwise trade.

This project moves the deep sea bulk carrying industry to the very threshold of the oft-discussed "compoundable ship." In the U.S. coastal trade the advantages of such a vessel are probably chiefly regulatory—both construction and manning standards for barge systems are substantially more liberal than those for conventional deep sea ships. But the system's flexibility offers real economic advantages as well, and it will be most interesting to see whether the configuration, once operationally tested, may not find application in other trades as well.[8]

Transhipment Systems

The systems described above utilize unmanned, unpowered barges as the means for assembling cargoes for transoceanic shipment. An alternative approach, also finding increasing application in the industry, is to deploy a fleet of small, self-propelled vessels to bring locally-generated cargoes to a central dispatch port for transhipment to a bulk carrier for the transoceanic movement.

Improved cargo handling systems have greatly enhanced the attractiveness of using feeder vessels for large bulk carriers whenever cargoes are geographically dispersed or ports or land transportation are inadequate. Overseas Container Lines plans such a system for distributing container shipments from Singapore through Southeast Asia. The Livanos group has plans for a fleet of 100 "mini-bulk carriers" (operated with eight man crews) to work in the same area, collecting lumber and other bulk products for through shipment on the company's larger vessels.

The petroleum industry has long used transhipment as a means of achieving economies of scale for long hauls.[9] Ships in the 30-70,000 dwt range are now being used chiefly for such local distribution, and several companies are following Shell's lead in making direct ship-to-ship transfers of the cargo.

Unit Load Systems, General Cargo

The diversity of means for consolidating bulk shipments in order to achieve economies of scale is mirrored in the movement of general cargoes. On the major routes among the industrialized nations, the container has gained a commanding lead. Elsewhere, it is not clear what system or mix of systems is likely to find greatest acceptance.

Containerization and roll-on, roll-off shipping may be regarded as the Cadillac and Lincoln of the general cargo freight business. Both are capital intensive and wasteful of shipping space, but offer extremely efficient means for cargo handling. The full cycle time for the best container gantries is only two minutes; two gantries working in tandem can take 1,000 containers from a ship and load 1,000 others in about thirty-six hours. A steady stream of drivers can work the ramps of a roll-on, roll-off vessel in approximately the same time.

Because the principal savings through these systems is achieved in cargo handling, they found their first applications in services in which handling costs were high: U.S. military shipments, the U.S. coastwise and noncontiguous trades (Puerto Rico, Hawaii, and now Alaska) and the trades of Great Britain,

Australia, Canada, and the Continent.[10] Countries with important trade with these nations, in particular, Japan, quickly followed suit and container systems now are rapidly spreading throughout the world.

The economics of containerization is the subject of an enormous literature as well as considerable dispute, which cannot be settled here. Suffice it to say that the investments being made worldwide in container facilities indicate that, for better or worse, this will be the principal mode of general cargo transport on all principal sea routes by the mid-1970s and that shippers and receivers which do not have access to such facilities will consider themselves relatively disadvantaged in world trade.

The rapid spread of containerization appears to have been more the product of competitive pressures than of the system's immediate economic return. Operators who are making money in their new container services are doing so because they can offer more convenient, rapid, and safer service and therefore achieve higher load factors than they previously enjoyed. Indirectly, their conversion to container shipping has been subsidized by port authorities, which have invested well over a half billion dollars in new facilities that are only partially charged against their users,[11] and by tax and credit incentives which favor investment in new ship construction vis-a-vis current outlays for ship operation and cargo handling. Accounting treatment of conversion costs and depreciation schedules for the containers and necessary supporting equipment also are subject to variations which make it exceedingly difficult to make cost comparisons with other unit load systems.

Containerization was pioneered in those services where the potential economic gain was largest and the potential competitive advantage most telling. As institutional obstacles—customs procedures, insurance, conference practices, labor rules, and so forth—have been cleared away, other routes have become attractive. More important, containerization itself has gained an internal momentum which is leading to applications even where the economics are uncertain. Large shippers who have adapted the majority of their export business to containers press for services which will permit their entire business to be handled in this fashion; manufacturers in less developed areas see container shipments as necessary to maintaining their share of overseas markets; ports fear a deterioration of their position if they do not convert; internal transportation systems, improved to accommodate containers shipped from the U.S., are available also for handling containers to other destinations; and so forth. The transition, in sum, involves such a breadth of economic interests that the cost-benefit calculations of any single decision-making element are meaningful only in relation to that organization's assumptions regarding the development of the system as a whole. The general assumption, as noted above, is that container systems will sweep the main East-West belt of general cargo transport and progressively penetrate North-South trades linking developed and less developed nations during the 1970s. It is an assumption which bears the marks of a self-fulfilling prophecy.

Table 13-1
Planned Container Services on Major Trade Routes, 1972

Route	No. of [a] Ships	Container[b] Capacity (thousands)	No. of Firms[c] 4 or More Ships	Total Firms	Est.[d] Penetration (%)	Conventional Ship Equivalents[e]
Europe/Aust. & N.Z.	22	182.4	2	8	90	144
Europe/E.C.N. Amer.	74	915.9	9	15	75	245
Mediterranean/E.C.N. America	11	117.9	1	4	75	29
Europe/W.C.N. Amer.	11	70.2	1	3	75	27
Far East/W.C.N. Amer.	28	288.2	3	10	60	84
Far East/E.C.N. Amer.	9	50.0	1	3	70	19
Japan/Australia	8	89.3	0	6	80	21
Europe/Far East	20+	201.9+	1	11	60	148
Aust. & N.Z./N. Amer.	14	114.6	1	6	50	36
	200		19	66		753

Source: Lambert Bros. survey "Displacement of Conventional Liner Tonnage on Major World Trade Routes," 1970.

[a]Full container, roll-on, or LASH ships with a container capacity of 400 20 ft. units or greater.

[b]20' container equivalents which can be moved each way. 10 tons per container x 2 approximates total trade flow that can be handled.

[c]Each consortium counted as one.

[d]Proportion of general cargo (as defined in OECD study) susceptible of being carried by containership. Penetration of 75 percent or greater probably represents saturation of containers' potential.

[e]Estimated in reference to liners typical of the trade. Numbers in most cases exceed number of liners which actually had been operated.

Roll-on, roll-off systems may be regarded as a variant of containerization in which the bogeys are left attached to the container in order to be able to load and unload with even greater efficiency. Originally used only for military vessels, short sea ferry services, and trades involving large shipments of automobiles, large "ro-ro" vessels have been placed in North Atlantic service by a consortium of European owners, and a dozen such ships have been ordered for use in other deep sea trades.

The second principal alternative to containerization is palletization, a system for handling small, standardized cargo units (usually 4 by 6 by 4 feet) on multideck ships equipped with side-ports and serviced by fork-lift trucks. Such systems may be regarded as an intermediary stage between conventional cargo handling methods and containerization. They involve more handling than container systems, but offer greater flexibility and lower initial outlays. A major advantage is that they may be used where there are imbalanced cargo flows, since wooden pallets are expendable, and the more expensive steel platforms are easily stowed for return. A variety of ingenious methods for packaging pallet loads have been developed to protect cargoes from damage at sea and while awaiting transit ashore. Although costing less than containers for sea voyages, pallets are generally more expensive to move overland and are therefore most attractive in serving destinations where there is only a short land haul.[12]

Pallet-oriented lines have organized to try to persuade shippers, port authorities, and other shipowners that the shift to containers is not inevitable. They have been successful in winning new, specially adapted terminal facilities in the Port of New York and at a number of Scandinavian locations, where the pallet is particularly favored.

About 20 to 30 percent of the cargoes now moving by liner are acknowledged by both container and pallet operators to be unsuitable for utilization.[13] This includes both cargoes too large to fit within a container and those, such as pig iron, steel scrap, waste paper and pulp, which are of such low value in relation to their weight or bulk as to make container shipment clearly uneconomic. Pallet carriers, operating a somewhat slower schedule with less investment, are in a better position to provide a mixed service but will also face competition from tramps, bulk carriers, and conventional liners for these noncontainerizable goods. An additional twenty-odd percent of the cargoes composed of such items as vegetable oils, chemicals, refrigerated goods, and pipe are inappropriate for pallet shipment but are considered "potentially suitable" for shipment in specially designed containers. A major question in the industry is whether cargoes of this sort can justify the expense of containerization or will shift to other types of ships.

Numerous minor advances in technology have accompanied the introduction of unit loads and undoubtedly further refinements will be developed in the future, particularly in packing techniques and in equipment for handling specialized cargoes. Increasing standardization of equipment, permitting interchange among operators between modes, has also been important, and further progress here may also be expected. Development of an economical collapsible container would facilitate the introduction of container services in badly balanced trades. Yet the main thrust towards the spread of cargo unitization in the decade ahead as in that just past, is likely not to be technology at all, but competitive factors and changing economic relationships which force use of labor-saving devices.

Both container and pallet systems may be regarded as methods of "bulking" cargoes by assembling large amounts of material for shipment in a homogeneous form. Although emphasis to date has been on offering frequent, high speed services to permit rapid delivery of high value goods, container ships are growing steadily larger in order to capture economies of scale wherever the traffic volume permits. The eight thirty-three knot 43,000 dwt. 2000-container ships ordered in September 1969 by SeaLand have received the most publicity but are likely to prove only the vanguards of the next generation container fleet.[14] Other British, American, Scandinavian and German owners have, in fact, already placed orders for twenty container ships only slightly smaller and less speedy than the SeaLand vessels.

These ships are much closer cousins to the fastest and biggest passenger liners than to the freighters which they replace. Prodigious amounts of premium cargo

Figure 13-3. Evaluation of Service Systems for Liner Cargoes.

Systems Alternatives	Factors Affecting Choice	Likely Outcomes
Variables which may be controlled by the transport operator in organizing a transoceanic service	Variables associated with the particular market in which the firm operates which affect significantly the economics of systems choice.	The pattern of choices which may be observed in surveying the more successful operations.

1. Vessel characteristics
    size   speed
    hold design, stowage
    factor, etc.
2. Cargo handling systems
    container   pallet
    roll-on, roll-off
    conventional
3. Cargo consolidation and packaging strategy
    port or inland consolidation
    center
    by shipowner, shipper, or
    freight forwarder
4. Connecting transportation
    rail   truck   ship
    pipeline   barge
5. Ocean service
    frequency   no. of ports
	1. Cargo characteristics
	    homogeneity and volume
	    physical characteristics (size,
	    durability, etc.)
	    value
	    origins and destinations
	2. Port characteristics
	    longshore labor costs
	    work practices and hours
	    hazard of delay
	    terminal facilities: cranes warehousing,
	    lay-out
	3. Voyage characteristics
	    distance
	    weather
	    ship operating costs
	4. Customer preference
		1. Container Systems when high volume of high value cargoes. Competitive pressures for investment. High port and ship labor costs with good inland transport links. Greater distances requiring larger ships higher speeds.
		2. Pallet Systems when less opportunity to concentrate cargo loading and discharge. Imbalanced trade. Little emphasis on inland transport link.
		3. Conventional Systems when low port cost; port congestion. Cheap cargoes. Long voyages. High cost of money and institutional barriers.
		4. Mixed Systems when low cargo throughout. Many ports of call. Mixed cargoes and conditions enroute.

will be required to support their operation. Yet, with the trade growth estimated to develop over the 1970s, there are at least a dozen routes on which such superfreighters could be employed advantageously.[15] In these trades, the introduction of very large, fast and perhaps nuclear-powered, container carriers in the late 1970s could create dislocations fully as serious as those created by the present generation of container ships over the past four years.[16]

Scale economies in container operations could also create a branching of container services into two classes, somewhat analogous to the dual trends forecast for dry bulks (see above). In one category would be sea-express service, which would provide frequent scheduling and high speed in order to compete with air cargo for premium goods; the second would be a low cost, high volume system patterned on bulk cargo operations but designed to consolidate small, container-sized shipments for which speed is less important than economy. Indeed owners of small "newsprint-type" bulk carriers might be attracted to this trade, which would appear to have the potential for filling a major gap in the present spectrum of sea transport services.[17]

Paperwork Management and Cargo Control Systems

Typically, in the introduction of new technology, software and control systems tend to lag behind the development of new hardware. Shipping is no exception. The paperwork burden on the industry, imposed partly by government requirements, banking terms, and legal practice and partly the product of the industry's own design, is estimated to involve costs which approximate the costs of ocean transport for many shipments.[18] Document simplification is an objective of a large number of government and commercial groups, which are examining specific documentation problems encountered in international trade.[19]

Simpler documentation will be essential to permit papers to be processed rapidly enough to stay abreast of container shipments. Several lines now are using telex to forward bill of lading information to receivers overseas; the Atlantic Container Line sends such information on magnetic tape, ready for computer processing on receipt, by air.

All the large container services now are supported by computerized cargo and container control systems. These systems at a minimum record the location of all containers in the system, the cargoes which they are carrying, their present location and anticipated destination. The more sophisticated also provide reservations and routing information. The U.S. Lines system, for example, provides the client with shipping information to the port, reserves space on an appropriate vessel, and identifies an overseas rail or truck line to transport the container to its final destination. It also controls the container's onboard stowage, and answers all questions on the status of equipment and bookings.[20]

The companies which are most successful at meeting their paperwork and control problems are likely to be those which achieve the greatest competitive success in liner and container shipping. Convenience looms large in any shipper's calculations and savings in paperwork are savings which are realized in the transportation manager's own immediate office. A good routing and control system also permits the shipping company to capture potential cargo at its source rather than exposing itself to the uncertainties and bearing the extra costs of employing cargo brokers and freight forwarders. This is a competitive factor (discussed at greater length in Chapter 14) which appears likely to be a major influence in the shipping industry's development during the next decade.

New Ships and Services

While technological development in shipping may be expected to be concentrated on improving existing systems, the search will continue for wholly new ship types and routings to better serve commercial needs or meet threats from other modes. At this time it does not appear that any of these possibilities will have a major impact on the industry within the time span (to 1980) here being considered. Yet they are in the news, they contribute to the dynamism of the industry, they may develop into major factors in the longer term, and they are likely to create at least some dislocation during the decade immediately ahead.

Advanced Ship Designs

Competitive pressure to offer ever-faster delivery coupled with the growing power and efficiency of propulsion systems is stimulating interest in a variety of new high speed, low displacement hull forms. Such designs range from narrow, monohulled displacement ships with unusually high cubic to weight relationships to the more radical multihulled vessels and "ground effects machines" (GEM's) which may be said to have no displacement at all. Higher speeds are made possible by reducing weight and frictional resistance in relation to volume and/or by introducing lifting devices such as fans or planes as well as by increasing power. For each type of vessel, there is a set of speed-range-capacity parameters within which it can perform most effectively.

GEM's (alternatively surface effect, or air cushion vehicles or hovercraft) have been pioneered by the British, and vessels of up to 165 tons with a cruise speed of sixty-one knots and a range of 290 nautical miles have been placed in operation.[21] Many alternative configurations are being considered for future development, including amphibious models and a 5,000 ton craft proposed for transoceanic service. However, to be competitive in routes also served by aircraft, GEM's must operate in the range of $.05 to $.10 per ton mile and overcome many environmental problems. As with all high-speed craft, the ratio of fuel to cargo is a limiting factor on range. Applications within the decade therefore appear likely to be restricted to more modest sizes (perhaps to 500 tons) over shorter routes (perhaps 500 miles).[22]

Hydrofoil ships have been constructed in substantial numbers and in sizes of up to 300 tons in Russia, Italy, the Scandinavian nations, and elsewhere. Speeds are on the order of 40 to 60 knots but payload remains a small fraction of gross weight, particularly due to high fuel consumption. Despite severe problems related to cavitation and structural stresses, Litton Industries projects the commercial feasibility of a 3,000 ton displacement craft by 1983 with a payload 20 to 30 percent of gross weight and a range of 3,600 nautical miles.[23]

The catamaran, whose weight is suspended above water on a pair of buoyant hulls, is a third member of the new family of specialized, high-speed craft. The principal advantages are large deck areas and good transverse stability. Construction costs are, of course, higher than for conventional monohull ships but, at high-speed, wave-making resistance and horsepower requirements are lower. There is interest in extending the use of catamarans from their present applications as car ferries and ocean research ships into other uses where deck area is important, including quick-load, shallow-hold container ships.

Another variant, with a potential for taking larger cargoes, is the TRISEC design developed by Litton Industries. This design provides a large, above-water cargo hold which is connected by an intermediate wave-cutting structure to two or more wholly submerged buoyancy pods. Litton Industries sees applications in carrying passengers and low density cargoes at 50 knot speeds.[24] Some recent Japanese designs for high-speed cargo vessels appear to be premised on concepts similar to TRISEC, although these ships are of more conventional appearance and hydrodynamic characteristics.

An approach potentially suitable for cargoes of slightly less density than sea water is total submergence of the cargo-carrying hold. Although the submarine offers greater propulsive efficiency than conventional ships at 25-30 knot speed ranges, the power requirements (and therefore costs) for achieving such speeds in an underwater system are very great, and there are numerous operating problems. Incentive to develop a commercial submersible would therefore have to proceed from some special need, such as under-the-ice transport of Artic oil being advanced by General Dynamics.[25] Litton Industries has concluded that even this application is likely to await development of a suitable nuclear power plant and will be realized only in a time frame of fifteen to thirty-five years.[26]

Improved ice-breaking ships may offer an alternative to the submarine tanker. The voyage of the "Manhattan" proved the technical feasibility of using strengthened, high-powered displacement vessels for transits through ice with thicknesses of up to 15 feet. The economic feasibility of such applications is still under study.[27]

New Routings

The possibility of opening a sea route through the Northwest passage illustrates both the problems and opportunities for modifying the flow of trade through pioneering of new routes. Passage across the Canadian Arctic would reduce the sea voyage from Europe to Japan by over 4,000 miles. On the other hand, almost this large a distance would have to be run at reduced speed and substantial investment would be required to create the necessary ice-strengthened ships. These factors, plus the increased cost of insurance and discomfort to the crew, have been sufficient to quench the enthusiasm of most shipping men.

A passage through the Siberian Arctic was formally opened to commercial navigation in 1968; however, use of this route has been limited almost entirely to ships providing service to the area itself.

Improved ice-breaking will probably have its largest practical effect in extending the season during which cold weather ports can be visited. The Port of Leningrad, for example, can now be kept free of ice for eight months of the year. By 1980 improved icebreakers are anticipated to permit both Leningrad and St. Lawrence Seaway ports to be operated on a year-round basis.

Particularly in the bulk cargo trades, port development and channel depths have a major influence on cargo routing and indeed on whether cargo can economically be handled at all. Japan, which enjoys favorable natural endowments, also has done the most to create deep water terminals and has been able fully to realize scale economies in her imports of heavy raw materials. Of the large maritime nations, the United States has done the least to help her ports keep pace with transoceanic bulk cargo shipping, although very large investments have been made by the U.S. in improving internal waterways. These investments may yield unexpected dividends as ship and barge systems become more popular, particularly for short haul, deep sea transport to Canada, the Caribbean and South America.

The future use and development of major international waterways—particularly the Suez and Panama Canals—create major uncertainties in the maritime transport picture. Over the past several years, the deployment of increasing numbers of very large tankers has largely offset the impact of the Suez closure. Since giant (250,000 dwt. and up) supertankers can deliver oil to Europe more cheaply than the smaller (up to 150,000 dwt.) tankers able to pass through the Canal, most forecasters conclude that the Canal's reactivation would initially have minimal effect on oil transport markets and costs. Other bulk and general cargo services would, however, be immediately affected. Were the Canal to be deepened to fifty or fifty-five feet, as projected by Egyptian authorities, it could also recapture much of the enormous Persian Gulf to Europe tanker trade and release the equivalent of 250,000 ship days now spent transiting the Cape of Good Hope.

Panamanian nationalism concurrently is creating some concern that the Panama Canal might be temporarily closed in the course of negotiations with the U.S. on the status of the Canal Zone. The interest of the Panamanian government in industrial development, however, could also lead during the 1970s to activation of a trans-Panamanian pipe line and/or an overland system to move containers across the Isthmus. Construction of such facilities would help overcome the congestion and draft limitations (forty feet) of the present Canal, but also might encourage the Panamanian government to try to close the Canal in order to capture its traffic for an overland route. Though an overland alternative might be economically feasible for some classes of cargo, it would not for others (e.g., most dry bulks). Already iron ore from Africa and Brazil is being shipped to Japan around Cape Horn.

The ease with which container cargoes can be transferred from one vehicle to another has stimulated great interest in developing new routes combining sea and overland transport to offer more rapid and in some cases more economical service than could be provided by sea alone. The most heavily utilized land bridge to date is the Rotterdam to Milan unit train link for distribution of transatlantic container cargoes into the Mediterranean area. Containers are also shipped overland from Europe to the Persian Gulf and from Halifax into the Canadian interior. The Japanese government is reported to have negotiated a through service to Europe via the Trans-Siberian Railroad, and Canadian railways are quoting through rates for Atlantic to Pacific container cargoes. However, neither these projects nor the much discussed cross-U.S. land bridge appear likely to offer serious threats to all-sea container services, since high speed ships can achieve almost as rapid delivery at substantially less cost.[28]

Where there is a flat terrain and high throughput, large-diameter oil pipelines offer a cost-effective alternative to sea shipment. The efficiency of pipeline operations has increased over the past decade at an even more rapid rate than that of tanker shipment. Experiments also are going forward in the use of pipelines for movement of liquified solids and even of small package units.[29]

New Services

Alert and technologically progressive shipowners will continue during the 1970s to seek out ways in which new technology can be used to offer wholly new services to the industrial world. Some of these innovations, which are likely to have high profit potential, may relate to means for transport of cargoes such as phosphorus and certain highly volatile petrochemicals which cannot now be moved by sea at all; others will involve integrated hook-ups of land, sea, and air services to facilitate through shipments under computer control. There is a clear potential for new feeder services to consolidate bulk, container, and package cargoes, particularly in island (Indonesia, Caribbean) and less developed areas having poor internal transport. Improved lighter services or other means of offloading pallet and container cargoes where direct ship to shore discharge is impossible is another area in which there is an economic need apparently solvable with new technology.

While ships are becoming more specialized, means for quick conversions to alternative uses should prove a fertile area for attention. Perhaps the potentially most versatile ship is the modern "newsprint" carrier which combines large open hatches with easy access and an easy cargo loading procedure. Such ships can be easily fitted out to carry cars, timber, containers, or any other cargo susceptible of being assembled into large units. With knock-down cargo holding gear it may be employed in carrying unitized goods in one direction and bulk-loaded materials in the other. Its potentials are only beginning to be explored.

A final interesting possibility involves processing materials while on board ship. To a limited extent, this already is done. Factory ships accompany fishing fleets; bananas ripen while in transit. Automation of industrial processes creates possibilities for refinement of ores, preparation of wood pulp, and the like away from populated areas while concurrently moving the material from its source to its market.

Systems Aspects of New Technology

Large scale technological development inevitably affects and is affected by the systems within which it is conducted. Systems considerations are particularly pertinent to transport innovation and ship services because of the multiple interests touched by change. Thus the ship itself is a system which must be engineered to perform with complete reliability in a harsh and impredictable environment. But the ship is only one component in the much larger system of ports, cargo handling facilities, storage depots, and feeder networks needed to support overseas transport. Transport in turn constitutes only one phase of the production and marketing process; the organization of production, location strategy, packaging and inventory control are equally crucial components of distribution. All these activities, when geared to export sales, must be geared in turn to the overall system of commercial rules and facilities pertaining to international trade.

The complicated systems attributes of marine technology can operate as a heavy brake on innovation. Once such new developments as containerization or the introduction of supertankers become established, however, these same attributes may contribute to the rapid transmission of the new technology throughout the industry.

The International Standards Association standards for container dimensions and fixtures and the effect of Suez and Panama canal rules on ship size are interesting cases in point—one emerging from formal negotiation and the other from the physical limitations of important waterways. Adoption of the ISA standard provided an enormous stimulus to the container movement by offering a firm basis for multimodal operations and equipment interchange. Yet it seriously hurt some operators and may prove over time to inhibit future improvement. In somewhat similar fashion, depth limitations for transit of the two Canals for many years established an effective ceiling on the size of ships, and a large proportion of harbours around the world continue to be geared to the 41 foot "Pan-Max." In both container and bulk carrier operations, however, standards-breakers have moved out beyond the norm to pioneer more ambitious systems on their own terms.

Breaking with industry, which is a necessary element of all real innovation, requires corporate strength as well as courage. Technological leaders in an industry such as shipping must be well enough financed to be able to absorb the inevitable risks and setbacks encountered in pioneering a new idea and must be backed up with sufficient technical know-how to be able to thoroughly check out all aspects of their proposed program. The Overseas Container Line entry into container operations, for example, is estimated to have involved an investment of over 100 million pounds. Although the technology involved was all well known, a research and development team of sixty persons worked for two years to assure that there would be no mishaps in introducing the new system.

System considerations put a special premium on ability to integrate production, port, and transport facilities. Although independents like Ludwig, Onassis, and Naess have often provided the stimulus for innovation, actual implementation has required the cooperation and support of the "Mr. Bigs" of international industry—the major oil and steel companies—in providing finance and the conditions which would make new development economically feasible.

In many cases systems modification requires the support of governments as well. The effective partnership between government and industry in Japan must be credited with having been a major influence in that nation's maritime achievements. It provided both the staged production goals and the means for mobilizing the trained manpower and finance necessary to obtain the materials, make the steel, organize the yards, dredge the ports, and design and operate ships in a dramatic upward spiral of development.

As sea transport systems expand in complexity and scope, international cooperation will become increasingly crucial to effective innovation. Such cooperation now is most easily accomplished within the corporate empires of international business, which have been able to establish fully integrated systems for production and transport of bulk commodities. The same level of systems optimization has not yet proved possible where cooperation must take place at the governmental level.

Stimulus to technological improvement is a priority objective for maritime affairs. To accomplish this objective, institutional frameworks must be provided to encourage and reward innovation by facilitating both adjustments in trade rules and the investments in port and internal transport systems which are necessary to accommodate change.

Transport innovation has the dual result of increasing productivity and generating diversity and dynamism in a key sector of industrial life. As will be pointed up again in the following chapter, trade, technology, and the shape of the shipping industry itself operate in a highly interactive system. This always has been so. It is only the pace of the interaction which has changed in recent years and which promises to continue to accelerate in the decade ahead.

14 Implications for the Shipping Industry

Shipping in the seventies is emerging as a very different sort of industry than that which shipowners have known in earlier years. The most dramatic changes are occurring within that sector of the industry, liner shipping, which has heretofore been the most conservative. The adaptations being made by this portion of the ocean freight industry to the container age are the chief focus of this chapter. It also deals briefly with issues in intermodal transport and with the outlook for the independent operator in bulk cargo trades. New conditions in every sector of the industry are creating a management challenge of imposing dimensions. The quality of management which will be required of the industry in the years ahead is identified in the chapter's concluding pages.

Adapting to the Container Age

In 1966-67, two American consulting firms (A.D. Little and McKinsey and Co.) rendered a series of controversial and prescient reports to the British Ports Council and Transport Docks Board assessing the likely impact of containerization, a movement which then was only in the very early stages of development in international trade.[1] The consultants laid out a startling scenario for the transition of a fragmented, technologically static industry to one organized around a small number of very large enterprises providing a standardized product—in this case container transport services—on a worldwide scale. The factors which would force this change were described as: (1) the competitive necessity to offer a more convenient, reliable, and rapid service, and (2) the economic necessity to circumvent escalating long shore charges by automating the loading and discharge of cargoes. During the transition, the consultants forecast a period of temporary overtonnaging, rate wars, jockeying to gain control of cargoes, mergers, liquidations, interport competition, and progressive internationalization.

When a new development such as containerization grips an industry, the initial impact is likely to be felt most strongly within the industry itself. Here the rush to get on the bandwagon in order to secure a place before being overtaken by the competition is likely to result in hasty decisions and a kind of mob psychology. The North Atlantic package cargo industry provides a classic case. Here about three dozen well established liner companies a few years ago shared a stable trade of about 4.3 million tons per year (both directions

175

summed) which was serviced by 160 to 175 ships. By December 1970, approximately fifty new or converted container and roll-on ships had been introduced, providing a total cargo capacity on these ships alone about a third greater than the total pre-existing fleet.[2]

The overcapacity on the route (particularly for containerizable cargoes) is such that the new container ships are reported to be sailing half empty—though in most cases they are still making money for their owners.[3]

The resulting shake-out has assumed dramatic proportions. Over 100 conventional liners have been retired from North Atlantic Service within the past three years. At least three old, established European companies have decided on voluntary liquidation rather than buck the trend. In the U.S., Moore McCormack Lines, which had made a heavy commitment to the containers, sold its four brand new cellular/roll-on ships, discharged 280 employees, and announced that it was abandoning the North Atlantic trade. U.S. Lines shifted its best ships to a Far Eastern service and concurrently attempted to sell or lease its entire container fleet to the SeaLand organization.

The lessons learned in the North Atlantic may prevent this pattern from occurring elsewhere as the container infection spreads to other trades. Indeed, a very different experience has been achieved in the pioneer container service from the U.K. to Australia, a matter of which we will have more to say below. Both cases, however, emphasize the need for careful planning combined with fast footwork in order to adapt successfully to the container age. The strategies selected by individual companies may differ, but everyone caught up in the scramble unleashed by "the box" has been forced to face up to difficult decisions which will fundamentally affect his position in the industry for at least the next decade.

Changes in Industry Structure

For those companies which decide to enter the container race, the first question to be faced is whether to go it alone or in cooperation with others. For many shipping firms—perhaps most—this is not even a debatable issue. The size and risk of the financial commitment compels a cooperative agreement. Furthermore, mounting a sufficiently large container operation to maintain a weekly or biweekly schedule, which is a competitive necessity on most heavily traveled routes, requires an assurance of more cargo than individual operators typically can control.[4]

With a few exceptions in which individual companies have either enjoyed an unusually large market share (e.g., U.S. Lines to Great Britain), or adopted an unusually aggressive posture (e.g., SeaLand, Sea Train), companies have joined forces in order to introduce container service. The forms of cooperation vary from outright mergers between companies sharing similar trading interests (e.g.,

Hamburg American and North German Lloyd) to cooperative arrangments in which companies continue to own and operate individual ships pledged to a container service pool, but coordinate sailings and share revenue according to agreed-on formulae. Most of these cooperative agreements are limited to a single service on a single route. Several now embrace companies of different nationalities, and have developed substantial subsidiary management organizations to operate the container service. At least one of the consortia, Overseas Container Ltd., has been mandated by its sponsors to design and implement new ventures on its own. Others are more circumscribed and confine their attention to the service areas previously covered by their members.

About one fourth of the world's 300-plus liner companies are participating in one of the approximately twenty-five major consortia organized to provide container service in transoceanic trade. Another twenty companies have launched major container operations on their own. Container services are now offered on all trade routes linking developed nations. Because several of the major container groups have organized operations in two or more routes, a total of sixty-six services are offered by thirty-two to thirty-five companies and consortia.

These services have already fairly well saturated the immediate potential for container transport on the routes to which their ships are assigned (See Table 13-1). Furthermore, many of these firms are operating only a minimum container service, based on only two to three full container ships (or on a half dozen vessels able to take on a partial container load). Although they handle a large cargo volume by traditional standards, these smaller units face the likelihood of being overwhelmed if faced with competition by one of the major container groups. This likely second stage consolidation will almost certainly have to be across national lines and even across regional divisions, joining Americans, Europeans, and Orientals in a common enterprise. When this occurs—the mid or late seventies seems a reasonable guess—container shipping will have achieved full internationalization.

Corporate Strategies

For a development which gained force only three to four years ago, containerization has already realized a surprising penetration of its major markets. Overtonnaging has soured the cream in the North Atlantic trades and appears likely to spread to the Mediterranean and, with curtailment of shipping to Vietnam, could infect the trans-Pacific trades as well. Yet container operators regard themselves as participating in a growth industry. Several have ambitious plans for expansion to establish operations on a worldwide scale.

There are several reasons to believe that of consolidation and competition within the container industry will ultimately result in the emergence of a few very large organizations with worldwide interests. Perhaps the most compelling is the need to achieve effective utilization of the containers flowing within the system—an objective which requires in most cases that the system be a large one.

The managers of expansion-minded companies are particularly emphatic that successful container operations depend on maximizing utilization of "the box." Containers may represent more than half the capital cost of the total system.[5] A control system which keeps containers moving, prevents losses, and provides for a steady flow of cargoes into consolidation points, to staging areas and thence onto the ship is an absolute prerequisite for a profitable system. Also, it is the container, not the ship, which is the vehicle for obtaining cargo. The major deep sea operators all own and manage their own stock of boxes.[6]

Effective interchange arrangements have been developed in a few trades, (notably Europe/Australia) but are absent in others. By and large, it is up to the individual operator to see that his containers get reloaded and back into service as a revenue-generating unit. The larger his network, the greater the number of optional routings he can offer his potential shipper. Also, as containerization moves toward the outer limits of its cargo potential, carriers will face an increasing number of situations in which cargo flows are imbalanced which will add to the pressures to allow the container to flow out into other trades. Operators that offer a wide network of transportation services will enjoy a significant competitive advantage in these situations over those which maintain only a point to point shuttle.[7]

The apparent surplus of container equipment on the main trunk routes may also operate as a force towards development of a few large organizations with worldwide interests. The more aggressive, growth-oriented companies are likely to be the ones that will buy out the less successful competitors on the older container routes, and, they will be in the best position to redeploy the ships onto new routes on which, for one reason or another, the established lines have not chosen to introduce container services. These will be mostly routes to less developed areas. It will be of interest to see whether the ship lines and governments in the affected countries will accept or resist the efforts of a SeaLand or an OCL to bring them the economic advantages of a tested and highly efficient container operation.

The third factor pushing container shipping toward a still further consolidation (and one which may influence the attitude of less developed nations) is the expansion of international business and trade interests. To the extent that cargoes being moved through container systems are generated by firms with worldwide manufacturing and distribution facilities, the stage will be set for worldwide container transport nets. By any economic test, the less developed nations have much more to gain than to lose by being tied into international business and transport systems. Linking up the seventy-six less developed states in an international container network will, however, be at best a tortuous process likely to require many years.[8]

Some interesting strategies have been developed to accommodate local sensitivities in expanding container services. For example, early in the planning of the consortium to handle Australian container trade (which will be discussed at greater length below), the OCL group invited the Australians to participate through the construction of an Australian Flag container ship. The consortium also gave positive support to enactment of regulatory legislation by the Australian government providing for governmental surveillance of its rate-making activities and ultimate authority to disapprove agreements found detrimental to Australian foreign commerce. The consortium in effect recognized that the total rationalization of the trade depended for its long-term stability on public acceptance and that its interest would be best served by promoting the development of orderly mechansims for public review.

Competitive Patterns

Containerization has developed largely within the framework of the conference system. The scale of development has been such as to alter radically the character of the conferences to which the sponsoring lines have belonged. Each case has demonstrated a somewhat different pattern. Organization of new cooperative arrangements, however, has proved much easier within the "closed conferences" operating out of Great Britain and Northern Europe than within the framework of the "open conferences" regulated by the Federal Maritime Commission in the American trades.[9]

The evolution of container services from Europe to Australia provides an illuminating example of the former situation. Interest in using containers first emerged in Great Britain, and the Australian service was deliberately selected by British planners to provide a testbed for container operations. It appeared to offer a manageable test since it involved only two nations which had common traditions and a stable trade serviced by a half-dozen British companies operating within a closed conference which was well insulated from competition from nonconference lines.[10] Containers, however, were destined totally to reshape the nature of competition in the Australian trade. Rather than being able to assess the competitive problem solely in reference to the United Kingdom services, the British progressively have been plunged into negotiations with the French, Dutch, Germans, Italians, and Scandinavians. In fact, even Russia has entered a competitor for the trade.

The planning of container service to Australia was initiated by the OCL group in 1967. The Australians were first to demand a position in the new undertaking; then a second group of British lines, Associated Container Transport, was brought into the OCL plan. By the time the nine OCL/ACT/Australian vessels were ready for operation, orders had been placed for five more container ships by continental lines. Concern that these vessels might either capture some British cargoes by transshipment through continental ports or seek directly to enter the UK-Australia trade was heightened when the French announced orders for still additional container capacity (for which the French Line had no apparent cargo base). Concurrently, due to a strike at the Tilbury docks, OCL was demonstrating that a transshipment service to Britain could successfully be provided from a cross-Channel port. As a result, serious discussions were initiated between British, continental, and subsequently, Scandinavian shipping interests to see whether agreements might be reached to coordinate rates, services, schedules, and tonnage to be employed in the overall Europe to Australia trade. These negotiations involved some two dozen lines located in ten nations and operating about seventy ships under a half dozen conference agreements. The outcome was a broad service agreement embracing all container shipping from the UK and the Continent on the one hand and the formation of a joint operating company to consolidate the noncontainer services of the three major Scandinavian lines on the other. This "Grand Solution," as *The London Times* saw it, nicely balanced the technical requirements of containerization, the need to maintain some competition and alternate services for those not able or wishing to use containers, and the interests of the many participating lines.[11]

A quite different model has developed in the North Atlantic, where conferences have never been as strong as those in trade from Europe to Australia and the Far East. The trade is also larger and more widely dispersed over a larger number of ports than is the Australian trade, and sea transport constitutes a smaller fraction of total distribution costs. Most important, the possibility of cooperation is inhibited by the variety of vessel types offered by participating firms and by the sheer number of companies offering container services: three consortia (of which two are of multinational composition) operating 24 container and roll-on vessels, an additional half dozen companies operating about 50 LASH and container ships on their own account, and a dozen others offering pallet and breakbulk services.

Despite some concern that the established conference rate structures were inappropriate to this new mode, the North Atlantic container ship operators (including SeaLand) initially all maintained their conference memberships. Rather than seeking to restructure the trade, effort was directed principally to working within the existing system to gain more favorable terms for containers vis-à-vis conventional breakbulk service. Modest success in this effort yielded a plethora of special rules and discounts, which helped encourage container traffic but which also tended to make the conference agreements unwieldy and more difficult to enforce.[12]

Concluding that this patchwork approach was inadequate, the eight major container ship operators in August 1969 filed a proposal with the Federal Maritime Commission for a new agreement designed to provide a uniform framework for all container ship operations between U.S. North Atlantic ports and Europe—a range theretofore covered by eight conferences.[13] In transmitting the proposed agreement, the attorney for the participating lines emphasized the need to coordinate operations over a larger geographic area and to establish more uniform terms and conditions suitable to the practices of the new container trades.[14] The agreement, pursuant to U.S. law, was to be open to all applicants; it was silent regarding the anticipated future of existing conferences but did provide for regional rate-making committees, which were pledged to recognize the natural advantages of competing ports.

In U.S. trades interline agreements must be approved by the Federal Maritime Commission before they can be implemented and the proposed super conference of North Atlantic Lines was met by immediate opposition from certain of the smaller lines and ports and from the Anti-Trust Division of the U.S. Department of Justice. As of September 1971, the proposal was still pending before the Commission. Meanwhile, two of its sponsors had withdrawn their conference memberships and such discipline as had prevailed under the old agreements was being badly eroded. But in contrast to the U.K.-Australian service, for which rates were increased by fifteen percent in 1970 to help cover the heavy new capital costs of AECS operators, rates in the North Atlantic have been reduced on most container shipments.[15]

Container trades from the U.S. to the Far East appear also to be developing in a competitive pattern despite the strong desire of the Japanese to stabilize the business and allow a more measured pace to container investment. The difficulty in designing grand solutions to the trans-Pacific trades lies partially in the strong position already enjoyed by the American Lines and partially in the political geography of the area. Most Europe to the Far East services also involve port calls in several nations, and in these trades too the possibilities for organizing a fully rationalized service appear likely to be frustrated by the diversity of national interests involved, and the sheer complexity of the problem.

The competitive thrust of leading container ship operators is reinforced by the strong competitive interests of major ports. In container systems, access to efficient terminal and inland distribution systems is crucial to commercial success, since the onshore portion of the operation both represents the major portion of through shipment costs and is the component within which effective performance is most visible to the customer. Relatively modest modifications in truck and rail services have been required to support international container shipments, but major investments have been required at the port gateways. A fully-developed container berth, including cargo distribution and consolidation centers, staging areas, and handling gear, may involve a cost of up to $10 million.[16] Adequate port facilities, as the British Shippers' Council has pointed out, can encourage competition among container carriers,[17] on the other hand, construction of specialized container facilities without firm leases from shipping lines can cause large losses to a port.

Anticipating that their commercial future was at stake, ports have made heavy investments—probably well over half a billion dollars worldwide—in their bid to capture container cargoes. The number of ports entering the race, particularly in Great Britain and on the European continent, generally is considered in excess of that which would be economically justified and their facilities are more extensive than is required to support existing trade. This overcapacity has created a rigorous competition among ports to attract new shipping services and to stimulate rail, trucking and barge lines feeding in cargoes to upgrade services and offer favorable rates.[18]

The ease with which containers can be transshipped has revived the 18th century concept of an entrepot port where cargoes are assembled from a wide area for shipment to their final overseas destination. A fully rationalized system might be built around perhaps eight to ten such points around the world. In fact, there are three times this number of ports vying for the entrepot role, each one of which is a terminus for one or two major services. Particularly in the Far East, the many different routings of new and planned container services tend to complicate planning and encourage competition both by making it less attractive to ship operators to pool their resources in a single system and by increasing the options open to shippers.[19]

In summary, introduction of containers has evoked a variety of competitive responses. This reflects both the diversity of the industry and the diversity of the environment in which it operates. In this respect, the container has not altered the basically uneasy balance between collaboration and competition which has always existed in liner shipping, but only changed the scale. The volume of cargo necessary to support competitive services has moved upward, but, with the flexibility of routings which the container shipper enjoys, the size of markets has moved upward as well.[20] Indeed, from the shipowner's viewpoint, the relevant market may be the entire world.

As has been stressed throughout this chapter, both competitive forces and the logic of the system appear to be moving the industry toward a small number of operators with worldwide interests supplemented by regional carriers on particular routes. These few operators are potentially vulnerable to competition from other modes of sea and air transport as well as to the breakdown of such arrangements as they may be able to develop among themselves. If this be a proper forecast, public policy should be aimed at encouraging the process of merger and consolidation in order to facilitate the growth of a few strong competitors with widespread interests. At the same time, it should seek to develop the means for assuring that these firms maintain their independent power in ways which are compatible with international commercial interests.[21]

Pricing Policies

Pricing issues are closely linked to competitive questions and, like the conference structure, are being reshaped through the introduction of containers. The

McKinsey study and many others have forecast that shipment of goods via containers will lead in time to adoption of a cost-based rate (also referred to as an FAK, or "freight all kinds" rate to denote that the charge is based solely on the dimensions of the box rather than the classes of commodities inside it). Deep sea operators, on the other hand, stoutly defend the use of commodity differentiated rates (demand pricing) which have been carried forward from the liner conferences.[22] However, they also acknowledge the need to simplify tariff structures, if only to facilitate bringing documentation and billing systems under computer control. Thus, the OCL/ACT group did seize the occasion of launching its new service to Australia to revise and simplify tariffs, and cut the number of freight classifications (in bound and outbound) from over 300 to only 75. Rates quoted for these broader classifications continue to reflect fully the differences in values of the commodities included in each. Pricing in other words continues to be geared basically to what the traffic will bear.

Container ship operators have an even stronger incentive than conventional liner companies to adopt demand-based pricing. For them, fixed costs may represent 90 percent or more of the cost of service, once the ship is committed to the voyage. Furthermore, with the amount of capacity becoming available, container ship operators have to use a value-rated scale to attract cargoes which might otherwise be shipped via conventional liners or tramps at rates substantially below that which they could quote on an average cost (or FAK) basis.

Yet, the container companies are also faced with the fact that their cargo can be considered simply to be a box, and can be handled like a box by any ship wanting to take the business. Hence a demand-based rate system exposes the container companies to the risk that other, low cost carriers might move in to "skim the cream" of high value containerized cargoes by offering an FAK, per container rate.[23] The only defense available to the container lines against such competition is to win customers through a superior service and then to compel their exclusive patronage through a dual rate, loyalty contract. The success of this strategy is likely to depend on a strong conference to assure that the same terms are observed by all liner companies serving the trade. This condition has been lacking in the North Atlantic and the container ship operators in this region now speak openly of shifting their vessels into an FAK or contract operation if better discipline cannot be established. Furthermore, for high value goods the potential spread between a class-rated tariff and an FAK rate is so great that it is uncertain whether there is really any way in which existing tariffs can be fully protected.

On short sea routes, container ship operators already have been forced to abandon demand-based pricing in favor of FAK.[24] During a short period in 1966-67, at the insistence of the British Shippers' Council, deep sea operators also received containers which had been consolidated by freight forwarders on a flat rate basis.[25] Most operators still impose a per container minimum charge, but one which falls substantially below the normal tariff and which becomes relevant, therefore, chiefly for containers containing less than full loads.[26] Any one, or all, of these three deviations from demand pricing could conceivably expand to a more dominant position.

The competitive position of freight forwarders vis-à-vis the large container operators is of particular interest. SeaLand's key commercial strategy, copied by other major container lines has been to market a through transportation service in order both to capitalize on the unique advantages of container shipment and to build their cargo base through direct sales of services to shippers. At least for large shipments, forwarders and agents have been superceded by this strategy. In the U.S., major forwarders have responded by buying into shipping firms and vice versa; in Europe, the freight forwarders historically have been a more dominant force and have sought to maintain their independence by concentrating on service to small and medium-sized shippers.

European forwarders are well organized and collectively control a large block of business—informally estimated to be in the range of 50 to 60 percent of all liner-type cargoes. It is not beyond the realm of possibility that they could shift their container business to chartered ships if the container lines continue to refuse to carry these cargoes on an FAK basis.[27]

Pressure for an FAK rate also may develop with expansion of intermodal services. Shippers and forwarders can now obtain a flat, per container charge from railroads (in the U.S., the so-called Plan III trailer-on-flat car arrangement), contract truckers, barge operators, and short sea shipping services. In time, they will demand the same arrangement from transoceanic carriers.

Air competition provides another factor which must be considered in pricing container ship services. Air freight rates are differentiated by commodity class, but the number of classes is much smaller than pertains at sea, and the rate spread is much more modest. Furthermore, both container ships and certificated air cargo carriers face competition from air freighters operated on contract, which can offer an attractive price to shippers able to arrange full aircraft loads.

Finally, the container ship company must consider possible loss of customers to contract sea carriers. A few large shippers provide the core for most container operations, just as they have for most liner services. Rates set too high can also encourage large container shippers to make their own transportation arrangements, even at some loss of the efficiencies inherent in a large integrated container system.

Steamship conferences always have had to deal with difficult pricing questions, and their durability demonstrates their ability to find some basis for accommodation amongst their members. The past few years and those immediately ahead, however, have exposed and will continue to expose the conferences to new orders of complexity in trying to devise pricing formulae. The formulae they must now devise must be satisfactory to a much more varied membership (pallet, container, breakbulk, roll-on, and so forth), effective in staving off competition, responsive to pressures from ports, understandable to shippers, susceptible to adjustments necessitated by automation, and appropriately related to rate structures on alternative routes and offered by alternative transport modes.

Some have suggested that governments should get into the steamship rate-making business.[28] Lord help them! Given the number of tariffs which now apply, it is intellectually impossible to derive a wholly rational set of rates which also will reflect the competitive realities of the container age. Matters as complex and competitively sensitive as this simply are not suited to the normal governmental process.

In fact tariff classification structures have become more complicated than can be handled efficiently even by the steamship conferences and major efforts being made both in the U.S. and Europe to consolidate classifications and mesh tariff classes with standard classifications used also for statistical reporting.[29] This is a long, tedious task. Ironically, success by shipping managements in their aim to simplify tariffs may make it possible also for governments to do what has in a practical sense been impossible for them heretofore: i.e., effectively to oversee the reasonableness of steamship rates.

Through Transport Systems and Services

Both the gains and the difficulties accruing from governmental participation in the technical aspects of transport management are amply illustrated in reference to through transport systems and trade facilitation.[30] The problems are both regulatory and commercial.

Nature of the Through Transport Problem

Everyone concerned with transportation—shippers, carriers, forwarders, and government agencies—has long shared the objective of achieving through services in international trade. Containers could make this objective a reality, but their advent has simply highlighted the gap between the possible and the actual situation.

The gap has a variety of dimensions. One might be termed a "credibility gap." Trade journals are replete with the advertised claims of shipping and forwarding companies claiming to offer complete, intermodal service. These same companies are amongst those most vocal in their assertions that banking practices, government regulations, and insurance rules make such service impossible.

A second dimension might be called a "confidence gap." Many observers feel that the real barrier to intermodal transportation is the struggle between land and water carriers, terminal operators, and forwarders for control. With each sector suspicious of the others' objectives, collaborative action to overcome institutional impediments has been extremely difficult.

Third, there is a performance gap for some sectors of the transportation industry, which simply have not given intermodal movements the priority necessary to encourage this category of shipments.

Another gap is in statistics, because there are very few hard data to describe cargo origins and destinations, or how transportation between them actually is achieved. The statistical problem also reflects a real problem—i.e., the number of handling operations which accompany most movements of goods.[31] Lacking good statistical benchmarks, it is impossible to say to what extent containerization has already eliminated handling costs preceding arrival of cargo at the quay and whether so-called through shipment under a single bill of lading will yield significant additional economies.[32]

Amongst government agencies there are jurisdictional gaps (and, in the U.S., jurisdictional overlaps as well). And finally, there are real gaps, as in principles for settling claims on cargo damaged while in a sealed container which was handled by several carriers while in transit.

The many dimensions of intermodal transport make it difficult to appraise the extent to which through shipments actually are impeded by such problems. Both commercial practice and government regulations have, to be sure, reflected a concept that land and sea transport are fundamentally different. Thus, U.S. law continues to discourage common ownership of multiple transport modes; abroad there are fewer legal constraints but public ownership policies, as applied to rail and water transport, have the same effect.[33] Similarly, while through service tariffs may now be filed with the U.S. regulatory agencies, the statutory requirement upon the Federal Maritime Commission to assure that rates do not unduly discriminate among shippers, ports, and shipowners has caused the Commission to insist upon a division of the rate into its sea and land components.[34] Some observers regard such rules as evidences of institutional lag which seriously inhibit implementation of rational transport services. Others conclude that such rules are needed to maintain fair competition among carriers and, by protecting competition, indirectly stimulate development of cooperative arrangements between modes.

A survey of 500 major shippers recently was completed by the Maritime Research Board of the U.S. National Academy of Sciences. Of this group, only 8 percent reported having experienced *significant* legal impediments to intermodal transport. Interestingly, replies ranged from an assertion that "there is no intermodal transportation service" to assertions that no problems at all are encountered in arranging intermodal shipments.[35]

Service Arrangements

In practice, a host of techniques are being used by carriers and forwarders to coordinate the land and sea components of through transport. The efficiency and economy of these arrangements are widely (and properly) regarded as the keys to competitive success. Thus, this phase of the transport process can confidently be predicted to be the focus for much more attention over the next several years.

Virtually all transoceanic shipments require some overland transport and most liner companies accept responsibility for moving cargoes at least from the terminal warehouse to the quay and aboard ship.[36] With containerization the terminal from which shipments originate may now be located 1,000 miles from the coast and may be operated by a shipping line, a carloading firm, a forwarder, a rail or truck company, or a government agency.

Great Britain has to date organized the most formal system for consolidating container cargoes, but other nations may find it advantageous to follow suit. The British system revolves around six inland clearance depots (container bases). These are privately operated but must be available on a nondiscriminatory basis to all ships and lines as a condition to customs facilities being maintained on location. The ocean carrier will either pick up and deliver cargoes at the shipper's premises or take custody at the depot, where he issues a through bill of lading.[37] Similar arrangements have been developed in Australia and are being promoted by the joint British/Continental consortium, Atlantic Container Line, in its North Atlantic service.[38]

American operators have taken a different tack. Following SeaLand's lead, they have sought to work out interchange agreements with rail lines and truckers operating within their service areas and to advise shippers on rates and routings available to convey their cargoes to the piers. For the most part, the American container lines have resisted formalization of internal cargo consolidation and routing arrangements, and have been cautious in assuming the responsibilities (and exposure to regulatory difficulties) associated with issuance of a through bill of lading. As the leading advocate of this point of view, SeaLand Service argues that the variety of rates and routings is so great that the shipper and carrier need complete flexibility to work out the most advantageous package on a case by case basis. SeaLand also expresses concern that, were joint or single factor rates for overseas transport from inland points to be listed in the official tariffs, they would then come within the scope of liner conference rules and have to be agreed upon by all concerned.[39]

The conferences have recognized the threat to their authority posed by individual negotiations between their members and shippers for through transportation services. Some have reacted by trying to limit the sales activities of their members to port-to-port services.[40] Others have adopted the alternative approach of seeking to develop common rate standards for service in inland points.[41] This latter approach, incidentally, will be mandatory for conferences embracing operators of barge-carrying vessels, virtually all of those cargoes are expected to be delivered to up-river points, if any real discipline is to be maintained over the rate quotations of their members.

A third line of approach to the problem of coordinating transoceanic intermodal movements is to authorize a third party both to handle arrangements and to assume all responsibilities associated with the shipment. Certain European freight forwarders have undertaken to perform such services for some time. In the U.S., the system has been formalized through certification of Non-Vessel-Operating Common Carriers (NVOCC's) which are authorized to issue through bills of lading for multimodal transportation they arrange via their own carriers or via carriers not owned by them.[42] The NVOCC enjoys a very flexible role in packaging through transportation services on behalf of shippers but, except to the extent that it can make special arrangements outside the framework of the regular common carrier and steamship conference systems, it lacks any independent rate setting power. In effect, most NVOCC's are carloading or forwarding services, which have extended their offerings, usually at a fee, to assume full responsibility for all phases of the shipments they arrange.

A few NVOCC's have been established by carriers as subsidiaries to arrange through bookings as a supplement to their usual port-to-port services. Such vertical corporate integration is a fourth response to the problems and opportunities for intermodal movement. For years, the Canadian Pacific and Canadian National Railways were considered to be the world's only fully integrated intermodal transportation services. They have recently been joined by a half dozen others (Overseas Container Lines, American Export Isbrandtsen, the Coast Lines, and Furness Withy), which control and/or operate trucking firms, carloading companies, and inland terminals and warehousing services. As yet none of these companies has been able to fashion its diverse components into a true, internationally recognized through-transport service.[43] Given the extraordinary scale and diversity of intermodal operations, and the fact that each mode remains subject to separate regulatory frameworks, vertical integration through mergers and acquisitions may not be a sufficient or even an efficient strategy for offering an improved intermodal service.[44] Even large, diversified, multimodal transport companies are unlikely to be able to offer the full range of services which their shippers require; having a stake in land transport could prove a disadvantage if it complicates reaching cooperative agreements with other truck and rail firms. Yet direct ownership of land services may also offer shipping companies opportunities to improve services, cut costs, and develop direct sales link with their customers.

Trade Facilitation

Successful development of international intermodal transportation will require a high degree of governmental cooperation to facilitate meeting customs and documentation requirements. Within Western Europe, North America, and Japan good progress is being made in these matters. For example, sealed containers can now be forwarded directly to consignees subject only to a declaration and sample inspection upon delivery. Through cooperation between the U.S. and the Economic Commission for Europe, a standard format for listing shipping information has been adopted which will be accepted for most inland surface transportation as well as for overseas shipment. Efforts are underway to better coordinate legal regimes applying to land, sea, and air shipments and, through adoption of a Combined Transport Convention (CTM), to fill gaps in the responsibilities of carriers of shipments being handled by several modes.[4][5]

To date the less-developed nations have not been actively involved in these efforts, and their governments have a tendency to be suspicious of their intent. Unfortunately, customs and documentation formalities in many of the l.d.c.'s are unduly cumbersome and vulnerable to being used for private gain. Through UNCTAD, however, the less-developed nations are beginning to give some organized attention to their trade formalities. Progress in these matters is likely to be an important influence on the willingness of shipping companies to extend modern container services to these nations.

Progress in simplifying intermodal documentation also will be necessary to save the shipping industry from being overwhelmed by the kind of back office snarl which has plagued the securities industry. With the introduction of 25-knot ships and 24-hour turnarounds, goods can now move faster, and sometimes at less expense, than the accompanying documentation.

The difficulties which have been encountered in the trade facilitation program have illuminated numerous commercial interests and rivalries. Shippers are eager to obtain fully guaranteed through service by a single carrier at a single rate if this can be achieved without sacrificing the opportunity to shop around for more economic transport packages. Each carrier, on the other hand, wants to preserve its own direct relationship with its customers, while carloaders and forwarders are fighting to prevent the carriers from assuming their traditional role.

Intermodal transport is an extraordinarily complex process. Physical compatibility, commercial practice, liability, rate-making, consular procedures, customs and standards of government regulation must all be taken into account. The complexity of the problem tends to work against those companies which seek total solutions in favor of those which adopt a more pragmatic approach to trying to fulfill priority shipper needs. It also encourages reliance on established practice and precedent as the surest and safest way for getting the job done.

It is of interest that, while the shipping lines have been establishing depots and consolidation points in the interior, forwarders have been attempting to extend their activities onto the docks, and railroads have opened cargo solicitation offices overseas. In effect, the several transport modes are increasingly encroaching on each other's turf. Through a wide range of arrangements, they are in many areas offering effective intermodal service. The problem, at least in the U.S., may be as much as one of understanding exactly what can and is being done within existing law as with the law itself.

Survival in Bulk Cargo Trades

Vertical integration of transportation and cargo interests in order to achieve through point to point service has existed for a long time in the bulk cargo trades, and has become even more common with the increasing specialization of ship types and services over the past several years. Although no data are available upon which to base a definitive judgment, industry sources are agreed that the proportion of shipments via vessels controlled by cargo interests is increasing, and that a diminishing role is being played by vessels, particularly general purpose tramps, spot chartered on the open market.

The independent shipowner has not by any means been squeezed out but he is being cast in a new role and faced with new problems, in many cases analogous to those in the general cargo field.

The most obvious development common to all branches of shipping is the trend toward consolidation of ownership and management responsibility. This is proceeding almost as rapidly in the tanker and dry bulk sectors as in the liner component of the industry.[45] The trend toward consolidation in the bulk cargo trades is caused by the same economic factors which lead to consolidation in the general cargo trades: the increasingly capital intensive character of shipping and the consequent need for financing; the quite limited number of very high capacity ships required to service particular markets; and the need for new, highly specialized management skills. The forms of consolidation found in the bulk trades are also similar to those found in the liner trades, including consortia, revenue pooling, joint management agreements, and ownership participations.

In the bulk shipping world, these arrangements are tending to separate the entrepreneural functions of investment and finance from day to day operation and management of the ships. The small shipowner who personally attended to all aspects of his operation still can find a place in the spot charter market. Elsewhere, however, he is increasingly being superseded by a growing class of professional managers who are knowledgeable about ship operations and shipper requirements, but who do not participate as owners or in arranging the finance.

Specialization of bulk carriers, particularly of very large ships, requires their owners to make a careful assessment of the specific markets the ships have been designed to serve. The need for such planning is in sharp contrast to past practice in bulk shipping.[46] Furthermore, the outlook, noted in Chapter 13, is for the 1970s to bring increasing specialization in order to capitalize on the growing sophistication of bulk cargo handling technology. The more specialized the ship and stable the run, the more likely that an industrial producer will decide to provide for his own shipping requirements rather than depend on charters or shipping contracts.

In the tanker trades the present mix of company-owned, time and spot chartered vessels appears to be grounded on reasonably stable underlying conditions.[47] In the dry bulk trades, the outlook for independent owners is less clear. Rapidly growing cargo tonnages and new cargo handling technology could encourage certain iron ore and coal shippers to acquire company-owned fleets. Bulk products companies also are likely to become increasingly alert to the importance of transportation to their overall operations and ways in which transportation functions can be better integrated with other phases of their production planning. Over the next several years, independent bulk carrier owners also expect the Japanese to curtail their present massive call on the charter market. Some progress may be made by the U.S. in carrying forward plans to develop a bulk cargo fleet.

Independent bulk carrier owners also may face increasing competition from industrial owners of bulk cargo fleets. Kaiser Aluminum, for example, has announced plans to expand its already strong base of operations in the Pacific to offer a full range of trading services, including finance, shipping, terminaling and inbound freight and delivery service. Several oil companies have added OBO tonnage to their company-owned fleets, which will cater to the dry cargo market in the event that a surplus develops in tankers. The British Steel Corporation, though moving its ore supplies wholly on ships under long-term charter, has taken a large minority interest in the ships.

On the other hand, many cargo interests have come to know and value the ingenuity of the shipping community in designing transportation systems suited to their trade; sheer technical virtuosity is an important element to a contract shipowner's survival. Also the number of participants in many of the raw products industries relative to the size of cargo flows offers a distinct advantage to utilizing specialized ships on an "as needed" basis rather than becoming committed to a wholly-owned fleet.

The same factors which are drawing the major industrials into more intimate involvement in bulk cargo shipping may be expected to attract the interest of governments as well. Shipowners are probably in a better position to buffer potential nationalistic pressures than companies whose investment is committed ashore. Yet, if a less developed nation can establish the likelihood of a predictable raw material export flow, it may be strongly induced to take direct action to grasp hold of this business on behalf of a nationally owned, chartered, or syndicated ship.

Finally, bulk carrier operators face the prospect of sharply increased public interest in the technical aspects of their operations—ship safety, the efficiency of officers and crew, insurance coverage, and so forth—in order to protect against oil spills, underway pollution, and other hazards. Such technical regulation usually acquires economic and competitive undercurrents. For example, the major underwriters' fear of navigational risks already has brought action raising insurance premiums for older ships which was regarded as unwarranted and discriminatory by their owners. In general, financially sound, stable, and technically competent operators will gain from regulatory pressures to upgrade the safety of marine operations; fringe operators and those unable to command good technical help will be relatively disadvantaged.

The Management Challenge

By any standard the transformation occurring in international shipping is impressive. Translated into personal terms, it has created a panorama of electrifying experiences; youthful managers catapulted into the presidencies of hoary old companies, other established personalities as rapidly let out, ex-truck drivers and fur merchants outperforming experienced shipping professionals in organizing new services, and whole companies bought and sold over breakfast. Such has been the pace suddenly imposed on an industry, most of whose firms, up to a few years ago, still bore the marks of their original founders. Nor does any relief from this explosion lie ahead. All told, what has been described in this book boils down to an imposing challenge to management.

The business of management of course is to cope with uncertainty, respond to new circumstances, and be able to plan for and implement change. It is a business, however, for which many executive personnel have proved poorly prepared. The scope of the transformation in shipping, furthermore, has propelled its management staff into wholly new fields of endeavour—systems analysis, computer control, and raw materials handling to name a few—and forced them to shift their basic orientation from ships and cargoes to product distribution and transportation services. Large rewards have been earned by those managements which responded successfully to the challenge and heavy penalties by those which did not.

The industry has undoubtedly been strengthened by the shake-out and will be better able in the decade ahead to build and consolidate its role. Yet, as shipping organizations grow larger, they will demand still higher orders of executive ability. And in some cases the character of executive leadership will need to be adjusted in order successfully to shift from a period of innovation and expansion to one of more competitive and cost-conscious operation.

For the most part the challenge to shipping management in the 1970s is a piece with the challenge faced by all industrial organization.

There is a basic requirement, first, for professional competence in a variety of technical fields. The shipping industry in the past has relied heavily on on-the-job training to bring its personnel up in the traditions of the industry. For the years ahead, this kind of training may be counter productive. The need is for new skills and improved knowledge of commercial, industrial, and public affairs beyond the immediate bounds of the industry's activity. The requirement for a broader management base, indeed, may be one of the principal factors forcing consolidation in the industry.

Second, the industry will require new emphasis on and techniques for selling its services. In both the general and bulk cargo fields, the added options available to shippers demand that the shipping company be prepared to take the initiative in demonstrating that it can provide superior transportation service and to see that the service is in fact provided when a contract is secured.

A third need is a capacity for planning under conditions, in most arms of the business, of extreme uncertainty. A nice balance is required here in both procedure and attitude. Together with good luck, the fortunes in shipping are the product of astute and nimble reflexes of well-informed individuals equipped to size up risks and take them. More than most industries, successful shipping management requires an extraordinarily broad grasp of the commercial and political environment within which the business is conducted. A good intelligence network to provide the basis for quick tactical decisions is as important in the bulk trades as more fundamental economic analysis to guide capital investment.[48]

Fourth, shipping managers in the seventies will require a thoroughly international orientation. We have argued throughout this volume that shipping companies which are oriented solely to national trades or tied to government support programs will lack the scope and flexibility to step ahead in the face of the hurricane of competition on the international scale. The comparative experience of the internally versus externally oriented U.S. flag lines over the past five years most vividly demonstrates the point, but the same pattern may be observed in Britain, Japan, France or a dozen other situations.

Finally, shipping managers will require a sensitive appreciation of the valid interests of the clienteles which they serve, including both shippers and the public at large. Self-discipline and reasonable means for accommodation to other interests will be essential to protect the industry from political action to obtain more favorable terms of trade.

It is self-evident that as an industry becomes more capital extensive, management skill becomes the most crucial element in a company's performance. The more advanced sectors of shipping are now amongst the most capital intensive industries of the world. Yet it should be recognized that in this chapter attention has been focused on developments occurring at the industry's leading edge. As of this date, more than 40 percent of the world's ship tonnage is still more than ten years old, and a heavy component of conventional shipping operations can be expected to be maintained throughout the decade. Whether the managers of these fleets, which include American, British, and Greek tramp owners and the majority of the liner companies from the less-developed world, can update their operating methods and mobilize the capital needed for modernization will largely determine whether this portion of the industry can survive over the longer term.

Concluding Remarks: New Dimensions in Sea Transport

The foregoing chapters have described developments in both trade and transport which are radically reshaping both the deep-sea shipping industry and the setting for its operations. International trade and shipping are becoming geographically more diffuse, the range of cargoes to be handled more varied, and the pattern of shipments more unstable as more and more raw material sources are discovered, and as the pace of industrial development quickens around the world. Companies which heretofore have been able to think in terms of a single region or product being forced to expand their own base of operations or merge with other firms. Comparative advantage based on natural endowments has for virtually all commodities been overtaken by the development of substitutes for which price competition is possible on a world-wide scale.

Rather than simply providing a vehicle by which goods available only, say in Australia, can be moved to Great Britain to satisfy a relatively inelastic demand, shipping is entering a period in which—like land transport—it becomes one of many variable elements in the costs of offering goods for sale. Australian wool competes with petrochemically-derived synthetics from Connecticut. Indirectly, in serving British mills, container carriers from Australia are in competition with chemical tankers from the U.S. And both are under pressure from producers to improve service and lower costs in an economy which extends to shippers a much wider range of possible markets, production technologies, and locations for their plants than has previously been the case.

We have argued in this study that the internationalization of the world economy has gained an irreversible momentum. Shipping is caught in the tide. As an UNCTAD study points out, there is no point in a nation such as Liberia trying to exercise the leverage which it may enjoy as the host country for large-scale mining operations to insist on nationally owned shipping arrangements if such arrangements are not acceptable to the purchasers of her ores.[1] And since markets change, the transport requirements may also change in a manner which simply could not be handled by a small country maintaining a small fleet. The shipping world of the seventies will definitely favor those owners whose organizations are both sufficiently large and flexible to be able to move quickly to capitalize on new trade opportunities as they develop anywhere in the world. It will deal harshly with companies which have allowed themselves to become captive to ponderous government bureaucracies or specialized to a particular trade, because no specific trade, however stable it may appear, is beyond being swept away in the accelerating pace of international competition.

The dynamism of the international trading scene presents a particularly difficult dilemma for the less developed states. During the fifties and early sixties these countries had focused their maritime ambitions toward gaining a place among the conference lines. By the time they had gained acceptance, the action had shifted elsewhere: to container shipping and the bulk cargo trades.[2] The organization, technical skills, and capital requirements for participating in these sectors of the shipping industry are simply out of reach of the LDC's in the absence of massive external aid.

The 1970s are unlikely to solve this problem. Indeed, the quickening rate of technological change is widening the gap between the have and have not nations. This outlook holds particularly portentous implications for shipping, since the less-developed nations continue to be involved (either as shipper or receiver) in about two-thirds of the world's dry cargo shipping measured in terms of tonnage moving in international trade.[3] The pressures which they may bring to bear to protect the position of less efficient national flag fleets will significantly influence the rate at which new investment will be made by the industry's more advanced components.

The rapid pace of development in shipping has the effect also of yielding a great diversity of shipping services, geared to different operating methods and reflecting very different patterns of factor costs. The prospect that some nations may try to protect continued operation of outmoded fleets rather than surrendering the business to better financed and more efficient competitors is only part of the story. The vast difference in labor costs in the developed and less-developed parts of the world clearly provides less incentive to the latter to invest in a new, automated seagoing plant. Good conventional ships, pushed off the main trunk routes, are likely to be available for operation at close to scrap prices. Also technology is offering a greatly enlarged range of ship designs—containers, LASH, pallet-loaded, and so forth. The novelty of these equipments will require a period of experimentation by operators to determine which ship types may be employed most profitably in which trades.

Institutional arrangements will need to reflect this diversity as well as the very different interests of nations participating in shipping and trade. Liner conferences will no longer be the almost exclusive conveyors of general cargos nor will chartered tramps be the dominant handlers of vessel lots. Tramps and conferences will continue in the picture through the 1970s to be sure. But increasingly they will be overshadowed by consortia of container carriers competing to establish global transport networks in order to secure their position in trade; by versatile all-purpose vessels poised to capture the important business of the paper manufacturers, coffee growers, steel companies, and freight forwarders able to assemble container shipments in vessel lots; by minibulk carriers and barge operators; and by generously financed industrials seeking new outlets for their capital and markets in which to employ OBO's and ore ships surplus to their immediate needs.

Part IV:
Issues for Public Policy

Introduction to Part IV

Merchant shipping is too vital a part of the world commercial scene for any trading nation to be indifferent to the metamorphosis which the industry is now experiencing. The stresses and strains within the industry as it adapts to new technology inevitably command the attention of governments, as the various parties in interest search for means to cope with new and unfamiliar situations. Governments themselves are of course also part and parcel of the transition, both as sponsors of national flag shipping and as the instruments through which the ground rules for economic enterprise are established.

The issues for international shipping policies in the 1970s however run to more fundamental questions than simply finding a basis for accommodating the changing patterns of maritime trades. It is not just shipping, but the entire span of international trade and business practice which is in flux. Internationally, as well as on the national scene, social and political considerations are increasingly accepted as legitimate and often over-riding aspects of economic policy. The goal of providing equal opportunity and full employment at home is mirrored internationally by a commitment to accelerate the growth of developing nations and stimulate their industry and trade. The shipping business, like most other enterprises, is to some degree being swept along by forces which lie beyond its immediate ken or control.

Questions of public policy in the field of marine transport reflect these two needs: first, for laws and institutions which will assist the ocean freight industry more effectively to exercise its necessary and important economic role, and second, for means to enlist international shipping in support of broader public goals.

The purposes of this part are to examine the issues which shipping's changing character raise for the international community and to consider alternative means for reconciling divergent interests. The part begins with an analysis of the appropriate objectives for public policy in this area, considering the needs both of the ocean freight industry and its clientele. Chapter 16 assesses the adequacy of a legal framework resting solely on the sovereign powers of independent states for guiding the development of this essentially international industry. Chapter 17 reports how analogous problems are met in international aviation, satellite communications, and fishing. In this book's concluding chapter the author has set forth his own conclusions regarding steps which might be taken in shipping to achieve more efficient, reliable, and equitable international transport services and to overcome some of the uncertainty and dissension which now confound this industry.

15 Policy Alternatives and Goals

In the concluding remarks to Part II, two questions were raised: (1) what framework of public and private institutions will sustain a "healthy, workable" level of competitive enterprise, and (2) how can the requirements for a private, competitive international shipping industry be reconciled with the accompanying need to stimulate the economic development of the disadvantaged nations of the world? It was noted that these questions need to be addressed in the context of the industry's likely future development, and that this development itself may raise further issues.

The outlook for the coming decade, reviewed in Part III, makes clear that long-standing policy issues in shipping are assuming new dimensions and that new issues are emerging as foci of concern. Will the powerful systems attributes of container shipping, for example, lead to conditions requiring these services to be brought under some type of international surveillance and control? Is there any reason to limit the size of shipping firms, their relation to other industrial interests, or their control by other transportation modes? With large scale organization and technological sophistication assuming such importance in deep-sea shipping, what is a proper posture towards enlarged participation in shipping by less-developed states? Is indeed the notion of national flag participation in the industry itself an anachronism and, if so, with what mode of organization may it be replaced?

These are real issues which are currently being debated in various forums throughout the world. It is unlikely that these debates will yield any single set of answers, for judgments vary as do local traditions and conditions. But some decisions can be expected on important shipping questions over the next few years, and those which are reached will shape the industry for years to come.

This chapter is designed to provide a conceptual base for analysis of shipping policy questions by presenting criteria for evaluation of sea transport systems and setting forth the range of alternative approaches to organizing this industry's international activities and governmental relations. The chapter concludes with discussion of the special problems which must be faced in framing an appropriate role in ocean shipping for less-developed nations and with a statement of objectives which might be set for public policy in the light of these and other needs.

Criteria for Sea Transport Systems

The basic role of sea transport services should be as the vehicle for transport of goods moving in international trade. In selected situations the industry, to be sure, may serve other purposes as well: e.g., it may be a source of employment, prestige, or extension of political power. But the commercial role is central. The analysis set forth in this section rests on the hypothesis that, to the maximum possible extent, arrangements for conduct of shipping services must be geared to the industry's central function of carrying goods moving in trade.

In considering the performance of this function, it is useful to think of sea transport in systems terms. Its physical components include ships, terminals, tugs, navigation systems and waterways, warehouses, and connecting land transport links. Its operations affect both production and marketing functions and are dependent upon a great variety of supporting activities—insurance and credit arrangements, forwarding houses and the like—which are closely coupled to the system.

For its smooth operation, the system requires a measure of stability and predictability, and it is chiefly in order to provide such predictability and to protect investments that such arrangements as conferences and shipper associations have developed. These institutional arrangements are themselves key elements of the system. They also provide the principal means through which governments may influence the system's operation.

Although it is popular to talk in terms of "system's optimization," practical questions for public policy inevitably concern the pros and cons of a range of sub-optimum alternatives. Also, it must be recognized that what benefits one part of the industry may be disastrous for another. At best, these trade-offs are made consciously with an eye to their impact on the system as a whole. In as vast and rapidly changing activity as ocean shipping, however, even this may stretch practical capabilities.

Furthermore, the ultimate objectives for an effective system of international sea transport (see Figure 15-1) are qualitative, multi-dimensional, and partially incompatible one to another. (Reliability, for example, almost always costs more money; efficient use of capital, viewed narrowly, is likely to limit the system's adaptability to changing needs.) More important, these objectives raise very difficult problems of definition. In the absence of any better guidelines, what constitutes "adequate," "efficient," and "equitable" service has tended to be resolved in terms of what the system is prepared to provide. Except in the U.S., Australia, India, and South Africa, there has been little or no effort on the part of governments to impose their judgments as to the adequacy of the sea transport serving national trades.

Nor are there any generally accepted objective measures upon which to evaluate the status of sea transport services. From some viewpoints, the industry has been performing remarkably well. Certainly there is no lack of capacity. At

Figure 15-1. Objectives for International Sea Transport.

System should be:	In reference to:
1. Adequate	Capacity, routes, and schedules. Responsiveness to shipper requirements.
2. Economic and efficient	Pricing Investment Operations
3. Equitable (or nondiscriminatory)	Shippers, ports, and nations Ship operators
4. Acceptable	Participants, users, and sponsor governments
5. Adaptable	Changing needs
6. Reliable	Safety, performance and predictability

least during the past decade technological improvements have been made at an astounding rate, which has moderated the rate of inflation in liner shipping rates while the costs for moving most bulk products has actually declined. In fact, except for the brief period in 1970 when Middle East developments sent charter rates skyrocketing, shippers appear to have fared well. The loosening of bonds within the conference system together with a systematic tendency towards over investment throughout the shipping industry have created a buyers' market in most trades.

From other viewpoints there are problems. To shipowners, today's buyers' market suggests a prolonged period of low profits and excess capacity. In the liner sector, these conditions will exacerbate the pressures on conferences and may be expected in some trades to destroy the delicate balance between collaboration and competition which the conferences have achieved. In the bulk trades, persistent overcapacity may force consideration of some sort of rate-setting mechanism to protect over-extended owners from financial ruin.

The lack of any real structure to regulate international shipping permits both an extraordinary diversity and instability in its operations. Thus, the world fleet includes some of the most sophisticated, expensive equipment to be found in any industry and also some of the worst. Ship charter rates remain excessively volatile and port services in many parts of the world are notoriously poor. There are isolated examples of procedures to regulate shipping rates and services which are as thorough and ponderous as are to be found in any industry; yet in most trades there are absolutely no mechanisms to shield either shipowners or the shipping public from potential abuse of monopoly power. Furthermore, rather than being one of the avenues through which developing countries may be brought more fully into the mainstream of the world's economy, the shipping business appears to be regarded by the governments of most such nations to constitute a barrier to their development.

A laissez faire approach to shipping policy has served reasonably well in years past. However, there is concern that it will not be adequate to guide the operation of the highly integrated shipping systems expected to develop during the decade lying ahead. The concerns are entirely pragmatic: specialization and consolidation within the industry will tend to increase shippers' vulnerability to interruption or curtailment of transport services; the economics of containerization may cause some ports of call to be dropped; countries not located on the main service trunklines are likely to find their transportation becoming relatively more expensive; and it will become increasingly important to firms dealing in bulk materials to secure the cooperation of their governments in deepening ports and making other improvements necessary to assure their access to the most economic bulk cargo service.

Such possibilities have sufficient reality to assure that governments in the future will monitor ocean shipping matters more closely than heretofore. The industry's concern (and the concern of many of its clients) is that this interest be expressed in a manner which respects the need both for greater consistency in the overall policy framework within which the industry operates and for greater flexibility in the actual conduct of shipping operations. A common understanding amongst governments of the economic needs and characteristics of the industry is essential to their exercising a positive influence in the industry's affairs. Lacking this common understanding, even well-intentioned actions are likely simply to prove disruptive. With it, even those governments concerned only with immediate gain for their nationals will tend to moderate their actions so as not to undermine the long term health of the shipping serving their trade.

While the criteria set forth in Figure 15-1 do not yield any single set of policies which are appropriate for all circumstances, they can contribute to a more analytic approach to shipping questions. By orienting discussion towards the qualities needed in the system for it effectively to serve international trade, agreed criteria for evaluating the industry's operations can help in resolving the conflicting interests of sovereign states. Such criteria can also establish some outer bounds for public policy: the bidding preferences used to support the aging U.S. flag tramp fleet, for example, appears to fail on any test and fortunately may be phased out.[1] The multiple goals reflected in the criteria also highlight the need for sensitivity and restraint in framing shipping policy and the difficulty of devising operationally useful tests for evaluating a policy's results.

Systems of Economic Control

The objectives selected to guide development of the ocean freight industry must be supported by some system of economic control. Such a system may be based

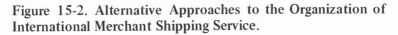

Figure 15-2. Alternative Approaches to the Organization of International Merchant Shipping Service.

totally on decision-making within the private sector or may rely on legal sanctions to shape the industries activities toward specific public goals. In either event, some system is required in order to provide a framework of expectations (regarding such matters as exposure to competition, access to ports and cargoes, and freedom to discontinue or expand services) within which to make business decisions. Even the absence of any explicit policy on these matters can be regarded as a policy of sorts—i.e., that any practice which does not strain public tolerance too far is permissible.

The range of alternative approaches towards establishing a policy framework for international shipping is schematically indicated in Figure 15-2. These alternatives are relatively independent of one another: i.e., highly formal public regulation may be required to maintain competition whereas an administered system may be regulated through rather informal, private controls. In theory, the taxonomy presented in the figure would therefore yield sixteen different policy combinations ranging from the extreme "international public utility" model (formal, international, government administration) to a pure laissez-faire solution (informal, private, international competition). A brief comment regarding each of these variables will highlight the variety of available policy choices.

Competition Vis-à-Vis Administrative Controls

This study has emphasized the importance of competition for sustaining the adaptability and vigor of international shipping. Competition is likely also to be the most acceptable basis for shipping operations.

This is in part because competition offers the only well established, neutral and impersonal means for resolving the multitude of competing interests arising between governments and among private parties in export-import trade and in part because most shippers, as businessmen themselves, are more willing to accept the decisions of other businessmen than of a government regulatory body. Private decision-making within a competitive system also offers unequalled flexibility for meeting customer needs and is, of course, regarded by economists throughout the western world as the preferred means for assuring the adequacy, efficiency, and equity of sea transport services.

The competitive system, however, also has built-in limitations, including its vulnerability to cyclical effects, dependence on good market information, and incapacity for dealing with natural monopolies. A decisive advantage is usually enjoyed by large and established firms and, in the absence of restraints, these companies may tend to collaborate rather than to compete.

Each of these limitations to competition apply also in shipping. However, in evaluating the role of competition in this international industry, five more particularized limitations of the competitive system must be cited:

The first relates to the unequal economic conditions prevailing in the world community at large. The barriers to free trade in goods and services which are found throughout the international economy propagate inequalities in economic capacity, currency values, and working conditions which make the comparative profitability of shipping firms poor indices of their comparative efficiency. To the extent that ship operating costs are tied by national laws to the costs of the domestic economy, the variances in national economic conditions tend to shift the basis for competition in shipping from a commercial contest between firms to a competition between governments.

Fortunately, such intergovernmental competition is muted by the realization that governments, like firms, are also ultimately bound by economics, and that an unchecked subsidy race profits no one. Also governments appear to be loosening the restrictions which they heretofore have placed on the operations of their shipping firms in order to permit them to realize the economies of drawing on a world market for ships, insurance, cargoes, and crews. The disparities in opportunity available to shipowners of different nationalities, previously accepted as normal and inevitable, are consequently gradually being overcome. American shipowners have demonstrated they can operate successfully without subsidy under the U.S. flag. Norwegians with ships built in Japan compete toe to toe with Greeks operating used tonnage built in Norway. Taiwanese obtain capital in London and New York to launch major shipping enterprises that are successful competitors to state supported Indonesian ships, and so forth.

Second, within the broad range of sea transport requirements, there are at least a few in which the economics of the situation clearly require franchising a single "chosen instrument" to handle the trade. Usually these are situations where a certain specialized type of ship must be completely integrated into a larger system—the distribution of military supplies to Arctic areas might be an example. In such cases, the vessel is usually owned by shipper interests; the impact on the overall sea transport picture is minimal.

Third, there are within shipping also many situations in which competition could be supported but in which limited entry holds promise of substantial economies of scale or efficiencies in equipment utilization. In theory, port or shipper interests could in these situations ask for bids from shipping lines for an exclusive concession to handle the trade. In a few instances this procedure has in fact been followed. In the typical case, however, shipper interests are too poorly organized and the lines too well established to comtemplate such a procedure.

Fourth, the absolute dependence of important commercial interests on the reliability and efficiency of ocean freight services is believed by some persons to require some mechanism to moderate the instabilities of competition and to provide for appropriate surveillance of industry practice. Shipowners frequently have demanded such protection as a precondition to making further investments and small shippers have repeatedly expressed a preference for reliable service at predictable and nondiscriminatory rates over the longer term benefits which economists argue might be gained through greater competition. In the real world, businessmen may simply be more comfortable with arrangements providing something less than the economic optimum.

Finally, there are cases in international shipping, as in international air transport, in which sponsor governments to national flag lines are simply unwilling to allow competition to determine flag shares. Fortunately these cases are the exception rather than the rule. At least the pretense of gauging fleet operations to economic and commercial criteria is almost always maintained.

Thus, whereas competition can and should provide the basic mechanism for governing rates and services in international shipping, there will be needs, at least in selective cases, to reinforce or supplement the competitive system with machinery to exercise administrative controls. Also, competition itself must be understood to be a positive objective which requires positive action for its fulfillment. As Gunnar Myrdal has phrased it, "equality of treatment can be equitable only among equals."[2] Maintaining such an environment, as we will note further in the final chapter, requires its own strategy of economic control.

Government Vis-à-Vis Industry Roles

A major objective of emphasizing competition in shipping is to minimize both needs and opportunities for government interference in the business. But achieving conditions in which competition can successfully operate is likely to require an enlargement of the present role of many governments in shipping affairs.

Consideration of the roles properly assumed by government and industry in shipping affairs often is confused by the variety of activities which may be conducted under public sponsorship. For purposes of our discussion here, governmental functions refer only to those concerned with the regulation of foreign affairs, commerce, and public safety and welfare. Governments of course also are frequently directly involved (as shippers and shipowners) in transport operations, but this is usually through some sort of quasi-public corporation which typically has more in common with private enterprise than with the central public functions.

The minimum essential governmental functions in support of international sea transport may be regarded as of three kinds: first, to assure that the infrastructure of facilities and institutions is sufficient to support safe, adequate, and efficient marine operations; second to assure that these operations do not contravene any larger public interest; and third, insofar as possible to protect its nationals engaging in the business from mistreatment or unfair and discriminatory practices on the part of any other government. These basic public functions are well accepted. Although mobilizing the concerted efforts of many governments to deal with the technical, environmental, and legal problems associated with the operations of an international industry such as shipping is a slow and difficult process, it can be done and is being done with increasing frequency and effectiveness.

In domestic affairs, governments typically fulfill a variety of other functions in support of industry and commerce as well. The courts provide a forum for hearing cases, scientific bureaus offer research support and standardization services, public works agencies develop necessary supporting facilities, and legislative regulatory processes assist in defining industry structure and practices. These functions are not well established with reference to international industries. In particular, some minimum framework or international law is a prerequisite for investment in international business operations. National governments share with the industry a common interest in and responsibility for participating in international negotiations to this end.

Realistically, the capabilities of governments to make an independent contribution to the legal regime for international shipping operations are quite limited. The number and skills of the personnel which can be assigned are too scanty and the processes too slow to rely on intergovernmental negotiation to solve the operational problems of the industry in the international sphere. Furthermore, such negotiations are vulnerable to political posturing and must usually reflect principles of representation in the selection of delegates that fail accurately to reflect the real economic interests involved. Given these conditions, it simply is not realistic to look to governments as a vehicle through which an elaborate international system for public regulation of sea transport functions might be enforced.

Recognizing these limitations, major emphasis has been placed both by governments and industry groups on strengthening procedures for self-regulation in shipping.[3] The major effort in this regard has been development of shippers' councils, but over the past decade considerable strengthening has been achieved in shipowner associations as well. These industry organizations have been structured to function at national, regional, and international levels and in some cases have quite well developed procedures for selecting delegates, preparing agenda, hearing cases, and reaching decisions.

The readiness of governments to permit industry groups to exercise regulatory powers depends on how representative such groups are of the interests at stake and on the acceptability of their decisions. Developing nations, for example, have been suspicious of the work of the Comité Maritime Internationale, contending that its membership is drawn principally from the industrialized states. But they have accepted procedures for commercial arbitration which afford reasonable opportunities to both parties to a dispute to present their case to a mutually acceptable board.

Most procedures for self regulation in international shipping are based on organized arrangements for bargaining collectively within a framework of agreed principles.[4] Governments play an important role in promoting arrangements for such consultation. Ordinarily government personnel will not participate directly, but they may be asked to observe shipper/conference negotiations and to mediate particularly obstinate questions. In Australia and India, government agencies are specifically required to approve agreements reached in collective bargaining. Elsewhere, governmental influences are exercised only indirectly.[5]

Despite the emphasis given by UNCTAD, organization of shipper councils has lagged. Councils are now well established throughout western Europe and in the dozen largest trading nations of Asia. Machinery is at least in place within nine leading South American nations. Elsewhere little appears to have been accomplished, suggesting a reasonable measure of satisfaction with the existing commercial arrangements and services offered by conference lines.[6]

National, Regional and International Organization

Unfortunately the ease with which regulatory machine can be organized appears to vary inversely with its ability to cope with important issues. In deep ocean shipping, these issues are essentially supra-national in scope. But the industry's international (i.e., worldwide) organizations are also its most cumbersome and, with respect to economic issues, its most ineffective. Indeed, it is almost certainly a direct reflection of the difficulty of organizing effective international action that there should be so many open questions regarding international shipping policy and competitive practices.

Figure 15-3 lists some of the subjects in which agreements should be developed internationally, if possible, to establish common groundrules for the

Figure 15-3. Targets for International Planning and Coordination.

1. Maintenance of Competition
   preservation of free access to markets
   equalization of tax burdens and subsidy advantage
   formulation of competitive standards*
   suppression of abuses of monopoly power*

2. Improvement of Commercial Practice
   trade facilitation, documentation and customs implication†
   availability of insurance and finance*
   coordination and enlargement of statistical services*
   standardization of commercial law regarding sea transport*
   articulation of ethical standards and business practice*
   non-discrimination among nations, ports, and shippers*

3. Coordination on Technical Matters
   ship safety, traffic separation and control, hazardous cargoes*
   navigation systems*
   waterways maintenance and improvement
   ship and cargo unitization systems standardization*
   tonnage measurement & other matters of a technical nature related to customs
      and taxation†

4. Environmental Protection
   oil spills, tank cleaning, sewage†
   multiple use of coastal waters
   nuclear hazards*

5. Dispute Settlement
   commercial disputes
   local issues bearing on status of waterways and interpretation of international
      conventions*
   expropriations and investment guarantees.

6. Labor Standards
   wages and working conditions*
   training and certification*

7. Development Assistance
   improvement of ports and waterways*
   organization of new, economically justified fleets and services*

*Currently receiving some attention at international level.
**Currently receiving major attention at international level.

industry's operations. Although economic and commercial issues present the greatest challenge, the list includes a heavy representation of technical matters as well.

The obstacles to effective international action in relation to the economic and commercial aspects of shipping are formidable. A very large number of interests of a political and strategic nature, are involved; the questions themselves are inherently complex and relate to a global trade. Furthermore, international collaboration inevitably involves some surrender of national prerogatives, a matter on which we will comment further in Chapter 16.

Nonetheless, international collaboration gradually is coming to be accepted as a necessary response to international business problems, and experience demonstrates that the challenge is not impossible. Agreements have been reached in other fields (the experience in air transport, communications, and fisheries is discussed in Chapter 17), and promising developments are under way within regional groups (notably the EEC) to delegate to supranational bodies economic control responsibilities in such difficult areas as antitrust policy and regulation of land transport. In shipping, there is a well-developed (though perhaps outdated) body of law dealing with rights of innocent passage, ship safety, and carrier's liabilities. Also, the OECD nations have successfully negotiated an agreement to limit shipbuilding credits and subsidies.[7]

In relation to technical matters, the obstacles to international collaboration are of a different genre. Important economic interests may be involved, but these generally do not touch sensitive nerves of national interest. Progress is more a function of the professional manpower resources which can be applied.

The tempo of international attention to the technical aspects of shipping has quickened during recent years. Nonetheless the backlog of needed projects is growing. To improve analysis and planning throughout the industry, priority attention is needed particularly to the improvement of shipping statistics.[8]

The industry shares with governments a common interest in port and waterway improvements. Major gains in investment efficiency would appear within reach through a fuller exchange of planning information in this field. Development assistance through multilateral channels for port and waterway improvements now stands at roughly $15 million per year, with an additional $5 to $10 million provided through bilateral channels.[9] The investments of industrial shippers in the construction of specialized cargo loading facilities in less-developed countries probably exceeds the amount provided through all public channels. Unfortunately, improvement of general cargo facilities, from which several carriers might benefit, is not so easily organized, and many ports in less developed nations remain poorly equipped, congested, and shoal.[10]

The avenues for international planning and collaboration are as varied as the problems to be addressed. Particularly in technical matters, informal consultation through private channels may prove more effective than the ponderous procedures of formal intergovernmental negotiation. Procedures for dispute settlement tend to emphasize informal, ad hoc arrangements rather than judicial processes under international law.[11] The practice which has evolved to harmonize commercial law with respect to technical standardization couples preliminary industry discussion with subsequent review and ratification under the auspices of an intergovernmental group.[12]

Accords do not have to be universally accepted in order to be effective. An agreement strongly supported by a few powerful nations is likely to be more potent than one weakly supported by a larger group. Agreements do, however, need to gain at least the tacit acceptance of all major groups of nations in order to gain the status of international law. In shipping, the suspicion with which the less-developed nations have viewed policies of the traditional maritime states has complicated development of internationally recognized codes.[13]

Consultation and cooperation are more easily achieved among persons sharing common purposes and a common heritage, and when limited to reasonably modes objectives. Particularly in the area of economic and commercial affairs, there may be such formidable obstacles to achieving comprehensive international agreement that more limited regional arrangements provide the only workable vehicle.[14]

As pointed out in Part II, a surprisingly large proportion of international trade is conducted within fairly well-defined regions. This component is growing. Through the UN Economic Commissions and the regional development banks, there also are facilities for organizing regional consultation which can serve a useful role, particularly in the less developed areas of the world. Thus, regional agreements may offer an approach which is both politically realistic and reasonably compatible with the needs of the industry.

National legislation, although often troublesome in reference to international shipping operations, may also have a constructive influence which may extend beyond those activities which fall within its direct control. Thus, proponents of the Federal Maritime Commission have argued that if its program had not been supported by the U.S., some other nation would have had to invent one.[15] In fact, many of the improvements to conference practices which have been achieved within the past decade (e.g., procedures for publication of tariffs and for due notice in adjusting rates) were initially spearheaded by the Commission and despite much grumbling, the conditions established by the Commission for offering preferential rates to shippers entering exclusive patronage agreements have been met by all conferences serving U.S. trades and are gradually spreading to other trades as well.

These more successful elements of the U.S. program are each geared to establishing a framework to preserve opportunities for competition within the conferences and between conference and nonconference lines. In other cases, as when the Federal Maritime Commission has attempted to review specific rates or the shares of trade which should be taken by the participating lines, its machinery has broken down. The lesson of the FMC experience therefore is twofold: first, that the leverage even of the world's most powerful governments to influence the conduct of shipping affairs is limited and is likely to be counter productive if it over-reaches realistic goals; second, that rules and practices which do not discriminate between carriers but are geared solely to assuring them a more equal opportunity to compete may be accepted by a sufficient proportion of the industry to be enforceable on an international scale.

This latter finding is important since it suggests an avenue for framing an international legal regime for shipping which would be consistent with the limited capabilities of governments. Neither the industry nor governments working alone are likely to be able to effect any major improvements in the present, unequal terms of shipping competition. The industry lacks the political clout necessary to overcome flag discrimination or to equalize subsidy aid to national fleets; governments are ill-equipped to cope with the nuts and bolts aspects of commercial practice or to upgrade the ethics of the ocean freight business. However, if the goal of a more competitive open system could win acceptance by a significant portion both of the industry and of the governments interested in shipping affairs, the two groups working in partnership should be able in important ways to reshape and improve the conditions under which shipping operations must be conducted today.

A Role for Less Developed States

A maritime program for the 1970s must take account of the aspirations of the less-developed states both in recognition of their legitimate interests and because the cooperation of third world nations will be necessary for the healthy development of the international ocean freight industry.

Priority objectives of the developing nations include increasing the flow of development capital and expansion of their foreign trade. These are objectives in which the international shipping industry also has stake, inasmuch as the huge, untapped markets and productive potentials of the less-developed lands constitute one of the most promising potential sources for growth in seaborne trade. A number of the industry's more forward-looking lines (for example, in South America, the W.R. Grace Company and the Royal Netherlands Steamship Line and in Africa, the Elder Demster Line) have recognized this stake and have taken an active interest in the development of the foreign trade of the nations which they serve. Other companies which conduct integrated transportation and trading operations have invested large sums in developing raw materials industries overseas.

The stimulus which capital input in primary industrial facilities can give to underdeveloped economies far outweighs the gains which less-developed nations can achieve through greater participation in a service industry such as shipping. The majority of the poorest developing nations have recognized this fact and have been content to rely chiefly on foreign-based lines for transportation services until higher priority needs might be met at home. Other developing countries, which have already achieved a reasonably diversified domestic economy, see fewer opportunities to expand their exports through domestic investment and look to shipping as a means for conserving or earning foreign exchange. There is surprisingly broad agreement that these initiatives also need to be supported insofar as they reflect sound economic planning for development.[17]

There will, of course, be differences of opinion regarding the circumstances which cause investment in shipping to constitute a sound development strategy. Indeed the UNCTAD Shipping Committee has concluded that the variables are so numerous that an evaluation can only be made case by case.[18] The Committee also emphasized that the most important variables, which also are the most difficult to quantify, are those concerning the effect which sponsoring a national flag merchant marine may have on other facets of the developing nation's foreign trade.[19]

It is much more likely that developing countries will benefit from investment in an entirely new services rather than from investment in a service which attempts to compete with (or displace) an existing foreign flag line.[20] Yet, curiously, most liner services of less-developed states operate over routes also served by others. Under such circumstances, the national flag carrier must provide a better service at lower cost than its competitors to benefit the nation's balance of payments.[21]

Local and regional shipping services, on the other hand, can be a quite rewarding investment for a developing country and can typically be managed for less capital outlay than improving transport with rail or roads. Furthermore, success in operating coastal, interisland, and regional cargo services can help build the organization and skills required before attempting to break into the more competitive deep sea trades.

Even the most promotionally minded of the less-developed nations have placed portions of their national flag fleets in domestic and intraregional services. Other nations have gradually equipped themselves to engage in international shipping by participating in those particular facets of the business in which they enjoy a comparative advantage by reason of skills, language, or locale. Foreign nationals are increasingly being used by the European lines as local agents for their business. India and Pakistan have long operated maritime schools to train personnel for service aboard both national and foreign flag ships.

These are significant programs which are consistent with a sound international division of labor. They need to be strengthened and expanded on their own merits and to provide an outlet for the legitimate maritime ambitions of the less-developed states. Over time, they can and have established the broader base of sea-going competence which has allowed nations such as Taiwan, India, Israel and Yugoslavia to become respected competitors in more far-ranging deep sea trades.

For less-developed states seeking to bootstrap their way into fuller participation in the international economy, having access to fully adequate and efficient shipping services is much more important than whether these services are locally owned or owned abroad. A progressive developing nation can attract such services—by contracting with a foreign line, by granting development concessions, or by simply improving its ports. It may also sponsor a national flag line but must avoid policies which would discriminate against competing lines. To quote Myrdal once again:

Underdeveloped countries have too little bargaining power to hope ever to gain much by resorting to monoplistic practices. Their great hope of pushing ahead is in competition. If ever the world political climate again improves sufficiently for the issue of international control over industrial cartels to be fruitfully discussed, the underdeveloped countries should be among the strongest proponents.[22]

From the viewpoint of the less-developed nations, an internationally competitive system of sea transport would have three definite advantages: (1) it would relieve concerns that conference rate structures discriminate against their foreign trade; (2) it would provide a better means for assessing the economic soundness of national investment in shipping and for rewarding those enterprises which are properly conceived and executed; (3) it would eliminate any basis for maintaining cargo reservation systems which in the long run promise to be most deleterious to the developing states.

For the developing nations to achieve an enlarged role in international shipping, they will need capital funds and technical assistance. These are more likely to be more forthcoming if the developing states will renounce protectionist policies (specifically the policy of flag discrimination) which now threaten to drag large segments of international sea transport system into the morass of bilaterally negotiated agreements. The developing nations in turn can hardly be expected to take this action without tangible assurances that their locally organized activities will not be suffocated by established elements of the industry or starved by lack of adequate development aid.

The political realities of the situation are such that the initiatives must probably be taken by the industrialized nations. The maritime interests of Europe, the United States, and Japan should take positive steps to enlist the facilities and personnel of the nations served by their lines wherever possible. This needs to be done in a way which recognizes the equality of both partners to the enterprise, even when this may involve some risk. With proper assurances that discrimination would also be abandoned on the other side, the industry might well take the further step of offering development capital to cooperating governments to permit them to take an equity position in local service and feeder lines.

The gap between the level and less-developed world must be narrowed; governments appear unable to mobilize the resources for the task. Perhaps forward-looking elements of the private sector can point the way.

Objectives for Shipping Policy

In this chapter we have examined some of the main policy options for shipping in terms of international trade requirements and of the special needs of less-developed nations. From both viewpoints, shipping policies geared to preserving open access to the world's cargoes and a reasonable degree of fair competition among deep sea carriers appear preferable to a public utility model as a means for economic control. Although maintaining an equitable environment for competition will require new levels of international cooperation to establish and enforce some basic rules of fair practice, we will argue in the next several chapters that this is more feasible than trying to reconcile competing national interests through any formula for dividing up world trade.

Taking a long view, the competitive model will prove most beneficial also to the industry itself. Shipping is a far more complex and dynamic industry than, say, a water works, an electric power station, or even a fleet of trucks. Systems of direct bilateral or multilateral franchising and regulation of rates and services not only may be expected to block the essential process of technological adaptation and change but, given the highly unstable character of international trade flow, may also expose franchised operators to intolerable oscillations in freight revenues. Particularly now, when the industry is in the throes of shaking down into new patterns of service, it would be disastrous to freeze operations into a particular regulatory mold. Furthermore, the pace of the industry's development, the number of rates, and the variations in service are such as to raise doubt whether any administrative system could be devised to cope rationally with the problem.

Nonetheless, the pressures to curb the effects of competition are too powerful to be ignored. Many governments are making substantial investments in national flag fleets and wish to be sure their vessels get a fair share of the trade; ports are insistent that the use of their facilities not be curtailed; maritime labor, particularly in the high-cost countries, appears to favor government regulation; and the less-developed nations, despite Dr. Myrdal's admonitions, feel their position is stronger in political negotiation than in competition in the commercial sphere. Given these pressures, unqualified acceptance of competition as the means for regulating the provision of shipping services is simply not in the cards. Since the probability of agreement on a comprehensive scheme of a public utility type of regulation is at least equally remote, policy makers will need to continue their search for compromise approaches which will absorb nationalistic pressures and other special interests without undermining the essential opportunity for shipping entrepreneurs to enter or enlarge their share of a trade by offering a better service or a lower rate.

16 Legal Framework for International Shipping: Problems and Issues

One of the principal impulses to the development of nation-states, historians tell us, was the need for a common framework of law for conduct of commerce over an area larger than the local province or duchy. Commerce today has burst beyond the boundaries of nations with a ferocity which has caused one respected research organization to conclude that "under present conditions, the nation-state is becoming obsolete; tomorrow, given anticipated changes in technology, in market distribution, in raw material availability, it will in any meaningful economic sense be dead—and so will the corporation which remains essentially national."[1]

Shipping has operated as an international business for 150 years, but under a carefully developed code of national rights and obligations that depended in the final analysis on the independent power of each sovereign over ships flying its flags. The system worked tolerably well through World War II. But in the postwar years both the methods for conducting business and the role served by the industry have outgrown the older conventions. International maritime law is impotent to deal with tax shelters, convenience registries, and container through-shipments. The international shipping industry appears unable to mobilize the authority of law to curtail unfair competition and unilateral extraterritorial regulation. With respect to international shipping economics and competition as practiced in 1970, there is essentially a vacuum of law.

Lord Rochdale's Committee of Inquiry in 1970 reached the conclusion that "a multilateral inter-governmental agreement on shipping will increasingly be seen as desirable by all concerned with the future efficiency and prosperity of shipping."[2] The Committee noted also that such an agreement can be reached only if a package sufficiently attractive to most maritime nations can be negotiated and that the necessary negotiations may be protracted. In the meantime, shipping companies must do the best they can to develop and operate an international sea transport system under the separate, conflicting and often inadequate laws of independent maritime states.

This chapter begins with a brief exposition of basic principles of maritime law and probes some of the jurisdictional and other problems which flow from its almost wholly national orientation. It then reports the recent effort of the CSG ministers to formulate an international code of conference practice and comments on the problems of framing standards for fair competition in shipping or, alternatively, of formulating any better basis for determining proper national shares.

Legal Responsibilities and their Enforcement

International maritime law is a subject of uncertain content, elusive boundaries and often intangible but far-reaching effects. In shipping, as in other fields of international jurisprudence, there is no single agency empowered either to develop, codify, interpret, or enforce agreed-upon principles of international law and practice.

The chief source of maritime law is the great body of rules of practice concerning freedom of navigation, access to ports, custody of cargoes, and the health, safety, and moral conduct of captain and crew developed over the centuries by individual maritime states, particularly Great Britain. These conventional rules and practices, including agreements regarding access to ports, have to some extent become embodied in a network of bilateral treaties of friendship, commerce and navigation. Considerable progress over the past 100 years has also been made in imparting an international character to these rules through the adoption of international conventions on the law of the sea and through the accretion of a substantial body of international custom and case law. In the last analysis, however, the integrity of maritime law depends on its interpretation and enforcement by the courts of individual nations.

Rights and Obligations of Registering States

The cornerstone to the legal regime of merchant ships is the reciprocal recognition of jurisdiction which states exercise on the high seas over the vessels which fly their flag.

In granting registry, nations assume a responsibility to exercise effective jurisdiction and control in "administrative, social, and technical matters." By implication, they also must see to it that vessels flying their flag respect the various rules regarding the safety of navigation, liabilities for carriage of passengers and cargo, internal discipline, and commercial practice which have been formulated through international consultation or enacted in municipal statutes.[3] In effect, the international community depends upon the responsible action of individual sovereignties to maintain public order on the high seas. As stated by Colombos: "The possession of a nationality is the basis for the intervention and protection by a State; it also is a protection for other States for the redress of wrongs committed by those on board against their nationals."[4]

With the emergence of convenience registries, serious questions were raised by maritime lawyers as to whether the principle that nations are free to establish the terms of registry was compatible with the responsibilities of these nations under international law for the operation of ships flying their flag. The Committee of the International Law Commission which undertook the preparatory work for the 1958 Geneva Convention, for example, concluded that for a state to exercise effective control, (a) it should at least require that a national be retained as captain of any ship registered by it, and (b) the vessel should be owned by nationals or by persons (including corporations) domiciled in the state. The Committee acknowledged that its aim was to harness "runaway ships" by establishing a regime in which vessels would be under the jurisdiction of responsible consular officers in foreign ports and would return to their home ports at regular intervals.[5] However, the Committee stopped short of recommending complete international standardization and enforcement of such registry standards, and the 1958 Geneva Conference, to which it rendered its report, refused to write into its draft Convention on the Law of the High Seas even the guidelines for registry which the Committee had recommended. The Conference settled instead on the vague injunction that there should be a "genuine [but unspecified] link" between the ship and the registering state. This decision, followed by a World Court ruling which recognized Liberia and Panama to be major shipowning nations entitled to representation on the IMCO Council, in effect has legitimized the flag of convenience system and helped open the way to the enormous increase in convenience registries which marked the past decade.

The 1958 Law of the Sea Convention's confirmation of the rights of individual states to establish the terms of registry was, however, accompanied by strong language as to the responsibilities which such states then assumed for the performance of ships under their control. This language was reinforced by the militant interest of the International Federation of Transport Workers in securing more favorable terms of employment aboard PANLIBHON ships. In effect, the owners of these ships were put on notice that their favored position would be tolerated by the international community only so long as they adhered to high, internationally sanctioned standards of safety and financial responsibility. For the most part, they have lived up to this expectation.[6] Many American owners of Liberian vessels have gone even further and voluntarily made formal pledges to their government that they will conform to U.S. regulations regarding the use of their ships and make them available to the United States in a national emergency. These actions have aligned a sufficiently powerful segment of the international community behind the flag of convenience system that the opposition to such arrangements for the time being appears to be effectively defused.

The consequence of these developments is to create a curious admixture in the legal framework for international shipping of complete national autonomy in the formalities of the industry's operation together with a high degree of internationalism in its practice. The convenience registries in many respects approach an international registration, since the rules applying to such registries are probably more influenced by the rules developed by IMCO and the policies of international labor unions and of associations of marine underwriters than by the interests of the nominal host governments. But officially Liberia is a sovereign power, exercising the same authorities as the United Kingdom or

France. Because neither of these latter two governments, nor those of any of the other established maritime powers, have been willing officially to subordinate their own sovereignty in shipping matters to the authority of an international body, it has been necessary for them to recognize the fiction of flags of convenience as a modus vivendi for reconciling the needs of an important segment of this essentially international industry to the political structure of our system of nation states.

With 22 percent of the world's tonnage now operating under convenience flags, it is difficult to see how the use of such registries will ever be suppressed. Nonetheless, the Rochdale Committee has identified curtailment of these registries as one of the necessary elements in a workable code of international maritime law.[7] The more likely development, and one which already is well under way, is that other nations will increasingly be forced by competitive necessity to liberalize their own terms of registry or offer sufficient inducements through subsidy and credit aids to offset the attraction of essentially tax free operations under convenience flags.

Scope of National Authority

Sole reliance on national authorities to regulate international shipping affairs creates a crazy-quilt of jurisdictional questions, which themselves have spawned a large body of international law. The ancient principle that each sovereign should enjoy complete and unchallenged authority within its territory (extended by analogy to include ships flying the flag) constitutes the central theme of this field of jurisprudence, but one which is proving increasingly inadequate to the realities of international shipping operations. With the disappearance of colonial ties, virtually every overseas voyage has come to involve a physical contact with another independent state. More importantly, the voyage involves commercial contacts which create important extraterritorial interests for the trading nations. Finally, both transport and trade now commonly involve still other parties as charterers, operators, cargo owners, and the like, whose participation further complicates the identification of the nation which may properly assume jurisdiction in the event of a legal controversy.

On the high seas, jurisdiction is established by the flag, subject only to the rights of other states to prevent acts clearly destructive of their interests. An international convention, signed in Brussels in 1952, established rules for ascertaining jurisdiction in the event of collision between vessels of different nationalities on the high seas.[8] A companion convention establishes penal jurisdiction for cases involving alleged negligence,[9] while still other rules are enunciated in the 1958 Geneva Convention on the High Seas to spell out situations in which a vessel may be detained or boarded by a foreign power. Although occasional dramatic controversies still occur, it may be said that the law is well established in relation to this category of cases.

In territorial and internal waters, the authority of the registering state is compromised by the concurrent jurisdiction of the adjacent state. A right of innocent passage through territorial waters is guaranteed by the 1958 Geneva Convention on the Territorial Sea and is generally accepted as a universal rule of international law. Free and equal access to ports was guaranteed by a 1923 Convention sponsored by the League of Nations. Unlike innocent passage, this is not an absolute guarantee but one which, under the Convention, may be withdrawn if the nation in which the port is situated has encountered discrimination against its ships or commerce.[10] Furthermore, a vessel entering a foreign port comes under the civil jurisdiction of the host nation and, under another international convention first negotiated in 1926, and updated in 1952, it is subject to detention or seizure if necessary to enforce claims against it.[11] In effect, the control which nations exercise over the commerce passing through their ports is the principal weapon available to them to influence the conduct of international shipping. However, it is one which may precipitate a direct conflict with the registering state.

Extraterritorial Jurisdiction and Conflict of Laws

Conflicts are almost inevitable when states attempt to assert an extraterritorial authority. Such efforts are easily perceived by the affected nations as unjustified meddling in internal affairs and as affronts to their national sovereignty. Yet even the most restrictive interpretation of the territorial principle acknowledges that acts abroad may so threaten the financial or political security of other states as to require an assertion of extraterritorial jurisdiction, and European courts as well as American have undertaken to adjudicate controversies occurring beyond their shores.[12] To the extent that any rule may be said to apply in such cases, it is that the overseas transaction must have "substantial effects" upon the contesting nation in order to be subject to its laws—a test which obviously can be applied only in proportion to the ability of the nation to enforce it.[13]

In shipping, the question of extraterritorial jurisdiction has been a longstanding irritant. For centuries, the kings of England claimed absolute dominion over the seas, and, as recently as 1805, Admiralty regulations required merchantmen to salute her Majesty's warships within waters considered within the imperial domain.

Currently, of course, controversies regarding extraterritorial regulation of shipping swirl principally around the attempts of the U.S. government to control the actions of foreign shipping companies serving its trade. Spokesmen for the United States stoutly maintain its right under international law to take whatever action it may deem necessary to protect its shipping or trade.[14] For the most part, they assert, the U.S. regulation—however distasteful it may be to the individual companies affected—is not inconsistent with any foreign statute and therefore is unambiguously applicable to companies wishing to participate in

U.S. foreign trade. However, the American authorities readily acknowledge the concurrent right of foreign governments to enact statutes to protect *their* interest in mutual trades. They realize that, if such statutes were enacted, implementation of the U.S. program might create a conflict of laws and might place companies caught between the conflicting instructions of opposing sovereignties in an untenable position. This, of course, is exactly the situation which developed in 1964-65 when several European nations enacted legislation prohibiting locally domiciled shipping companies from complying with orders of the Federal Maritime Commission to produce information regarding their tariffs in inbound trades. This effectively frustrated the FMC program, but it also placed the noncomplying conferences in violation of an FMC order and hence in jeopardy of prosecution under U.S. antitrust law. The impasse was eventually resolved by negotiation. The incident demonstrated that unduly offensive action will be met by counteraction costly to all concerned. Its principal lesson, however, is perhaps that assertions of extraterritorial jurisdiction in shipping are less a question of legal principles than of international comity. In fact, the only jurisprudential rules which have been developed to deal with conflicts of overlapping jurisdiction essentially call upon each state to reconsider its position in the light of the other's vital interests.[15]

Other Jurisdictional Issues

The maze of national laws and international conventions regulating shipping contains a host of other gaps and contradictions which complicate the day-to-day operations of the industry. A pervasive problem is establishing the proper jurisdiction for hearing and settlement of cases. The operating arms of the international consortia or container ship operators, for example, are typically incorporated in Bermuda or Holland, whereas the members are domiciled in England, France, Germany, and Scandinavia. Holding companies based in London or New York may fulfill the terms of an affreightment contract using ships registered in Liberia, Norway, and Greece. A collision of a Portuguese vessel under bareboat charter to an Italian operator and commanded by a national of Spain could bring all three nations into the case, depending on the cause of the accident, and so forth. Even where national laws are not directly in conflict, their differing interpretations within the alternative jurisdictions within which the case may be heard may give an advantage to one or another of the parties to the dispute. Establishing a proper venue in such cases can therefore be a critical phase in their adjudication, for which international law provides few guidelines.

Intermodal transport presents a variety of novel questions regarding the responsibilities and liabilities of the various carriers participating in the shipment, and the manner in which their tariffs and bills of lading are to be constructed.[16] Such shipments, spanning several countries as well as several transport modes, are vulnerable to regulation under several different systems of laws, yet realistically none of the various agencies which might claim jurisdiction enjoys sufficiently broad authority to exercise effective control. Even the conferences have encountered difficulty in maintaining rate discipline over rates to inland points offered by their members.[17] Governments, in turn, are forced to recognize that whatever influence they may be able to wield over rates for port to port shipment may in effect be cancelled by arrangements for overland transport abroad to the final destination.[18] Within U.S. foreign trades, regulation of intermodal shipments has been further complicated by the overlapping jurisdictions and differing attitudes of the three independent agencies charged with transport regulation.

The practical limits on governmental authority over shipping are illustrated by the difficulty governments encounter in establishing jurisdiction over the activities of steamship conferences, which are often unincorporated, composed chiefly of foreign flag lines and domiciled abroad. Yet these conferences adopt tariffs, conduct arbitral proceedings, and implement rules in which other parties may have a substantial interest. In order to bring conference activities under legal discipline, the United States has required that each conference agreement approved by it contain an identification of an individual upon whom legal process may be served. However, the conferences typically have few, if any, assets against which a judgment might be enforced and little formal authority in any event over the actions of their membership.

In sum, the conduct of the business of shipping brings into play a plethora of legal and jurisdictional questions which threaten to overwhelm the classic simplicity of traditional legal doctrines. Substantial efforts have been and are continuing to be made both to harmonize national laws bearing on maritime affairs and to work out rules to clarify which nation's laws are to apply to the case. Ad hoc arbitration panels may be composed through mutual agreement of the parties in interest to deal with important cases involving multiple jurisdiction. The dispute settlement mechanisms provided for in most conference agreements provide an additional forum which is adequate for a large number of more routine commercial matters. International negotiations have led to the adoption of many recommended practices as well as formal agreements as to the rules which should apply in such technical areas as ship safety, labor standards, and pollution control. Interpretation and implementation of these agreements, however, remains a matter for individual states. Settlements ultimately depend upon the willingness of the disputants to abide by the decision of an informally selected arbiter, or upon the ability of the government representing one of the parties to the dispute to assert effectively its authority over the case.

Standards for Fair Competition and
Business Practice

The absence of any recognized international legal authority in shipping has particularly inhibited the development of any generally recognized standards for fair competition and business practice. Such standards are in any event exceedingly difficult to translate into law. The difficulty is magnified in shipping both by the inherent complexity of the industry and by the widely different commercial traditions of the many nations participating in it. Yet, within the past several years, some progress has been made in developing some basic ground rules for conference operation and relations between shipowner and shipper interests.

Public attention to competitive practices in shipping was stirred in the early 1960s by the step-up in U.S. regulatory activity following the 1961 reorganization of the Federal Maritime Commission and the formation three years later of the UNCTAD Shipping Committee. The potential threat to the conference system which the Europeans saw in these developments led to a meeting in 1963 of the senior government officials of Europe's major maritime powers. The meeting concluded with adoption of a resolution which affirmed the need for coordination of these governments' policies regarding the commercial aspects of shipping and which recognized their responsibility to assure that conference agreements incorporate appropriate standards of good business practice and provide necessary mechanisms for impartial settlement of disputes.[19]

The work of the ministerial group (now known as the Consultative Shipping Group or CSG and composed of ministers concerned with shipping of twelve major European shipowning countries plus Japan) was quickly followed by development of a memorandum of understanding between the European shipowners and the Councils of European Shippers emphasizing the desire of both groups to continue to work within a self-regulated conference system.[20] Concurrently, a newly organized Committee of European National Shipowner Associations (CENSA, formed in 1963 in response to the Transport Ministers resolutions) developed model clauses dealing with malpractices and adjudicatory machinery to be incorporated in conference agreements.[21] In 1964 the principle of self-regulation through the conference/shipper council system received a further endorsement by the UNCTAD Working Party on Shipping.[22]

As conceived by the UNCTAD staff, satisfactory collective bargaining procedures between shipowners, shippers, ports, and other interested groups must be accompanied by arrangements to assure that agreements are in the national interest as well as in the interest of the direct parties to the agreement. Representatives of the developed nations, on the other hand, have urged that government participation be kept to a minimum "in order to allow the most natural expansion of existing [private] institutions and to avoid the inhibiting effect of cumbersome bureaucracies."[23]

The emphasis of the past six to eight years on self-regulation and consultation as an alternative to public supervision has led to the general acceptance of certain basic regulatory principles for liner shipping. All parties agree on the necessity for publication of tariffs, on the need for due notice prior to making rate changes, on the utility of impartial arbitation machinery, and on the importance of a public accounting of conference activities. However, the understandings developed on these matters have been almost entirely of an informal, voluntary character, and actual implementation in conference practice has not always followed the lofty admonitions of industry groups.[24]

Noting that existing machinery was not fully effective (particularly with respect to disputes regarding admission to conferences) and that many governments were still not convinced that self-regulation would work, the Transport Ministers of the Consultative Shipping Group met again in Tokyo in February 1971, with observers designated by CENSA and the Council of European Shipper Councils to determine what further steps might be taken to reinforce industry efforts to improve business practice. At this meeting, the Ministers concluded that the shipowners within their jurisdiction should be required to formulate a detailed code of fair dealing in conference activities. This code was to apply initially in trades served predominantly by European lines, but it was to be suitable for eventual international adoption. The Ministers proposed that the code be directed in particular to attaining the following objectives:

a. Conferences should publish annually full reports about their activities . . . and include important consulations held with shippers, changes in membership, overall trends in costs, and major changes in services, tariffs and conditions of carriage;

b. Conferences should maintain close contact with shippers with a view to the establishment, strengthening and extension of consultative arrangements on all matters of common concern . . . not ruling out the possibility of independent panels to which commercial issues arising between shippers and shipowners might be referred. They should further ensure that shippers in developing countries have easier access locally to responsible conference representatives with whom to take up questions concerning the trade. As a background to their consultations, conferences should where practicable and appropriate arrange for the preparation on an aggregated basis of a financial analysis designed to indicate the trend of costs and profits.

Bearing in mind differences in regional circumstances, shipowners are asked to consider various possibilities for application of the consultation machinery, with a neutral chairman if requested by one of the parties, such neutral chairman not to be a governmental official or an official of an intergovernmental body;

c. Conferences should refer all unresolved disputes over admission to a separate panel of conciliators;

d. Conferences should adopt and apply the Good Conduct model clauses and machinery for complaint and adjudication recommended by CENSA in 1963 . . . this is particularly important with the development of unit load systems;

e. Conferences should make their tariffs publicly available at reasonable cost.[25]

In advancing these proposals, the Ministers noted that, "while their intention was to avoid in principle any governmental interference in commercial shipping matters, they should nevertheless wish to stress the necessity for shipowners and conferences to comply with the provisions of these decisions and for the code to be functioning satisfactorily."[26] They further stated that their governments would give consideration to supervising implementation of the code of conference practice on a continuing basis (for example, by requiring reports by their shipowners) and to its amendment from time to time as appropriate.

In short, the governments of the major maritime nations have now declared themselves in support of an internationally applicable code to govern competitive practices within conferences and between conferences, ports and shippers. The system which they envision would be highly decentralized and would rely heavily on arbitration by "neutral bodies" designated by the interested parties. However, in time it might be expected that these bodies would seek to rely upon the precedents established by one another's decisions, which would establish the basis for the development of a new field of international commercial law.

Given the context within which the procedures for self-regulation of liner shipping are developing, it may be anticipated that the main thrust of a shipping Code of Fair Practice will be towards more orderly and equitable accommodation of interests within the conference system. In negotiations with conferences, however, shipper groups have strongly asserted their privilege to use nonconference carriers if available on more favorable terms. The gradual strengthening of shipper organizations as a countervailing force to the conferences may be expected to be accompanied by increased interest in maintaining opportunities for competition between shipping lines. Furthermore, the difficulty within the shipper council system of providing adequately for representation of the smaller factors in the trade may cause governments to give more specific attention to their needs. Indirectly, therefore, a system emphasizing collective bargaining between the dominant commercial factors (conferences and major shippers participating in shipper councils) may over the longer term lead to adoption of appropriate restraints on their bargaining powers in order to protect the competitive position also of the smaller factors (nonconference lines, freight forwarders, and small shippers) in the business.

The Problem of National Shares

The evolution of guidelines for competition in shipping is vastly complicated by the strong political interest which attaches to national flag lines. The problem feeds on itself, since the governments' concern usually reflects a conviction that their flag ships are not receiving a fair share of the trades. Government action to redress the supposed discrimination through subsidies or cargo reservations in turn erodes further whatever objective basis may exist for setting a standard. The problem of flag shares arises principally in relation to liner traffic, where competitive mechanisms are not adequate to dispose of it automatically, but it is beginning to be raised in reference to selected bulk commodities as well.

Any nation which is sufficiently determined to expand the scope of its national flag shipping services can find means to channel a substantial portion of its trade to its national flag ships. However, the costs of such action—in money, in trade opportunities, and in international goodwill—may be very large, especially if the objective for national flag participation is set above 30 or 40 percent. As a general proposition, liner traffic must be shared both with the ships of the trading partner and with so-called "third flags"—ships of other nations which service the trade as part of a more far-ranging liner service. There is, however, no international agreement which requires such sharing and certain nations (e.g., Japan, East Germany, and perhaps the USSR) have embarked on programs aimed at capturing substantially more than 50 percent of their total import-export trades.

The stakes of other nations in the business make it unlikely that any country will be able to lift its share in the transport of its import-export trade above 50 percent on the basis of superior service alone. Some sort of economic incentive or administrative directive will almost certainly be required to cause large numbers of shippers to change their routing policies in favor of the national flag. This implies adoption of cargo preferences, which run counter to the objectives of an international regime for shipping as phrased in Article I to the IMCO Convention.[27]

Through the UNCTAD Shipping Committee, certain of the less-developed states have pressed hard for international acceptance of the legitimacy of cargo preferences if necessary to assist their fleets to gain "an increasing and substantial participation in the cargoes generated by their foreign trade." Rebuffed in these efforts, these countries, under Brazil's leadership, argued alternatively in 1969 for international machinery along the lines of the ICAO/IATA air transportation system to oversee shipping services, allocate routes and sailings, and assure that developing countries were not discriminated against by the major maritime states. A proposal to form a working group to examine the feasibility of drafting such a general instrument was placed before the UNCTAD Shipping Committee, but also was rejected.[28]

Although they have been unable to gain international acceptance for any system of publicly determined flag shares, the governments of certain less-developed nations have persisted in efforts to negotiate national flag shares in their export-import trades through bilateral agreements. Brazil has been a leader in this field. During the two years following its abortive efforts to sponsor development of international machinery, it has successfully negotiated an enlarged share for its national flag ships in almost all its overseas foreign trades. This result was achieved primarily through agreement reached between Brazilian interests and their counterpart national flag lines to share reciprocally in cargoes which their governments might reserve for their respective national flags.

Although shipping authorities of the major maritime nations have strongly resisted direct governmental action to fix flag shares, they have tacitly accepted various devices used within the industry to accomplish essentially the same results. Discussion of flag shares is a major concern of most closed conferences. Within the conferences, the apportionment may be direct (through cargo or revenue pooling) or indirect (through allocation of ports and sailing schedules). It may be expressed in terms of fixed quotas or in terms of formulas which have some built-in self-adjusting features to allow expansion of the more efficient lines.[29] There are, of course, some conferences, particularly in the U.S. trades, which do not deal with flag shares at all but which confine their activities solely to harmonization of rates and practices.

Little is known regarding what criteria, if any, the conferences may employ in establishing trade shares. The historical position of the participating lines and the cargo tonnages contributed by each of the trading partners appear to be the most significant factors. Other criteria which may be used are listed in Figure 16-1.

None of these alternatives offers a fully satisfactory means for dividing up a trade. The several criteria are mutually inconsistent and oriented to different ends. For the most part, they escape exact quantification; where quantification is possible (as in reference to cargo volumes), there are options as to what measure is to be used. The extreme difficulty in establishing any objective basis for a fair division of business among national flags is, in fact, one of the strongest arguments for rejecting an oligopolistic system for providing shipping services in favor of a system which allows shares to be established through competition, assuming the competition is fair and equal and that some means can be developed to correct for externally created differences in factor costs.

Figure 16-1. Alternative Criteria for Establishing National Flag Shares.

1. Cargoes generated by the participants in the trade.

2. Present and projected fleet capacity.

3. Historical position of the participating lines.

4. Importance of merchant shipping to the sponsor states.

5. Relative efficiency of the participating lines.

6. Opportunities for specialization (cargo categories and port ranges) among the participating lines.

7. Optimization of sailing schedules and routing.

8. Numerical rules of thumb (40-40-20, etc.).

These qualifications, of course, lie at the heart of the problem. As pointed out in Part II, international financial arrangements do not currently permit relative costs to be used uncritically as a yardstick for the relative efficiency of different national flag operations. A country which has artificially propped its domestic economy and imposed inflated costs on its maritime industries will have difficulty selling a shipping service in international competition, even though the service itself may be efficiently operated. It may be argued that this is simply one of the penalties which such nations must pay—or conversely, that such nations should welcome the opportunities which the world shipping market affords to obtain foreign flag services at less cost than if they undertook to provide the service themselves. But such arguments are likely to be particularly unpersuasive to third world nations that are convinced anyway that they are systematically exploited by European and American-dominated arrangements for international finance and trade.

Pending broad reforms in international economic institutions, problems of flag shares will continue to demand the sensitive and creative attention of governments as well as of leaders within the shipping industry in order to achieve equitable and sensible solutions. Discussion of specific issues is undoubtedly best left to the give and take of private negotiation; governments, however, can provide guidelines to give added credibility to the competitive setting and to recognize legitimate national interests. Such guidelines might include:[30]

a. a right for ships of every nation to participate in the conferences serving its trade, including wayport conferences closely related to the nation's foreign trade;
b. access to "third flags" to pick up and discharge cargoes at intermediate points in connection with a more far-ranging service;
c. acceptance of direct subsidies to shipping in such amounts as may be required to offset competitive disadvantages associated with conditions attached to their flag registry, so long as such aid does not restrict the opportunity for all flags to share on equal terms in the trade;
d. provision for periodic renegotiation of conference agreements in order to accommodate new entrants into the trade and to permit expansion by the more efficient operators;
e. avoidance of cargo quotas and preferences either within conferences or at the governmental level in favor of more flexible techniques, such as partial open-ended revenue pools, coordination of port calls, and capacity limitations where participating lines agree as to the desirability of such arrangements to improve services to shippers;
f. establishment of time limits on any exceptions to these principles which may be permitted to assist the development of infant shipping lines.

It may be hoped that the increasing internationalization of shipping may allay some of the present preoccupation with flag shares. Shipping lines which are largely owned, managed, or manned by overseas interests are unlikely to be able to evoke the active support of their registering governments. Nor are international shipping consortia likely to maintain strong national ties.

As presently organized, vessels operated by the container ship consortia fly the flags of their sponsor lines; participation in these groups has been roughly in proportion to the traffic previously handled. But as the Rochdale Committee has pointed out, this cannot be a static formula. Trade will expand; shares will change; and some accommodation must be found within the consortia to spread the resulting benefits equitably among the members. The Committee suggests that these developments will inevitably cause a more intimate integration of the consortia, if they are to continue to exist at all.[31] Since it will be impossible to make even reasonably exact adjustments in the number of ships operated by each partner, the participation of the members will need to be set on other grounds—perhaps in terms of their subscriptions of capital, cargoes solicited, services furnished, or some combination of these. Dealing with the problem in these more conventional business terms should help to diminish the emotional overtones which are aroused when dealing with flags and ships, and in this way contribute to the resolution of the problem.[32]

Thus, as technology reshapes the organization of international shipping, the familiar problem of national shares may for large sectors of the liner industry be translated into a new and unfamiliar problem of devising means for representing national interests through financial participation in international consortia. Such arrangements should provide for representation of the interests of those less-developed states serviced by the international firms as well as of those of their principal financial sponsors. Within each consortium, the participants might be expected to develop a common interest in maximizing the efficiency of their fleet operations with only secondary regard for the ships' flags. Between consortia, competition on a fair and equal basis should be entirely feasible, since the fleet operations need not be bound by the economic policies of any single national participant.

In sum, if the major operating elements of the merchant shipping industry can successfully achieve a true international personality, one of the industry's most persistently vexing problems should tend to disappear. Other problems, revolving around means to influence and control these new entities, may however be expected to emerge in its place, for there are real divergencies in national interests which no organizational arrangement can reasonably be expected to overcome.

17 Experiences in Related Industries

The problems encountered in international shipping have analogs in many other industries. Collectively, the various institutional arrangements which have been developed by these industries to reconcile diverse public and private interests can yield a very valuable body of exerience and they constitute a rich opportunity for comparative research. Unfortunately, there appear to be no published studies which systematically assess the effectiveness of alternative institutional approaches to international economic regulation: perhaps the field is simply too complex and compartmentalized to permit it. Also, the solutions devised by each industry necessarily reflect circumstances peculiar to the case. A brief report on experiences of other industries can nonetheless provide a useful perspective on the problems faced in shipping. In this chapter, three widely different cases—aviation, satellite communications, and fishing—are briefly analyzed in terms of each industry's special characteristics; its institutional arrangements for determining national shares, rates and services; and its success in meeting economic and political objectives.

International Aviation[1]

Industry Structure and Characteristics

Aviation is an even more politically sensitive industry than shipping. Outside of the United States, a very high proportion of the scheduled carriers are either government owned or government controlled. Also, landings and departures must be made within national boundaries. A basic principle of international air law is that a scheduled air service may be operated over and into the territory of a foreign state only with the permission of that state. International air operations accordingly must be conducted entirely within the terms agreed upon amongst sponsor states.

Other characteristics of the aviation industry also have contributed to an unusually high degreee of public visibility and government involvement. In its early days the industry was strongly promoted by governments as a means of improving postal services. At least up to World War II, commercial aircraft were regarded as having potential military use, and a national flag airline was still valued for its contribution to national prestige. National flag carriers are maintained by eighty-one nations. Over the past two decades the number has been expanding at the rate of three new entries per year.[2]

Aviation shares with marine transport a relatively high proportion of fixed to variable costs. Being tied through international agreement to specified routes, there is perhaps an even stronger incentive in aviation to set rates jointly at levels which will support profitable service. On the other hand, aircraft are smaller and more flexible units than ships, and many economists argue that, were services to be competitively priced, capacity would be brought into better balance with demand.

International air operations, like shipping, show a high variation in operating costs. These variances, however, are less a product of national economic policies than of the firms themselves—their equipment, routes, operating efficiency, and equipment utilization. Large, well capitalized firms appear to enjoy decisive advantages. Thus, in 1965 the industry's four largest firms (Pan Am, BOAC, Air France and TWA) controlled 38 percent of the business.

The relatively small number of firms in the industry (roughly 125 as compared with 300 to 400 liner firms alone) and their concentration on scheduled passenger services have caused international air operations to be relatively susceptible to government oversight and regulation. Yet even here, public bodies have found themselves hard pressed to cope effectively with the plethora of special promotional fares and services. Difficulties also have been encountered in regulating charter flights, air freight, and contract services.

Finally, air safety and the coordination of air navigation systems are major problems in international aviation. Framing regulations concerning them is the principal task of an extensive apparatus of international and regional agencies.

Institutional Arrangements

International air transport regulation is conducted through a combination of bilateral and multilateral mechanisms involving both the carriers and their sponsor governments. The general patterns of their relationships, depicted in Figure 17-1, embrace numerous case to case variations which are built into the terms of specified bilateral intergovernmental agreements. These agreements set out the reciprocal privileges granted by each nation to the carriers of its contracting partners and the procedures by which rates and services are to be regulated and routes fixed.

In negotiating "bilaterals," questions relating to the capacity which may be offered by carriers of the contracting nations and their access to traffic destined for en route or "beyond" points (the so-called fifth freedom traffic) have presented particular difficulties. In general, those countries with large, efficient air fleets have argued for a liberal system, free of capacity limitations in competing for any traffic originating at the points they have been certificated to serve. Smaller countries have resisted such arrangements and have been sensitive in particular to allowing fifth freedom services, which they fear will squeeze out

Figure 17-1. Institutions for Regulation of International Air Operations.

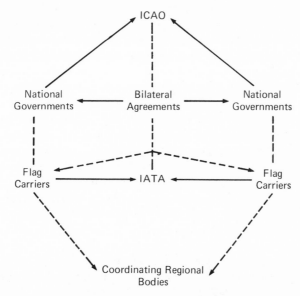

any realistic opportunity to develop their own national lines. In the absence of any general multilateral agreement, which has proved impossible to achieve, these questions have had to be worked out in bilateral negotiation.[3] This procedure has undoubtedly impaired the overall efficiency of the industry by limiting the carriers' flexibility to work out a rational route system. In effect, in international avaiation third flag carriers can operate only if agreement can be reached between three governments; that of the carrier's sponsor nation, the government of the nation where the cargo originates, and that of the nation where it is discharged.

Rates to be charged by international air carriers are required in most bilateral agreements to be approved by the governments of both contracting parties. The 1946 Bermuda Agreement between the U.S. and Great Britain, which has provided a model for any other reciprocal understandings in this field, spells out elaborate procedures for coordinating the actions of the contracting parties and provides, in the event of disputes, that the questions shall be referred to the International Civil Aviation Organization (ICAO) for an advisory report.[4]

In actuality, the process for developing agreement on air rates is infinitely more complex, since rates on different routes involving other carriers and other governments must be properly related to one another. This is achieved through the three regional traffic conferences of the International Air Transport Association (LATA), a private association of 104 of the world's leading international airlines. Agreement within these conferences must be unanimous.

Even such questions as inflight meal services or movies can consume weeks of negotiation.

Once unanimous agreement is reached, however, there is a strong likelihood that the IATA recommendation will be accepted by governments.[5] And despite the ponderous nature of its machinery, in its 25 years of operation IATA has been successful in reaching more than 1000 rate agreements, including specific fares and formulas covering some 150,000 pairs of points in the world network.

Intergovernmental consultation in aviation affairs is conducted through the International Civil Aviation Organization (IACO) which, like IMCO is one of the specialized agencies of the United States. Like IMCO, ICAO is concerned with administrative and technical aspects of the industry's operation. However, ICAO is a substantially larger agency, has been designated to perform a number of operational services, and is empowered to issue binding regulations regarding the airworthiness of aircraft and competence of flight personnel.

Comment

The ICAO/IATA system has husbanded the development of international aviation from its infancy following World War II to the dynamic and largely successful industry it is today. Equipment has been upgraded, new carriers absorbed into the system, and routes extended throughout the world with relatively little controversy. At the same time, the system's rigidity has permitted the growth of some fundamental maladjustments. Overcapacity has been a chronic problem. Also, many observers feel that rates have been held too high and that innovations in rates and services have been unduly inhibited by the rule of unanimity.

The inadequacies of the system appear most vividly in relation to air freight. IATA does not attempt to set individual commodity rates (it reviews only overall levels of tariffs). Nonetheless, coordination of cargo charges presents a substantially more complicated task than that of passenger fares. It involves more complicated cost relationships and more routing factors, and must take into account a great variety of materials and packaging options. Most importantly, there are more competitive alternatives in the cargo business. In fact, some IATA members doubt that the problem should be tackled by IATA at all.

A 1967 report issued by the British Shippers Council (a group generally friendly to the ocean freight conferences) takes a particularly critical position towards the present IATA system on the grounds that it is (1) slow and conservative in reaching tariff decisions, (2) unresponsive to shipper interests, (3) unduly protective of high cost carriers, (4) overly restrictive in its attitudes toward charter arrangements, (5) biased toward stimulating excessively high levels of service, and (6) productive of overcapacity and economic waste.[6] One evidence of the lack of initiative in rate matters cited by the Council is the airlines' reliance principally on cargo weight in setting freight tariffs. The Council suggests that a more flexible system geared both to "what the traffic will bear" and "what the equipment can carry" would stimulate much faster growth in aircargo business.

The shortcomings of the ICAO/IATA system may be traced principally to the insistence of governments on controlling access on a wholly bilateral basis, requirements for government approval of rates, the unanimity rule in IATA, and the excessive formality and privacy of its procedures. On the positive side, the complex machinery of ICAO and IATA does bring questions of essentially international concern to an international forum and protects national governments from becoming directly involved in rate and service negotiations.

International Satellite Communications

Our second example presents a very different set of circumstances, problems, and solutions. In this case, the international community has had the opportunity to design an institutional framework for launching a wholly new enterprise.

The technological requirements for a satellite communications systems are quite straightforward. All that is basically required is a network of ground stations to send and receive communications and a system of satellite relays. However, organizational arrangements were required which could mobilize massive technological and financial resources and accommodate the diverse interests of a large number of governmental and commercial participants. An interim solution was adopted in 1964 which provided for an international consortium (INTELSAT) functioning within policy guidelines established by interested governments and managed through an operating contract with its U.S. signator (COMSAT). This interim arrangement will soon be superceded by Definitive Arrangements which provide more formalized procedures for oversight of INTELSAT's affairs.

Industry Characteristics

The need for special arrangements to manage the international deployment of communications satellites relates chiefly to the technological characteristics of the system itself. Its space segment is a resource in which many nations share an interest and which requires a large, international market to generate the level of use needed to write the large fixed investment. The system's ground components must be coordinated both with the satellite relays and with conventional communications also dictated developing some kind of special mechanism to involve a large number of nations as joint sponsors of this unique effort. Large amounts of capital were required; some means was needed to assure communications companies with large fixed investments in older technologies (cable and microwave) that the introduction of the new system would be handled intelligently. Perhaps most important, the cooperation of these companies, which control the flow of message traffic, was needed to provide a base for the new enterprise. Finally, like sea and air transport, satellite communications represent a service of considerable economic importance to the world community. There is a general interest in assuring that the service is efficient, reasonably priced, and provided on an equitable basis to all users.

Institutional Arrangements

In the early 1960s when these problems were being considered, the United States enjoyed a commanding lead in the development of communications satellite technology. Extended debate had culminated in 1962 with Congress authorizing creation of a unique private corporation (COMSAT) to lead the U.S. effort in this field.[7] The enabling legislation stated that the principal purpose of the new corporation was to "establish, in conjunction and in cooperation with other countries, . . . a commercial communications satellite system, as part of an improved global network, which will be responsive to public needs and national objectives. . . ."[8] It did not spell out in detail how this was to be achieved.

The design of institutional arrangements to fulfill the purposes of the Act therefore was left largely in the hands of the new corporation, working with the Department of State, the Federal Communications Commission, and its private incorporators. A series of draft agreements were developed.

The first, opened for signature by governments in August 1964, established objectives for a global satellite system; provided for designation of a communications firm or agency to sign a supplementary Special Agreement for each signatory country; established an Interim Communications Satellite Committee as INTELSAT's governing body with responsibility to design and operate the space segment of the system; specified the composition and voting rights in the Committee; and provided that financial participation in INTELSAT and ownership of the space segment would be lodged in the signatories to the supplemental Special Agreement.

The second, a supplemental Special Agreement, concurrently opened for signatures, set forth in some detail the ground rules of financial participation in INTELSAT, specified the role to be played by COMSAT as its agent deploying the space segment, and (in a further addendum) provided for arbitral procedures in case of disputes.[9]

Subject to the policies and specific determinations of the Interim Committee, COMSAT has acted since 1964 as Manager for INTELSAT. This management function, together with COMSAT's controlling financial interest in INTELSAT, afforded COMSAT a dominant role in the consortium under the Interim

Arrangements.[10] Nonetheless, seventy-nine nations subscribed to the INTELSAT agreement. The eighteen largest subscribers (some representing groups of nations) took seats on the Interim Committee.

As INTELSAT grew, the desire of its participants to have a greater share in its control and management also increased. This desire constituted the central issue in the recently concluded negotiations of Definitive Arrangements for INTELSAT, which are expected to supersede the Interim Arrangements during 1972. The Definitive Arrangements achieve some dilution of the control of the organization by: (a) providing two new policy organs which will work on the one man, one vote basis, and by (b) limiting the maximum weight which can be given to the vote of one participant in the Board of Governors, where weighted voting will be continued, to a maximum of 40 percent of the total.

Under the Definitive Arrangements, INTELSAT will no longer be a consortium, but, instead, will be an organization with its own legal personality. The responsibility for the Management of INTELSAT under the Definitive Arrangements will eventually be assumed by a Director General. However, until then, management will be divided between a Secretary General responsible for financial and administrative matters and COMSAT responsible for technical and operational management under a six-year contract with INTELSAT.

Figure 17-2. Institutions for Communications Satellite Operations under the Definitive Arrangements.

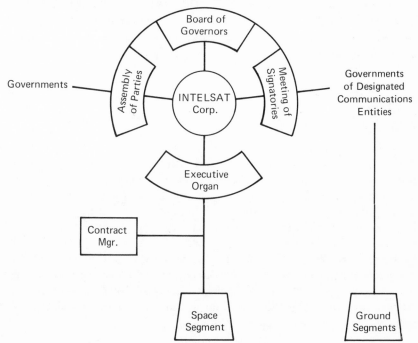

Comment

The INTELSAT consortium represents a wholly new approach to coordinating international economic activity, which was carefully tailored to the particular requirements of the case. By centering very substantial authority and responsibility in one member (COMSAT), the consortium has been successful in fulfilling its technical and operational mission. Its international superstructure under the proposed Definitive Arrangements may prove unwieldy, and those associated with the enterprise are fearful that shifting to a one-man, one-vote system in the governmental Assembly of Parties and in the Meeting of Signatories will undercut the sense of management responsibility which accompanies financial commitment, will exacerbate tensions by providing a forum for raising underlying political issues, and will diminish the effectiveness of the entire venture.

The outcome of the Definitive Arrangements' negotiations illuminates the political pressure to which any intergovernmental enterprise is exposed.[11] To the extent possible, international revenue-producing ventures need to be shielded from direct government participation. Where such participation is necessary, it should be limited to a modest number of like-minded countries who share substantial financial risks. These partners must be willing to delegate operating responsibility to a compact management team and reserve only the long range planning function to themselves.

In container shipping, the present consortia are organized somewhat along these lines. Perhaps the chief lesson of INTELSAT is that the consortium form does not necessarily protect the commercial character of the business if the enterprise is allowed to grow too large or attract an undue amount of governmental attention.

Fishing

Industry Characteristics

The fishing industry presents another very different case. This is an old industry composed of many small units. National identification is strong and fishermen look to their governments to help protect traditional fishing grounds. Although the industry conducts its activities in international waters, operations tend to be localized to particular areas. This permits its regulation to be approached largely through regional agreements.

Although an old industry, fishing also has been caught up in technological change. New equipment permits fleets to range further, locate fish schools more quickly, and harvest them more efficiently. This has brought new entrants into the industry, sharpened the interest of developing nations, and placed severe pressures on established fisheries.

Conservation is the fundamental problem necessitating fisheries regulation. Ineffective conservation regulations can involve large costs both by permitting unnecessary depletion of stock and by forcing fishermen to adopt uneconomic techniques. However, a fully rational approach to fisheries management would also require coming face to face with the problems of coastal state preferences and of national shares. Because governments have, with only one or two exceptions, refused to face up to these issues, major segments of the industry are plagued by a chronic overcapacity which yields an uncertain and usually inadequate return on investment.[1,2]

Institutional Arrangements.

The institutional framework for conduct of international fisheries is a patchwork of inadequately enforced regional conventions supplemented by fragmentary international law. An effort to strengthen the system was advanced in the 1958 Geneva Convention on the Law of the Sea, which prepared a special Convention on Fisheries and Conservation of the Living Resources of the High Seas. This instrument would have authorized a single state whose economic interests appeared threatened by depletion of a fishing stock to force multilateral development of appropriate conservation measures and to take reasonable unilateral action should this effort fail. The Convention itself, however, failed to gain enough adherents to gain a secure position in international law.

The failure of the 1958 Geneva Fisheries Convention throws the burden for fisheries regulation onto regional conventions. These conventions are typically concern with reducing the catch by prohibiting certain types of fishing gear; fixing fishing seasons; specifying allowable overall catch; and restricting age and size of catchable fish. Most of these "accepted" conservation techniques also unnecessarily impair the economic efficiency of the industry.

To carry out the provisions of the agreement, the conventions establish various fishery commissions as administrative agencies. Generally, such an agency's only power is to make recommendations, which must be agreed to by all parties to the agreement before becoming effective. Enforcement of agreements is through the facilities of the signatory states and is difficult even when all the parties are fully committed to the terms of the convention.

Enforcement problems are further aggravated by the fact that not all nations participating in a fishery necessarily are parties to the conservation conventions. There are no regularized procedures in most cases for settlement of disputes. The scientific basis for establishing conservation measures is in many cases inadequate, and the geographic coverage of the conventions may be insufficient to the need.

In sum, most fisheries conventions are quite inadequate even to their limited conservation purpose. In reference to the larger economic problems of the industry, they are almost irrelevant if not counter-productive. Most fisheries typically still are treated as "open ranges." The abundance of the sea is a common property resource available for the taking by whoever can make the catch.

Comments

A laissez-faire approach might have been appropriate to the fishing industry so long as stocks were sufficient to satisfy all comers. Under modern conditions, however, some form of rationing becomes essential.

The fishing case dramatizes both the •need for and the difficulty of establishing an appropriate legal framework for conduct of international economic activity. The conference carrier may argue that his situation is similar to that of the fisherman. If another vessel arrives on the berth before him and depletes the cargo stock, he suffers a loss. Agreements to limit liner sailings have a parallel in agreements to limit fishing efforts.

Considering the economic stakes, it is surprising that cooperation has not developed more fully within the fishing industry. Within the U.S., economic pressure is currently forcing small operators to merge with larger firms or retire from the industry. Large, well organized deep sea operations are being mounted by Russia, the Scandinavian states and Japan. The emergence of a relatively small number of internationally-oriented fishing firms may establish a basis for more rational management of the sea's living resources.

Summary

The one thread which links the three case studies sketched above is a concerted effort on the part of governments to establish a framework for competition within each industry of firms linked to a host of sovereign states. In fishing, the legal framework, such as it is, has evolved slowly in response to felt needs within the industry. In satellite communications, institutional arrangements are the product of conscious and explicit design.

The cases make it clear that there is no one "right" approach to international economic control. Institutional arrangements need to build in a sensible way upon the established practices and needs of the industry. There is little point, for example, in postulating a vastly expanded role for intergovernmental organizations if such organizations will in reality be unable to assume such tasks. It is equally futile, however, to expect that a complex industry with high investment requirements and a critical role in world economic affairs can operate successfully without some organized structure to regulate its affairs. Reaching agreement upon such arrangements is a necessary stage in the development of any large scale industrial endeavor.

18 Approaches to a Workable System

The complicated machinery which has been fashioned to reconcile divergent interests in aviation, communications, and fishing is largely absent in the merchant shipping industry. In shipping, a far more diffuse medley of law, custom, political pressure, and commercial organization modulates the industry's performance and shapes the manner in which individual firms respond to international sea transport needs.

Shipping's reliance upon the more informal mechanisms of liner conferences, freighting contracts, and the various international consultative bodies reflects this industry's very different roots. Until very recently, those controlling the vast preponderance of the world's tonnage have resisted any governmental interference in their affairs. Necessary arrangements to protect investments and to develop new trades could be worked out informally and be made to stick in most cases without overt governmental interference.

This is changing. Shipping men everywhere now recognize the necessity for close collaboration among themselves and with governments in order to maintain favorable conditions for their trades. Yet there is great uncertainty as to where their new collaboration with government may lead and great concern that poorly conceived arrangements may impair the industry's essential flexibility and freedom of maneuver.

Basic differences in philosophy divide the shipping world. These reflect the many different facets of the industry, the conflicting interests of developed versus less-developed nations, and the opposing political traditions and methods of capitalist and socialist countries. No single comprehensive system of public regulation is likely to be able to satisfy these many interests. Yet because shipping is a global enterprise, some core of common approaches is needed to undergird the continued operation and development of a healthy and efficient international sea transport system.

The competitive principle can and should fill this role. Competition has the great advantage as a method of economic control of being a relatively well-accepted and impersonal means for maintaining a workable division of labor amongst nations and between industrial firms. In this field, even the Russians endorse the idea. Allowing competition to regulate the market is probably the only way in which national rivalries can be overcome, and undue interference by governments in regulating rates and services avoided. The maritime industry therefore has a substantial stake in protecting opportunities for fair and equal competition wherever this is possible.

In this concluding chapter, we will summarize some of the main themes of this study by considering steps which are realistically available to policy makers to overcome some of the irritations and inefficiencies of the present legal/political framework for shipping operations by emphasizing the common interests of all nations in an efficient, equitable, and competitive sea transport system.

The Outlook for Shipping Competition

Is it realistic to stake the institutional arrangements for shipping's development during the 1970s on the principles of commercial competition? There are many shipping men and public officials who believe not. Some point to competition's inherent limitations in relation to certain sectors of the industry and argue, for example, that the powerful systems aspects of containerization will create monopoly opportunities for the leading firms. Others consider free entry to shipping markets to be a prescription for chronic overtonnaging and, together with the industry's cyclical characteristics, for enormous economic waste.

The most pervasive concern, however, regarding the adequacy of competition as the fundamental principle for a strengthened legal/political framework for shipping operations relates to the great difficulty of disciplining firms and governments which refuse to abide by the rules of the game, which in turn undermines confidence in the validity of the competitive principle itself as applied to international economic affairs. Thus, we find a high official of the U.S. government at a recent international shipping meeting concluding that his country's shipping companies "are too valuable a national asset to allow them to be victimized through an unrelenting adherence to a slogan or concept such as freedom of the seas."[1]

Together with the less-developed nations, whose abilities to support successful deep-sea shipping operations in today's capital intensive industry are severely limited, there is real danger that the U.S. government may conclude that its shipping firms simply cannot withstand the rigors of the international scene. With its high costs and broad national security responsibilities, the U.S. has at best demonstrated a wavering commitment to liberal shipping policies through the post-war years. In accepting the proposition that subsidies and cargo preferences were essential to its national interests, the U.S. has created a situation in which the greater portion of its shipping industry has become totally dependent upon such aids for its survival.

We have argued previously that the less-developed nations cannot afford to rely on bilateral arrangements as the vehicle for expanding their participation in international shipping.[2] The United States cannot afford this approach either, for it has proved to be self-defeating within the context of the competitive pressures on both its shipping and trade.

In a very real sense, it is as difficult to maintain protected national flag shipping operations in a competitive trading environment as it is to be competitive in shipping if potential cargoes are being diverted into vessels favored by flag preferences.

Surveyed internationally, the great preponderance of world shipping continues to be in the competitive mode. And, though there are countertendencies, this proportion is widening. Thus, we see an increasing variety of materials—including perhaps the ubiquitous box—whose shipment is coming to be arranged through contracts for shipment in vessel lots. Furthermore, technology is offering an ever-greater range of transport options, and in an expanding world economy a wider variety of raw materials sources and markets.

In the liner sector, the weakening position of the "old line" conference is clearly leading to sharper competition amongst both conference and nonconference firms. This is in part simply a function of the rate of change within the industry. In part it reflects the overtonnaged condition of many trades and the competition being encountered by the new container ship companies from other modes.

Those liner and container trades which have been cast firmly into a die of administratively controlled services and markets exist essentially on the periphery of the industry's main stream of operations. Compared to the great and growing trans-Pacific services and services from Europe to the Far East, the sea trades which are limited by national preferences or bilateral agreements are both small and growing relatively slowly.

The trends toward specialization and consolidation of shipping firms, which can be observed in both the bulk and general cargo sectors of the industry, should also tend to enhance competition, even though sharply reducing the number of firms. For these trends to have such an effect, however, they must be viewed in their broadest, international context. In relation to a particular, narrowly-defined bilateral situation, for example, containerization may lead to the total elimination of all direct shipping competition. The same technology, however, creates realistic possibilities for indirect competition from carriers equipped to move container cargoes over other routes and by air. And, within the ocean freight industry, a smaller number of strong, well-financed and expansion-oriented shipping enterprises promise to bring a more dynamic competitive outlook to the industry than has been tolerated in the past by the more numerous lines, each trying to hold onto its small share of the trade.

Specialization can also strengthen competition on an international basis by offering shippers a greater diversity of transport options. Within a single bilaterally-organized trade, traffic may not be sufficient to justify LASH, plus roll-on, plus regular container service. But nations which open their ports freely to the facilities of the entire international shipping industry can look forward to a wealth of opportunities to experiment with new services and routings.

For competition to be a workable basis for organization of shipping, it must be allowed to operate over a broad, multinational market; conversely, to be able to look with confidence to the shipping industry for adequate, efficient, and equitably-priced sea transport services, the international community must be able to rely on an effectively functioning competitive mechanism. In this situation, the two concepts—internationality and competition—are highly inter-dependent.

The increasing internationality of the ocean freight industry—and of the entire system for commodity production and distribution throughout most of the world, as well—provides a basis for optimism that international transport can be developed in the competitive mode. In the industry's most advanced sectors, leading companies and consortia are shedding their national flag identification. With ships, crews, management, and marketing organizations drawn from whatever nation can perform each part of the job most effectively, these international transport operations are in a position to compete on a fully equal basis with one another. Their customers, which increasingly are companies maintaining facilities throughout the world, are in a position to insist upon such competition.

Programs to Support a Competitive System

Building a competitive system in shipping is an objective which requires positive action and its own strategy of economic control. This strategy needs to embrace at least the following elements: means to assure shipper choices among alternative transport services, means to maintain approximate parity in the economic opportunity among the suppliers of these services, international agreement regarding standards of business practice, preservation of independent action among competing firms, and of course free access by all shipping companies to cargoes throughout the world. A brief comment on each is in order.

Diversity of Transport Services

Maintaining a diversity of shipper options does not imply that multiple services need be offered on every route; the traffic in many cases simply is not sufficient to support it. However, potential competitors must be allowed access to port facilities and shippers must be free to use their services without fear of undue economic reprisal.[3] Also, a sufficiently large number of independent entities should offer container services all over the world to make competitive quotations (perhaps through shipping via different routes) a realistic possibility.

New technology has added significantly to the range of shipper choices and should be encouraged. Thus, lighters from LASH vessels offer an efficient alternative to shippers in backwater ports which heretofore may have been confined to a monthly call. The new fleet of 3,500 dwt., minibulk carriers being built by Livanos will provide economical alternatives to shipping commodities via conference liners.

Port development policies are a second means through which governments can influence service patterns and encourage diversity. For example, some overcapacity in berths may be justified to preserve competitive sailings, and shipper options can be expanded by providing up-to-date facilities for break-bulk, tramp, pallet, and ro-ro operators as well as full container ships. Port dues and pier leases need to be geared to real costs and administered in a manner which assures equal access to all comers.

Third, governments might promote competition by subsidizing the operation of nonconference lines in the shipping serving their trade. Several authors have advocated this policy, but despite its apparent practicality, it has not been adopted on any significant scale. The obstacles are several: (1) wherever the conferences are sufficiently powerful and arbitrary in their traffic policies to be a source of real concern to the nations which they serve, they are also powerful enough to make organization of a nonconference competitor a hazardous and expansive undertaking: (2) whereas the costs of supporting a nonconference line are tangible and substantial, the benefits are intangible and largely confined to those engaged in foreign trade; as a result, public enthusiasm for such a project is likely to wane before its purposes can be accomplished; and (3) both governments and shipping managements generally have preferred to work through the conferences to achieve rates favorable to their trade rather than to buck the tide through rate competition. None of these factors, however, suggests that governments or their client shipping lines need give the conferences their unqualified support. The threat to withdraw from the conference is an effective weapon, as is the suggestion that major shippers (including government agencies controlling significant volumes of import-export trade) may shift their business to other modes.

A fourth means for supporting diversity and competition is the provision of marketing information regarding the rates, capacities, and sailings of irregular carriers, and also regarding the cargoes offered by shippers. There currently are no general clearinghouses for such information, and, in most parts of the world, tramps make only very modest efforts to publicize their sailings or to secure "topping off" package cargoes. With the industry shifting increasingly toward the use of affreightment contracts (under which the shipowner retains operational control over the scheduling and deployment of his vessel) in lieu of voyage charters (which limit opportunities to take on extra loads), more aggressive marketing by irregular carriers would appear to hold significant potential for diversifying options available to small and middle-sized shippers and forwarders.

Fifth, governments can encourage diversity through restraint in the promulgation of mandatory technical standards. Even the best intentioned and soundly based standardization programs, if made mandatory, can have deleterious long term effects. The container standards imbroglio provides a classic case. A mandatory international standard would have facilitated container interchange and allowed significant economies of scale. But such action would also have penalized some of the most efficient operators then in the trade and inhibited adaptations of container shipping to changing situations and to the varying conditions of different parts of the world.

Finally, diversity requires mobility in the deployment of shipping services. It is in reference to this need that government-to-government bilateral shipping agreements are most damaging. Such agreements segment markets, narrow opportunities for competition, and tend to spawn further bilateralization of shipping services. Hence, we have argued in this study that flag preferences are neither necessary in nor compatible with a properly functioning sea transport system.

Equality of Opportunity

Avoiding discriminatory measures is, of course, the sine qua non for maintaining parity of economic opportunities. This is an obligation which lies particularly heavily on established firms, since their position in the market may itself be argued to be discriminatory against new companies attempting to enter a trade.

Senior shipping officials of the major maritime countries have recognized that steps to assist in the organization of new sea transport services by the less-developed states can, when done according to sound economic criteria, be a positive factor for enhancing shipping competition.[4] Development assistance in such cases can both help to deflect potential tendencies within the less-developed world to promote national flag shipping through other, less acceptable means, and help to create broader support within international bodies for a liberal shipping policy. A more active program by the international development banks to assist nations pledging to develop national flag shipping in a manner consistent with overall industry interests would be a particularly effective way to promote competition in shipping.

Economic conditions vary so greatly around the world that this competition can never be entirely "equal." Indeed, even within domestic industries, studies have revealed an extraordinary spread in the costs of doing business between the most and least efficient firms and in the quality of their products. While a complicating factor, variances in costs do not of themselves make competition infeasible. Furthermore, granting the presence of practical barriers to any direct action to offset national differences in ship operating costs, there are nonetheless certain policies through which nations can cooperate to bring about greater equality indirectly.[5] For example, nations domiciling profitable companies should be expected to take a larger tax than those with unprofitable operations under their flag. Interest rates on ship mortgages might be adjusted to reflect anticipated operating costs or alternatively these cost factors might be considered when establishing the time period over which new equipment is allowed, for tax purposes, to be written down. Also, national laws regarding such matters as manning tables, safety standards, and insurance may be brought more closely into line both through international collaboration or action by individual nations to examine national maritime legislation in order to be sure that there are real reasons from the viewpoint of national policy for any significant departure from the international norm.

Standardization of ship operating and registry conditions would of course be most effective if brought under a single code of international law. The major elements of such a code have, in fact, already been put in place through the work of the technical committees of IMCO, the Comité Maritime Internationale, and the ship classification societies. Although the political ramifications would be far-reaching, it would not be a large step administratively to require that all ships be licensed by an International Shipping Authority after a determination that they met these technical standards and would be operated in conformance with an international shipping code.[6] This license would supplement the usual national registry. Its introduction would both establish minimum standards for the industry throughout the world, and provide a benchmark against which any special national requirements set forth in national legislation might be assessed. As noted later in this chapter, a licensing procedure also might provide the revenue basis for expanded internationally organized services to shipping and for qualifying shipowners to receive such existing services as insurance and vessel classification.

In effect, an international licensing procedure already exists today through the facilities of the Liberian Government. What is required is only a more explicit recognition of the international character of the convenience registries and more thorough and comprehensive inspection of the flag of convenience ships to be sure that they do indeed meet the standards which have been set.[7]

Standards of Business Practice

Through negotiations in UNCTAD, CENSA, and the Consultative Shipping Group, considerable progress has been made over the past several years in developing a common understanding regarding conference practices and relations with shippers.[8] This work needs to be extended to embrace standards for fair competition amongst shipping firms (and between conferences and independent lines), principles for container shipping, and procedures for monitoring on a continuing basis the operations of the system as a whole.[9]

The U.S. Federal Maritime Commission, supported by the Department of State, is one of the few official bodies which has attempted to deal seriously with this latter group of questions, and its efforts have been marred by the largely national orientation of its work. Thus, the SeaLand-U.S. Lines merger has been evaluated chiefly in reference to its impact on other U.S. flag lines rather than its impact on the structure of the international shipping industry, which includes several firms larger than SeaLand and U.S. Lines combined. Similarly, the long debate over the structure of shipping services and role of third flags in the U.S.-Brazil trade was necessarily focused chiefly on U.S. interests, including its desire to assist Brazilian development and to support competition in shipping.[10] The Maritime Commission has, however, developed some legal standards regarding unfair pricing policies and service requirements which might serve as models for broader application.

Anti-Monopoly Rules

Perhaps the most sensitive and contentious aspect of the U.S. Maritime Commission program has related to its effort to place bounds on the monopoly powers of shipping firms and conferences. The difficulties have reflected both deep-seated differences in viewpoints over the role of competition in the liner trades and scepticism that a public agency can, in even the best of circumstances, successfully monitor competitive relationships among business firms.

Looking ahead, the potential cartelization of container shipping looms as a far more difficult problem than regulation of shipping conferences. If a consortium of cooperating lines, such as has emerged in the Europe to Australia run, is able to saturate an entire trade, who is to say whether it has effectively monopolized the business or, for that matter, whether such a monopoly is detrimental to the region's foreign commerce?

A Free Market in Ships and Cargo

From an international perspective, the fact that a monopoly situation may develop in a particular trade needs to be of general concern only if such situations are sufficiently prevalent as to undermine the dynamism of the overall market in ships and cargoes. Thus, international shipping has been able to retain its basically competitive character, despite the presence of grossly discriminatory practices in some trades. Where such practices have appeared, the firms previously competing for the business have been able to relocate or to liquidate their operations on at least somewhat acceptable terms. The damage created by flag discrimination to date, therefore, has been perhaps greater to the countries which have denied themselves the services of the international shipping industry than to the industry itself.

Flag discrimination and bilateralism, however, have a multiplier effect. If any substantial portion of the ocean freight market should come under such terms, there could easily be a sudden burst of bilateral arrangements as other nations react to the potential loss of adequate trade connections with the affected region by themselves agreeing to a bilaterally-negotiated service. It is this kind of domino effect which is most feared by those seeking to preserve competition in shipping by maintaining the broadest possible market in ships and services.

Implementation of International Shipping Policy

To establish a more effective legal/political framework for international shipping, the general principles outlined above will need to be translated into a specific code of shipping practices. This step in turn must be followed by formation of appropriate machinery to monitor the industry's operations, arbitrate disputes, and develop new policies to adapt to changing conditions.

An International Shipping Code

Consideration of shipping problems at both the national and international levels has for many years been inhibited by the absence of clear statements on basic principles. The most positive result of the work of the UNCTAD Shipping Committee, the U.S. regulatory program, and similar efforts elsewhere, is that they have raised and forced serious discussion of some real issues, the existence of which had previously only grudgingly been acknowledged. This discussion has developed a sufficiently strong and widely-held conviction regarding the inadequacy of present arrangements as to establish the basis for acting on a more explicit set of principles to govern the industry's future operations.

The official initiative of the Consultative Shipping Group to lay out a set of principles for world consideration has been an important second step towards adoption of a meaningful shipping code. These principles are to be debated by the UNCTAD Shipping Committee in its sixth session in April 1972. If agreement can be reached within this committee, a basis will have been established for more formal action—perhaps an international convention or congress—to adopt a statement of principles and to consider means for overseeing their application in shipping operations.[11]

If nothing else, the adoption of a statement of principles can help to clarify future discussion of shipping questions by providing a single reference point and defining terms. Such a statement should be helpful also in giving some identity and expression to the interests of *international* shipping as an industry which is to some degree separate from and greater than the sum of its component parts. Finally, a statement of principles would help to upgrade business practice and protect conforming operators from unwarranted criticism.

Institutional Apparatus

To be effective, any international agreements regarding standards for shipping competition will need to be accompanied by agreement on mechanisms for their interpretation in the light of changing conditions. Competition is an elusive concept. Even within the U.S., where antitrust law has been developed and refined over a period of seventy-five years, standards for measuring workable competition are highly flexible, varying from industry to industry as well as from time to time.

For a complex international industry such as shipping, it will almost certainly be advisable to provide maximum flexibility in administrative arrangements: (1) by emphasizing self-regulation wherever possible, (2) by relying chiefly on case law progressively to refine and interpret the industry code of practice, and (3) by setting up appropriate arbitration and review machinery at national and regional levels as well as at the level of international organization.

Specialized arbitration machinery to deal with shipping issues would have many advantages which should gain it the support of the parties in interest. Properly organized, it should be able to provide a faster, more expert, and reliable interpretation of the applicable principles of international law; it would provide a central facility for publishing relevant findings and codifying cases; it would promise greater consistency in decisions; and it would provide an avenue for overcoming the present questions of proper jurisdiction.[12]

Arbitration machinery might be of two types: one, sponsored by the industry itself and charged with hearing disputes amongst shipping companies and the second, sponsored by an appropriate intergovernmental group to hear cases involving shipper interests or governments. In the first case, enforcement of judgments might be arranged entirely through private channels. Informal mediation may also be possible in intergovernmental disputes but arbitration generally is not fruitful if the issues relate to matters of national policy.

Some sort of International Shipping Review Board should therefore be organized in parallel to privately sponsored arbitration machinery in order to provide a forum for considering matters of broader industry concern. This Board, for example, might be the instrument for surveillance of subsidies and preferences to national flag shipping. Although the Review Board would have no direct authority, it could review and comment upon national shipping policies insofar as they affect international interests and, in concert with other international agencies, consult with the interested parties to work out arrangements for terminating objectionable practices.[13]

Reporting and fact-finding procedures analogous to what are being suggested here for shipping have for many years been built into the GATT and International Monetary Fund machinery. They recognize that, realistically, a workable system must be broad enough to tolerate a variety of different approaches including unilateral preferences and bilaterally negotiated arrangements in selected situations. Exceptions to an international code's general competitive objectives, however, should be subject to justification and scrutiny.

As a policy body, the Shipping Review Board should also give continuing consideration to the overall efficiency of the international shipping industry and to the need for additional legislation at the national and international levels. The Board might assist also in organizing regional approaches to shipping problems both in terms of assisting interested shipping, shipper, and governmental interests to form the Regional Coordinating Committees mentioned later in this chapter and in cooperating itself with the World Bank and the various regional development banks in assisting protected national flag fleets to become more competitive. Thus, in addition to its quasi-judicial and policy roles, the Board might also exercise a more pragmatic, problem-solving function.

So influential a body as the Shipping Review Board sketched above would clearly need to be very carefully formed. It could not be too large without blunting its effectiveness, yet it should also be broadly representative. It should enjoy a professional detachment and authenticity in its work but cannot become mired in legal procedure. Although visualized as a public agency (in order to facilitate ties with other agencies within the UN and World Bank groups), it should be oriented chiefly to dealing with economic problems. In designing its structure, particular attention will be needed to devising appointment procedures which will yield a membership committed to reaching solutions to the industry's problems and will shield the members from undue political pressures. The Board's success or failure will depend more upon stature and quality of its personnel than upon the details of its organization.

A third element needed at the international level is an administrative agency, which might be built around the existing Intergovernmental Maritime Consultative Organization:

1. to standardize statistical reporting systems, and to collect and analyze data as necessary to understand and report on the overall operation of the world sea transport system;
2. to promote and coordinate introduction of improved navigational systems and canal and harbor projects, and to provide for operation of multinational technical systems;
3. to continue and expand on the technical work of IMCO to assure ship safety, environmental protection, and proper indemnity against losses;
4. to provide administrative support to the Shipping Review Board;
5. to sponsor appropriate arbitration bodies to consider more specific competitive and operating problems.

An International Maritime Authority charged with the foregoing functions will require firmer financial underpinnings and somewhat geater autonomy from its sponsor governments than now is enjoyed by IMCO. Financing might therefore be partially through the UN and partially through a small licensing fee on ships and/or shipping companies supporting its activities and benefiting from its services.[13]

International organizations can deal effectively only with that core of common principles which should apply more or less uniformly across the entire industry. Specific rate and service arrangements should not come under their jurisdiction, but should be worked out regionally.[14] Appropriate Regional Coordinating Committees, organized to respond to both governmental and commercial interests, should therefore assume a key role in developing intra-regional trades and may serve also as the vehicle for negotiating service arrangements for shipping between regions. Particularly for container shipping, a regional approach appears to be a practical necessity as well as a means for improving prospects for intraregional cooperation.

Consider, for example, the problems involved in organizing container service between Europe and the Caribbean. The service cannot possibly be justified unless cargoes originating within several countries at both termini can be brought into the system; within the Caribbean, a feeder network would probably be required to funnel cargoes into one or two main container ports. Any oversight by the Caribbean governments of rates and services would almost certainly have to be through a single regional body to be acceptable to the carrier, and any financial participation by the Caribbean states in the enterprise would have to be similarly coordinated. It might be noted that the area currently does not enjoy long haul container service because it has not been able to develop this degree of cooperation.

To take another example, services to the U.S. and Europe from the East Coast of South America are at present separately negotiated with Brazil, Uruguay, and Argentina, and they suffer seriously as a result of these nations' narrow bilateral approach. The scale economies of high-volume container shipping can be realized fully only if the entire area can be brought within a single service or pattern of coordinated services (as from Europe to Australia and New Zealand). National rivalries amongst the American nations have to date prevented this development. The consequences have been particularly serious for the smallest of the three countries, Uruguay.

The principal hazard of a regional approach to shipping regulation is that it might provide impetus to formation of competing blocs of shipowner nations. If a few basic standards can be developed for comprehensive application, however, such competition could have a healthy effect upon the industry. While the long term outlook for the Peruvian National Line for example, is not encouraging, there is no reason why a consortium of Latin lines should not become a force in the container trades. The competition of such a consortium would stimulate traffic from the area with the development of port facilities. Furthermore, it would establish a more progressive situation than would be likely to develop if a hopelessly outclassed national flag company operating obsolete vessels were left the sole competitor of an advanced containership or LASH service.

Enforcing International Responsibility

For any regulatory system to be workable, the majority of affected interests must want to make it work. This principle is valid at both the national and international level. The greater difficulties encountered in enforcing conformance to international law reflect the diversity of interests and lack of traditions of voluntary compliance rather than lack of formal sanctions. As more and more economic activity is brought under international surveillance, voluntary acceptance of procedures for international oversight of shipping policy should gradually increase.[15]

Cooperation will be gained more quickly if effective sanctions can be brought to bear against those who fail to comply. A variety of measures could be invoked in shipping. At the international level, a mild deterrent could be introduced by withholding cargoes whose shipment is financed through multilateral aid programs from noncomplying companies. A more severe sanction would be to withhold the aid itself.

In its report on international aid and development the Pearson Commission stressed the need for closer cooperation amongst the international agencies concerned with finance and trade in order to promote consistent and effective responses by the international community to the particular situation of each nation benefiting or seeking to benefit from multilateral aid.[16] National shipping policies should come within the scope of this review.

International agencies already offer significant technical assistance to the ocean freight industry; should an International Maritime Authority ever be formed and granted licensing and/or registry powers, it would be in a position to build a financial base adequate to raise its services to the industry to an even more critical level.[17] These services might be denied those found by the authority to be in noncompliance.

An International Authority would also be in a position to exercise considerable pressure on noncooperating nations through interpretations of international conventions and law. In the most severe cases, it could deny a noncomplying carrier the protection of the law, which would vastly complicate its ability to collect payments due, enforce claims, acquire insurance, or even resist seizure on the high seas.

Sanctions are available to regional groups as well as to enforce good faith collective bargaining with respect to practices in specific trades. The most potent weapon at the regional level is the opportunity to coordinate countermeasures by national governments if met by discrimination abroad.[18] Also, a regional group seeking to negotiate terms of container shipments, for example, can threaten either to shift its trade to another area or to transport it via another mode (e.g., conventional liners, small bulk carriers, etc.).

In short, isolated deviations from internationally accepted practice can be disciplined if there is the will to do so. The sanctions suggested above, however, can hardly be applied on a broad scale basis. Nor are they likely in a practical sense to be quickly brought to bear on a nation or national flag carrier which in other respects is fulfilling its international responsibilities.

In summary, the steps which may prove workable to achieve a more orderly framework for the conduct of international shipping are analogous to those which may be used in other areas of international relations and trade. As in trade, shipping would benefit if an international convention or code could be formulated to clarify what practices are acceptable to the world community and which are to be condemned. The main themes of this agreement should center on standards to protect opportunities for competition and to equalize insofar as possible the economic situations of competing lines.

Buttressed by adequate checks and balances, greater competitiveness in the supply of ocean shipping services is in the interests of the less-developed nations as well as of the established maritime states. In fact, a system which rewards business prowess and penalizes inefficiency would appear to be the only means for reconciling the divergent interests of these two groups and for establishing a basis for the international cooperation necessary for making any arrangement work well.

Concluding Remarks: A
Prospectus for the Next Decade

This study has sought to survey developments in sea transport in terms of the issues which such developments are creating for the shipping industry and for public policy. It has reflected a conviction that institutional arrangements for the industry's operations must be reshaped to reflect changing technologies, trade practices, and national aspirations particularly within the so-called "third world."

The drama of merchant shipping's transition from a loosely organized, contentious, nationally-oriented family of small and medium sized· firms to today's highly mechanized, systems-conscious international enterprise has unfolded with remarkable vigor and speed. It represents a global revolution in business methodology analogous to the displacement in the 1930s of the independent grocery by the national supermarket chains. That such pervasive changes could be accomplished are indicative of the flexibility and adaptability of shipping institutions.

Economic opportunity may be anticipated to continue to provide the leading edge to the future development of international shipping. Some conferences, labor groups, small producers, and regulatory agencies may continue to fight a rearguard action against the march of container and bulk handling technologies, but the economic advantage offered through these improved methods is such that they will not be able to hold out for long. In sharp contrast to as recently as five years ago, present concern is not that technological development may be inhibited by institutional restraint but rather that the astounding success of container shipping may lead to overinvestment, too rapid a shake-out in the industry, and a premature freezing of operations in this new mode.

While the infection of technological change has already swept through most of the advantaged segments of the shipping world, there are many pockets within the industry which continue conventional operations of old ships on narrow profit margins. Particularly in the less-developed world, entire trades are vulnerable to remaining locked into obsolete transport systems. Unless action is taken by local authorities to consolidate cargoes at regional ports and to update facilities for loading and discharge, service to those areas may be expected to deteriorate further in absolute as well as relative terms.

With a few exceptions, no nation can now expect to organize and maintain a competitive merchant fleet solely through its own resources. The most successful enterpreneurs are those who have mobilized capital, ships, manpower, and markets on an international basis. By 1980, the concept of a wholly indigenous national merchant fleet may seem anomalous. Certainly, one of the long range problems which faces this industry and others is how enterprises of an essentially international character are to be licensed, taxed, and regulated by appropriate public authorities.

The advantages to the world community which are potentially available through introduction of truly efficient, fast, low cost through transport services are enormous. Realizing these opportunities will require closer international collaboration and organization of more tightly integrated transport systems than has been accepted in this industry heretofore. Attention is particularly urgently needed to facilitating through shipment services, simplifying documentation, improving terminal and shoreside operations, and reducing the number of shipping rates. Different approaches are being taken to these tasks. In the short run, the careful planning conducted by the OCL/ACT group within the sheltered environment of its closed conference service to Australia has probably been the most productive. In the longer run, this study has argued that competition must be allowed greater play.

One approach which almost surely will not work is direct action by governments to assign routes, set rates, and regulate terms of transport. Although shipowners acknowledge the critical importance of their services to trade and are anxious to work informally with governments to sweep away impediments to more efficient and lower cost transport, they argue persuasively that to impose on shipping a regulatory system analogous to that applying in international air transport would destroy the very flexibility which is most needed to assure that services meet changing commercial needs.

International shipping is a highly complex industry, sensitive to political pressures, trade policies, and (in the U.S.) to regulatory attitudes. In the past, the industry has enjoyed a certain mystique, and government policies toward it have been colored by a mixture of national pride and nostalgic recollections of sailing ships. Shipping today is moving rapidly away from its romantic roots into the world of big business operations. It is an industry which occupies a key role in the world's economy. By and large, the problems it faces are similar to those of other critical national interest industrial undertakings which operate on an international scale. As with steel, chemicals, aircraft manufacture, and finance, shipping interests are big and powerful enough to surmount most political impediments to their development. But the progress of the industry could be greatly facilitated, to the benefit of all concerned, by government policies which recognize the industry's essentially international character, protect opportunities for competition on fair and equal terms, and respect its need for flexibility in its commercial relations with shippers, ports, and connecting carriers.

Learning to deal with international business operations appears likely to become one of the foremost problems for governments in the decade ahead. With reasonable economic stability and intergovernmental cooperation, it is a solvable problem. But it needs priority attention.

Notes

Notes

Introduction to Part I:
The Industry and Its Setting

1. Despite the legal theories of such representatives of small trading powers as Hugo Grotius, deep sea shipping was conducted on thoroughly mercantilist lines through the eighteenth century. With the repeal of the British Navigation Act in 1849, these mercantilist restrictions were largely cleared away, and international shipping entered a period of freer competition undergirded by relatively free access to cargoes and ports. The mercantilist tendencies of earlier years, however, have never been wholly eradicated, and owners based in countries such as Greece and Norway, which enjoy only a limited commercial base, have had to offset this disadvantage through superior operating and trading skills.

2. The term "flag of convenience" lacks an authoritative definition, and different persons may embrace different national registeries within the term. One textbook definition denotes "convenience" registeries as those available to foreign shipowners "by a simple administrative formality, such as the mere registration or grant of a certificate of registry." (Columbos, *The International Law of the Sea*, 4th ed., rev., as quoted in B.A. Boczek, *Flags of Convenience: An International Legal Study*, Cambridge, Mass.: Harvard University Press, 1962, p. 3.) Actually all nations impose a registry tax, and it is the revenue to be gained therefrom which motivates some states to make their flag available as a convenience to foreign nationals. For many years only Liberia, Panama, and Honduras were considered to be flags of convenience by most authorities, but other nations (Somali, Bahamas, Cyprus, Lebanon, and the British Crown Colonies of Bermuda and Hong Kong) are now recognized to fill the same function. About 22 percent of the world's deep sea cargo tonnage flies these flags.

Additionally, ship owners—particularly the international oil and minerals companies—may register vessels (either owned directly or by foreign subsidiaries) in nations other than the domicile of the parent company. These registries are usually motivated by a commercial or operating interest rather than simply the easy (or "convenient") terms of the registering nation. Such registries account for an added 10 to 15 percent of international shipping tonnage.

Chapter 1
The International Ocean Freight Industry

1. It was not until the 1847 Treaty of Paris that piracy was officially condemned in international law, or until 1849 that Great Britain repealed the

Navigation Acts restricting British trades to British vessels except where specific exceptions had been granted under reciprocity agreements.

2. Both in the eighteenth and nineteenth centuries and now, the merchant shipowner has operated in a great variety of ways. Thus, some have bought and sold goods along their voyages both for trading profit and to fill their ships; others may take goods owned by others on consignment or even lease out the vessel as a whole for specific voyages or blocks of time. With this variety of practice, the analogy between the "merchantman" of yesterday and the great oceangoing fleets of modern industrial corporations is at best a rough one.

3. In recent years, the tanker business has come to overlap dry cargo operations, since tankers are equipped to carry grains, and a number of bulk carriers are being built with both dry and liquid capabilities.

4. Liner rates are typically five to ten times greater per cargo ton than are the rates for goods shipped in large quantities by tramp. The differential reflects not only the safer, faster service, but also the relatively larger handling costs of a speciality service and the fact that liner rates typically include loading and discharge costs, whereas tramp rates do not.

5. Container ship design favors a long, relatively beamy and tapered hull which may be driven at high speeds and which has a relatively small displacement in relation to the size of the ship in order to offset the space loss associated with stowing large containers. The greater efficiency of container ships, therefore, stems from their faster turnaround time in port (about two to three days on the North Atlantic run versus ten to fifteen days for a conventional ship) and their higher service speeds (twenty to twenty-six knots versus fifteen to sixteen knots for early post-war designs). On a ton per ton basis (dwt.) the container ships can therefore provide two to three times the carrying capacity of the ships which they replace. Because the new ships typically also are roughly twice the size in deadweight, four to five conventional vessels may be displaced from service with a single new container vessel.

6. Figures are for the period from 1956 to 1968. Data on number and tonnage of ships relate to ships 5,000 gross tons and over and are by the U.S. Maritime Administration. The increase in "carrying capacity," a statistically elastic concept because it depends on the manner in which vessels are employed, is estimated from examination of UN data on cargoes actually carried in seaborne trade and of data published by the Maritime Transport Committee, OECD, regarding average shipment distances and ship productivity.

7. The economic role of conferences and their pricing procedures are discussed further in Part II, Chapters 7 and 9, and in Part III, Chapter 14.

8. The conference does not necessarily embrace all lines serving the trade nor can it exclude the possibility of a new entrant. Additionally, the conference carriers face indirect competition from tramps, air carriers, and other conferences which may be able to offer alternative routing. The conference also faces the potential defection of its own members if it sets rates so high as to tempt a

participant to cut rates in the hope of enlarging his share. Excessively high rates may also reduce trade volume. More important, the conferences have come to occupy a quasi-public role and face the displeasures of the governments of the nations which they serve if they act in an arbitrary or discriminatory manner. In the highly political milieu of ocean shipping, this can be an important check on the misuse of conference power.

9. Major trade routes were defined as those long distance routes carrying large tonnages, the minor routes as those long distance routes carrying small tonnages, and the intermediate and local were short distance and intraregional trade routes. Conferences operating between Ivory Coast and U.K., for instance, would fall into the major trade route of West Coast Africa to Europe.

10. Considering the amount of governmental and academic attention which has been directed to conferences, there is surprisingly little systematic information available as to the extent to which they control the world's liner trades. This may be due in part to the fact that conditions vary in both time and place and that nonconference liner services are often unstable and not always distinguishable from tramp operation. In general, it appears that the conferences hold a dominating position in most U.K., West European, American, and Japanese trades, and an important role throughout the world, including even the Socialist Bloc.

In his dissertation, *The Economics of Ocean Liner Conferences* (Boston College, 1965) John Walgreen suggests that the conferences can usually effectively resist any real threats to their custom (often by bringing the competitor within the conference tent) but may choose to ignore minor operators who sporadically enter the trade (op. cit., pp. 113 ff.). Such data as are available, tend to support this thesis and show nonconference lines to handle less than 10 percent of the liner trade (See Dag Tresselt, *The West African Shipping Range*, UN Sales Doc. 67. II.D.24, p. 69, and for U.S. trades, statistics prepared by the Federal Maritime Commission showing almost half the conferences serving the United States to be free of any nonconference liner competition, and about half of the remainder to face the competition of only one line). It should be noted that these data are now over five years old.

11. Effective January 1, 1971, INTERTANKO was reorganized as the International Association of Independent Tanker Operators, and its headquarters moved to Oslo. The new grouping represents 60 percent of the world's independent owners but is not currently planning to work with rate stabilization schemes.

12. There is, to the author's knowledge, no single compendium of national laws applying to the ownership and registry of ships. The variables are simply too numerous, applying not only to the conditions relating to registration of the ship itself, but also to the tests of domicile of partnerships and corporations and of citizenship to individuals. Thus, whereas U.S. law is among the most strict in the tests applied for granting nationality to ships, Aristotle Onassis was able to

satisfy its requirements by transferring his shipping interests during the mid-1950s to a trust on behalf of his two children, who were both U.S. citizens by birth. British legislation determines the eligibility of a corporate body to register a ship under British flag by the combined elements of principal place of business and national incorporation; these tests generally provide the model for commonwealth nations. Countries which have modeled their laws on the French system allow a larger measure of foreign capital so long as there is local management. Based on this principle, certain South American nations grant their nationality to ships even though wholly owned by aliens.

In addition to ownership and management criteria, some nations impose requirements regarding national crews, particularly to assure representation of nationals among the ship's officers. A very few (chiefly only the U.S.) require that the vessel be constructed in a national shipyard.

13. *Shipbuilding and Engineering Log*, 74, no. 7, p. 201.

14. The difference between the effective control estimates shown in Table 1-3 and those which might be implied by the *Shipbuilding and Engineering Log* data appears to derive chiefly from a different approach to ascertaining the nationality of owning firms. Thus the *Engineering Log* data include ships owned by the foreign affiliates of U.S. forms; Table 1-3 does not.

15. The history of the "genuine" link requirement of the 1958 Geneva Conventions and its interpretation under international law are reported in Chapter 16 and by B.A. Boczek in *Flags of Convenience: An International Legal Study* (Harvard University Press, 1962) and by T.K. Thommen, *International Legislation on Shipping* (UN Document, Sales No. E.69.II.D.2). The former source also includes a partial survey of national requirements regarding corporate domicile, build, manning, management and use of national flag ships. No complete compilation of such matters has been discovered by the author.

Chapter 2
Government Interests and Roles

1. Japan and India have developed their merchant marines as a matter of national policy through budgeting credit and subsidy assistance in a series of five-year plans. Japan has emphasized liberal credit aids to private owners, including foregoing interest payments on government loans, and also has given direct subsidies for participating in cross-trades. India has supported wholly government-owned as well as private shipping through subsidized credit and tax remissions to assist in new construction. For details of these and other programs, see Irwin Heine, *Maritime Subsidies* (U.S. Government Printing Office, 1969).

2. Tax considerations are of special interest to shipowners in these high tax nations. In general, such special provisions as apply to shipping reflect the

unique policy to offer a preference to promote the national flag fleet. However, in Sweden shipowners are granted complete freedom in applying depreciation charges—an important advantage—while German ship construction and charters are exempt from the value-added turnover tax. Belgium grants a modest construction subsidy and has exempted shipping from a 6 percent corporate income tax applicable to other transport industries.

3. The British investment grant was established in 1966 to replace an allowance of 40 percent excess depreciation designed to cushion the impact of rising prices for replacement equipment. The grant initially was available to any British corporation building ships for registry under the British flag. In 1969 standards were tightened by requiring evidence that the allowance would have a favorable effect on the British balance of payments and in 1970 it was eliminated altogether. There now is pressure on the Heath government to reinstate the grant.

4. Both the French and Italian governments hold major interests in the principal national flag lines and provide substantial subventions to these lines to support "national interest services." The Italian subsidy is reported by Heine to total $38 million per year (ibid., p. 59); French payments include a $7 million amount to equalize the operating costs of French vessels with their competitors.

5. Flag discrimination practices of less developed nations are detailed in a paper, "Flag Discrimination," prepared by the Maritime Transport Committee of the OECD (DAF, MTC, 69.44, issued on a restricted basis 5 December 1969) and are summarized in Phillip Franklin, *The Economic Impact of Flag Discrimination in Ocean Transportation* (unpub. diss., The American University, 1969). See also below, part 5 of this chapter.

6. During fiscal year 1971, direct operating subsidies to U.S. operators totaled $268 million, net of recapture. Indirect aid through favorable charter rates for carriage of government bulk cargoes and other tax, training, and medical benefits would bring the total to $400 million or over. The vessel operating expenses of directly subsidized carriers during the same period totalled $585 million, net of cargo expense, overhead, and depreciation.

7. For description of these programs, see *Consultation in Shipping* (UN Document, Sales No. 68.II.D.1) and the report, *Shipping Conference Arrangements and Practices*, of the Canadian Restrictive Trade Practices Commission (Ottawa: Queen's Printer, 1965), p. 11. It should be noted that, although formal procedures exist in the countries mentioned, they are frequently used in most cases. Even the United States, which has had regulatory legislation on the books for over fifty years, has taken an active interest in shipping regulation only during the past decade. Conversely, governments of countries lacking formal procedures may from time to time intervene in conference affairs in order to protect their nationals' commercial interests.

8. Competent reports on this interesting case are to be found in T.J. May, "The Status of Federal Maritime Commission Shipping Regulation Under

Principles of International Law," *Georgetown Law Journal*, 54 (1966), 794, and a note, "Rate Regulation in Ocean Shipping." *Harvard Law Review*, 78 (1963), 636, and in two more recent papers by James Gordon published in *The University of Chicago Law Review*, 37, nos. 1 and 2 (1969).

9. Although the Brazilian Merchant Marine Commission was established in 1941, it did not actively seek to regulate overseas shipping until 1967. In that year, legislation was adopted to empower the Commission to disapprove conference and pooling agreements in Brazilian trade. The Commission then acted promptly and aggressively to dissolve those shipping conferences in its key trades (Europe, North America, and Argentina) which refused to grant a larger share of the cargoes to the national flag carriers participating in the trade. The Brazilian action, in contrast to the U.S. effort, appears to have been taken entirely in support of its shipping interests (rather than shippers) and has therefore had a particularly direct and painful impact upon the maritime industry per se, and in particular upon the so-called "third flags" serving her trade.

10. The Indian and Australian programs are described in *Consultation in Shipping*, pp. 73-112. Both governments require prior notice of rate increases and make provision for independent investigation of their economic justification and for arbitration as to the manner in which allowable increases are to be applied.

11. See footnote 3 of Chapter 3 for references concerning the failure of the proposed postwar International Trade Organization.

12. Franklin, *The Economic Impact of Flag Discrimination*, Chaps. 4 and 7.

Chapter 3
International Trade and Financial Policies

1. Jan Tinbergen, *Shaping the World Economy* (New York: Twentieth Century Fund, 1962), p. 137.

2. Ibid.

3. The failure of the United States to ratify the ITO charter scuttled the most promising opportunity of the postwar period to establish some order to international trade and undermined the ability of GATT to exercise more than a tenuous moral force upon its contracting partners. There is a large literature on international trade policy and the influences of the GATT. Early postwar aspirations are recorded by Clair Wilcox in *A Charter for World Trade* (MacMillan, 1949); their disintegration in a 1954 article by William Diebold, "The Death of the ITO" (Princeton University Press). A recent appraisal of the outlook for international cooperation in trade in the face of nationalistic and protectionist tendencies is found in Gardner Patterson, *Discrimination in International Trade: The Policy Issues 1945-1965* (Princeton University Press,

1966). The work of GATT is described in *Everyman's United Nations*, a manual to that organization's structure and activities published by the Secretariat. Another description is found in Gerald Curzon, *Multilateral Commercial Diplomacy: The General Agreement on Tariffs and Trade and its Impact on National Commercial Policies and Technique* (London: Michael Joseph Ltd., 1965).

4. It is extraordinarily difficult to develop any overall gauges as to the trend in trade agreements or the extent to which tariffs, exchange controls, preferential arrangements, and so forth affect the flow of trade. The difficulties are both conceptual and empirical. While there have been a number of interesting economic studies on tariff levels and their effect on demand, judgments regarding the impact on nontariff barriers are almost wholly qualitative or directed solely at particular commodities in particular trades.

In this connection it is useful to remember, for example, that until 1961 the United States firmly opposed any type of commodity or trade agreement designed to stabilize supplies or pricing. In subsequent years it has taken the lead in negotiating international marketing agreements for cotton textiles and coffee, encouraged informal restraints in export of steel, and actively considered similar arrangements regarding electronic components, shoes, and fibers. With a deteriorating international trade position, the U.S. is under severe pressure to accept still more restrictive measures to protect industries threatened by rising imports from abroad.

5. The functions of UNCITRAL include coordination of the work of organizations already working in this field, preparing new international conventions and model laws, promoting ways of ensuring uniform interpretations of existing law, and collecting and disseminating information on national legislation and legal developments. Its initial emphasis has been toward harmonizing legal practices applicable to the international sale of goods, commercial arbitration, and payments settlements. However, UNCITRAL also has specifically committed itself to working with UNCTAD on shipping bills of lading, charter parties, and marine insurance, and appears likely to continue to show special interest in this field.

6. "Model conventions" have been available for international agreement on principles for direct taxation since 1928. These have been periodically revised and expanded, chiefly under the auspices since World War II of the OEEC and OECD, to include such income, capital gains, and estate taxation. Between 1939 and 1957 the number of bilateral agreements among OEEC countries rose from twenty to sixty-two. By 1966 it had grown to 102, and the negotiation of additional agreements is under way. These agreements are most effective in reference to the direct taxation of individuals; less so in reference to the more complicated corporate tax problems. They do not reach indirect taxes at all, although these are in some measure regulated under GATT rules. See *Report of the Committee on International Trade and Investment* of the International Law Committee at the Helsinki Conference (1966).

Specific tax problems related to shipping have been identified and compiled by the Baltic and International Maritime Conference in a publication, *Double Taxation of Non-Residential Shipping* (Copenhagen, 1968).

7. Recognizing that economic recovery from World War II would necessarily require a period of years, the authors of the Bretton Woods Agreements provided for successive stages in assuming the full obligations of membership in the Fund. Even following accession to Article VIII, which pledges the member state to maintain a freely convertible currency, nations may invoke exchange restrictions, import surcharges, and multiple exchange rates with the approval of the Fund to meet temporary conditions.

8. The Agreements express a delicate balancing of sovereign national privileges and international controls. On the critical matter of exchange rates, for example, only a member—not the Fund—can propose a change which is then accepted by the Fund. Should the Fund find the member's proposal unacceptable, the new par value may nonetheless be put into effect without contravention of the Articles of Agreement, but the member taking such action exposes itself to the same possible sanctions as one which has failed to perform Treaty obligations. See Joseph Gold, *The International Monetary Fund and International Law*, monograph published by the Fund (Washington, D.C., 1965), p. 14.

9. International Monetary Fund, *1969 Annual Report*, p. 31.

10. James Tobin, "Economic Progress in the International Monetary System," in *Changing Patterns of U.S. Foreign Trade and Investment*. Edited by Bela Belassa (New York: Norton & Co., 1964), p. 120.

11. The manner in which monetary and currency management has influenced shipping operations is difficult to trace but has undoubtedly been substantial. Capital commitments, for example, have often been required by national authorities to be undertaken only within the nation or with other nations with which there was a favorable monetary balance. The Germans have recently placed orders in British yards in part to balance off British expenses (stemming in part from troop commitments) in Germany. In other cases, the currencies used for capital outlays are dictated by commercial interests to protect against the possibility of revaluation of debt service, to balance debt service and anticipated revenues, or to meet the requirements of potential longterm charterers.

In day to day management, shipping companies must continually adjust their currency holdings and policies. Being immersed in the business, some engage in extensive currency speculation as a sideline. By providing an avenue through which currencies may be manipulated, the industry has undoubtedly attracted some investment primarily interested in freeing blocked currencies for wider use or repatriating earnings.

Most companies engaged in international shipping operations now require freights to be paid in dollars, francs, or sterling. The national flag fleets of soft currency countries, on the other hand, accept shipments from nationals paid for in local currencies and receive special authorization from their governments to convert specified amounts of soft to hard currency to meet their operating expenses abroad. Such procedures obviously afford the national flag a substantial advantage.

12. International Monetary Fund, *1969 Annual Report*, p. 32.

13. Free currency exchange is accepted within currency "areas" and certain regional groupings, though such exchanges do not create a fully free market. Within the Common Market also, steps are underway to coordinate more actively the domestic economic policies of the member countries. In effect, economic integration appears to generate its own momentum. If trade is to be conducted freely, it is convenient for currencies to move with equal ease. If currencies move, they must reflect common values. This implies monetary coordination.

14. Fear that the governments might become involved in the economic aspects of shipping has caused the industry to resist the formation even of specialized intergovernmental structure for dealing with maritime affairs. The Intergovernmental Maritime Consultative Organization, a specialized agency of the United Nations, was finally established only after ten years of tortuous negotiation severely limiting its functions. (For a fuller discussion of the Intergovernmental Maritime Consultative Organization, see Chapter 4 under "United Nations Agencies"). An interesting statement of a common industry point of view during the period when the IMCO charter was under consideration is to be found in Viscount Runciman's Annual Shipping Lecture to the Chamber of Shipping, 19 April 1955 *(Journal of the Institute of Transports*, 26, no. 5, pp. 145-158). His Lordship concludes by quoting Lord Melbourne, "Try to do no good and then you won't get into any scrapes."

15. Johan Horn, "Nationalism and Internationalism in Shipping," *Journal of Transport Economics and Policy*, 3, no. 3 (September, 1969), 6. Horn is chairman of the Norwegian Shipowners Association. See also the *Annual Report of the U.K. Chamber of Shipping* for 1969, for a similar line of argument and a statement of the objective of workable competition.

16. Norwegian Shipowners' Association, *Review of Norwegian Shipping, 1969*, pp. 11-12.

17. Ibid., p. 11.

Chapter 4
International Shipping Institutions

1. Complete and up-to-date anthologies of international shipping organizations are not publicly available except in a special survey prepared for limited distribution by Saguenay Research. The most comprehensive material is to be

found in N. Singh and P. Colinvaux, *British Shipping Laws* (London: Stevens & Sons, 1967); vol. XIII, UNCTAD Documents TD/32, TD/B/C.4/48, and TD/B/C.4/49; and the *Yearbook of International Associations*, Brussels: Union of International Associations, 1969). A listing of some 200 national and international organizations of interest to shipping, with very brief descriptions, is found in the *Annual Report of the Baltic and International Maritime Conference, 1968-69* (Copenhagen, 1970), pp. 306-323.

2. The Convention for the Safety of Life at Sea (1960), Conventions for the Prevention of Pollution of the Sea by Oil (1954, and amended in 1962, 1967 and 1969), Convention for Facilitation of International Maritime Traffic (1965), and Convention on Load Lines (1966).

3. Declarations were filed by ten countries (Greece, Yugoslavia, four Scandinavian countries, Poland, Iceland, Spain, and Morocco) stating in substance that their participation in IMCO was conditional upon that organization's refraining from intervening in the commercial and economic aspects of shipping.

4. The work program of the legal committee, though focused on matters relating to insurance liability and facilitation, anticipates also cooperation with UNCTAD and UNCITRAL for studies of commercial and trade policy issues.

5. The Committee's work program is organized under nine heads as follows: establishment of consultative machinery (substantially completed with the approval of a report on this subject in November 1966); level and structure of freight rates; conference practices and adequacy of shipping services (a category which embraces a variety of studies and is the main facus for staff work); improvement of port operations and related facilities; merchant marines in developing countries; technological progress in shipping; annual reviews of current and long-term aspects of maritime transport; seminars on shipping economics; international legislation on the UN system, in particular regarding technical assistance and international financing and aid.

6. With 77 of 124 votes, the developing nations have a clear majority in UNCTAD whereas developed states enjoy effective control of the twenty-seven member Economic and Social Council of the UN. The latter agency has demurred on giving UNCTAD as large a role in intergovernmental development planning as it seeks. (See "Rift Could Spell End of UNCTAD," *N.Y. Journal of Commerce*, 6 February 1969).

7. UNCTAD, *Report of the Committee on Shipping*, UN publication, Sales No. E/Conf. 46/C.3/13), p. 30.

8. Printed studies available through the UN Sales office listed in the bibliography. Numerous other working papers are available in multilith through the UNCTAD library and are referenced in the *Report of the Committee on Shipping on its Third Session* (TD/B/C.4 (III)/Misc. 5).

9. The Shipping Committee's conference and rate studies depend for their success almost entirely on data voluntarily submitted by the conferences. Although cooperation has been good in some areas, many of the conferences

have refused to furnish data on rate-making and commercial policy issues. (See ibid., p. 7, 14).

10. Resolution 7 (III), creation of a working group of international shipping legislation, adopted by the Committee on Shipping at its Third Session, ibid., p. 47.

11. The ILO standard for minimum wages is related to the economic and cultural development in each country, subject to a floor of U.S. $70 monthly, an amount which exceeds the wages of most Asian seamen. It was proposed in 1969 that this floor be raised to U.S. $91.

12. The Hague Rules draw their name from a preparatory conference of the Comite Maritime International (CMI; see description in the section of this chapter entitled "Nongovernmental International Associations.") conducted at the Hague, at which they were formulated. They were subsequently reviewed for governmental approval by the Brussels Diplomatic Conference. The Conference is an ad hoc body but has standing as a repository for international conventions.

13. The International Shipping Federation initially was organized in 1909 to provide a vehicle for indemnifying participating shipowners for losses incurred through labor disputes. Following the organization of the ILO, it radically broadened its purposes and membership to provide for consultation among national steamship owners associations on the whole range of industrial relations issues before the ILO.

14. CENSA was established in 1963 in response to a resolution of the European Ministers of Transport stressing the need for improved liaison between conferences and shippers. It also considers general shipping policy questions, positions to be taken before international governmental agencies (e.g., UNCTAD), and other matters, such as the impact of containers, as appropriate. For several years CENSA's staff support was provided by the ICS. There is now a separate staff but close links have been maintained.

In addition to the shipowner associations of twelve European states, CENSA also includes the shipowners group from Japan.

Chapter 5
A Regional Review

1. Article 84 of the Rome Treaty, which concludes that Treaty's transport section, states: "The Council may unanimously decide whether, to what extent, and by what procedures, appropriate procedures may be made in respect to sea and air transportation." The EEC Transport Commissioner recently has been quoted as stating that he will ask that common policies be extended to sea and air transport "as soon as the circumstances seem favorable." (M. Bodson before the Council of the European Economic Community, as quoted by Tristan Vieljeux in "Common Market and Ocean Shipping," a report to the General

Meeting of the Baltic Maritime Conference, Munich, May 1969, reprinted in the *Norwegian Shipping News* (October 1969), pp. 63-67.

2. Although Market authorities may have a valid basis for their contention that Article 84 of the Rome Treaty does not limit the application of other elements of the Treaty to shipping, their interpretation has been opposed by several of the participating governments. See Nigel S. Despicht, *Policies for Transport in the Common Market* (London: Lambarde Press, 1964), p. 201.

3. See Tristan Vieljeux, "Common Market and Ocean Shipping." Vieljeux argues that the Market's economic integration, without complementary action to harmonize policies with respect to shipping, could lead European owners to shift to Dutch registry as a Common Market "flag of convenience," an outcome which is unlikely to be acceptable to the other participants. He also points out that the Authorities will be led increasingly into shipping matters as an extension of internal transport and port policies, as a defense against potential "plundering" of Western European cargoes by East European ships, and as a means of enhancing trade terms and foreign exchange earnings. These latter forces could potentially cause adoption of more protectionist shipping policies, or at least the development of special arrangements for covering the transport requirements of the Market's trade with other regions.

4. In his study, *British Shipping and World Competition* (London: Athlone Press, 1962), pp. 12-14, S.G. Sturmey cites four factors as having exercised a determining influence: Britain's world-wide colonial ties, its early and rapid industrialization, its rapid population growth, and its tightly knit commercial establishment. Although acknowledging the presence of relatively unfavorable economic and political factors, Sturmey emphasizes the conservative attitudes of British shipping management in explaining Britain's subsequent decline. (See Chapter 15.)

5. Governmental aids to shipping are carefully documented by Irwin Heine in *Maritime Subsidies* (U.S. Government Printing Office, 1969). A useful supplemental *Report on Indirect Government Aids to United States and Foreign Maritime Industries* was prepared by Ernst and Ernst for the Shipbuilder's Council of America and is available from the latter organization in multilith.

6. Committee of Inquiry into Shipping, *Report* (London: Her Majesty's Stationery Office, May 1970).

7. J.J. Oyevaar, *Dutch Merchant Shipping*, Report to the Board of the Royal Netherlands Steamship Association (multilith, 1968).

8. It is interesting to note that a number of international container consortia are based in Bermuda or the Bahamas not to avoid tax but to ensure that just one of the participating countries does not get all the tax as would be the case if the parent company were based in one of those countries. By basing the parent company in a tax haven, the participants are able to ensure that all the proceeds go back to the participating members where they are taxed by the home government.

9. PL 91-469, approved October 21, 1970.

10. The Philippine statute to develop a national merchant marine, for example, is closely modeled on the U.S. statute; a number of statements also have been made by officials of South American governments suggesting that they have been influenced in their decisions to impose preferences by the U.S. example. (See Committee of European National Shipowners' Associations, *Study of U.S. Cargo Preference and its Harmful Effects* (multilith, October 1968).

11. The figure for U.S. flag participation in liner shipping usually cited by the U.S. Maritime Administration is 22 percent. However, this calculation excludes military and certain other cargoes moving under cargo preference statutes which have been classified as "non-commercial." Their inclusion raises U.S. participation to the 25 to 30 percent level noted in the text. If the calculation is made on a cargo value or freight revenue basis, the percentage is slightly higher.

12. Statistical studies have been conducted only in reference to cargoes carried by foreign flag vessels officially listed by the U.S. Navy as under U.S. effective control. These ships carry roughly 20 percent of U.S. tanker and dry bulk cargoes. To qualify for inclusion on the Navy list, however, the vessel must be registered under Panamanian or Liberian flag and be specifically pledged by its owner to be available to the U.S. government in the case of emergency. In addition to vessels on the Navy list, therefore, there is probably an equivalent amount of bulk cargo tonnage not on the Navy list which is operated under foreign flags by U.S. owners in U.S. foreign trade, indicating an overall participation in the range of 30 to 40 percent. See U.S. Maritime Administration, *Effective U.S. Control of Merchant Ships, A Statistical Analysis, 1970* (Washington: U.S. Government Printing Office, 1971) tables 1-4.

13. For details of the 1960 economic plan see R. Furuta and Y. Hirai, *A Short History of Japanese Shipping* (Tokyo News Service, Ltd., 1967), p. 157.

14. A small subsidy has been provided for many years to encourage cross trading, which is considered advantageous from the viewpoint of balance of payments. In 1968, Japanese ships carried 7.9 million metric tons of cargo in such trades.

15. Data presented in this section are drawn chiefly from essays prepared by Dr. Czeslaw Wojewodka of the Polish Institute of Shipping Research and published in English by the Bergen Institute of Shipping Research, 1967.

16. For example, see V. Bakaev, "Problems of International Navigation," *Journal of Merchant Marine* (Paris, 2 February 1967). Bakaev was Minister of Merchant Marine, USSR.

17. Economic Commission for Latin America, *El Transporte en America Latine* (multilith, Santiago, 1969), p. 172.

18. Among the new African nations, Nigeria enjoys the largest GNP at $4.5 million, roughly that of a U.S. city of 1.1 million population.

19. Data from Dag Tresselt, *The West African Shipping Range* (UN publication, Sales No. 67.II.D.24) which provides an extremely useful case study of shipping problems and opportunities during the early stages of development.

Introduction to Part II:
The Economics of Sea Transport

1. Recent books presenting analyses of shipping economics include: E. Bennathan and A.A. Walters, *The Economics of Ocean Freight Rates* (New York: Frederick A. Praeger, 1969); Carleen O'Loughlin, *The Economics of Sea Transport* (London: Pergamon Press, 1967); Thomas Thorburn, *Supply and Demand for Water Transport* (Business Research Institute of the Stockholm School of Economics, 1960); and Alan Ferguson et al. *The Economic Value of the U.S. Merchant Marine* (Chicago: Northwestern University, 1961). C.F.H. Cuffley, *Ocean Freights and Chartering* (London: Staples Press, 1962) has useful information regarding tramp practices. Z. Zannetos, in *The Theory of Oil Tankship Rates* (Cambridge: M.I.T. Press, 1966) deals with the economics of tanker chartering. R.O. Goss treats selected economic problems in his book of essays, *Studies in Maritime Economics* (Cambridge University Press, 1968).

In addition to the above, a large volume of economic studies has been published by the UNCTAD Shipping Committe, and a series of monographs on economic subjects has been issued by the Bergen Institute for Shipping Research, which includes many excellent papers.

2. Major studies undertaken by Saguenay Research and reported in this chapter include a study of cargo origins and destinations in international seaborne trade, prepared by Barbara A. Thompson, and a study of ownership and registry patterns in the world merchant fleet, prepared by Thomas James. Research undertaken by a Saguenay team on the behavior of ship charter markets in 1970-71 provided additional background although the results of this proprietary work cannot be reported here.

Chapter 6
The Cargo Base: Demand
for Shipping Services

1. This estimate reflects the proportion of ton-miles provided by ship vis-à-vis rail, truck, or air service. Because data are not available to establish the total volume of international trade in tonnage terms or to define the relative contributions of different types of carriage in shipments involving several modes, the estimate had to be developed from examination of the origins and destinations of major categories of international trade and must be considered an approximation only.

In view of the relative economy of sea transport, the proportion of transport cost attributable to ocean freights in international shipments falls far below the estimated percentage of ton-miles of transport performance by sea. (An OECD study, *Ocean Freight Rates as Part of Total Transport Costs*, published in 1968, found that for typical overseas general cargo shipments, sea freights accounted for only half the total transport cost although the sea leg was many times the length of the inland transport.) In terms of the value of goods carried, sea transport is also a less dominant element, since high-value goods constitute a larger proportion of the short distance intraregional trades than of long-haul shipments and have been diverted in some cases to air.

2. In this study, the term international seaborne dry cargo is construed to exclude U.S.–Canadian Great Lakes traffic (roughly twenty-seven million tons per year), government-owned and military transport, international river traffic, services to off-shore colonies and territories, and services along the coasts of such nations as the U.S., USSR, Australia, Brazil and Chile.

3. International air freight shipments were estimated by the International Civil Aviation Organization to have totalled 2.4 billion revenue ton miles in 1968. This is less than .04 percent of the total ton miles of seaborne international trade (including tanker movements) and only about 0.5 percent of the breakbulk cargoes carried by liners. On the other hand, international air cargo revenue is reported by ICAO to have been in excess of $650 million in 1966, an amount which approximates some 8 percent of the estimated revenues of international liner shipping. The competitive position of sea and air carriers is discussed further in Part III.

4. Accurate commodity breakdowns of "short-sea" intraregional shipments are not available. It may be supposed that manufactures loom larger in such services than in the long-distance interregional trades. Because they draw higher rates than most semi-processed and bulk commodities, manufactures and related "liner-type" goods also represent a far more significant element in the ocean freight business than tonnage data indicate. See Figure 1-2.

5. Liners as a matter of practice absorb a substantial portion of the imbalances identified here, sometimes returning to port virtually empty. Unless some return cargo can be generated, however, a vessel ordinarily can more profitably be employed in the tramp mode. Calculations prepared by Saguenay Research suggest that tramps may actually move less than half of the surplus of cargoes on the heavy leg of major general cargo-trade routes; cargoes remaining for liners, according to this calculation, still would be imbalanced roughly 2 to 1.

The Saguenay Research calculations are based on cargo *tonnage*. In most liner operations, cargo *volume* is the more critical measure. Unfortunately, volumetric data are not generally available. A special study for the U.S. Maritime Administration has found that on a volumetric basis in the North Atlantic, liner utilization on the average, however, is only 33 percent higher on the heavy leg than on the light. (Ernst and Ernst, *Selected Commodity Unit Costs for Oceanborne Shipments via Common Carriers* (Washington: Federal Clearinghouse, 1966).

6. Considering the cubic capacity of typical deep sea tramp and liner vessels, the weight-volume characteristics of typical cargoes, and the space loss due to broken stowage, about 4,000 long tons of general cargo may be considered a full load for a conventional 16,000 dwt. (11,000 grt.) breakbulk ship; 3,000 tons provides a reasonably satisfactory payload. Trades generating less than 300 thousand tons of cargo in both directions (summed) are therefore adequate to support less than fifty sailings per year; those generating 300 thousand to 3.0 million may support from 50 to 500 sailings a year.

7. The fact that container ships are not physically able to carry all commodities now handled by liners further emphasizes the need to approach ship routing and scheduling on a regional basis. Some of the less developed nations in particular have expressed concern about how cargoes "left over" by container ships can be handled.

8. The volume of shipments peaked in 1966 at 76 million metric tons, but the subsequent two years showed a decline to 65 million metric tons. Such low value commodities as pyrites, salt, and phosphate rock cannot be moved economically over long distances and have enjoyed rapid growth, as have fertilizers, timber, wood pulp, paper, and steel. Demand has not grown so rapidly for such staples as rubber, wool, coffee, and tea.

9. In a study of the economic effects of international trade instability, Joseph Coppock found that between 1946 and 1958 median national incomes from export of minerals (including fuels) varied from year to year by an average of 27 percent (exclusive of changes attributable to secular trend), those from manufactures by 19 percent and those from food products by 16 percent. See J.D. Coppock, *International Economic Instability; The Experience After World War II* (McGraw Hill, 1962), p. 23.

Chapter 7
Ships and Services: Supply

1. Lay-up and breakout costs may be in the range of $40 to $50 thousand and, in addition, expenses of several thousand dollars per month must be anticipated to guard and maintain a decommissioned vessel. The extent of the loss which an owner will be prepared to take on a particular voyage therefore depends in part on his estimate of the future market. The elements entering this calculation are set out in H. Gripaios, *Tramp Shipping* (London: Thos. Nelson & Sons, 1959), pp. 153-162. An interesting thesis also has been developed by Claudio Escarpenter in his *Economics of International Ocean Transport: The Cuban Case before 1958* (University of Wisconsin Press, 1965) that freights tend to deteriorate during periods of sustained peace because there is no mechanism unequivocally to dispose of the surplus tonnage which tends to be accumulated as the world industrial plant achieves full capacity by owners who are attracted

to the industry by the recollection of past profits and the expectation that future emergencies may renew demand (Escarpenter, p. 152).

2. Author's estimates from a working paper prepared November 1969 by Saguenay Research.

3. The major assumptions on which the model is built are the following: (a) About 15 percent of the tonnages of ships 1,000 gross tons and over are employed in intraregional and domestic trade and are accordingly excluded from the model. This estimate appears consistent with the size distribution of ships (about 15 percent of the fleet capacity is in the one to five thousand ton range) and Saguenay Research estimates of intraregional vs. interregional transport performance. (b) The net cargo carrying capability of liners is two-thirds their rated gross tonnage; that of other ship categories, 88 percent of their rated deadweight (allows for bunkers, engine room, etc.); average speed is 90 percent rated maximum; and fifteen days per year is required for dry docking, maintenance and repair. (c) Including an allowance for broken stowage, liner general cargoes require an average of 120 cubic feet (3 measurement tons) for each weight ton. Tankers and bulk carriers are assumed to carry cargoes in one direction only.

4. The utilization pattern indicated here and used in the model is an adjustment of estimates prepared in 1958 by A.S. Svendson and cited by the UN Department of Social and Economic Affairs in its study, *The Turnaround Time of Ships in Port* (UN publications, Sales No. 67. VII.5), p. 6.

5. Data on utilization of U.S. liners was analyzed on a sample basis by Ernst and Ernst, *Selected Commodity Unit Costs*, pp. 34-35) for 1964 and, comprehensively, by the Maritime Administration in a special study made five years earlier (S.B. Unander, "Estimated Savings in Dollar Exchange from Possible Increased Cargo Carryings in U.S. Flag Ships," U.S. Maritime Administration News Release 60-83, Nov. 27, 1960). Both indicated utilization in the range of 80 to 90 percent outbound and 50 to 60 percent inbound.

6. UN, *Turnaround Time of Ships in Port*, p. 9.

7. Influences creating a tendency toward overcapacity in liner service are identified later in this chapter.

8. Seventy-five percent of the six major bulk products are carried by bulk carriers.

9. the Schultz study, reported in *Maritime Transport, 1968* (Organization for Economic Cooperation and Development, Paris) involved analysis of nineteen commodity classes to determine the proportion of interregional movement in each class which generated a volume of over 300,000 tons per year (500,000 tons annually for manufactured fertilizers and iron and steel products). Schultz argues that volumes of this magnitude in products which do not require packaging should permit their being handled in shipload lots, but acknowledges that his methodology may substantially overstate the bulk cargo potential since: (1) the cargoes may not be homogeneous, and (2) liners with surplus capacity may underbid tramps for cargoes to fill their ships. The cargoes analyzed by

Schultz roughly parallel those classified in the Saguenay study as "sometimes handled in bulk."

10. Financing terms applying in 1967 are summarized in an UNCTAD study, *Establishment or Expansion of Merchant Marines in Developing Countries.* (UN publication, Sales No. E.69 II.D.1), p. 45. Since this date, terms have generally been tightened. OECD governments in particular have cooperated in curbing unduly liberal sales arrangements. Effective January 1, 1971, builders in OECD countries were asked to require at least 20 percent cash and a 7.5 percent interest rate with eight year repayment term on ship mortgages.

11. It will be noted that these terms assume 100 percent mortgage financing of new vessels, an arrangement which is viable in Japan because of the close business relationships linking shipyards, operators, and banking institutions. Beginning in fiscal year 1969, terms were changed to require 5 percent of total construction cost to be met through internally generated funds or equity capital.

12. Achievements under this plan are reviewed by Kenji Akasaka, "Bottoms Form Sound Foundation," *Shipping and Trade News* (Tokyo, October 1968), p. 102. The program brought 82 percent of Japan's merchant tonnage within six management groups. Depreciation shortages, which had totaled almost fifty billion yen at the program's beginning, were eliminated, and almost ten million dwt were added to the fleets of the participating companies. Akasaka attributes these accomplishments primarily to "such national subsidy measures as the interest subsidy and grace period as well as shipping enterprises' efforts toward efficient operation of ships and towards reducing expenditures."

13. Irwin Heine, *Maritime Subsidies* (U.S. Government Printing Office, 1969), p. 13.) Heine notes that this offer would appear to apply only to twenty-four vessels being built for the coffee trade.

14. It should be noted that in most European nations, it is the character of shipping investment in relation to generally applicable tax principles which creates the favorable investment opportunity, rather than any special tax incentive for shipping. Thus, all of these nations allow some form of accelerated depreciation; most either levy no tax on capital gains or allow reinvestment of the gain in a replacement asset without tax. The U.K. allows depreciation to be charged at the owner's option. Sweden provides for tax-deferred payments into a tax equalization fund. Norway allows capital gains and 25 percent of corporate earnings to be placed in special tax-deferred funds for reinvestment in depreciable assets. All of these systems are available for any industrial investment but are particularly favorable in reference to investment in ships, which are easily financed, purchased, written-down, and sold. In West Germany, shipping has enjoyed a special tax benefit since the industry was exempted from the "value added" tax applied to wholly domestic enterprises.

15. Sections 954-955, SubPart F, Revenue Act of 1962. (76 Stat. 1012-5).

16. *Marine Engineering Log, 28th Annual Yearbook Issue* (15 June 1969), p. 201, cites a fairly typical example. In this case, an American movie company had

accumulated a substantial amount of retained earnings in a blocked currency which it traded to an American oil company which planned a ship construction program in the nation's yards. Unfortunately, there are no data to indicate the extent of such practices, but one suspects that they may be widespread.

17. R.T. Brown, *Transport and the Economic Integration of South America* (Washington, D.C.: The Brookings Institution, 1966), p. 118. For a summary of the findings of the ECLA study mentioned in the text, see Remarks of Arturo Israel before the Fifth Transport Management Institute, the American University, June 1969.

18. E.g., A.A. Walters and E. Bennethan, *The Economics of Ocean Freight Rates* (New York: Frederick Praeger, 1969); D.L. McLachlan, *Pricing in Ocean Transportation*, University of Leeds, circa 1963; and various studies of S.G. Sturmey, the UNCTAD Shipping Committee, and the Bergen Institute for Shipping Research.

19. When rate discipline breaks down within conferences, price competition typically occurs outside the official tariff structure. In a rate war, when individual firms or groups of firms are scrapping for cargoes and seeking to force an unwanted competitor from the trade, price cutting also is likely to be selective with favorable deals extended to important customers or those whose business is most critical to the competition. The overall impact of competition on rates in liner shipping is therefore impossible to gauge. While specific rates may be halved, it is unlikely that the overall level will be reduced by more than ten to twenty percent. Competing lines may even be able to maintain a profitable position in such circumstances, even though profit margins usually fall. Interesting material on pricing behavior in liner shipping may be found in the report of the Antitrust Subcommittee of the House Judiciary Committee, *The Ocean Freight Industry*, Report 1419, U.S. House of Representatives, 87th Congress, 2nd session (Washington: U.S. Government Printing Office, 1962).

20. Probably the most ambitious effort to assess the economic justification for an administered rate structure was the Northwestern University study, *The Economic Value of the United States Merchant Marine* (Northwestern University, 1961), initially chartered by the U.S. subsidized shipping lines. The Northwestern University group did examine market size and the interest of shippers in stable rates, frequent services, and the like but did not examine the economic value of holding extra space. Instead the study adopted the position that in economic terms these service features can only be justified as a competitive response to shipper demand. The study concluded further that, in U.S. liner trades, competition was feasible and was the preferred means for achieving optimal use of national resource.

21. For example, the Northwestern study (p. 180), found the optimum economic speed for liner shipping in U.S. trade to lie in the range of thirteen to sixteen knots, depending on the routes and ship size. A more recent mathematical study by Jan R. Getz et al., "Design of a Cargo Liner in Light of the

Development of General Cargo Transportation," prepared for the Diamond Jubilee Meeting of the Society of Naval Architects and Marine Engineers, cites the economic optimum for conventional liners as only eleven to twelve knots. Yet, because the conference system excludes opportunities for price competition, the commercially most successful operators have sought to expand their share of the business by offering even faster services and now are employing vessels with speeds of sixteen knots to up to twenty-six knots in order to gain a competitive margin.

22. E.g., the Northwestern University study (p. 264) and the S.G. Sturmey "Economics and International Liner Services," *Journal of Transport Economics and Policy*, 1, no. 2 (1967), 190-203.

23. E.g., W. Grossman, *Ocean Freight Rates* (Cornell Maritime Press, 1956) and Carleen O'Laughlin, *The Economics of Sea Transport* (Pergamon Press, 1967).

24. This argument is developed by B.J. Abrahamsson in an unpublished Ph.D. dissertation, *Developing Nations and Ocean Transportation: An Analysis of the Cost and Pricing of Ocean Transportation*, University of Wisconsin, 1966, and is illustrated through the use of a mathematical model.

25. Reasonably complete public data are available only for U.S., British, and a few other publicly-owned or publicly-held lines. These data are summarized in S.A. Lawrence, *United States Merchant Shipping Policies and Politics* (Washington, D.C.: The Brookings Institution, 1966), appendix tables, A-11 to A-14 and (for British industry) in the *Report of the Committee of Inquiry into Shipping* (Her Majesty's Stationery House, 1970) (The Rochdale Report), Chapter 18. These data indicate average rates of return on capital employed in liner shipping of 3 to 5 percent. Similar results are reported for Norwegian shipping by the Norwegian Shipowners' Association.

26. A team at the University of Lyons has made statistical studies of the sensitivity of trade in seven primary products to changes in ocean freight rates over twenty-two French trade routes. The team's principal findings were: (1) little correlation exists between rate changes and changes in cargo volumes, (2) a fairly strong relationship exists between freights charged and the demand for the final product; and (3) there similarly is a positive correlation between the freight rate for specific products and the possibility of competition either from substitute products or from alternative transport services. See S. Wickham, *La Sensibilité des Exportations de Produits primaires aux Variations de Frets Maritimes* (University of Lyons, multilith, 1967).

27. Three basic developments in the character of foreign trade, discussed further in Part III, are relevant here. Historically, the overwhelming preponderance of trade has been rooted in distinctly different natural endowments and economies of trading partners. As a single world economy develops, these differences tend to disappear, the number of substitutes increases, and the margin of advantage of one source over another is narrowed. Second, the

reduction in sea transport expense in reference to other aspects of production allows traders to reach out to a greater variety of sources over a greater range of routings. Finally, our increasing affluence is probably bringing into foreign as well as domestic trade an increasing proportion of luxury commodities, for which demand is particularly sensitive to price.

Chapter 8
Organization of Sea Transport Markets

1. Above this size a second propeller must be added, which creates a steep increase in expense and some loss in propulsive efficiency.

2. C.H.F. Cuffley in *Ocean Freights and Chartering* (London: Staples Press, 1962) provides extensive material on the character of tramp freight markets. An analysis of the extent to which the many submarkets are linked within a total world market was examined by Hector Gripaios in a master's thesis for the London School of Economics (1949) quoted by D.L. McLachlan, *Pricing of Ocean Transportation* (dissertation, University of Leeds, circa 1963), p. 196.

3. This aspect of cost arising from flag discrimination has not been systematically examined, but would appear likely to be substantial in view of the marked instability in both the routing and volume of shipments of specific products. Costs of discriminatory practices are discussed at greater length in Chapter 10.

4. Presence of a second deck within the holds of the older tramps permitted these vessels to take some portion of their cargo in breakbulk form and eased the loading of semi-bulk cargoes shipped in barrels or bags. The sagging popularity of this type vessel in favor of single deck bulk carriers would suggest that shippers increasingly are using bulk handling techniques and that certain breakbulk commodities, formerly handled by tramps, have shifted to liners.

5. Data furnished the author by Fearnley and Egers Chartering Co., Ltd. show industrially-controlled carriers to make roughly 50 percent more trips with cargo than those owned by independents. Interestingly, the larger ships in both categories show slightly more voyages than those under 35,000 dwt. The data suggest that the industrials and the larger ships, representing very high capital investment, are loaded and discharged with maximum speed. The data may be biased through a higher proportion of short voyages in the industrial category, but this seems unlikely since these vessels are on the average also larger and hence presumably economically more suited to longer voyages.

6. Although bulk cargo vessels in the range of 35-40,000 dwt. can enter a high proportion of the world's ports, the number of ports with drafts and facilities to accommodate larger ships is quite limited, even in the developed countries. An analysis by D.J.M. Nolan in *Bulk Carriers: Past, Present and Future* (special thesis study prepared for the London Institute of Chartered

Shipbrokers, pp. 4-1), shows 27 percent of the world's 291 principal ports to have drafts at mean low water of less than 30 feet, 52 percent to have between 31 and 40 feet, and only 21 percent to have drafts in excess of this amount. A 15,000 dwt. vessel typically requires 30 feet of water; a 40 foot draft is necessary to safely accommodate a 50,000 dwt. bulk carrier.

7. However, such dual purpose tankers are no longer favored by the grain houses and they are no longer considered "combination carriers."

8. In a survey of the 1968 operations of 129 combined carriers, Fearnley and Egers found only fourteen voyages (approximately 1 percent of the total covered in the review) in which multiple cargoes were coupled in a single trip (letter dated 3 December 1969, from Mr. Birger Nossum to the author).

9. Ibid.

10. Cuffley, *Ocean Freights and Chartering* p. 334, reports 60 percent of tramp charters in 1960 to have been for grain, coal, and ore shipments. A report of his Ocean Freighting Research Service, quoted by the UNCTAD staff in *Freight Markets and the Level and Structure of Freight Rates* (UN publication, Document No. TD/B/C. 4/38) shows an even higher percentage of shipments to be in these classes in 1964-1967. However, there are inconsistencies in the volume of shipments shown in the two series which make a year-to-year comparison suspect.

11. Willi Frischauer, *Onassis* (New York: Meredith Press, 1968), pp. 90-96, describes the negotiation in vivid terms.

12. The homogeneity of liner rate behavior has been studied by McLachlan, (*Pricing of Ocean Transportation* op. cit.) by the UNCTAD Shipping Committee staff, by the Anti-Trust Subcommittee of the U.S. House of Representatives Committee on the Judiciary, and by others. McLachlan has constructed correlation indices for changes in rates of inbound and outbound conferences and of conferences serving separate trades (pp. 192-195). The UNCTAD Shipping Committee Report, *Freight Markets and the Level and Structure of Freight Rates* pp. 74-124, emphasizes the manner in which changes in commodity price levels influence rates with similar effects in various trades. The Anti-Trust Subcommittee of the U.S. House of Representatives Committee on the Judiciary, in its study, *The Ocean Freight Industry* (Report 1419, 87th Cong. 2d sess. Washington, D.C.: Government Printing Office, 1962), details interconference agreements.

13. Factors contributing to the spread of containerization and other unit load methods are discussed in detail in Chapter 14.

14. Analysis of liner itineraries published in trade journals suggests that the geographic zones serviced by liners typically are sufficiently large to generate at least 500 thousand tons of general cargoes annually. Twenty such zones (e.g., the United Kingdom; Europe; Bayonne to Hamburg; Western Baltic and Scandinavia; etc.) have been identified by Saguenay Research. Typically, liners operating in these areas will service the entire zone, although some services may

call at only selected ports within the zone and others may combine port calls within the zone with calls in an adjacent zone. Additionally, there are at least twenty smaller, more remote areas (e.g., Eire, Iceland, the Red Sea, Alaska) which support liner services on a more limited scale.

15. A larger number of countries engage in liner services within their local area. The numbers cited here refer only to countries offering long-distance sailings.

16. The size of liner markets in U.S. foreign trade was analyzed in the Northwestern University Study (see note 20, Chapter 7), Chapter 10. In the high volume U.S. trades, only seven of the twenty-seven official foreign trade routes, accounting for less than 15 percent of total cargo tonnage, were found to support less than fifteen vessels (able to provide approximately two sailings per week). Interestingly, even in these trades from four to nine firms were represented.

Chapter 9
Competition in Shipping

1. The only systematic analysis of optimum firm size in shipping which has come to the author's attention is that of Walter Oi reported in Chapter 9 of the Northwestern University study (A. Ferguson et al., *The Economic Value of the U.S. Merchant Marine*, Northwestern University Press, 1961), pp. 278-311. Oi's finding, related to liner firms, is that scale economies in this branch of the industry are small and tend to diminish after firm size reaches forty ships and the number of vessels assigned to a single service reaches ten to twelve. The UNCTAD staff, in *Establishment and Expansion of Merchant Marines in Developing Countries*, p. 16, concur in this general view and point out that even smaller firms may be organized successfully by supplementing in-house management competence through contracts with agents and other ship operators. E. Bennethan and A.A. Walters in *The Economics of Ocean Freight Rates* (Praeger, 1969) p. 40., on the other hand, stress the strategic importance of a firm's having sufficient resources to sustain a prolonged period of stiff competition from the conference operators when seeking to establish itself in a trade. Thinking within the industry at this point definitely favors the view that competitive success demands consolidation and strength.

2. Less-developed nations which have adopted targets for participation of national flag ships in their foreign trade generally have not legislatively distinguished between liner and bulk cargoes. Chilean legislation, in fact, explicitly states that its 50 percent objective includes ore shipments, and the Venezuelan government is considering a bill which would require half of Venezuela's oil to be exported in national flag ships.

3. The six largest private operators of liner vessels included three Japanese

companies (NYK, Mitsui-OSK, and Japan Line), the British Peninsula and Orient Lines, Norway's Wilhemsen Lines, and the Danish Maersk-Möllen operations.

4. The six giants of the liner industry participate in 128 of the transoceanic conferences listed in Croner's *World Directory of Freight Conferences* (London, 1970). These 128 conferences cover virtually all the world's major liner trades.

5. Voting patterns within conferences were analyzed in 1960-61 by the staff of the Anti-Trust Subcommittee of the Judiciary Committee, U.S. House of Representatives. For the conclusions of this analysis, see the staff report, *The Ocean Freight Industry*, H. Report 1419, 87th Cong., 2d sess. (Washington, D.C.: Government Printing Office, 1962).

6. The U.S. Merchant Marine Act of 1920, section 28, sought to make the preferential rail rates granted for export cargoes available only for cargoes subsequently to be shipped via U.S. flag vessels. The section was challenged in the court and has never been implemented.

German rail rates are often considered to favor German lines. These rates do promote shipments through German ports but do not discriminate between carriers.

7. George W. Stocking, *Workable Competition and Anti-Trust Policy* (Nashville Tenn.: Vanderbilt University Press, 1961), p. 190, and C.E. Ferguson, *A Macroeconomic Theory of Workable Competition* (Durham, N.C.: Duke University Press, 1964), p. 20.

8. One of the most interesting critiques of conference economics is found in S.G. Sturmey, "Economics and International Liner Services," *Journal of Transport Economics and Policy*, 1, no. 2 (1967), pp. 190-203, on which the text discussion draws heavily. See also the Northwestern University study and Bennethan and Walters, *Economics of Ocean Freight Rates*.

9. Although various computational models have been developed, no one to the author's knowledge has attempted a calculation of the economic costs and benefits of the conference system. The difficulties are partially conceptual and partially due to lack of data. As noted in the text, means for supporting prices may be a necessity in an activity which almost always operates with excess capacity. Such excess capacity in turn is an inevitable aspect of providing a scheduled service, if all cargoes presented for shipment are to be accommodated. Thus, whereas conference arrangements may create significant economic costs, these costs may be no larger than would be created through any other means for discharging a valid economic function.

10. Conferences have been studied by interested governmental groups since the turn of the century when Edward VII convened a Royal Commission on Shipping Rings, which submitted its generally favorable report in 1909. Recent reports on conference practices include those of the U.S. House Judiciary Committee, *The Ocean Freight Industry*, 1962; the Canadian Restrictive Practices Commission, *Shipping Conference Arrangements and Practices* (Ottawa: Queen's Printer, 1965); the 1970 report of the British Committee of Enquiry

into Shipping (Rochdale Report); and a 1970 report of the UNCTAD Shipping Committee, *Conference Practices and the Adequacy of Shipping Services* (UNCTAD Doc. TD/B/C. 4/62, 19 January 1970, multilith).

11. Public Law 87-346, section 2 (75 Stat. 763).

Chapter 10
The Economics of Government Aid

1. In the shipping field, the classic statement of this economic doctrine is found in F. Eversheim, *Effects of Shipping Subsidization* (Bremen Institute for Shipping Research, 1958).

2. See the Northwestern University study and S.G. Sturmey, *A Consideration of the Ends and Means of National Shipping Policy* (Bergen Institute for Shipping Research, 1965).

3. Sturmey, ibid., p. 25.

4. Estimates of the differential resource value of money prepared in the mid-fifties by OEEC staff (Milton Gilbert and associates) and subsequent calculations attempted by other authors are surveyed by H. Linneman, *An Econometric Study of International Trade Flows* (Amsterdam: North Holland Publishing Company, 1966), pp. 69-70, 220-222.

5. The most dramatic example is furnished by the United States, whose prices for new ship construction are more than double those of lowcost yards abroad but which nonetheless requires the employment of such ships in all its subsidized services.

6 See L.R. Prest, *Financing Transport in Developing Countries* (Unpub. MS of the Brookings Institution, 1967), p. 233.

7. A misallocation of resources occurs when the level of subsidization of shipping exceeds that of other sectors of the world economy so that an excess investment in shipping, followed by depression of rates, invites more goods to move in transoceanic trade than is economically optimum. In reality, it is unlikely that transportation costs will ever be reduced to a level which offsets the burdens on trades imposed by tariffs.

8. This is the basic strategy of the United Nations Conference on Trade and Development as first formulated by Raul Prebisch in *Towards a Global Strategy of Development* (UN publication Sales No. N.E.68. II.D.6) which argues for a basic shift in the pattern of the world economy to utilize more fully the manpower and resource potential of the less-developed world even though such action may displace apparently more efficient, developed industries, because in time new markets and new industries will emerge. The economic basis for the Prebisch doctrine is articulately examined in Virginia L. Galbraith's *World Trade and Transition* (Washington D.C.: Public Affairs Press, 1965).

9. An interesting example is provided by Cuba, whose shipping enterprises

have been heavily dependent upon sugar exports, which in turn were the major element in its economy. See C. Escarpenter, *The Economics of International Ocean Transportation: The Cuban Case Before 1958* (University of Wisconsin Press, 1965).

10. Efforts were made during the preparation of the Convention to Establish the Intergovernmental Maritime Consultative Organization to formulate standards to govern the provision of government aid to merchant shipping, but without success. The thoroughly compromised language which emerged has been interpreted by the Indian lawyer, Nagendra Singh, in *British Shipping Laws* (Singh, N. and Colinvaux, R., vol. 13; London: Stevens & Son, 1967), as sanctioning subsidies to shipping so long as such subsidies do not restrict the "availability of shipping services to the commerce of the world on a competitive basis."

During the same period, the smaller Organization for European Economic Cooperation adopted a Code of Liberalization of shipping to establish a standard of fair competition among the member European states. This code has subsequently been taken over by the OECD, whose overseas members include Canada and Australia. The Code calls for "free circulation of shipping in international trade in free and fair competition" and proscribes restrictions in cargo routing through "exchange control, by legislative provisions in favor of the national flag, by arrangements made by governmental or semi-governmental organizations giving preferential treatment to national flag ships, by preferential shipping clauses in trade agreements, by the operation of import and export licensing systems so as to influence the flag of the carrying ship, or by discriminatory port regulation or taxation measures." The Code does not proscribe direct cost-reducing subsidies, such as those extended by France and Italy; the United States, however, found it necessary to state a reservation to the Code in favor of its statutes for cargo preference.

Also, the General Agreement on Tariffs and Trade recognizes that "special governmental assistance may be required to promote the establishment, development or reconstruction of particular industries" but prohibits "quotas, import or export licenses or other measures" to restrict the free exchange of products. The 1958 Geneva Conventions require equality of treatment amongst foreign vessels passing through territorial waters; and clauses proscribing flag discrimination are to be found in many bilateral treaties of friendship, commerce, and navigation and in national laws. (See Franklin, *Economic Impact of Flag Discrimination*, pp. 45-47 and 348-353.)

11. Classifications of shipping subsidies by Franklin, ibid., Sturmey, *A Consideration*, etc., and Eversheim, *Effects of Shipping Subsidization*. A useful classification and treatment of economic effects also is found in O. Henell, *Flag Discrimination: Purposes, Motives and Economic Consequences* (Helsingfors: Soderstrom & Co., 1956).

12. Investment incentives may, of course, also be used to promote sales by

shipyards, and here the impact is direct and substantial. Thus, whereas a 10 percent investment grant is likely to create only a one or two percent margin in ship operating costs (and hence exercise only minor influence on an owner's decisions whether to build), a 10 percent differential in building costs between acquiring a vessel in Japan or in Britain is substantial in reference to deciding where the vessel is to be obtained.

13. This line of argument assumes free flow of capital across national borders so that owners are able to exercise the option of convenience flags. In fact, there are both formal and informal inhibitions which tend to restrict owners to national registries, particularly in Europe, Japan, and the less-developed states.

14. The economic effects of the U.S. subsidy system are discussed in the Northwestern University Study and S.A. Lawrence in *United States Merchant Shipping Policies and Politics* (Washington, D.C.: Brookings Institution, 1966).

15. The terms "flag discrimination" and "flag preference" are used interchangeably in this study, although some persons make the distinction that the former term denotes only mandatory decrees which discriminate formally between national and foreign flag vessels, whereas the latter denotes measures designed to cause shippers to route a stipulated portion of their cargoes via national flag. A definition which embraces both terms is: governmental action which, either directly or indirectly, imposes unequal requirements on national versus foreign flag vessels and/or affords them unequal opportunities to secure cargoes.

16. Franklin, *Economic Impact of Flag Discrimination* for details of cargo routing practices and legislation, see also the reports on this subject issued by the Maritime Transport Committee, OECD, and the International Chamber of Commerce.

17. For example, Guatemala under a 1965 law waived a 100 percent import tariff surcharge on cargoes carried by Guatemalan vessels—an incentive large enough to cover the entire freight expense of a typical shipment. A similar incentive is offered importers by Peru. In the Philippines, exporters are allowed an income tax credit twice the amount of shipping freights when using Philippine vessels. Uruguay waives half of its ad valorem import tariff if the consignment is carried on a national flag vessel, and also charges foreign ships higher port and stevedoring fees. Brazil exempts freight from the ad valorem tax base for customs duties when shipment is via a national company.

18. Since conference rate-making is a private negotiation, there is no direct evidence that cargo preferences cause an escalation of liner freight rates. There is indirect evidence, however, drawn from the relative level of rates for commodities covered by preference schemes. The influence of preferences on conference rates was studied in the mid-1960s by the U.S. Federal Maritime Commission and was extensively reviewed in a series of hearings before the Congressional Joint Committee on the Economic Report (see *Discriminatory Ocean Freight Rates and the Balance of Payments* Hearings and Reports, 88th and 89th Congress (10 volumns). Washington: U.S. government Printing Office, 1964).

19. A few states (e.g., Columbia, South Korea; similar legislation is being considered in Thailand and Taiwan) require exports to be handled on a freight prepaid basis (c.i.f.) and imports to be handled f.o.b. so that routing can be controlled by domestic companies and preference given national ships. Others (Indonesia, U.A.R., Guinea, and Ghana) use export-import licenses and trading corporations to gain control of cargo routing. Commercial realities, however, may defeat the most elaborate scheme. Bulk commodities, for example, are frequently sold for export well before their production or distribution has been arranged. A study performed by the UNCTAD staff noted some tendency for such products to be shipped f.o.b. and for manufactured products to travel c.i.f. Principally, the study noted, however, that enormous diversity characterized shipping terms and that the terms were far more sensitive to commercial factors than to policies to promote national merchant marines. (UN Conference on Trade and Development, *Terms of Shipment*, (UN publication No. TD/B/C.4/36, December 1968).

20. Franklin, *Economic Impact of Flag Discrimination*, p. 255. Franklin's data is calculated for Free World shipments only.

21. Ibid., pp. 267 and 314. Franklin's estimate is essentially arbitrary, being based on an estimated portion of the freights estimated to be paid for shipment of cargoes under preference schemes. If one accepts the premise advanced in this chapter that such preferences fundamentally distort the shape of world shipping, however, the order of magnitude Franklin cites would appear, if anything, to be conservative.

22. An example is provided by Greece which in the mid-1960s initiated a concerted program to repatriate citizen-owned ships. Such ships were guaranteed permanent exemption from all income taxation but were required to pay a modest tonnage tax in currencies earned in their foreign operations. Incentives were built into the scheme also to encourage formation of management offices in Greece and the use of Greek shipyards for modification and repair. Subsequently, the plan was made available also to foreign companies agreeing to domicile in Greece. Generous credit terms were concurrently extended to Greek owners agreeing to undertake new construction in domestic yards and to cover the amortization with hard currencies earned abroad.

23. Flag discrimination measures which disrupt and segment shipping markets place a double burden upon the domestic economy: first, in increased cost of shipping services and second, in less favorable transport arrangements for the nation's exports. The United States has on several occasions lost opportunities to make important sales of surplus wheat because of the reluctance of the potential buyer to take delivery in high cost U.S. flag ships; coffee imports to the U.S. are said to have shifted towards Africa from Brazil in part because of unsatisfactory shipping arrangements in the Brazilian coffee trade; both Burma and Uruguay have notoriously poor shipping services, and a declining foreign trade in part because of their insistence on discriminatory shipping practices; and so forth.

24. Johan Seland in "International Shipping, Sources of Invisible Earnings," *EFTA Bulletin* (June 1962) p. 12, has illustrated the extreme consequences which can flow from this method of fund accounting by pointing out that it would be possible for a nation owning not a single ship to show a credit in its transportation account were the freight payments for imports to be lower than the value of the goods and services furnished foreign vessels visiting her ports. This situation could actually occur in an oil-rich country offering popular bunkerage facilities or in a country enjoying substantial earnings through canal dues.

Introduction to Part III:
Developments in Trade and Technology

1. E.R. Schlesinger, "The Long-Run Outlook for U.S. Merchandise Imports," *Staff Papers of the International Monetary Fund* (February, 1954).

Chapter 11
Outlooks in International Relations and Trade

1. Trade between the industrialized nations has assumed a steadily larger share of total world trade during the past twenty years, growing from less than 60 percent of the world total by value in 1945 to 70 percent in 1965. This trade meanwhile has tended to shift from exchange between product groups to exchange within the same product line—i.e., chemicals, machinery, and automobiles sold both by Europe to the U.S. and by the U.S. to Europe. This shift supplants economic necessity with consumer preference and drastically narrows the gap of comparative advantage on which trade depends.

2. Sir Dennis Robertson, as quoted by Business International, *Corporate Planning Today for Tomorrow's World Market*, (BI Research Report, 1967), p. 34.

3. Econometric models of international trade are reviewed and evaluated by Grant B. Taplin in "Models of World Trade," *Staff Papers of the International Monetary Fund*, 14, no. 3 (1967). Additional, more recent contributions are referenced in an OECD study by F.G. Adams, *An Econometric Analysis of International Trade*, OECD Economic Studies Series, (January 1969).

4. In effect economists now regard comparative advantage to be an economic phenomenon, rather than the product of resource endowments. The latter are rather widely spread and substitutes are readily available. Demand for specific products is a function of their price, and willingness to commit resources to their production is a function of demand. In effect, comparative advantages are manmade or, as Kindelberger puts it: "Trade explains factor endowments

rather than factor endowments trade." Charles B. Kindelberger, *Economic Development*, (New York: McGraw-Hill, 1958), p. 243. Econometric studies accordingly have largely eliminated factor endowments from their calculations.

5. Hans Linneman, *An Econometric Study of International Trade Flows*, (Amsterdam: North Holland Publishing Co., 1966).

Working with 1958-1960 data, Linneman developed equations to describe trade flows between eighty countries (6,300 trade pairs) solely in terms of the gross product and population of each country, the distance separating them, and their participation in preferential trading systems. In a supplemental analysis, he also introduced a "commodity composition" variable, but found that, other than for oil-producing countries, it was not of major importance.

A number of pilot studies preceded the Linneman study and a group of Finnish economists under the direction of P. Poyhonen published their results concurrently. Other recent work is reported in papers presented at a meeting of the Ad Hoc Group of Experts on Import/Export Projections, sponsored by UNCTAD, Geneva, 29 May to 2 June 1967.

6. Linneman's calculations ignore per capita income, in part on the grounds that it is not an independent variable which must be represented separately in his equations and, in part, because different per capita income levels appear not to affect the propensity to trade. A rich country represents a larger market in relation to its population than a poor one, to be sure, but it also demands a greater variety of products and offers more surplus production for use abroad. The per capita income factor therefore is nondeterminative. Linneman, *An Econometric Study*, pp. 19, 211.

7. Ibid., p. 180. Of course, this diminution may be offset by the stimulus to overall economic activity which integration would provide.

8. Ibid., pp. 28, 180-188.

9. Ibid., pp. 188-196.

10. Although he did not include secondary effects in his calculation, Belassa has presented estimates of the imported component of goods exported by major trading nations, which range from a low of 5 percent in the case of the United States to highs of 21 percent in the case of Japan, and 40 percent in the case of Israel. It should be noted also that Belassa found that the stimuli to trade would be broadly shared by the nations participating in tariff reductions so that such reductions would have little effect on their net trade balances. Interestingly Japan would stand to gain most in expanding exports versus imports. (See B. Belassa, *Trade Liberalization Among Industrialized Countries* (New York: McGraw-Hill, 1967), chapter iv.

11. See note 24 of this chapter.

12. The effect is very simply demonstrated in reference to the Japanese steel industry, which is built almost entirely on imported materials. A purchase by the United States of steel from Japan will be followed by purchases of coal from Canada and ores from Chile and Australia, each major trading partners of the

U.S. Assuming their earnings from sales to Japan were translated into imports of U.S. automobiles, built from Japanese steel, a closed feedback loop is created which expands the economic activity of all concerned by the extent to which the trade rationalized production and permitted new markets for the final product (U.S. cars in this case) to grow in Chile, Australia and Canada.

13. F.G. Adams, *An Econometric Analysis of International Trade*, p. 50.

14. Ibid., p. 58. See also R.R. Rhomberg, "Short Term Trade Model," *Econometrica*, 34 (1966) pp.

In practice, the adjustment and feedback mechanism noted in the text may not work as smoothly as in the economists' models. For nations which are heavily trade dependent, recessionary phases are likely to require unacceptable internal adjustments and create pressures for protective arrangements to buffer their effect. The fiscal policies used by industrialized nations during inflation also tend to frustrate the natural operation of the corrective cycle, due to the proclivity of governments to resort to temporary trade restrictions as a means for postponing the necessary action to restrain internal demand.

15. Judd Polk, "The Rise of World Corporations," *Saturday Review*, 22 November 1969, p. 32. At present market values Polk estimates the accumulated overseas investment of multinational companies, defined as companies making 25 percent or more of their sales abroad, to be in the range of $300 billion, of which a bit more than half has been originated by U.S.-based firms. About one-third of the U.S. investment is in manufacturing, one-third in oil, and one-third in other activities. Although chiefly concentrated in already industrialized economies, the investment has been an important force in the industrialization of less developed areas and nations, where foreign companies plan an even more prominent role in relation to the scale of locally-based activities. Despite political instability and expropriations, the flow of investment funds from developed to less developed states has grown at the rate of 18 percent per year from 1963 through 1968, when it reached the level of $5.8 billion.

16. This shift has been spurred in part by the formation of EFTA and the EEC, and by U.S. investment in Europe which has increased at a rate of 15 percent per year between 1950 and 1967 (ibid., p. 33).

17. According to data compiled by the U.S. Department of Commerce, affiliates of U.S. firms had sales abroad in 1964 of $37.2 billion; their exports to the United States alone were $2.7 billion. (We may assume that at least this level of production was also distributed to other European nations.) Imports by the affiliates from the U.S. were reported at $3.7 billion, or almost 10 percent gross production (see U.S. Department of Commerce, *Survey of Current Business*, Dec. 1965).

18. Business International, *Corporate Planning Today*, p. 37.

19. Kindelberger, *Foreign Trade and the National Economy*, (New Haven: Yale University Press, 1962), chapter 12.

20. Commission on International Development, *Partners in Development* (New York: Praeger, 1969), p. 45.

21. For an excellent survey of actions during the period through 1955 to remove restrictions to trade, see *The Quest for Free Trade* (United Nations publication Sales No. 1955 II.C.S.). Subsequent actions have been summarized in annual reports published by the U.N. on current events in international trade and development.

22. Forecasts of foreign trade activity are commonly included as a component of national development plans. Such forecasts, however, may represent more a level of aspiration than a realistic estimate of levels which can actually be achieved.

23. See Organization for Economic Cooperation and Development, *The Outlook for Economic Growth* (Paris, 1970).

24. The Kennedy Round tariff reductions are to be spread over the period 1968-1971. It may be assumed that the trade effect lags to cover roughly the period 1969-1975. Preeg has estimated the tariff reductions on dutiable trade in nonagricultural commodities (excluding fuel and trade flowing within EFTA, EEC and the British Commonwealth Systems) would permit a reduction in c.i.f. prices averaging 4.3 percent. The 1964 level of this trade was $25.6 billion. Preeg assumed a demand elasticity of −2 (so that each percent change in the relative price of imports yields a 2 percent increase in their sale) and that the tariff reduction is fully reflected in relative import price. Using the 1964 base, the increase in trade due to the Kennedy Round would calculate to roughly $2.2 (or almost $4.0 billion extrapolating to 1969 trade levels and prices). To this amount one must add the increased trade in agricultural products flowing from reductions in this field, the effect of the lowering of nontariff barriers, the effect on trade with nations not included within the $25.6 billion base figure cited above, and the increased opportunity for nonmembers of the EEC and EFTA to penetrate these markets which resulted from the Kennedy Round. Except with respect to this last, Preeg did not attempt estimates of these effects. See E.H. Preeg, *Traders and Diplomats* (The Brookings Institution, 1970), chapter 14.

25. Aluminum products, for example, typically involve four stages; raw bauxite may be shipped to Arvida for reduction to alumina, the alumina is smeltered to ingot in Norway, rolled into sheets in England, and fabricated into a finished product in Germany.

26. Alexander Eckstein, *Communist China's Economic Growth and Foreign Trade* (New York: McGraw-Hill, 1966), p. 47.

Chapter 12
Cargo Trends and Implications

1. Detailed trade statistics are published by only about 60 percent of the world's nations. Adequate data are not available from Communist nations, India, Pakistan, or many of the small, less-developed countries of Africa and Asia.

2. It should be noted that port authorities are unable so easily to adjust their capacity to changing trade levels and ports consequently have become the most vigorous supporters of shipping research. Results of port studies are generally available to and are used by the liner companies.

3. UNCTAD Shipping Committee staff in "Review of Recent Developments and Long Term Trends in World Shipping" (UNCTAD TD/31, 27 December 1967) published their projection of worldwide dry and tank ship cargoes through 1975. These estimates were subsequently adapted by Litton Industries in a report to the U.S. Department of Transportation (Litton Industries, *Oceanborne Shipping: Demand and Technology Forecast*, Report to the U. S. Department of Transportation, June 1968). Both the UNCTAD and Litton data are essentially only extrapolations of past-year trends in oceanborne commerce. The UN statistical staff, at the request of the UNCTAD Shipping Committee, have formulated a proposal for an ambitious project to build the statistical base for a worldwide econometric model of cargo flows but have not yet received funding support.

4. Consumption rates of various products per thousand of population are presented in the appendices of Bela Bellassa, *Trade Prospects for Developing Countries* (Homewood, Ill.: Irwin Press, 1964).

5. The global outlook for container shipping has been surveyed by a British ship brokerage firm, Lambert Bros., in a publication titled, "Displacement of Conventional Liner Tonnage on Major World Trade Routes, 1970" (London: mimeo., 1970). See also Table 12-2.

6. "747–Vast Promise, Some Problems," *Transportation and Distribution Management*, (September 1969), p. 38. The L-500 has a cargo payload of 150 tons; the B-747–100 tons.

7. The aircraft manufacturers have forecast sales of 200 all cargo jumbo jets by 1975 and an additional 250 craft by 1980. Added to the anticipated belly capacity of passenger aircraft, this would provide cargo capacity of roughly 14 billion ton miles in 1975 and 30 billion ton miles in 1980, perhaps two-thirds of which would be available for international service.

8. The rule of thumb estimate that cargoes moving in volumes in excess of 300,000 tons per year will tend to be handled in bulk was developed by Reinhold Schulz, secretary of the OECD Maritime Transport Committee, and has been used as a base point for subsequent studies by the British Shipbuilders Association and others. See, footnote 9, chapter 7.

9. See remarks of S.G. Sturmey, "The Impact on World Seaborne Trade of Changes in Shipping Costs," presented to the International Symposium on Middleterm and Longterm Forecasting; multilithed distribution by Stichting Maritime Research, The Hague, June 1970.

10. Estimate developed from data on number of container ships in operation or under construction by A/S Shipping Consultants, Oslo.

11. The outlook for major bulk commodity shipments has been assessed in detail by Saguenay Research for its annual studies of world ship charter markets.

Continual surveillance of bulk movements is also maintained by the Norwegian firm, Fearnley and Egers. Several major U.S. consulting firms (Arthur D. Little, Litton Systems, Stanford Research Institute, and Booz, Allen, Hamilton) also have prepared bulk cargo estimates for the Maritime Administration.

12. Represents the transport performances which might be provided by a tanker fleet of six million tons.

13. World Bank, "Recent and Prospective Trends in the World Petroleum Industry," Commodity Note 57, and G. Norstrom, *The World Demand for Merchant Shipping Tonnage and the Swedish Shipbuilding Industry 1964-1980* (Stockholm: Almquist and Wiksell, 1965).

14. UNCTAD, *World Commodity Survey, 1968*, (United Nations publication TD/ B/C.1/Rev. 1, Sales No. E. 69 II.D.%) pp. 81-84.

15. For example, Rotterdam's marine industrial area has become the most rapidly growing industrial site in Europe. In the United States, there has been a pronounced shift of population from the interior to the coastal counties.

Chapter 13
Developments in Marine Technology

1. In an economic study of tramp shipping, Thomas Thorburn has demonstrated that the justification for greater investment for larger vessels and higher speeds increases as the size and distance of the cargo increase. Thus, the long distance, deep-ocean trades establish the leading edge for marine technology. Their growth will encourage innovations which would have payoff on the short sea routes only at sharply higher levels of business, but which later may be transferred into the shorter trades as the technology is established. The models presented by Thorburn are a classic case of demand leading technology with feedback to demand. Thomas Thorburn, *Supply and Demand of Water Transport* (Stockholm Institute of Economics, 1960), chapter 3.

2. Erich Jantsch, *Technological Forecasting in Perspective* (Paris: Organization for Economic Co-Operation and Development, 1967); Raymond S. Isenson, "Technological Forecasting: A Management Tool," in *Management, A Book of Readings*, H. Koontz and C. O'Donnell, eds., 2d ed. (New York: McGraw-Hill Book Co., 1968), p. 85.

3. Thomas Thorburn, *Supply and Demand for Water Transport*, pp. 95, 200.

4. Design of very large ship structures actually presents fewer problems than that of smaller vessels since environmental forces are distributed more evenly. The potential liabilities which would be incurred in the event of an oil spill three to five times that of the *Torrey Canyon*, on the other hand, may act as a check on tankers larger than those now in service.

The application of the latest type of bulbous bow has permitted the construction of much beamier vessels in order to maximize deadweight capacity for a given set of dimensions. The optimum hull speed for ships of this design is in the region of 16 knots, which can be achieved through a single screw in vessels of up to about 325,000 dwt.—the largest size now in operation. Since twin screws are somewhat less efficient and the gains to be derived through further increase in size diminish in upper ranges, a step increase to the 500,000 dwt. is required if further scale economies are to be realized.

5. The modal size of bulk carriers in operation, 1 January 1969, was in the 30,000 to 40,000 dwt. range. The surge in new orders for smaller vessels therefore represented an interruption in the general trend toward larger size, which is in response to the need for replacements for aging warbuilt Liberty and Victory ships to handle secondary trades.

6. Several such configurations are described in *Ship Types of the Future*, Proceedings of the International Marine and Shipping Conference, 10-20 June 1969 (London: Institute of Marine Engineers, 1969).

7. J.A. Teasdale, *Survey of Tug and Barge Transport Systems in North America*, multilith report available from the author, University of Newcastle-on-Tyne, England.

8. Among the advantages claimed for a compoundable ship by I.E. Iozza in a paper presented to the International Marine and Shipping Conference, June 10-20 1969, are: greater flexibility in employment of the power unit and in drydocking and repairs, greater ability of the ship's units to enter small ports, and (for tankers) barge drafts which would permit transiting the Suez Canal with cargoes much larger than those now possible.

9. Michael Hubbard has calculated that it is more economical in shipping crude oil to use supertankers (150,000 dwt, and over) for the deepwater portion of any voyage in excess of 4,000 miles. See Hubbard, "The Comparative Cost of Oil Transport to and within Europe," *Journal of the Institute of Petroleum*, 53, no. 517 (1967). The calculation of course assumes that schedules are such that both the supertanker and local delivery ships can be fully utilized. An alternative much used in Europe is to offload a portion of the supertanker cargo at a deepwater port of first call and deliver the remainder to ports of lesser draft capacity.

10. Standard-sized containers have been used by the U.S. military since prior to World War II. However, SeaLand (then Pan Atlantic Steamship) is generally credited with initiating the "container revolution" in an experimental New York to Houston service in 1955. SeaLand's first, specially converted cellular ships were placed in service two years later. Grace Lines made the first attempt to use a cellular ship in foreign trade in 1958 and the following year, Matson successfully introduced containerization between the West Coast of the U.S. and Hawaii. It was not until March 1966, however, that a fully integrated container service was launched on the North Atlantic by U.S. Lines with ships partially fitted out with rails to carry containers as well as conventional cargoes. A

historical review of the various steps toward containerization is found in Hideo Iida, *Containerization, Theory and Practice* (published in Japanese by Seizando Bookstore, 1968; available in English only in multilith), which is perhaps almost the most comprehensive single source on the subject. See also A.A. Evans, *Technical and Social Changes in the World's Ports* (Geneva: International Labour Office, 1969).

11. The manner in which port investments are handled varies widely. The Port of New York Authority builds and leases dock and terminal areas but expects operators to install their own equipment; the Halifax containerport was built and equipped with government funds; the Port of London is a private corporation financed through borrowings; and so forth.

12. The economics of pallet versus conventional break-bulk and container ship operations have been elaborately developed, from a pallet operator's point of view, in J.R. Getz et al., "Design of a Cargo Liner in the Light of Developments in General Cargo Transportation," presented at the Diamond Jubilee meeting of the Society of Naval Architects and Marine Engineers.

13. The lower percentage applies to trades among industrialized nations; the higher to trades with less developed areas.

14. The SeaLand ships will carry 1,086 thirty-five foot containers. The ships are powered by two steam turbines generating a total of 120,000 shaft horsepower (SHP) and are 944 feet long by 105 feet beam with a 30 foot summer draft. Six vessels being ordered by British Consortia for their Australian service are twin screwed steam turbine vessels delivering 80,000 SHP for a service speed of 26 knots and designed to carry 1,800 twenty foot containers.

15. At 80 percent utilization, a single 43,000 ton container ship operated at thirty knots in transatlantic service can handle as much cargo as eight to ten modern 15,000 dwt. 18 knot conventional freighters. The entire North Atlantic trade in 1980 could potentially be served by only thirty-five of these super-carriers.

16. It is difficult at this time to estimate the economic advantage of employing large, high speed container ships. Because of their fine lines and relatively light displacement, high speeds can be obtained for large vessels at a relatively modest cost. In the container trades, however, cargo is definitely limited in supply. This means that economies of scale, which have fostered the development of the supertanker, will be of lesser importance in the development of container ships. Growth in ship size in the container trades has come as a side benefit of the high capital costs that have forced many competitors to form consortia and so consolidate the available cargo into fewer, larger ships. These new large high-speed ships have enormous horsepower requirements. The cost and weight of fuel oil is so great, particularly on long trade routes, that nuclear plants may well find their first real niche in this particular sector of the merchant marine.

17. The possibilities for development of this new type service are further discussed in chapter 14.

18. Export documentation is estimated by the U.S. National Committee on International Trade Documentation (NCITD) to cost about $3.5 billion per year, or 10 percent of the f.o.b. value of U.S. exports. Simplification of the Bill of Lading alone was estimated by the Committee to save exporters some $500 million per year. See Maritime Transportation Research Board, *Documentation for Cargo Movement* (Washington, D.C.: National Academy of Sciences/National Research Council, 1971), pp. 4, 7.

19. Both national and international agencies are involved in a concerted effort, which now is beginning to pay real dividends. Ibid., chapter 2.

20. Remarks of Vincent Barba, General Manager, Container Operations, Mareport '71, Baltimore, Md., 6 April 1971.

21. See P. G. Fielding, "A High Speed Ship for the 1970's," paper presented to the Society of Naval Architects and Marine Engineers, June 18, 1969.

22. The Litton Industries forecast is for a 1,000 to 4,000 ton captured air bubble GEM by 1983 to operate in coastal or interisland trade with a potential also for service to underdeveloped ports where delivery must be made inland. Litton Industries, *Oceanborne Shipping: Demand and Technology*, Report to the U.S. Department of Transportation, June 1968), p. 3.

23. Ibid., pp. 3-65.

24. Ibid., pp. 3-57. In addition to its reduced wave-making resistance, the TRISEC would appear to have a number of advantageous characteristics. The main body of the ship, for example, can be built as a plain rectangle permitting lighter and lower cost construction and improved cargo stowage. As with the catamaran, deck area may be enlarged.

25. The General Dynamics proposal envisions a 250,000 dwt., 18 knot vessel to provide a year round shuttle service between Arctic oil fields and a transshipment port in southern Greenland. The company estimates that a fleet of six such vessels might be built for roughly $1 billion. Its calculation of the total system cost for delivery of Arctic oil via its proposed mode is $1.25 per barrel, which it believes will be competitive with other practical alternatives. In addition, the Company argues that, once fully developed, the system would be more reliable than one which is exposed to the elements. Development and construction would require a minimum of three to four years.

26. Litton Industries, *Oceanborne Shipping*, pp. 3-77. Although Litton has identified the possibility of using submarines for moving Arctic oil, it should be noted that it published its forecast prior to the General Dynamics proposal.

27. Ice breaking involves both art and science, with many different characteristics of the ship, ice, and weather affecting the possibilities for safe and economical transit. For an interesting report of the Manhattan voyage, see T.C. Pullin, "We Smashed through the Northwest Passage," *Petroleum Today*, Winter 1970, pp. 4-11.

28. The economics of land bridge services are heavily dependent on the rate charged for services. In the U.S., this rate must be approved by the Interstate Commerce Commission unless the service can be shown not to concern domestic

interstate transportation. The SeaLand organization in 1967-68 participated in serious negotiations with U.S. rail carriers in an effort to bring rates down to $10/measurement ton for transcontinental service (approximately $150/35 foot container). The offering price of the railroads at the time was $500/40 foot container and the spread between bid and offered sufficiently large that no agreement was concluded. Although U.S. rails have continued to publish special land bridge rates, they have not yet brought rates to a level which seriously threatens sea carriers, although some analysts believe it to be economically feasible for them to do so.

29. An interesting state-of-the-art report, "Pipeline Transportation," may be found in the January 1969 issue of a trade magazine, *Handling and Shipping*. Pipelines have been used for many years to move coal slurries over relatively short distances. About 100 such lines are now being operated in the U.S. to move such materials as gilsonite, sulphur and limestone. A $35 million coal slurry is being constructed across the Arizona-Nevada border which will move 660 tons per hour over a 275 mile span. In Canada, slurry lines are being used to pump wood chips to paper mills. Following an experiment in which a 514 pound ball was successfully moved through a 109 mile oil pipeline, the Canadian Pipeline Research and Development Association has approved a five-year $4.75 million program to develop commercial methods of moving capsules in pipelines.

Chapter 14
Implications for the Shipping Industry

1. The consultants' studies were chiefly concerned with identifying cargoes which could economically be handled by containers and the routes upon which containerships would be most likely to prove economically feasible. Building on these findings, the consultants·projected the likely displacement of conventional liners with container vessels and the likely impact on ports and port labor. The principal source documents are: two reports by Arthur D. Little, Inc. to the British National Ports Council, *Containerization on the North Atlantic: A Port-to-Port Analysis* and *1970 Outlook for Deep Sea Container Service*, both dated November, 1967; a report presented to the Ports Council Operational Research Department of the University of Lancaster, *The Potential for Container Service Based on Physical Cargo Characteristics*, December, 1967; and a more summary, dramatic presentation to the British Transport Docks Board of the estimated impact of containerization on maritime industries by McKinsey and Co., Inc. *Containerization, the Key to Low Cost Transport*, June, 1967. A rebuttal to the McKinsey report by Eric Heirung of the Fred Olsen Lines titled, "Containerization: Key to Waste of Money," was published in the October 5, 1967 issue of the *Fairplay International Shipping Journal*. At about this same

time a statement also was issued by the Port of New York Authority titled *Container Shipping: Full Ahead*, expressing that body's commitment to a major investment in the Port Elizabeth container terminal.

2. An additional twenty-four container ships are anticipated to be placed in North Atlantic service by 1972. As a rule of thumb, one modern container ship, designed for a twenty-two knot service speed carrying 1,000 twenty foot containers, has a cargo capacity approximately equal to five conventional liners.

3. "Rate Troubles Beset Containership Operators on North Atlantic Route," *N.Y., Journal of Commerce*, Dec. 7, 1970, p. 5A.

4. As noted in Chapter 9, firm size within the liner industry shows a rather marked discontinuity, with a large number of companies operating less than twenty-five ships on only two to three routes and a very few controlling from forty to eighty ships each and being represented in a large number of trades. However, on a particular route, no single company typically has operated more than about fifteen ships and usually only enough vessels have been committed to one route as are necessary to provide sailings at competitive intervals. The result has been to spread available cargoes widely among a large number of companies, the number of participants being roughly proportional to the size of the trade.

5. Most container systems require two containers on shore for each container on ship—i.e., a ratio of three boxes per shipboard cell. At $3,000 a copy, the containers for a 1,000 unit ship would involve an outlay of $9 million versus $10 to $15 million for the ship itself. However, the wear and tear on containers is likely to be much higher than that on seagoing equipment, and companies typically are seeking to amortize the container units over a period of five to eight years.

6. Company-owned containers may be supplemented as needed to meet specialized requirements or fluctuations in demand with leased equipment. Also a number of the smaller operators have entered into container interchange agreements with one another. Shipowners will also carry equipment owned by shippers which meets technical specifications. Most, but not all, international container operations are now conducted with containers built to ISA dimensional standards. The major exception is SeaLand, which uses thirty-five foot design (but which has designed its new ships so that they can be converted to carry forty-foot lengths if desired). However, while operating with common dimensional standards, each operator by design or happenstance has also built into his system certain unique features which tend to complicate interchange arrangements.

7. A direct example of how the impulse to expand the scope of container networks is linked to the supply and movement of containers is provided by the recently announced agreement of the DART consortium (North Atlantic), Fabre Line (U.S./Mediterranean), and Columbus Line (U.S., New Zealand and Australia) to operate a joint container pool. Its title is Global Containers, Ltd.

8. An interesting example is provided by the OCL efforts to extend

container services to Hong Kong, a step which would be entirely rational from an overall transport systems point of view, but which is less attractive when viewed from the local perspective of a small, crowded island. Plans for a multimillion dollar container port have been under discussion in Hong Kong for over five years. Although OCL acknowledges "bringing maximum pressure to bear" to gain approval of this project, it has not yet been successful. Failure of the Hong Kong legislature to authorize construction has in effect choked off OCL plans to extend its container operations from Australia north and eastward across the Pacific Ocean.

9. "Closed conferences" are those which set their own standards, usually highly restrictive, for admission of new members. "Open conferences" are those which are required to accept any applicant willing to abide by conference rules, pay an initiation fee, and meet other reasonable tests. See chapter 4.

10. The U.K.-Australian conferences had long resisted intrusion by ships servicing western Europe into the trade, and, within the conventional liner system, European and British trades were almost fully insulated from one another.

11. In designing the Australia-European Container Service (AECS), a particular effort was made not to seem to overreach the opportunities for control of the trade which the combine enjoyed. The Scandinavian companies and the Australian government both were fully consulted and services organized in a manner which recognized these other interests in the trade. See "Interpreting the Logic of Containerization," *The London Times*, 27 October 1969, editorial.

12. See *Graphic Analysis of Rules Affecting Container Traffic* (Federal Maritime Commission, multilith, June 1969).

13. Agreement #9813, docket 69-58, Federal Maritime Commission.

14. Letter from George F. Balland to the Commission, 22 August 1969, docket 69-58.

15. In the North Atlantic, a 5 to 10 percent discount is allowed for cargoes presented in containers and the containers themselves are leased to shippers on rather liberal terms. Rates have also been opened by the conferences on several hundred commodities for which member lines now compete for cargo. See C.F. Davis, "Rate Troubles Beset Container Operators on North Atlantic Route," *N.Y. Journal of Commerce* (7 December 1970), p. 5A.

16. Providing that the ship is equipped with heavy lift gear, containers can be loaded and unloaded at any location which has sufficient storage area to handle incoming and outgoing containers. Realizing the economies of rapid cargo handling procedures, however, requires much more space than is available at most conventional cargo terminals, particularly those organized around finger piers.

17. British Shippers' Council, *Future Container Services: What Shippers Require* (multilith, 1967-68). The Council urged the Treasury to allow port investment beyond that which could meet strict cost-benefit tests on the

grounds that such surplus capacity would be the best protection the country could buy against monopolization of container trades by a few enormous consortia.

18. U.S. law requires both domestic and foreign conference rates to be nondiscriminatory between ports, and a similar standard is evolving with Great Britain and the European Common Market through its Transport Commission. The standard is a difficult one however to apply in practice, and there is a continual struggle among ports to expand their overlapping hinterlands. The nondiscrimination clauses also apply only to rates established by collective action and therefore are nonapplicable to contract carriers or nonconference steamship lines.

19. The pattern of overland feeder services within the large industrial nations mirrors these same pressures. Thus England has devised a program through which all container lines draw on cargoes flowing into seven major inland consolidation centers. But, within the U.S., each major container line has established its own network of consolidation points and forty or fifty cities are represented in one network or another.

20. For example, the AECS group may argue that the volume of cargoes from Europe to Australia, which was sufficient to support a half dozen competing liner services, is insufficient to support more than one adequate service using container ships, although this assertion remains vulnerable to challenge by a competitor line. Whether or not another carrier may choose to enter the trade, however, it would be entirely practical for Australians to make shipments to Europe either via Singapore or via the eastern route through the Panama Canal.

21. It can be argued that in shipping the participation of six or seven competitively weak carriers in a trade is more likely to result in monopoly conditions (since such carriers are strongly motivated to rely on the protection of the conference) than a smaller number of carriers whose competitive strength is bolstered by participation in a variety of trades. Also, competitive strength in today's shipping world requires a broader base than one or two trades can provide and must be assessed in reference to world competition rather than in terms of competition within any particular national flag group. From this viewpoint, the Justice Department position in opposition to the SeaLand acquisition of U.S. Lines appears to be contrary to the objectives which the Department seeks.

22. The argument is particularly well stated by Arne Koch, *Current Pricing Behavior in Liner Shipping* (Bergen: Institute for Shipping Research, 1968). See also chapter 7, for an outline of the basic rationale for a demand based price system in liner shipping.

23. The technical feasibility of providing a container service with newsprint-type bulk carriers, or indeed almost any ship, has been noted in chapter 13. The economic feasibility depends upon such intangibles as the willingness of port

authorities to provide suitable berthing space, of underwriters to offer cargo insurance, of dock workers to handle the cargo, and of shippers to permit this alternative routing. Modest amounts of package cargoes always have been loaded by tramps. The new condition is simply that the shipment can now be technically managed with more ease and safety, and in greater volume, than heretofore was practical.

24. Kerry St. Johnstone, managing director of OCL, likens the short sea route to a bridge on which the operator appropriately exacts a standard toll for use. The sea leg in this case accounts for a far smaller proportion of total port-to-port transport costs than in transoceanic service, with the results that (a) the charge bears less relevance to patronage than the frequency and convenience of the service, and (b) the operator can afford to average out his load factor over a much larger number of trips. Also the short sea operator faces competition in many routes from rail firms and overland services. See K. St. Johnstone, "The Impact of Containerization Upon the Structure of World Shipping," Speech before the Transportation Research Forum, Montreal, 1967.

25. In the early period, container operators were concerned about their ability to attract small package cargoes and offered the FAK rate as an inducement to forwarders to consolidate such cargoes into containers for shipment via their ships. It was unclear whether the forwarder should charge the regular tariff to his customers or alternatively pass some portion of the saving on. The practice consequently came under attack from the conferences and government regulatory agencies, which construed the practice as a means for providing illegal rebates to shippers. See Hideo Iida, *Containerization Theory and Practice* (Tokyo: Seizando Bookstore, Ltd., 1968), pp. 215 ff.

26. The minimum rate on North Atlantic services at 32¢/cu. ft. works out to a bit over $400 for a 20-foot container, which is about 60 percent of the revenue which might typically be expected for a full container load of paying cargo.

27. Shipping interests apparently fear and would be prepared vigorously to resist any action along these lines by the forwarders. A recent case provides some interesting perspectives. Two groups of N.Y. forwarders had in the late 1960s sought to organize container consolidation terminals in New York close to the port area and within the 50-mile radius covered by the N.Y. Shipping Association-International Longshoreman's Association contract agreement. The forwarders proposed to use ILA labor to stuff their containers, as required by the agreement but, after a false start, were informed by the ILA that its personnel could no longer work on the job. Containers originating within the 50-mile zone not packed by ILA labor are subject to a $250 surcharge when loaded on N.Y. Shipping Association ships, so the effect was to force the forwarders to abandon their plan. The forwarder group filed suit, which was later withdrawn in favor of a suit filed by an individual forwarder who had been faced by the same action. Although a final decision has not yet been rendered, a preliminary injunction was issued in March 1969 against the NYSA and the ILA to desist from discriminating against such forwarder activities.

28. During the summer of 1970 unsatisfactory conditions in the North Atlantic trade led the U.S. Federal Maritime Commission to consider seriously asking Congress for authority to suspend noncompensatory rates in international shipping. The proposal evoked a storm of protest even before it was announced, and was quietly dropped.

29. Rate simplification in North America was initiated by the container lines proposing the North Atlantic "super conference." Although this initiative has been dropped, the task has been taken up by a subgroup of the National Committee for International Trade Documentation (NCITD) and in Europe by a quasi-official unit, SITPRO, which is seeking to harmonizing steamship rate classes with the Brussel Standard Tariff Nomenclature.

30. The term "through transport" denotes point-to-point shipment under a single bill of lading and with a single carrier assuming full responsibility for the shipment's successful completion. The term is usually used in reference to shipments between inland points requiring coordination of the services of several carriers. The tariff for this service may or may not be the sum of the tariffs for its several components (quotations varying from the sum of the components are termed "single factor rates"). The scope of the term "trade facilitation" is very much broader than "through transport" since it embraces the whole range of techniques to facilitate point-to-point transportation of goods, of which a "through service" is but one.

31. SeaLand, for example, opposes through shipment tariffs on the grounds that more flexible and economical arrangements can be developed on an ad hoc basis tailored to the needs of specific customers and the availability of overland transport at the time the shipment actually must be handled.

32. The joint ownership of railroad and steamship lines, which had grown to large scale proportions during the late nineteenth century, was prohibited by the U.S. in the Panama Canal Act of 1912. In Europe statutory prohibitions were not enacted, but throughout the continent rail lines were brought under government control during World War I and the years immediately thereafter, effectively destroying the opportunity for private companies to control both rail and steamship lines.

33. Federal Maritime Commission General Order 13 (46OFR 536.16).

34. The survey is reported in Maritime Transportation Research Board, *Legal Impediments to International Intermodal Transportation* (Washington, D.C.: National Academy of Sciences, 1971), pp. 130-153. This report provides exceptionally thorough coverage of issues relating to intermodal shipments to and from the U.S.

35. In the days of sailing ships, ship masters accepted responsibility for cargo by issuing bills of lading when cargo was delivered to ship's tackle, and they were discharged of responsibility when the cargo was delivered to the overseas pier. As ship operators developed their own terminals, this practice shifted. Bills of lading were issued when goods were delivered to the terminal, and the costs of holding the cargo until the next ship's arrival and positioning it for loading onboard were

included in the tariff. In fact as long as fifty years ago, some ocean carriers would even pick up cargoes at the shipper's warehouse and issue a bill of lading for the through transport service.

36. At this point, the through bill, issued under the Hague Rules, does not cover all liabilities associated with the shipment, but improvements in the underlying international law were proposed following the 1969 Tokyo Convention of the Comité Maritime International (CMI). Also, although OCL/ACT attempted to back up its through bill with a standard cargo insurance form, British shippers refused to accept this limitation on their freedom to select cargo coverage of their choice.

37. See remarks of J.C. Moore in the proceedings of the Fourth Annual Maritime Management Institute, "Intermodal Transportation–Government Regulatory Policy?" March 4-5, 1970, published by the N.Y. State Maritime Academy, Fort Schuyler, N.Y.

38. See J.C. Moore, ibid.

39. This reaction is best illustrated by the efforts of the North Atlantic Westbound Freight Conference (NAWFC) to prevent one of its member lines, Container Marine Line (CML) from offering a through service independently of its conference service. The case was taken to the Federal Maritime Commission (docket 68-8) which found in favor of CML, commenting in its opinion that the Conference had a positive obligation to encourage such new developments in shipping.

40. Following the Commission's dicta in the CML case (note 39), nine conferences serving U.S.-South American trades filed proposed modifications to their conference agreements with the FMC seeking to extend the scope of the agreements' rates to inland points, and concurrently, barring independent action by individual member lines to develop such rates separately from the conference. The Commission in docket 69-33 accepted the conferences' proposals but on the condition that the conferences must demonstrate progress in developing such through rates or release their members to negotiate such rates independently. See remarks of Charles D. Marshall at the N.Y. State Maritime Academy Conference, op. cit.

41. The NVOCC has been recognized in U.S. maritime administrative law for about twenty years but, since it is a relatively invisible component of the total transport complex, it has never been recognized legislatively nor has its status been adequately defined. With the increased interest in this service stimulated by containers, the number of firms licensed as NVOCC's has climbed sharply, and a fact-finding inquiry to determine more exactly the conditions within which the NVOCC should operate has been initiated by the FMC. Concurrently a draft international convention to recognize a new class of intermodal carrier (the combined transport operator) and to authorize its issuance of through bills of lading has been drafted by the Intergovernmental Maritime Consultative Organization in cooperation with the Economic Commission for Europe. Some of the

sponsors for this proposal, on which they hope to obtain international action in 1972, see it as opening the way for a new concept of "transmodal" transport management in which the focus for commercial relationships would be shifted from carriers to transmodal container shipment firms which would in turn subcontract with carriers for transport services. See R.F. Morison, "Industry Views Sought on Transport Document," *N.Y. Journal of Commerce*, Dec. 15, 1970, p. 1, and remarks of Richard C. Cotton, "The Emerging Corporate Structure for the Intermodal Concept" before the N.Y. State Maritime Academy Symposium op. cit.

42. Even the Canadian Pacific has acknowledged difficulty in integrating the activities of its various modes, which has led to successive reorganizations aimed at encouraging better internal coordination.

43. Interestingly neither the Rochdale report in Great Britain nor the Oyevaar report on Dutch shipping even raised the possibility of vertical integration of transport services as an alternative to consolidation within the shipping industry. In the U.S. anti-trust restrictions on vertical acquisitions within the transportation industry appear to be relaxing, but there have been no official initiatives to repeal legislation which bars certain specific categories of joint ownership arrangements.

44. Authorization for carriers to operate as Combined Transport Operators and to issue a Combined Transport Document is the major means through which the present draft of the Combined Transport Convention seeks to fulfill its objective of facilitating through shipment (see note 41, above). Prepared by Comité Maritime International in cooperation with UNIDROIT, it is anticipated that the draft CTM convention will be reviewed by interested governments at an international conference on containers to be sponsored by IMCO in 1972.

45. The practice of creating separate entities to hold nominal ownership of individual ships may obscure the rather high degree of consolidation developing within the bulk cargo field (see Chapter 9, above). Owners also often participate in joint ventures or consortia, a pattern particularly prevalent in Scandinavia.

46. For a lengthier analysis of this point, see E.S. Engelstad, "The 1970's—a Period of More Planning for Shipping?" *Fairplay*, Scandinavian Review, May 8, 1969, p. 57.

47. Oil companies badly underestimated tanker requirements for their 1970 market and are strongly represented in the order books for new tonnage. Should the Suez be reopened or should shipment requirements be curtailed for some other reason, a very severe drop in the demand for chartered tonnage might be anticipated.

48. A corollary point is the need for balance in approaching shipping as a cash flow operation versus approaching the industry as a vehicle for money management and capital gains. So long as an owner could hold his operation together, the real dividends in shipping have been received in making occasional spectacular gains and in managing high risk transactions in a manner which allowed them to be leveraged upward without erosion from taxes.

Concluding Remarks to Part III:
New Dimensions in Sea Transport

1. Dag Tresselt, *The West African Shipping Range*, (UN Doc. 67 II D24), p. 47, quoting a report issued by the Liberian national planning office.

2. Some of the smaller nations are now shifting their sights to seek representation in these areas, particularly through stipulations in their concession agreements with the international mining companies. For such arrangements to have any economic validity in today's world, however, they must extend to the marketing organization so large a degree of operational control as to reduce the host government's role to an essentially token participation. International oil and minerals companies, in effect, can better afford to pay a penalty for cargoes taken on their own terms than to allow their operations to become tied up through unsuitable transport.

3. The participation of less-developed states in seaborne trade is of course heavily weighted toward lower valued exports of raw and semifinished cargoes. On a value basis, their share is less than one third.

Chapter 15
Policy Alternatives and Goals

1. The 1970 amendments to the U.S. Merchant Marine Act of 1936 did not alter statutory requirements that at least half of all U.S. government cargoes should be carried in U.S. flag ships. However, the amendments did emphasize the need to build a fleet of modern and efficient bulk carriers to replace the War-built tramp vessels now employed under the protection of the cargo preference statutes to carry U.S. exports of grain and other bulk products. The intent of the amendments was that the new ships should be able to compete for these cargoes on an equal basis with their foreign flag competitors and, if American wage rates were to make such competition impossible, direct subsidies should be provided instead of limiting competition only to U.S. flag ships. As of this writing, necessary regulations to implement this intent have, however, not been published so the exact procedures to be used remain unclear.

2. Gunnar Myrdal, *An International Economy: Problems and Prospects*, (Harper Bros., 1956), p. 291.

3. For example, see the "Common Measure of Understanding on Shipping Questions," adopted at the first UNCTAD session, 1964, which endorsed the liner conference system as necessary to secure stable rates and regular services, but which noted also that close cooperation between conferences and shippers, supported by well-organized consultation machinery, was required to make the system function properly. Promotion of shippers' councils and appropriate council-conference consultation has been one of the main aims of the UNCTAD

Shipping Committee. See Proceedings of the UN Conference on Trade and Development, vol. I: *Final Act and Report*, Annex A.14.22 (UN publication sales no. 64.II.B.11), pp. 54-55.

4. See *Consultation in Shipping*, report by the Secretary General of UNCTAD, N.Y., 1967 (UN Publication TD/B/C.4/20/Rev.1; Sales No. 68. II, D.1.).

5. Ibid., p. 24.

6. Progress in establishing consultation machinery was reviewed at the Fifth Session of the UNCTAD Committee on Shipping, April 1971, and will be reported in the minutes of that meeting.

7. OECD Council Resolution C(69)95, 23 June 1969, established outer limits for credit terms to be permitted in export sales (other than "special cases" in which concessional terms are arranged specifically to assist a less-developed country) and pledged the thirteen signatory countries to "progressive reduction of all factors which distort normal competitive conditions" in the shipbuilding industry.

8. A program to improve cargo statistics has been formulated by the statistical office of the UN, but its implementation depends both on increased funding and on cooperation of member states.

9. The UNCTAD Secretariat has summarized the work of international organizations in *Technical Assistance in Shipping and Ports* (United Nations publication Sales No. TC/B/C.4/49, Geneva, 10 January 1969).

10. Introduction of LASH type vessels promised to alleviate the port development problem in less-developed areas where shoal waters and inadequate docks have heretofore forced cargoes to be loaded from lighters.

11. For example, procedures established in U.S. law for settlement of conference disputes call for hearing before an arbiter appointed by the conference but also require a written record to be kept of the case and that the dispute be subject to de novo review by the government at its discretion.

12. See above Chapter 4. Typically, draft conventions have been developed by the Ship Safety Committee of IMCO or by the Comite Maritime International and forwarded to IMCO for intergovernmental review and for organization of a special diplomatic conference if necessary.

13. Interestingly, the socialist nations have generally supported efforts to develop international conventions in the shipping field.

14. For example, in South America the ALAMAR group of ship operators has been able to mount operationally practical discussions with the LAFTA Transport Advisory Committee, composed of governmental officials, regarding the application of cargo preferences in intraregional Latin American trade, while the UNCTAD meetings have not. It is interesting to observe also that, in the concrete negotiations conducted at the regional level, South American owners have implicitly accepted a more open and competitive system than their governments propound in the more rhetorical atmosphere of international political organizations.

15. This point has been made by U.S. government personnel in discussions with the author. See also T.J. May, "The Status of Federal Maritime Commission Shipping Regulation Under Principles of International Law," *Georgetown Law Review*, vol. 54, pp. 846-856.

16. An interesting treatment of the issues discussed in this section is provided in articles of L. M. S. Rajwar, M.G. Valente, Jan J. Oyevaar, and W.R. Malinowski published in a special issue of *International Conciliation*, "Shipping and Developing Countries," Carnegie Endowment for International Peace, No. 582, March, 1971.

17. The role of less-developed nations in shipping has been discussed in the UNCTAD Shipping Committee since the Committee's formation in 1964. Much of this discussion has revolved around the legitimacy of cargo preference as an instrument for facilitating the expansion of an underdeveloped nation's fleet. Representatives of the traditional maritime states have strongly opposed flag discrimination but have gradually broadened their support of other ldc objectives. Thus, the first (and by implication, primary) resolution of the CSG ministers at their February, 1971, Tokyo meeting was a statement: (a) noting with concern that cargo reservations have over the past four years become even more widespread and that such practices lead to increased costs and poorer transportation services; (b) acknowledging the legitimate aspirations of developing countries to expand their merchant marines and to increase their participation in the carriage of seaborne trade "on a competitive basis and taking into account in particular the special problems associated with the infant stage of development of certain merchant marines"; (c) implying that their governments would be prepared to provide technical and financial assistance for legitimate projects; and (d) pledging also to urge shipowners to invite shipping lines of developing nations into all conferences, (including way port conferences), which relate to these countries foreign trade; but (e) also reserving the right to take countermeasures should ldcs, despite these positive steps, persist in flag discrimination.

18. UNCTAD Shipping Committee, *Establishment or Expansion of Merchant Marines in Developing Countries* (United Nations publication, Sales No. E.69.II.D.1, New York, 1969), p. 54.

19. Ibid.

20. From the evidence marshalled by UNCTAD and others, it is fairly clear that there are no substantial positive benefits to be gained by a less-developed nation which undertakes to organize national flag services on foreign trade routes already reasonably adequately served by other lines. As members of the conferences, national flag lines are at best only one vehicle through which a developing nation may apply pressures to obtain improved transport services; their concurrent obligation to maximize their own revenues is, however, likely to diminish their effectiveness in this role and may lead a relatively inefficient operator to adopt policies within the conference which are detrimental to its

national trade. The few national flag lines, on the other hand, which have attempted to operate outside the conference on routes already served by other lines, have incurred substantial losses which have been hard to justify in relation to any demonstrable benefits to commerce.

21. Anomalies in international finance and in the value of money make it possible for investment in an unprofitable national flag shipping line to be advantageous as a means for earning foreign exchange. The amount of loss which can be tolerated depends entirely on the circumstances of the case but cannot be large. See also chapter 10.

22. Gunnar Myrdal, *An International Economy: Problems and Prospects*, p. 266. Myrdal has singled out shipping as one of the key industries in which more open competition would be consistent with both trade and development objectives.

Chapter 16
Legal Framework for International Shipping: Problems

1. Business International, *Corporate Planning Today for Tomorrow's World Market* (New York, 1967), p. 4.

2. *Report of the Committee of Inquiry into Shipping* (London: Her Majesty's Stationary Office, 1970), p. 411.

3. Article 5, 1958 Geneva Convention on the High Seas.

4. John G. Colombos, *The International Law of the Sea*, 5th ed., (New York: David McKay, 1962), p. 265.

5. International Law Commission, "Report on the High Seas," (UN publication Doc. No. A/CH 4/17, 1950).

6. The convenience fleets include some of the world's most modern and efficient vessels on which pay rates and working conditions are competitive with or superior to those applying in major European registries. However, the PANLIBHON fleets also include some 1.1 million tons of warbuilt and prewar vessels. These latter vessels have a significantly poorer safety record than the world fleet as a whole and are still regarded in some quarters as presenting a hazard to navigation. See Maritime Research Board, *Report of the Ship Safety Committee* (U.S. National Academy of Sciences, 1970).

7. Committee of Inquiry into Shipping, *Report*, p. 411. The status of convenience registries was also reviewed by the transport ministers of the consultative Shipping Group countries at their Tokyo meeting in January 1971, but no action was taken other than commitment to give further study to the problem. The ministers' resolution, however, did express concern that flags of convenience "encouraged in general a lowering of standards of safety and of social benefits to seafarers and were affecting the competitive position of their merchant shipping, and could lead to loss of capital, of employment, and of

taxable capacity." Also, the ministers formally went on record with a statement that "the registration of ships under flags of convenience was not in conformity with the principle reflected in the Geneva Convention of the High Seas, 1958, which required that a State must effectively exercise its jurisdiction and control in administrative, technical, and social matters over ships flying its flag."

8. International Convention on Certain Rules Concerning Civil Jurisdiction in Matters of Collision.

9. International Convention for the Unification of Certain Rules Concerning Penal Jurisdiction in Matters of Collision.

10. In fact, there are numerous inequalities in the operation of ports, and some cases in which ports have been effectively closed to vessels of particular registries by their governments and even by the governments of third parties.

11. See T.K. Thommen, *International Legislation on Shipping* (report prepared for the UNCTAD Shipping Committee, published as TD/32/Rev. 1, UN Sales No. E.69.II.D.2, N.Y., 1969), p. 8.

12. An excellent summary of concepts of extraterritorial jurisdiction is presented by Timothy May, former Executive Director of the U.S. Federal Maritime Commission in "The Status of Federal Maritime Commission Shipping Regulation under Principles of International Law," *Georgetown Law Journal*, 54 (1966), pp. 794-856.

13. Ibid., pp. 810-819.

14. Ibid., pp. 840, 846.

15. The principle expressed in the *Restatement of Foreign Relations Law* (Section 40, 1962) cited by May, "Status of Federal Maritime Commission Shipping Regulation," p. 846., is that "where two states have jurisdiction to prescribe and enforce rules of law and the rule they may prescribe requires inconsistent conduct upon the part of a person, each state is required by international law to consider in good faith moderating the exercise of its enforcement jurisdiction, in the light of such factors as (a) vital national interests of the states (b) the extent and nature of the hardship that inconsistent enforcement actions would impose . . . (d) the nationality of the person, and (e) the extent to which enforcement by action of either state can reasonably be expected to achieve compliance."

16. Legal problems associated with intermodal transport are summarized and placed in policy perspectives in a report published by the Maritime Transportation Research Board of the National Research Council/National Academy of Services, "Legal Impediments to International Intermodal Transportation" (Washington, D.C.: NAS/NRC, 1971).

17. The leading case involved a complaint brought by the North Atlantic Freight conferences against one of their member lines, Container Marine Lines, for filing a through rate for an intermodal service. The Commission determined that the service was entirely separate from the Conference agreement and must be allowed (Federal Maritime Commission Opinion and Order, docket 68-8, April 23, 1968). CML subsequently resigned from the conference.

18. The U.S. Federal Maritime Commission has announced that it will accept filings of through rates so long as they report the division between their sea and land components. This could lead to the unusual (and undoubtedly unacceptable) situation that a European rail or truck line might be called upon to justify its charges before a regulatory agency of the U.S. Government on the grounds that such charges affect U.S. foreign trade.

19. Resolutions adopted 15 March 1963 by the Western European ministers responsible for shipping, published in UNCTAD, *Consultation in Shipping* (UN publication Sales No. 68II. D. 1, 1967), p. 51.

20. Note of Understanding Reached between European Conferences Lines and European Shippers, December 1963, ibid., p. 54.

21. Ibid., p. 55.

22. UNCTAD "Common Measure on Understanding in Shipping Question," in *Report of the Working Party on Shipping*, (UN publication, Document No. E/Conf. 46/C.3/13), p. 30. This statement expressed the group's unanimous agreement that the liner conference system is necessary to secure regular services and stable rates but also that its proper functioning depends on close cooperation between shippers and conferences.

23. UNCTAD, *Consultation in Shipping*, pp. 2, 25.

24. The signatories to the various "understandings" noted here have been representatives of national shipper and shipowner councils, who have no formal authority to commit even their own associations, let alone the individual members of their group.

25. Decisions taken by the Ministerial Meeting in Tokyo, 1-5 February 1971, Paragraphs II, 7.

26. Speaking Note adopted by the Ministers to accompany their decisions, ibid.

27. For the text of this Article and Nagendra Singh's interpretation of it, see footnote 10, Chapter 10. Because this portion of the IMCO convention has never provided a basis for action, it is questionable whether it would be recognized as an operative part of international shipping law.

28. The proposal was co-sponsored by twenty-three developing nations in a resolution outlining tasks for a subcommittee on shipping legislation, but was withdrawn in the face of the strong opposition of the developed states.

29. Pooling arrangements, although reflecting a tighter organization of the participating lines, do usually provide a self-adjusting mechanism by allowing somewhat larger profits and hence opportunities for expansion to their more efficient members. Revenue pools therefore tend to be favored by economists over straight quota arrangements. See E. Bennathan and A.A. Walters, *Revenue Pooling and Cartels* (London School of Economics, 1969).

30. These proposed guidelines are gleaned from several sources. For example, the third suggested standard (that direct subsidies should be permitted that do not restrict the freedom of all flags to share in the business) is drawn from the IMCO Convention, Article 1 (b). The statements regarding participation of

national flag lines in the conferences serving their trade, including wayport conference, are derived from the Decisions of the Tokyo Meeting of Ministers, January 1971, Article I, 7.

31. In the last analysis, what nations seek to achieve when they promote a larger national fleet are primarily opportunities for earnings, commercial influence, and assurance that ships will be available in emergencies. Earnings are likely to be enhanced by participating in a larger international grouping, even if only through share subscriptions. Such participation is likely also to be the most effective means for maintaining commercial influence and there is at least a valid question whether container ships constructed for commercial service are really relevant to military needs.

32. Committee of Inquiry into Shipping, *Report*, p. 112.

Chapter 17
Experiences in Related Systems

1. A principal source for this presentation is M.R. Straszheim, *The International Air Line Industry* (Washington, D.C.: Brookings Institution, 1969). For a comparison of the economic justification for administered price systems in air transport and shipping, see Terrence Higgens, "The Regulation of Air Transport," *The World Today*; Nov. 1965, pp. 470-479.

2. There is a high correlation between ownership of national flag air and sea carriers, the principal exceptions being landlocked states, which usually do not register shipping and geographically small nations, which (outside Europe) tend not to support air carriers. Thus of the world's 150-odd nations, 65 participated in both air and sea transport; 16 only in air, and 22 only at sea.

3. The 1946 Bermuda agreements between the U.S. and Great Britain established a rather ambiguously phrased compromise on this issue which has been widely adopted in other bilateral air treaties. Under the Bermuda agreement, no restrictions were imposed on the capacity which carriers of the two contracting parties might offer in service to one another's territories except that there should be a reasonable relationship between supply and demand, a fair and equal opportunity for carriers of both nations to operate on the route, and restraint in taking any action which might "unduly affect" the services of a competitor. With respect to service to third countries, the agreement provided that, whereas passengers to en route locations might be carried, capacity should be geared basically to the requirements for service to the ultimate destination.

4. In fact, ICAO has refrained from participating in economic matters and has not been called upon to arbitrate rate disputes which are instead worked out within the traffic conferences of IATA.

5. Less than 5 percent of the 1,000 resolutions adopted by the IATA conferences have been disapproved.

6. British Shippers Council, "The Influence of IATA in the Structure of Air Freight Rates and the Development of Air Cargo" (occasional paper no. 245.67).

7. The Communications Satellite Corporation (COMSAT) is sometimes described as a quasi-governmental corporation because the President of the United States is empowered to name three members of its Board of Directors and because it operates as the U.S. participant in INTELSAT, the international system. In fact, COMSAT is entirely privately owned and operates for profit in a manner similar to any other government regulated private enterprise. The form of the COMSAT corporation (as well as agreements regarding the stock participations to be taken in it by the leading U.S. land live and radio communications companies) reflected a tortuous compromise in the Congress between those who wished the satellite program to be publicly managed and those who wished to transfer responsibility to private enterprise.

8. Public Law 87-624, section 102a, approved August 31, 1962.

9. National investment quotas in INTELSAT were established in the Special Agreement on the basis of projected international message traffic for the member nations through 1968. COMSAT's original quota was 61 percent, but has since been reduced to 53 percent in order to accommodate new members joining INTELSAT. Thus COMSAT presently contributes 53 percent of the capital required for INTELSAT, and has a 53 percent vote in the Committee, since voting rights in the Committee are based on investment.

10. COMSAT, by its 53 percent vote alone, cannot initiate action in INTELSAT, but does possess a veto in the Interim Committee. COMSAT, however, sought to avoid resort to the veto and, instead, worked to achieve consensus before a decision is taken.

11. One of the principal issues debated during the negotiations of the Definitive Arrangements was how to better insure distribution of contracts among the industries of member countries. The same question has come up in all other international agencies with large procurement programs. The developing nations in INTELSAT were strong advocates for awarding contracts by international tender solely on the basis of the best combination of quality, price, and most favorable delivery time. The Europeans on the other hand were the chief proponents for some scheme of more even distribution so as to enable their industry to compete more effectively for INTELSAT procurements with U.S. industry. The solution was a compromise which establishes the policy that contracts "shall be awarded so as to stimulate in the interest of INTELSAT world-wide competition."

12. If national shares of a predetermined catch could be established, each participating nation could then commission a limited number of vessels to conduct the harvest by the most efficient means available. Because governments have been unwilling in most fisheries to negotiate on this basis, conservation is effected instead by placing limits on the amount each fisherman can take or on the total catch to be permitted, with each boatowner in a race to see if he can

fill his boat before the season is closed. The problems involved in managing common property fisheries resources are discussed at length in the Panel Reports of the U.S. Commission on Marine Science, Engineering and Resources, Pts. 7 and 8, U.S. Government Printing Office.

Chapter 18
Approaches to a Workable System

1. The Honorable Andrew Gibson, Maritime Administrator and Assistant Secretary of Commerce, before the Gothenberg Conference on "Freedom of the Seas," April 1972.

2. See Chapter 15.

3. Loyalty (or "dual rate") contracts, designed to impose a modest, predefined penalty on shippers who choose to use a nonconference service, have not generally been felt to involve undue economic reprisal. An important aspect of the U.S. regulatory program, however, has been to define the terms of such contracts so that continued patronage is encouraged but can be broken without dire results.

4. See the Resolution Adopted by the Consultative Shipping Group at its Tokyo meeting, February 1971, which are paraphrased in Chapter 15, footnote 17.

5. The great difficulties of trying to appraise the cost differentials amongst different national flag fleets are illustrated by the problems encountered in administration of the U.S. operating differential subsidy program. For a description of some of these problems, see S.A. Lawrence, *U.S. Merchant Shipping Policies and Politics*, (Brookings Institution, 1966).

6. An International Shipping Authority, designed to perform such administrative functions on behalf of the industry as publish statistics, arrange for consular functions, and license ships, might be organized as an operating arm of IMCO or as an independent body with a board of governors drawn from a variety of backgrounds (e.g., international public and private organizations, the marine insurance industry, ship classifications societies, and so forth).

7. Most flag of convenience tonnage, as noted in Chapter 16, is modern, efficient, and scrupulously inspected to insure conformance to international shipping codes. However, these flags have also been used by some owners of old tonnage which could no longer meet U.S., British, or European standards and have been placed under a convenience flag as a last resort.

8. The decisions of the CSG ministers at their Tokyo meeting, February 1971, did include a policy statement regarding terms for admission into conferences and a section calling for further study of issues associated with use of flags of convenience. Otherwise, the decisions were concerned almost entirely with shipper-owner relations.

9. The need to be able to monitor the operation of the system as a whole springs from the need to be able to appraise overall effectiveness, to update standards in light of changing conditions, and to respond to specific problems in the context of their impact on the total system. Achieving this capability implies much enhanced statistical capabilities but does not imply a requirement for any central governing body to oversee the industry's operations.

10. Conditions in the U.S.-Brazil trade have been an object of FMC concern for many years, particularly with respect to pooling arrangements for handling the large coffee and cocoa business. Until 1967, a substantial portion of this business was handled by Scandinavian companies and the remainder by U.S. and Brazilian lines. When the Brazilian government embarked on its fleet expansion program, it sought to negotiate a division of trade with the U.S. which would gradually have forced the Scandinavians out of the business. The proposal initially was rejected by the FMC (docket 68-10) but with language which permitted the affected lines to renegotiate their proposed pooling agreements. In Docket 7-30, the Commission approved arrangements which provided for equal sharing by U.S. and Brazilian lines of cargoes controlled by their respective governments. The Scandinavians regarded this as a reversal of the earlier decision and have requested reconsideration.

11. The UNCTAD conference failed to reach the hoped for agreement in support of the Consultative Shipping Group code. Instead, the developing nation bloc within UNCTAD prepared a substitute code which stressed the rights of developing nations to take any needed action to promote their national flag shipping and the responsibilities of all shipping lines to submit proposed rates to appropriate public bodies for review. Unable to resolve the impasse between the two approaches, the developing nation bloc forced adoption of a resolution calling upon the United Nations to convene as early as possible in 1973 a Conference of Plenipotentiaries to "adopt a Code of Conduct for the Liner Conference System to be adopted by the Governments of all countries and to be implemented in a manner that is binding on them and can be suitably enforced." This resolution was opposed by all noncommunist developed nations participating in the Conference but was nonetheless adopted by a vote of 74 to 19 with two abstentions.

12. The suggestion made here for procedures for international arbitration in shipping obviously leaves many unanswered questions relating to the manner in which such a body might be appointed and supported, whether it should assert primary jurisdiction over any categories of cases or hear only matters voluntarily brought before it, and how it might enforce its decisions. Fortunately a growing body of experience is being gained on matters of this sort in other industries within which such procedures apply (e.g., international satellite communications) and within such multinational groupings as the EEC.

13. Discriminatory shipping policies are likely to be justifiable only in situations which involve more general trade and monetary problems. Corrective

action should therefore be planned in the context of the nation's overall economic situation and should be enforced as part of a program supervised by GATT or IMF to meet the nation's more fundamental problems.

14. Positive benefits might be expected to flow to individual shipping firms through affiliation with an international body as well as vice versa. Thus, such affiliation could be a basis for lower insurance costs, improved consular services, and ship market and cargo data.

15. Appropriate links between the regional bodies and the proposed international authority would be desirable both to promote local conformance with an international code and a realistic degree of tolerance in international regulations. Regional representatives, for example, might be constituted as a governing board to the international body.

16. The advent of international regulation of satellite communications provides one example; the comprehensive collective bargaining between oil companies and the organization of producing states another. International regulatory procedures also are being advanced with respect to such other diverse areas as marine resource development, energy transmission, and weather and climate control.

17. Lester B. Pearson et al., *Partners in Development*, Report of the Commission on International Development to the World Bank, (New York: Praeger, 1969), pp. 208-230.

18. The Authority, for example, could eventually assume responsibility for managing international waterways, for operating navigational and rescue systems, and even for maintaining computer-controlled container and cargo data exchanges.

19. Legislatures of several of the CSG countries already have authorized their governments to join in retaliatory actions against countries which employ flag discrimination against any member of their group. This posture was reiterated in the ministerial decisions reached in Tokyo (Article I, paragraph 10).

Index

Adams, F.G., 134
Africa, 55
Ainsworth, Gardner, xvi
Air France, 240
Alcan, Shipping Services, Ltd., xvi, 94
Alcoa, 94
Alumina, 56–57
American Export Isbrandtsen, 196
Antimonopoly rules, 256
Arab states, 54
Asian Development Bank, 54
Associated Container Transport, 187
Atlantic Container Line, 174, 195
Aviation, 239–43

BOAC, 240
Balfour, James, xvi
Balance of payments, 120–23
Ballast, 79
Baltic Coffee House, 8
Baltic and International Maritime
    Conference, 40
Baltic Shipping Exchange, 16, 100
Baltic and White Sea Conference, 16
Barge systems, 167–69
Barracuda Tanker Corporation of Bermuda,
    17, 22
Bauxite, 156–57
Belassa, Bela, 133
Benford, Harry, xvi
Bermuda agreements, 241, 318
Bethlehem, 94
Bergesen, Sigval, 3
Brazilian Merchant Marine Commission,
    81, 272
Bretton Woods Agreements, 32–33, 274
British Navigation Act, 1849, 267–68
British Petroleum Company, 22
British Petroleum Trading Ltd., 22
British Ports Council, 183
British Shippers' Council, 189, 191,
    242–43
British Steel Corporation, 199
Brown, R.T., 84
Brussels Diplomatic Conference for Private
    International Law, 39
Bulk cargo, 152, 158, 165–67, 198–200

CENSA, 41, 42, 232, 233, 277
CESC, 42, 233
COMSAT, 243, 244, 245, 319
CSG, 40, 42, 232
Canadian National Railways, 196
Canadian Pacific, 196

Cargo, 63–74, 92; air, 149–50; bulk, 152,
    158, 165–67, 198–200; categories,
    145–46; control systems, 174–75; trends
    and implications, 143–59
Center for Planning and Projectiles, UN, 35
Central American Common Market, 45
China, 52, 141
Coal, 154–55
Coast Lines, 196
Code of Shipping Conference Practice, 40
Combined Transport Convention, 197
Colombos, John G., 226
Comité Maritime International, (CMI), 41, 217
Commission on International Trade Law
    (UNCITRAL), 31, 35
Commission on Sea Transport, 41
Commission of Transport Users, 41
Committee of European National Steam-
    ship Owners Associations, see CENSA
Communist nations, 51–53
Competition: and administrative controls,
    213–15; and conference system, 111–12;
    outlook for, 250–57; standards for fair,
    231–34
Conference system, 13–16, 111–12
Consultative Shipping Group, See CSG
Containerization, 169–71
Contracts, terms, 101–102
Convention on the Law of the High
    Seas, 227
Council of European Ministers of Trans-
    port, 35
Council of European Shippers' Councils,
    see CESC
Council for Mutual Economic Assistance,
    52
Convention on the Recognition and Enforce-
    ment of Foreign Arbitral Awards, 31
Conventions on the Law of the Sea, 35
Costs, 82–86

Department of Economic and Social
    Affairs, UN, 35
Development Program, UN, 35
Dry bulk carriers, 97–100
Dutch Shipowners' Association, 47

ECA, 35
ECAFE, 35
ECE, 35
ECLA, 35
EEC, 45
EFTA, 45
East African Community, 45

313

About the Author

Samuel A. Lawrence served as Executive Director of President Lyndon B. Johnson's Commission on Marine Science, Engineering and Resources and assisted the Commission in the preparation of its 1969 report, *Our Nation and the Sea.* He is also the author of a Brookings study, *United States Maritime Policies and Politics.*

Dr. Lawrence's present study of the international shipping industry has been undertaken with the assistance of a grant from eight private firms concerned as shippers or shipowners with aspects of maritime transportation; an industry association; a consulting company; and the Government of Canada. The study's sponsors have given the author complete freedom in pursuing the research and in reaching his conclusions.

Dr. Lawrence holds his BA from Harvard and the MPA and Ph.D. from American University. He is currently a vice-president (administration) at Cornell.